Lecture Notes in Computer Scien

Edited by G. Goos, J. Hartmanis, and J. van Leeuwen

Springer
Berlin
Heidelberg
New York
Barcelona
Hong Kong
London
Milan
Paris
Singapore
Tokyo

Gérard Lacoste   Birgit Pfitzmann
Michael Steiner   Michael Waidner (Eds.)

SEMPER - Secure Electronic Marketplace for Europe

Springer

Series Editors

Gerhard Goos, Karlsruhe University, Germany
Juris Hartmanis, Cornell University, NY, USA
Jan van Leeuwen, Utrecht University, The Netherlands

Volume Editors

Gérard Lacoste
Compagnie IBM France, Centre d'Etudes et Recherches
Le Plan du Bois, 06610 La Gaude, France
E-mail: lacoste@fr.ibm.com

Birgit Pfitzmann
Universität des Saarlandes, Fachbereich Informatik
Im Stadtwald, 66123 Saarbrücken, Germany
E-mail: pfitzmann@cs.uni-sb.de

Michael Steiner
Michael Waidner
IBM Zurich Research Laboratory
Säumerstrasse 4, 8803 Rüschlikon, Switzerland
E-mail: steiner@acm.org, wmi@zurich.ibm.com

Cataloging-in-Publication Data applied for

Die Deutsche Bibliothek - CIP-Einheitsaufnahme

SEMPER - secure electronic marketplace for Europe / Gérard Lacoste ...
(ed.). - Berlin ; Heidelberg ; New York ; Barcelona ; Hong Kong ;
London ; Milan ; Paris ; Singapore ; Tokyo : Springer, 2000
  (Lecture notes in computer science ; Vol. 1854)
  ISBN 3-540-67825-5
CR Subject Classification (1998): E.3, C.2, D.4.6, K.4.4, K.6.5, J.1

ISSN 0302-9743
ISBN 3-540-67825-5 Springer-Verlag Berlin Heidelberg New York

SEMPER is part of the European Commission's ACTS Programme (Advanced Communications Technologies and Services). Funding is provided by the partner organisations, the European Union, and the Swiss Federal Department for Education and Science.

Springer-Verlag is a company in the BertelsmannSpringer publishing group.
© Springer-Verlag Berlin Heidelberg 2000
Printed in Germany

Disclaimer: Some of the systems mentioned in this book may be protected by trademarks, copyrights, or patents. They are the property of their owners.

Typesetting: Camera-ready by author
Printed on acid-free paper   SPIN: 10722159   06/3142   5 4 3 2 1 0

Foreword

Some years ago, businesses could choose whether to migrate to electronic commerce, however, today it seems they have no choice. Predictions indicate that companies that do not make the necessary changes will be overrun by competition and ultimately fail. Therefore, we see more and more companies undergoing tremendous transformation in order to adapt to the new business paradigm. At the same time new companies are being established. One thing these companies have in common is the increased dependency on security technology. The invention of electronic commerce has changed the role of security technologies from being merely a protector to being also an enabler of electronic commerce, and it is clear that the development of security technology is a key enabler in the growth and deployment of electronic commerce. This has been recognised at European level (European Union 1997e).

The launch of a comprehensive EU policy in the area of security in open networks is fairly recent with the adoption of a Communication on cryptography in October 1997 (European Union 1997c). A very important complement and support to the European policy is the European Commission's contribution to overcome technological barriers by giving special importance to R&D (Research and Development) activities.

The *SEMPER* project was launched in September 1995 and was funded partly by the European Community within the *Advanced Communication Technologies and Services* (ACTS) specific research programme part of the Fourth Framework Program (1994-1998). In this book the *SEMPER* project team presents in a coherent, integrated, and readable form the issues addressed, the motivation for the work carried out, and the key results obtained.

SEMPER is an innovative project in several aspects. What really makes it innovative and impressive is the integration of the following components into an overall security framework for electronic commerce:

– *SEMPER* is the first project aiming at securing electronic commerce as a whole by developing a technical security framework realised as a middleware. This brings forward two advantages. First, such a technical security framework supports multiple business scenarios by providing powerful security services to applications implementing the business processes. A novelty compared to other security middleware is the provision of security mechanisms through a more commerce-oriented application programming interface. Second, the development environment shields application designers from the security implementation details and their evolution over time.

- *SEMPER* provides an open security platform which can be configured with relevant modules in order to cope with national regulations.
- A trustworthy user interface, TINGUIN, which ensures that users can securely manage information. TINGUIN provides a single point of interaction between users and their secure platform. Such a single interface is essential to ensure users' consistent perception of their security.
- *SEMPER* has proposed a legal framework for establishing legal predictability of electronic commerce. An interesting result is the adaptation of the technical and legal frameworks to each other by enabling the user's tools to visualize important legal aspects and to manage legal parameters.

The results in this book constitute a major contribution to the development of secure electronic commerce and the work presented has set the scene for future directions in secure electronic commerce. The last chapter of the book highlights some open problems related to the work done by the project. However, many more exist and there is still a lot to be done before the goal of secure electronic commerce will be reached. This has been recognised at European level, and the security-related R&D activities will be intensified under the new 5th Framework Program (1998–2002). Within the 5th Framework Program, the Information Society Technology (IST) Programme addresses the technologies of the online world.

Everyone interested in investigating the state of the art and future directions for secure electronic commerce should find this book extremely valuable and it is without any reservation that I strongly recommend it.

May 2000

Spyros Konidaris
European Commission
Director a.i. – DG XIII-F

Preface

Since the invention of the World-Wide Web (WWW) in 1991, Internet-based electronic commerce has been transformed from a mere idea into reality. Customers browse through catalogues, search for best offers, order goods, and pay for them electronically. Information services can be subscribed online, and many newspapers and scientific journals are readable via the Internet. Most financial institutions have some sort of online presence, allowing their customers to access and manage their accounts, make financial transactions, trade stocks, and so on. Some countries already support filing tax declarations electronically. Electronic mails are exchanged within and between enterprises and often already replace fax copies. Soon there will be no enterprise left without some Internet presence, if only for advertisement reasons. In early 1998 more than 2 million web servers were connected to the Internet, and more than 30 million host computers (Zakon 1998). Internet business is estimated to have reached $50 to $100 billion in 1998, mostly in business-to-business trade, and continues to increase at a high rate of growth (Henry, Cooke, Buckley, Dumagan, Gill, Pastore, and LaPorte 1999).

Thus, doing some electronic business on the Internet is already an easy task. As is cheating and snooping. Several reasons contribute to this insecurity. The Internet does not offer much security per se. Eavesdropping and acting under false identity is simple. Stealing data is undetectable in most cases. Popular PC operating systems offer little or no security against viruses and other malicious software, which means that users cannot even trust the information displayed on their own screens. At the same time, user awareness of security risks is threateningly low.

The only well-accepted security tool for the World-Wide Web is the Secure Sockets Layer protocol (SSL), which provides a secure pipe between web client and web server (Freier, Karlton, and Kocher 1996). It cannot generate signed messages or signed receipts, which naturally makes it unsuitable to tasks like electronic online payments and contract signing. And even for SSL, the problem of *visualizing* security to the user is unsolved: most WWW browsers only distinguish between "secure" and "insecure" connections, but do not tell the users in a simple way with *whom* exactly they are communicating over an established "secure" channel.

Such user interface problems are amplified by the fact that today's electronic-commerce systems offer little support in maintaining consistency in data and security among the different parts of a business process. As in the paper world, users have to fill in the same data again and again, copy data on several forms, accumulate data from different transactions by hand, and so on. More problems are revealed if one looks at the legal aspects: often it is not clear—or not even decided—who bears liability and which country's law is applicable in a specific situation.

In 1994 we, the *SEMPER* consortium, came up with the idea that all these security problems could best be solved by grouping all necessary security technologies under a coherent and open software framework, and a single, consistent user interface. Such a framework should allow automatic linking of parts of a business process. Necessarily, it should support not only secure communication and payments, but also the negotiation of business and security parameters, fair exchange of documents (as in contract signing and certified mail), handling of disputes among the parties, etc. Besides keeping data confidential, it should also grant its users some degree of anonymity and unobservability—like users on physical marketplaces can act anonymously. All this should be based on requirements from the market, and should be consistent with the legal systems.

The idea was turned into a proposal to the European Commission, with the result that we started work on implementing this idea in September 1995. We concluded the project early 1999. Some partners are currently exploiting parts of *SEMPER*, but we also aim at more complete use of the framework in successor projects and products. This book summarizes our main results.

Part I gives an overview of our solutions, i.e., the technical framework and a proposal how to tackle the open legal questions. This part is intended to be readable by everyone, i.e., it does not presuppose a specific technical background except some basic familiarity with the Internet.

Part II covers topics for which fundamentally new scientific or engineering results were obtained, and looking at them in detail would be beneficial to everybody working in the field. See the introduction of Part II for more details.

The results of *SEMPER*, including the full architecture, prototype description, and results from expert surveys and trial evaluations, are documented in a number of public, formal deliverables. These are available online from http://www.semper.org, or by writing to: IBM Zurich Research Laboratory, Computer Science Department/Project *SEMPER*, Säumerstrasse 4, CH-8803 Rüschlikon, Switzerland.

May 2000

Gérard Lacoste
Birgit Pfitzmann
Michael Steiner
Michael Waidner

Authors of this report: Part I was written, based on the results of the entire project, by *Birgit Baum-Waidner, Gérard Lacoste, Birgit Pfitzmann, Michael Steiner, Michael Waidner,* and *Arnd Weber.* Chapter 5 was written by *Michael Waidner.* Chapter 6 was written by *N. Asokan, Birgit Baum-Waidner, Torben P. Pedersen, Birgit Pfitzmann, Matthias Schunter, Michael Steiner,* and *Michael Waidner.* Chapter 7 was written by *Dale Whinnett* and *Reinder Wolthuis.* Chapter 8 was written by *Akis Hamamtzoglou, Thomas Hecht, Giannis Papadopoulos,* and *Arnd Weber.* Chapter 9 was written by *Rolf Michelsen, Stig Mjølsnes, Petros Pantis,* and *Kostas Tzelepis.* Chapter 10 was written by *Matthias Schunter.* Chapter 11 was written by *N. Asokan* and *Michael Steiner* and is based on (Abad-Peiro, Asokan, Steiner, and Waidner 1998; Asokan 1998; Asokan, Herreweghen, and Steiner 1998). Chapter 12 was written by *Maria Gatziani, Torben P. Pedersen,* and *Kambiz Zangeneh.* Chapter 13 was written by *Birgit Baum-Waidner.* Chapter 14 was written by *Birgit Baum-Waidner* and *Rita Zihlmann.* Chapter 15 was written by *Michael Waidner.*

People and organizations who contributed to *SEMPER*: *Fabrice Clerc, Philippe Magliulo, Marc Mazoué,* and *Marie-Jo Revillet* from CNET - France Télécom. *Holger Erichsen* and *Bernd Horsch* from the Commerzbank. *Bjarke Dahl Ebert, Maria Gatziani, Peter Landrock, Kim Lueders-Jensen, Timmy G. Madsen, Jesper Drud Nielsen, Thomas Sepstrup Nielsen,* and *Torben P. Pedersen* from Cryptomathic. *Paul Dinnissen, Berry Schoenmakers,* and *Bryce Wilcox* from Digicash. *Akis Hamamtzoglou, John Katakis, Sophia Koutsoukou, Dimitrios Livas,* and *Giannis Papadopoulos* from EURO-COM EXPERTISE. *Christoph Baert, John Schey,* and *John West* from Europay International. *Michael Ehrl, Thomas Hecht,* and *Ralf Kuron* from FO-GRA Forschungsgesellschaft Druck e.V.. *Horst Ehmke, Matthias Enzmann, Rüdiger Grimm, Tobias Himstedt, Basawarai Patil, Wolfgang Putz,* and *Kambiz Zangeneh* from the Forschungszentrum Informationstechnik mbH (GMD). *Jean-Marie Blanchère, Sylvain Cornillon, Gerard Lacoste, Philippe Leblanc, Jean-Pierre Le Heiget,* and *Christian Navarro* from IBM France, Centre d'Études et Recherches; *Ulrich Einig, Karsten Riede,* and *Christian Thiel* from IBM Heidelberg; *Jose L. Abad-Peiro, N. Asokan, Andreas Fleuti, Ceki Gülcü, Günter Karjoth, Ferdinando Loiacono, Mehdi Nassehi, Thomas Schweinberger, Michael Steiner, Els van Herreweghen,* and *Michael Waidner* from IBM Research, Zürich. *Petros Pantis, Maria Tsakali,* and *Kostas Tzelepis* from INTRACOM. *Sylvain Cornillon, Sharon Prins, Jako Swanenburg, Matthijs de Vries,* and *Reinder Wolthuis* from KPN Research Netherlands. *D.M.A. Schaap* from MARIS. *Mathias Flenker, Stefan Liesem, Christian Petersen,* and *Ingo Saleck* from Otto Versand. *Mogens Rom Anderson, Birgit Baum-Waidner, Klaus Becker, Felix Jaggi, Thomas Mittelholzer, Armin Müller, Claus Rasmussen, Rainer Rueppel, Bruno Wildhaber,* and

Rita Zihlmann from Entrust/r3 security engineering ag. Rolf Michelsen and Stig Frode Mjølsnes from SINTEF Telecom and Informatics. Peter Bosch, Dick Bulterman, Ray Hirschfeld, Jaap Henk Hoepman, Sjoerd Mullender, and Louis Salvail from the Stichting Mathematisch Centrum (CWI). Matthias Schunter from the Universität Dortmund. Ingo Pippow, Jan Reichert, Arnd Weber, and Dale Whinnett from the Universität Freiburg, Institut für Informatik und Gesellschaft. Birgit Pfitzmann and Matthias Schunter from the Universität Hildesheim, Institut für Informatik. Tom Beiler, Jürgen Brauckmann, Lothar Fritsch, Birgit Pfitzmann, and Matthias Schunter from the Universität des Saarlandes, Saarbrücken, Fachbereich Informatik. Sponsoring partners of SEMPER were Banksys (Belgium), Banque Générale du Luxembourg (Luxembourg), Enyca (Spain), and Telekurs/Payserv (Switzerland). The project was led by IBM.

The following organisations provided the infrastructure for the SEMPER trials: in France: ACRI, Actimedia, Centre d'Études et Recherches IBM France, Centre International de Communications Avancées, France-Télécom, and IDATE; in Germany: Commerzbank, FOGRA Forschungsgesellschaft Druck e.V., Forschungszentrum Informationstechnik mbH (GMD), Gesellschaft für Zahlungssysteme (GZS), Otto Versand, Universität Freiburg, Institut für Informatik und Gesellschaft, and Universität des Saarlandes, Saarbrücken, Fachbereich Informatik; in Greece: EUROCOM EXPERTISE; in The Netherlands: KPN Research, MARIS, and Stichting Mathematisch Centrum (CWI); in Switzerland: IBM Research, Zürich; in the UK: Oil and Gas Product Library Ltd. (OPL); in the USA: GTE; and the members of the MOMENTS consortium.

SEMPER was part of the Advanced Communication Technologies and Services (ACTS) research program established by the European Commission for 1994-1998, and received funding under contract AC026 from the European Commission DGXIII and the Swiss Bundesamt für Bildung und Wissenschaft.

Acknowledgments: Interesting discussions with several people outside the consortium helped us to develop and to refine the ideas presented in this book. In particular, we would like to thank *Alain André, Patrick Aubry, Ali Bahreman, Philippe Bardet, Annarosa Baum, Joachim Biskup, Jay Black, Michel Bosco, Peter Büttner, Mario Campolargo, David Chaum, Anne Clarke, Marc Dacier, Michel Dauphin, Michel Fossaert, Renaud di Francesco, Michel Frenkiel, Philippe Garnesson, Mark Greene, Phil Janson, Spiros Konidaris, Jens Kristensen, Philippe Lefevbre, Karine Lieres, Mark Linehan, Jean-Pierre Meyer, Refik Molva, François Montagner, Kostas Papanikolaou, Peter de Rooij, Paul Rottier, Jukka Salo, Boris Saulnier, Tom Scanlan, Julia Sime, Hansrudolf Thomann, Paul Timmers, Gene Tsudik, Joep Van de Veer, Pierre Vannel, Hans-Dieter Zimmermann, and Rosalie Zobel.*

Table of Contents

Part I

The Vision of *SEMPER*

This Part I provides a condensed overview of the objectives, focus and results of the project SEMPER. It is written for a general audience interested in electronic commerce and does not require any particular technical knowledge.

Chapter 1 describes scenarios of electronic commerce and the special security problems that distinguish it from traditional commerce, reviews existing approaches and the most important basic security techniques, and presents the goals and focus of SEMPER.

Chapter 2 summarizes the technical part of the SEMPER approach. We provide a model of electronic commerce, identify the services needed for secure electronic commerce, and propose an architecture supporting these services.

Chapter 3 discusses legal aspects of electronic commerce and summarizes our proposal on how to tackle them: the SEMPER Electronic Commerce Agreement (SECA). A particularly important aspect is fair liability distribution for digital signatures given today's technology.

Chapter 4 summarizes the benefits and potential of the SEMPER framework from a commercial point of view, in particular potential product lines.

Necessarily, the presentation in Part I is rather high-level. In Part II we provide details on the most important and innovative issues.

G. Lacoste et al. (Eds.): SEMPER 2000, LNCS 1854, p. 1, 2004.
© Springer-Verlag Berlin Heidelberg 2000

1. Secure Electronic Commerce

This chapter sets the stage for the subsequent presentation of our results. We present examples of electronic commerce and the need for security, existing approaches and their shortcomings, and the overall goals and the specific focus of *SEMPER*.

1.1 The Notion of "Electronic Commerce"

The term *electronic commerce* is generally understood to span the whole range of business situations that are at least partially supported by a communication network such as the Internet. This includes the informative parts of commerce—like the provision of business directories, catalogues, and help desks—but also the legally more challenging parts, like signing contracts, transferring funds, executing contracts, issuing credentials, or delivering intangible goods. All the steps must be documented in a legally sound way, e.g., for taxation or as a provision for court disputes.

The project *SEMPER* focused on these security-relevant parts of electronic commerce. In an abstract sense, these are all those parts that transfer or generate values, rights or obligations. In order to see what this means more concretely, let us consider two important examples of Internet-based electronic commerce, shopping over the Internet and business-to-business commerce.

1.1.1 Example 1: Shopping over the Internet

Our first example covers the "standard" case of business-to-consumer electronic commerce over the Internet:

Merchants offer their products and services over the Internet, which means they make all the necessary information accessible via a World-Wide Web server (on-line catalogue), allow consumers to place orders electronically by filling in Web-forms or sending electronic mail, and link this new channel to their back-end system which finally fulfills the orders. Payment might be online, e.g., by sending credit-card details to the merchant, or out-of-band (i.e., outside the network), e.g., by invoicing, and it might take place before

G. Lacoste et al. (Eds.): SEMPER 2000, LNCS 1854, pp. 3–14, 2000.
© Springer-Verlag Berlin Heidelberg 2000

or after delivery. The merchandise might be CDs, books, computers, cars, nights in a hotel, flights over the Atlantic, stock shares, or Teddy bears.

Typically there is no pre-established business relation between the merchant and the customer. Thus they are unlikely to trust each other a priori: The merchant will require some guarantee of payment before delivering goods, and the customer will require some guarantee of getting the right goods before making a payment. Currently both requirements are satisfied in a very weak sense only:

- The merchant can ask the customer for a credit-card number, and can get an authorization from the credit-card organization for the amount the customer will have to pay, before processing the order. This creates some confidence in the customer, but since the customer does not "sign" a payment order the merchant has no real guarantee that he can capture the amount. The card holder might always revoke the payment subsequently. In theory the customer does not take any risk here, as he can always cancel a transaction (this is the regulation for MOTO = mail-order/telephone-order transactions). In practice, however, many people do not check their credit card statements carefully, and canceling a bogus transaction can be very cumbersome. In Europe it is not even clear that canceling succeeds in real life in spite of the MOTO regulations.

  The problem becomes worse by the fact that the Internet does not support identification of business partners, i.e., the customer cannot be sure whether he is talking with a respectable, honest merchant or a criminal, and thus criminals might easily collect lots of credit-card numbers. (SSL, a protocol for secure communication between client and server, has the potential to provide such partner identification. Section 1.3.1 discusses it and its limitations.)

- In contrast to just sending the credit-card number and expiration date to the merchant, real payment systems like SET (MasterCard and Visa 1997) generate some evidence for a payment. This improves the overall security as it becomes more difficult to forge payments. But it also often means that the customer has to take the larger share of the remaining risk (see Section 1.2.3 for such risks) as he cannot simply revoke a payment any more.[1]

---

[1]Originally SET was only intended for reducing the overall risk, without placing more of this risk on the customer. The SET specifications (MasterCard and Visa 1997, Book 2, Section 2, "Services/Caveat") explicitly state: *"SET does not provide non-repudiation."* But they also *"permit non-repudiation via rules and policies of individual payment card brand implementations,"* and some implementations use this to assign the full risk to the cardholder. For instance the Swiss SET registration form (UBS 1998) says: *"4. All initiated SET transactions which are based on a system-controlled, true legitimation, using the card number and the matching digital signature, may be charged to the Cardholder without reservation and are legally binding for him/her; this applies even if the SET transaction was not actually initiated by the Cardholder. [...] This legitimation*

- For catalogue retailing of physical goods, the merchant can ask for payment-on-delivery. Then he will always be paid for delivered goods, but he might still lose money on returned goods due to wasted production, handling and shipping. Usually the customer does not take any risk. Obviously, this approach is unsuitable for intangible goods. It is also unsuitable in cases where production, handling or shipping are expensive, or where the number of "fake" orders is not limited and thus even small expenses can add up to a substantial loss.
- For continuous services, like subscriptions, the merchant can ask the customer to sign a contract in writing, i.e., the relation between merchant and customer is established out-of-band, in the classical, paper-based way. (The same holds for the relation between bank and customer in home banking.) This is pretty safe for the merchant, but unsuitable for spontaneous purchases and in general for low-value transactions. Moreover, many such contracts are not very advantageous for the customer as they assign all liability to him, without ensuring that he is technically equipped for protecting himself accordingly (see Section 1.2.3).

In the following chapters, we show how *SEMPER* improves upon all these approaches by eliminating many risks and allowing reasonable limitations of the remaining risks for all parties.

1.1.2 Example 2: Business-to-Business Commerce

This second example covers the typical business-to-business electronic commerce.

The most basic way for business-to-business electronic commerce, electronic mail, is already well established and often replaces informal business letters, phone calls, and printed product documentation. Typically, payment is performed out-of-band through cheques or funds transfer, and the time of payment is unrelated to that of delivery. For instance, a customer's account is maintained and settled once a month based on the transactions performed during that period. Corporate credit cards are also increasingly used.

As soon as more formal business documents, e.g., orders, are also sent electronically, the question whether they are legally binding is quite similar to Example 1. However, for the near future, partners in business-to-business electronic commerce often have a formal trading partner agreement in place, and in such cases it is simpler to establish a secure communication channel between the partners or even to agree on specific liabilities.

In the long run, more flexible and spontaneous relationships are desired for electronic commerce, e.g., compare the goals of RosettaNet (RosettaNet 1998). There are several projects on using EDI (Electronic Data Interchange) over the Internet. Some, such as OBI (OBI Consortium 1998), are already

---

agreement means that the risks arising from the misuse of the password and/or the personal code are in principle incurred by the Cardholder."

deployed but only automate simple types of procurement, e.g., high-volume low-value goods in a business-to-business scenario. XML/EDI (Peat and Webber 1997) is much more general, but not yet concrete. Others try to structure the complexity and diversity of the business processes by supporting general supply-chain management and other inter-company workflows over the Internet. So far, none of these projects contains many security considerations. However, studies such as Schoder, Strauss, and Welchering (1998) show that lack of security is recognized in industry as one of the main impeding factors for electronic commerce in business scenarios.

1.2 What's Special about Electronic Commerce?

Both types of electronic commerce discussed in Section 1.1 parallel traditional, paper-oriented types, and thus the high-level security requirements are intuitively clear. But *satisfying* these requirements in the electronic world is quite different from satisfying them in the paper world.

1.2.1 Virtuality of Electronic Commerce

Electronic commerce takes place in a virtual world, where everybody is "equal." There is no difference between a message received from the office next door and one from the other end of the world, or between a message sent within the same country and one sent across the border. The web site of a respectable well-known company does not need to look more serious or trustworthy than the web site of a garage business—or a web site set up by some criminal. The Internet also does not ensure a standard semantics for names: www.XYZ.com does not necessarily belong to company XYZ.

Hence, even without any technical attacks on the network, establishing *trust* between business partners in electronic commerce requires additional effort. Similar effort is needed for collecting evidence for cases where a dispute occurs. The two problems are related but not identical: Trust can be in a purely "digital" entity, e.g., a certain web server becomes known for delivering useful and bug-free programs or beautiful pictures. Evidence more often needs to point back to a real-world entity, e.g., for paying compensation or other punishment in case of serious misbehavior.

Another aspect of virtuality is that electronic commerce can easily take place across borders. Typically this reduces the legal certainty; e.g., in many cases details such as which country's law is applicable, or who bears what liability under which conditions, are not clear and decrease overall security and trust. This is discussed in more detail in Chapter 3.

1.2.2 The Internet as a Hostile Environment

Typically, messages sent over the Internet are processed by several intermediate computers before they are delivered to the intended recipient. Nothing prevents these intermediate computers from screening traffic for interesting information; there is no confidentiality. Sender addresses are not verifiable: It is trivial to send an electronic mail under a wrong identity. In fact, "multiple personalities" are a built-in feature of many Internet mail clients. Attackers can also effectively change the meaning of addresses, redirecting traffic sent to www.XYZ.com to an address of the attacker's choice.[2]

1.2.3 Insecure User Equipment

There is a lot of literature on how to break into PC computer systems, e.g., Denning and Denning (1998), Denning (1990) and Neumann (1995), which is the usual type of device used for electronic commerce over the Internet (at least for consumers and small businesses). Apart from low-tech attacks by people who get physically near the PC, the main problem are attacks with Trojan horses and viri, i.e., malicious code hidden in useful code or data. Traditionally this kind of rogue code was mostly transported in free or pirated software and had to be explicitly loaded by the user. Propagation was slow and user education and virus checkers provided good countermeasures against these distribution media. However, with the advent of the Internet these attacks can propagate much quicker and can be much harder to detect and prevent. Standard browsers, emailers, and also the operating systems themselves have proved to have bugs that allow outsiders to place code on a user's machine while the user is doing his normal work and not intending to load code, e.g., while he is only browsing (Dean et al. 1998; Dean et al. 1996) or reading mail.[3] Once the attacker has malicious code on the machine, this code can in particular look for secret data and access codes used by standard electronic-commerce applications (or entered by the user into them) and send those out to the attacker.

If high-value transactions can be made from standard PCs, and become as legally significant and thus valuable as traditional ones, it would be very surprising not to see many attempts to break into such systems. There is no reasonable way for users to protect themselves from such attacks except by giving up all Internet access and thus electronic commerce (Weber 2000). Even smartcards do not help very far: Even if they protect secrets, the user's access data and commands to them go through the PC and can still be caught and modified there by malicious software.

Some users feel protected because they only use their PC for low-value transactions, but of course this is an illusion if an attacker can just as well do high-value transactions or a very large number of them with the same set-up. Similarly, some users do not seem to be aware that they are vulnerable to

---

[2]This last problem will be solved by the emerging Secure Domain Name Service (Eastlake 1999) and proper use of IPSEC (Atkinson 1995).

[3]See for example http://www.newscientist.com/cgi-bin/pageserver.cgi?/ns/980425/nwindows.html.

attacks from the Internet not only if they have servers running, but as soon as they use anything like browsers or email. Ignoring these risks makes them even more vulnerable.

1.2.4 New Opportunities to Commit Fraud

Today, fraud in electronic commerce is a relatively minor problem. But most likely the main reason is that the overall volume of electronic commerce has been too small. Attacking traditional commerce has been more cost efficient for serious criminals. But we are convinced that this will change dramatically: the more successful electronic commerce becomes, the more attractive becomes electronic fraud.

An additional argument is that electronic commerce has some properties that favor fraud: Electronic fraud can be highly automated, i.e., a single criminal might be able to simultaneously attack a whole user population, e.g., all the customers of a certain company. Some fraud procedures can be performed at a very high speed, which might make attacks on low-value services attractive that would never represent a risk in the physical world. Plausibility checks like "not too many requests from a single person" do not necessarily work, since criminals might be able to generate an unlimited number of new identities. Cheaters can commit their crime remotely, e.g., from countries with weak criminal laws or no interest to prosecute fraud committed abroad. Finding promising targets is also facilitated by the Internet, as it is usually quite easy to check which companies use which security mechanisms.[4]

1.3 Existing Approaches to Secure Electronic Commerce

Basically two security mechanisms are actually applied in today's electronic commerce: SSL as a means to establish secure channels between business partners, and Trusted Market Providers as a means to implement centralized security policies. Two further mechanisms are widely discussed and used in prototypes and trials, digital signatures with corresponding public-key infrastructures and secure payment systems.

1.3.1 Secure Channels

Most electronic-commerce solutions use the SSL protocol (Freier, Karlton, and Kocher 1996) to establish a secure channel between the business partners, e.g., a buyer's World-Wide Web browser and a merchant's server. At least

---

[4]One should also be aware that unprotected email and browsing can be a good source for conventional burglars and blackmailers to find attractive targets, e.g., by looking for vacation servers, or people who search for and buy expensive tangible goods.

the server, optionally also the client, are identified by means of public-key certificates. "Secure" means that all messages sent through this channel are integrity-protected and encrypted, i.e., any modification of the messages can be detected and outsiders cannot read the messages.

Although SSL is a useful tool, most of the security problems in electronic commerce cannot be solved with it:

- SSL uses *symmetric* cryptography for the main messages. This means that sender and recipient of a message have the same secrets. Therefore the recipient does not gain any evidence (e.g., for use in court) that the sender actually sent a message (e.g., made a binding offer or ordered expensive goods) because the recipient could just as well have produced the message himself.
- One design goal for SSL was to provide a *transparent* secure channel, i.e., after the set-up phase the application does not need to be aware of SSL. This is a very nice property for simple secure communication. However, for electronic commerce it means that even if asymmetric cryptography were used throughout, SSL messages could not serve as evidence in any easy way, because SSL would automatically sign all sorts of messages without clear relation to what the user actually saw on the screen and authorized.
- SSL is just a protocol (i.e., it defines message formats and other such technicalities). *No legal meaning* is typically associated to the keys used in it (compare Section 1.3.3). Of course, this is fine for its intended use as protection from outsiders, and it is the correct legal reflection of the technical facts in the first two items that prevent it from being used for protection of two communication partners from each other.
- The typical user of SSL clicks on a link to a certain partner in his browser, sees a lock symbol that shows that a secure channel was established, and believes he now has a secure channel to the desired partner. However, as long as he does not go to a particular window to check a certificate, an attacker can still just as easily cheat him as without SSL, because the lock symbol only means that there is a secure channel to *anyone*.

The last issue is not a problem of SSL as a protocol (and not even a limitation of secure channels in general, as the other issues are). But it shows that a secure user-interface design and secure linking between different steps, here between the name clicked on and the name of the partner on the channel, are important for overall security. These are two important topics in *SEMPER*; see below.

1.3.2 Trusted Market Provider

Many electronic-commerce solutions are organized around a central server which manages a marketplace and is responsible to ensure the security of *all* parties on the marketplace. For instance, Open Market (Open Market 1998) and existing auction and broker services use this model. Another example are workflow systems which support the co-operation between pre-defined entities according to pre-defined rules and procedures. Typically a workflow is seen as a single database process which interacts with different entities. Security of a workflow is primarily given by assigning each of the entities the necessary access rights, in the usual database sense. These rights are determined by the entity's role with respect to the workflow and by the current work item.

The disadvantages of this approach are that the players have to trust this central server, usually even without being able to detect fraud, and that this naturally results in closed solutions.

1.3.3 Digital Signatures and Public-Key Infrastructures

Proving that a certain action in the virtual world was performed by a certain entity is technically primarily facilitated by *digital signatures*, first introduced in Diffie and Hellman (1976). A digital signature scheme is a cryptographic mechanism that allows its users to attach certain bit strings, called "digital signatures," to digital documents such that, in principle, everybody can check signatures, but nobody can forge a signature under a document the supposed signer did not actually sign. The information necessary to verify signatures of a certain person is called the *public key*, and the information necessary to generate the signatures is called the *secret key*. For a secure signature scheme, nobody who only knows the public key and some signatures generated by the true holder of the secret key must be able to compute a signature under any additional document.

To link a signed document to a certain *real-world* entity, one has to know whether the public key actually "belongs to" this entity. This is facilitated by *public-key infrastructures* (PKI) (e.g., Ford and Baum (1997)). The typical solution is to establish one or a few *certification authorities* (CA). Their task is to verify that a certain public key *pk* belongs to a certain entity X and to sign a digital document, called *certificate,* that confirms this fact to others. The notion of "belong to" is vague, and there have been many discussions on the semantics of certificates. (The better way would have been to make the certificates real statements saying what is meant, instead of essentially pairs of a name and a key.) Naively, one would like a semantics that allows the recipient of a statement with a digital signature to treat it like a statement with a handwritten signature. Even more simplified, this would mean that the certification authority states in the certificate that the entity X is willing to take full responsibility for every statement that carries a correct signature with respect to *pk*. The phase where X agrees to this responsibility (because such liabilities should not be assigned to a person by third parties, and indeed cannot in most laws) is called *registration* and should involve a handwritten signature by X under a similar statement. The certification authority should verify this signature with respect to an identity document of X to make registration secure.

However, people would currently like to carry out electronic commerce with PCs only, and, as explained above, secret keys on PCs can easily be stolen or misused by attackers (and even smartcards do not help all that much). Hence such a strong liability is not desirable because it would expose consumers and small businesses to an incalculable risk. A special case of this liability question was already discussed for SET in Section 1.1.1, and existing solutions typically have the same all-or-nothing approach. *SEMPER* has come up with a much more flexible approach balancing the needs of all parties; see Chapter 3.[5]

At a more abstract level, keys are often seen as "identities" or "pseudonyms" under which the players can act on the electronic marketplace, and PKIs as a means to bind a digital identity to a real-world one. But one should keep in mind that this is just an analogy: Electronic identities are information, basically secret keys. Thus, unlike real identities, they can be stolen. A criminal who gets a secret key can create perfect counterfeits, where no expert witness can find a difference. Moreover, a criminal can create an arbitrary number of new secret keys, thereby possibly multiplying his own power to commit crime.

1.3.4 Payment Systems

There are a number of different proposals for secure electronic payment systems. One main class follows established paper-based systems where security relies on handwritten signatures by replacing those with digital signatures. Here SET (MasterCard and Visa 1997), favored by large credit-card companies, is best-known; cheques (e.g., FSTC (1995)) and home banking (e.g., Zentraler Kreditausschuss (ZKA) (1999)) are other subclasses. The second main class tries to imitate cash. Here the most interesting implemented system is ecash by DigiCash (Schoenmakers 1998), which, in contrast to others, also simulates the privacy aspect of traditional cash. This may become even more important in the virtual world with its additional threats. Payment models are explained in more detail in Chapter 11; for an overview of techniques and proposals see Asokan, Janson, Steiner, and Waidner (2000). *SEMPER* did not work on any new payment systems, but on a mechanism that allows users to handle the given variety in a flexible and secure way.

1.4 The Whole Picture of Electronic Commerce

The security mechanisms for electronic commerce considered so far concern individual *steps*. A payment is one such step, and sending a signed document is another. However, such steps do not exist in isolation in electronic

---

[5]The German Digital Signature Act (German Government 1997) and the European Signature Directive (European Union 2000) do allow limits on the uses of a certificate; here the *SEMPER* solution could be integrated.

commerce: They must be *linked* so that one can safely refer from one step to another. In other words, business consists of *processes*. This is already true for simple catalogue-based shopping over the Internet as described in Section 1.1.1: For example, the price paid should correspond to that in the catalogue. The buyer does not want to pay without receiving the merchandise, nor the merchant send it without being paid. Furthermore, if the buyer does get the merchandise but it is seriously different from the offer in the catalogue he may want to return it, which may result in a dispute in court. Many variants of such processes are possible, in particular in a business-to-business scenario. For example, there may be a longer negotiation phase; there might be different binding offers for the same good or service; and delivery might be in several installments.

In all such processes there are certain rules that a secure electronic-commerce tool should help to ensure: Many steps process certain *forms,* i.e., documents with fields with a fixed semantics, like "price" or "delivery date." Some rules, e.g., from accounting or tax laws, concern a form as such. Other rules, more important for security, concern the relation between the fields of different forms, e.g., that the price of a payment is the same as in the order, or the semantics of the fields, e.g., that something has indeed arrived at the delivery date. Each participant in secure electronic commerce wants his own tool to locally check this for him, or at least to aid him in checking and help him to remedy problems, without relying on the partner to run the same tool securely or simply not to cheat.

This means that records of the steps are needed in a meaningful context, i.e., within the processes they belong to. This is not only desired by both private and commercial users for managing their assets, but also to allow the extraction of meaningful evidence in the case of disputes, and to enable the concept of an "electronic auditor."

The process approach is similar to EDI and projects like XML/EDI or OBI mentioned in Section 1.1.2, but none of those focuses enough on the related multi-party security requirements.

How *SEMPER* and such projects could be integrated is mentioned in Chapter 6.

An additional issue with a process-oriented approach is user authorization. In principle, most steps need to be approved by the users, typically a human user in the case of consumers and small businesses. However, the user might not want to be bothered with each step, but want to give the approval once for an entire process. This means that rights to perform certain steps must be delegated to the user's secure electronic commerce tool, for example by means of *authorization and delegation policies.*

1.5 Resulting Goals of *SEMPER*

1.5.1 Security Requirements

Generalizing from concrete scenarios and concrete threats, and from user interviews in *SEMPER* (see Chapters 7 and 8) and outside surveys, one can see the following main security requirements for electronic commerce:

- Fairness: Ensure that situations like payment without delivery, or delivery without payment, do not happen.
- Authenticity: Ensure that partners cannot impersonate others or, where anonymous, ensure that they cannot act without having the proper rights.
- Availability of service: Ensure that all contracts and promises are fulfilled.
- Privacy: Ensure that partners do not collect or use data for unintended purposes. Ensure that outsiders do not get unnecessary information.
- Prevent misuse of goods, like infringement of copyright and illegal resale of information.

All these requirements are not only made on the internal technical system, but relative to how the real users interact with the system, from the user interface design to the legal environment.

1.5.2 The *SEMPER* Focus

As a result of the view on the current situation and future needs as described so far, *SEMPER* has set the following goals for its specific approach:

- *Entire processes*: *SEMPER* should support all the standard steps, linked into complete business processes as described in Section 1.4, such that the security requirements are fulfilled for the entire processes. For extreme cases, disputes must be supported, i.e., the tool must help to find the necessary evidence and must also help arbiters to evaluate it. Privacy must also be supported for entire processes.
- *Multiple scenarios*: *SEMPER* should be usable in a variety of person-to-business, business-to-business, and person-to-person scenarios. In particular for large businesses, it should be suitable for integration into back-end systems, i.e., for use without human intervention. In other cases, only export and import of data with other programs is necessary. The benefits of using one framework for all these scenarios is decreased development cost and increased confidence in its security due to more intensive scrutiny.
- *Openness*: For many of the services (e.g., payments, signatures, encryption) several protocols and products already coexist and will keep coexisting. The *SEMPER* architecture should be able to integrate them easily. It must also support business partners in selecting which protocol and product to use in a given situation.

It should also be possible to integrate less standard building blocks, e.g., anonymous communication (in particular for privacy in web browsing and prepaid low-value purchases) and time-stamping and other notary services.

- *Ensure that users can securely manage information*: All the security technologies need to interact with the human user (except in back-end integration): He has to agree to transfer a right or to give away certain private information to a certain other party, and thus he has to be convinced about this party's current role and rights. This requires a carefully designed user interface: Users must be made aware of security-critical facts, but still "normal" users should not be bothered with so many details that they start clicking "ok" regardless. Important aspects are a uniform look-and-feel for critical steps, and clear indications of "points of no return" where a negotiation or selection phase ends and a legally meaningful or privacy-critical step is taken. We call such an interface a Trustworthy Interactive Graphical User Interface (TINGUIN).
- *Multi-party security*: *SEMPER* must be a distributed system with no a-priori assumptions that everybody will trust particular entities. Where third-party services are needed, everybody should be free to choose them in the most suitable way, and it should be possible to hold such third parties accountable for their actions.
- *Legal framework*: The technical framework alone is insufficient for establishing a predictable security environment because national laws and regulations do not yet include specific and coherent provisions on electronic commerce. A legal framework, acknowledging the liabilities of digital signatures and the value of electronic records taken during business processes, is required. It should in particular provide clarity in cross-border situations (and situations where only the certification authorities are different). A fair and reasonable distribution of rights and responsibilities should be made that takes into account the current risks and vulnerabilities and can adapt smoothly to changed situations (e.g., more secure user devices) in the future.

Apart from developing the technical and legal frameworks, *SEMPER* also worked on particular protocols where no sufficiently secure or efficient technology was available yet. In the following chapters, we will see how *SEMPER* carried out this approach. In particular, Chapter 2 gives an overview of the technical approach and Chapter 3 of the legal framework, while Chapter 4 shows how this basis can be used in important scenarios. Some highlights are presented in more detail in Part II of this book.

2. Technical Framework

This chapter gives an overview of the technical framework of *SEMPER* and how this framework fulfills the goals derived in Chapter 1. The framework covers the whole scope of business processes from the standpoint of security and is flexible enough to integrate existing or future security tools.

2.1 The *SEMPER* Model

The technical provisions of the *SEMPER* framework are primarily designed for the users of the marketplace. Typically their roles are buyers or sellers, but *SEMPER* also supports other business processes besides purchases. The framework is also useful for third parties with security-relevant functions like auctioneers, notaries, and arbiters who evaluate disputes on the basis of digital evidence, but then some role-specific additional software will be needed.

The basis for the technical provisions is the model that

- the security-critical parts of electronic commerce are typically sequences of transfers or exchanges of information, and
- users might question the current state of affairs during or after a business process.

The concepts of transfer and exchange address the first point, while the concept of deal addresses the second one. These concepts contribute to the support of consistent business processes while implementing multi-party security.

A *transfer*, in *SEMPER* terms, achieves the transmission of one or more pieces of information like a document or a payment from one party to one or more recipients. The concept of transfer should be understood at an abstract level. Hence, a transfer may need one or several messages to complete. The model distinguishes three main types of items that may be transferred: (a) payments, (b) signed statements like offers, orders, receipts, contracts, and certificates, and (c) information like intangibles to be delivered. Each item or its transfer may be individually associated with security attributes such as confidentiality or non-repudiation of origin or receipt. Items may be grouped together under the concept of container for the purpose of performing a transfer. Security attributes may also be assigned to a container.

G. Lacoste et al. (Eds.): SEMPER 2000, LNCS 1854, pp. 15–21, 2000.

For example, an order with its corresponding payment can be packaged in a container which demands non-repudiation of receipt.

When several transfers need to be grouped together to represent the semantics of an indivisible operation among two or more parties, the concept of *exchange* is used. Payment against delivery is an example of an exchange. Typically, exchanges are associated with fairness guarantees so that a party's transferring an item will imply the reception of an item in return: payment against delivery implies that payment is received if and only if delivery occurs. Thus, a fair exchange will either complete successfully or everything will happen as if no exchange took place. (The simplest implementation would be to always send both items to a trusted third party, which only forwards them if they fit the expectations.) Figure 2.1 illustrates typical exchanges in electronic commerce.

	Payment	**Signed statement**	**Information**
Information	Purchase of information	Conditional access, certified mail	Information exchange
Signed statement	Payment with receipt	Contract signing	
Payment	Money exchange		

Fig. 2.1. Typical exchanges

A third key concept in *SEMPER* is that of a *deal*. A deal corresponds to a sequence of steps (also called transactions later at a technical level). It addresses the need to cope with an entire business process in a consistent manner, maintaining the link between steps as they occur. A deal is recorded both at the seller's and the buyer's side (or, in other types of business processes, similarly at each participant's side). This is illustrated in Figure 2.2. The record includes the information received and sent during each step, overall information about the process like negotiated security attributes and the digital identity of the parties involved, and the relations among steps.

Based on deal records archived at the buyer's and the seller's, exception handling by the parties themselves and disputes involving an arbiter can take place. By inspection of deal records, securely aided by his own installation of *SEMPER*, an arbiter will evaluate evidence and determine an appropriate resolution.

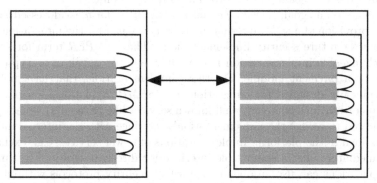

Fig. 2.2. A deal: Both parties record the steps and their relations

2.2 Approach

The *SEMPER* model described so far is the basis for fulfilling the goals
of considering entire processes and providing multi-party security (see Section 1.5.2). We now consider the *SEMPER* approach to cope with the following three goals: (a) allowing for multiple business scenarios, (b) establishing
an open security platform, and (c) ensuring that users can securely manage
information.

The first goal, *usability in multiple business scenarios*, is addressed by po-
sitioning the main part of *SEMPER* as a piece of middleware, which provides
security services to applications implementing business processes.[1] Security
services are offered in the style of a security tool box, thereby enabling applications to freely invoke individual services as needed. Hence, an application
where one pays after delivery can invoke the information transfer service
and the payment service in this order, while other applications could use a
fair exchange, or do the payment completely out of band. The division into
applications and security services through an application programming interface provides application designers with the flexibility to cope with as many
business scenarios as required. This division also brings them the advantage of shielding their applications from the security-implementation details
and their evolution over time. Hence, the approach of *SEMPER* divides the
support of business processes into two distinct, but complementary, types
of developments: (a) applications, including the integration of back-end systems, and (b) security means. A difference to other security tool boxes is that
SEMPER provides security means up to a higher, more commerce-oriented

---

[1] *SEMPER* has also provided prototypes of standard applications of this middleware part; see Chapter 4.

level with its transfers, exchanges, and deals, and also with the consequent provisions for meaningful records and dispute resolution.

The second goal, *providing an open security platform*, is addressed through the provision of a set of internal interfaces designed for the integration of existing or future security implementations. The *SEMPER* term for such an exchangeable implementation is a module, e.g., we speak of a crypto module or a payment module. For those implementations that have not been specifically designed for integration in a *SEMPER* platform (in particular implementations of already well-known services like payments), an adapter is required to bridge the implementation's interface with the internal interface provided in the platform. Implementations of newer services, e.g., exchanges, immediately offer a compatible interface for direct integration. In this way, applications can use an open-ended set of security protocols without being aware of their specificity. Users can populate their security tool box with the modules of their choice. The *SEMPER* framework itself performs overall functions like the automatic negotiation!of module of a module that both business partners have in their tool box and that best provides the desired high-level security and quality-of-service attributes.

The introduction of a trustworthy user interface, the TINGUIN, in *SEMPER* addresses the third requirement, *ensuring that users can securely manage information*. It clearly partitions, from the user's standpoint, information into trustworthy and unverified information. The *SEMPER* user interface is designed to be the unique point of interaction between users and their secure platform. A single interface is of paramount importance: Multiple ones, provided by each security implementation integrated in *SEMPER*, would introduce complexity and seriously endanger the user's consistent perception of his security context. This would significantly weaken security. The interface provides the user with means to interact with the other parties involved in electronic commerce, whether a business partner or a third party. It visualizes security-relevant information received such as party authentication, certificates, credentials, signed information, payments, or signed receipts. It empowers users to sign documents like offers, orders, or quotations, to authorize payments or the downloading of a business application, to register with registration authorities, or to request certificates from a certification authority. It also enables users to manage secure information stored locally like past steps of a deal, certificates, preferences, and to securely install new modules on the platform.

2.3 Architecture

The security functions offered by *SEMPER* are structured in three layers and a set of supporting services. The upper layer, named the Commerce Layer, offers security services to the applications and provides the process orientation. It relies on the middle layer for transfers and exchanges. That middle layer, noted the Transfer-and-Exchange Layer, relies itself on the bottom layer, called the Business-Item Layer, for protocols specific to the nature of business items exchanged. Figure 2.3 illustrates the overall architecture of *SEMPER*.

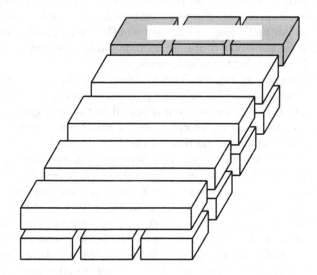

Fig. 2.3. *SEMPER* overall architecture

The *Commerce Layer* maintains the status of a deal and records its progress. It offers the business application, and thus finally the user, services to open new deals, to navigate across or within existing deals, and to retrieve and display previous and current steps. Deals can also be exported, e.g., to an arbiter for inspection and resolution of disputes. The arbiter has the same support for displaying and verifying steps of a deal by the Commerce Layer of his own *SEMPER* installation. Opening a deal includes the negotiation of the overall quality of service, in particular the security attributes. Additional security attributes may be set for individual steps. For example, if confidentiality was not set at deal level, it can be added for the delivery of information. Some attributes only make sense for entire deals, e.g., anonymity. In addition, general application-oriented specializations of lower-layer services are placed on the Commerce Layer.

The *Transfer-and-Exchange Layer* manages exchanges and transfers. In an exchange, each party specifies business items in the form of a description of what will be sent, and what is expected in return. Each party also specifies security attributes for the exchange. The exchange will complete only if two conditions are met: (a) the description of business items to be sent match the expectations, and (b) the security attributes required can be met. For the fairness of the exchange, i.e., the both-or-nothing property, the help of a notary may be requested. To this end, *SEMPER* designed efficient and novel optimistic protocols involving a notary only in case of exceptions.

For transfers, several arbitrary business items can be grouped into containers. Security attributes can be associated to both the container and the information within it. For example, sending a container with non-repudiation of origin will internally lead to a signature of the sending party on aggregated information for the whole container, including items like payments that may involve several rounds of communication.

The *Business-Item Layer* handles transfers according to the nature of the data being sent and received, whether payments, statements, or information. The description of the desired item is passed to the appropriate module for actual transmission and reception through a suitable protocol. For example, a payment to be made on the basis of the SET protocol is passed to a SET module that achieves the necessary three-party communication among the customer, the merchant and the payment gateway. A user can have multiple so-called purses, e.g., for several credit cards and anonymous stored-value payments, and manage and use them consistently with *SEMPER*. In the course of the project, implementations of seven different payment systems were integrated through the interfaces offered by the Business-Item Layer for payments. A similar approach was followed for statements and information.

The *Supporting Services*, including the trustworthy user interface, are available for access by the three main layers. Apart from the user interface, they include various services for cryptography, secure communication, and local bookkeeping. The cryptographic services mainly provide for key generation, encryption, and signatures. There are also provisions for handling certificates both for a public-key infrastructure and for trust management.

The communication services offer communication in a unified way, shielding service use from the specificity of the underlying network. A quality of service parameter enables the selection of the appropriate communication channel. Secure communication is implemented as a natural extension with security attributes as additional quality-of-service parameters. In addition, *SEMPER* provides for anonymous communication in the same framework by an abstract addressing scheme that comprises normal and pseudonymous addresses.

Among the local bookkeeping services, the archiving services manage secure storage and retrieval of certificates, keys, and the information pertaining to deals. The preference services maintain a consistent view of user preferences to modules in *SEMPER*. Access control services protect system and data integrity and confidentiality by verifying the rights of the *SEMPER* components as well as business applications wishing to access to critical resources.

2.4 Protocols and Implementation

The *SEMPER* architecture aims at securing electronic commerce as a whole, and is at present still the only architecture with this ambitious goal. A more technical overall description is given in Chapter 6. There it is also shown how other known projects would fit into our overall architecture. Within the project, a prototype of the architecture was implemented in Java. Trial experiences with this prototype and corresponding business applications are described in Chapters 7 and 8. New protocols and strategies invented in *SEMPER* within this architecture are described in detail in other chapters of Part II. This concerns in particular the payment framework, fair exchanges, trust and liability management and the deal concept.

3. Legal Framework

This chapter outlines *SEMPER*'s proposals for establishing legal predictability of electronic transactions. An important novelty is a method for assigning liability to digital signatures in a way that is predictable for all sides without requiring prior investment into highly secure hardware, the Commitment- and Liability-Cover Service. The proposals also cover most other legal aspects of electronic commerce, again with a focus on predictability even in cross-border scenarios, fairness to all parties, and ease of adoption. A model for implementing these proposals is given as the *SEMPER* Electronic-Commerce Agreement, *SECA*.

3.1 Introduction

Electronic commerce promises the ability to perform almost arbitrary transactions over information networks. However, this new support of business has not yet developed in the order of magnitude that was anticipated, partly because legal predictability is still not available. Because their computers are not secure enough, users are still facing many risks, in particular impersonation attacks through stealing private keys or, if the keys are stored on smartcards, through misuse of the smartcard via the insecure computer; see Sections 1.2.3 and 1.3.3. These risks will increase once electronic commerce is commonly used. This means that, technically, digital signatures cannot fully ensure non-repudiation until such attacks are really prevented. Nevertheless, most users wish to use their current PCs for all their actions on the Internet without even bothering to get a smartcard reader and a smartcard, and even less wait a few years for more secure devices.

SEMPER developed a suite of measures that allows all parties, both the holders of signature keys and relying parties (i.e., parties that accept signatures and rely on their validity), to limit their overall risk in a predictable yet flexible way. This represents a market-driven, in contrast to entirely regulation-driven, approach at liability assignment for signatures. It is described in Section 3.2.

Furthermore, while digital signature laws are indeed emerging, different countries are taking different attitudes. For example, the regulations enacted

G. Lacoste et al. (Eds.): SEMPER 2000, LNCS 1854, pp. 23–29, 2000.
© Springer-Verlag Berlin Heidelberg 2000

or planned in forty states of the United States have approached digital signatures in about six different ways. (Details about emerging regulations are given in Chapter 14.) Other legal issues like advertising, the applicable law and jurisdiction, consumer-protection laws, privacy and data protection, and copyright and trademark issues, would also need to be harmonized in order to encourage cross-border commerce. *SEMPER* proposes to compensate the current lack of regulations by establishing binding agreements for the immediate use of electronic commerce. Such agreements have a realistic chance to be recognized and accepted by the players and courts if they are clear, fair, comprehensible and practicable. A concrete model agreement is explained in Section 3.3. (Details can be found in Chapter 14.)

3.2 Predictable Liability for Signature Keys

Regulating the liability for digital signatures is the core question in a legal framework for electronic commerce. The concrete objectives in *SEMPER* were:

- To enable a key holder to limit his liability to an acceptable and previously known *overall value* in case the equipment used for signing is compromised.
- To enable relying parties to rely on received signatures regardless of whether the key holder's equipment was compromised.
- Not to require the parties to know each other a priori, or to make paper-based bilateral agreements for this purpose.

Recall that in cases of bilateral relationships that do start with personal contacts, e.g., in home banking or under a trading partner agreement, the first two requirements can be fulfilled quite easily by agreeing on an overall limit on the transaction volume between these partners. With the third requirement, *SEMPER* extends this type of security to the more flexible relationships desired in electronic commerce.

The following main measures achieve these objectives:

- Each party makes an agreement on its concrete liability with its CA (certification authority). This is called an *initial commitment*.
- Online services guarantee to relying parties that the value they rely on is covered by the overall value the key holder is liable for. This is called the *Liability-Cover Service*, short L-Cover Service.

The first measure means that the agreement on liability is made in the one place where an agreement has to be made anyway. Thus there is no significant overhead. In our legal view, the agreement requires a handwritten signature by the person incurring the liability (the owner of the signature key) under the terms of the agreement. For high liabilities, the person's identity and signature should be compared with an identity document. This makes identity stealing, as known with credit cards, as difficult as possible.[1] The CA includes the liability limit in its certificates. Several certificate standards and regulations already allow limits, in particular X.509v3 (ISO/IEC 1995), the German Digital Signature Act (German Government 1997) and the European Signature Directive (European Union 2000), but without giving them a clear meaning. (In particular, is the limit per transaction or overall? And in the latter case, how can the relying party know whether it is covered?) These fields can be utilized and made meaningful by the *SEMPER* commitments and liability covers, either by the policies of individual CAs or generally.

3.2.1 Commitments without Online Third Party

For cases where the overhead of the full liability-cover service is not deemed worth while, *SEMPER* proposes two simpler forms of commitment:

– *General liability limit:* The general rule is that a key holder is liable for digital signatures made with this key unless he claims his key was compromised. In that case, the key holder has to satisfy all relying parties that are not covered by higher-class commitments with an overall amount not exceeding the general liability limit he agreed to. Thus the relying parties cannot fully rely on the signatures, but they know that the key holder cannot revoke transactions with impunity.
  Considering that many users do not look at certificate details, the *SEMPER* model agreement *SECA* proposes that this limit could be fixed, depending only on the role of the party (e.g., private or business).
– *Partner-specific liability limit:* For business partners with whom a key holder deals regularly, he can agree to an additional limit on what he would pay this partner if his signature key is compromised. The function is similar to a bilateral agreement between these parties, but the CA mediates the initial agreement, so that the relying party need not verify an identifying document etc.

3.2.2 Liability-Cover Service

If a relying party requires a certain fixed liability per signature and the key holder has not committed to a partner-specific liability limit in advance, the full liability-cover service is needed. The key holder initially commits to a (freely chosen) overall liability limit for this service, e.g., on a certain value per month, to its CA providing this service. For a specific signature, the key holder contacts the CA and requests a commitment for the amount needed by the relying party. The request is digitally signed. Upon receiving a valid request, the CA verifies that the amount is still within the overall limit and

---

[1]However, in any case, a key certified with an overall liability limit is less dangerous for its supposed owner than one without. Hence the requirements on correct identification can be less strict if anything.

adds this amount to the total so far. The CA then signs a specific liability-cover certificate, which uniquely refers to the transaction to prevent re-use for other transactions. Upon receipt of a signed message and a corresponding liability-cover certificate, the relying party verifies that all signatures are valid and that the committed amount is sufficient for the purpose. Details are presented in Chapter 13.

3.2.3 Security and Market Effectiveness

For security, the important point is that none of the commitment types allows a criminal who has gained access to a signature key to increase the key holder's liability for this key by using the key itself.

The service fulfills multi-party security, i.e., nobody needs to trust the CAs unduly: A key holder is protected by the paper-based commitment procedure to the liability limit. (If criminals can subvert this procedure, they can cheat, but the procedure was required to be equally secure as other commitments to similar amounts in paper-based commerce.) The relying parties obtain clear guarantees in the certificates, and if the CA gave out certificates exceeding the key holder's overall limit, or certificates for which it cannot show the key holder's signed request, the CA should be liable.[2] The remaining, predictable risks may be insured at the discretion of the parties and insurance companies.[3]

The market incentive for using a liability-cover service is that recipients of signatures (typically service providers) will require non-repudiation, i.e., liability of the key holder, in some situations, or offer favorable conditions to key holders giving such guarantees. This will encourage key holders (typically customers) to agree to such liabilities with limits suitable to their financial status, if they can reasonably hope to recover the cost, bother, and risk of a getting a certificate. An organization of potential recipients might also sponsor CAs to make certificates with liability more attractive to customers immediately. Market forces can then also drive the development of more secure devices: When compromising keys with certain liabilities becomes attractive enough for criminals so that it happens often, the incentives that key holders need before agreeing to such liabilities will increase, and at some point buying more secure devices will be cheaper on average.

---

[2]However, it should not be liable for the key holders' financial abilities to fulfill their commitments—this is not the job of a legal framework, but of a credit-rating agency.

[3]In contrast, it is unlikely that insurance companies will insure key compromise without liability limits in the long run, as they cannot verify whether such a claim is true or not (similar to problems with insurances against luggage theft). Excluding key holders whose key is compromised more than, say, twice is not a solution because a criminal might indeed attack the same target several times.

3.3 The *SEMPER* Electronic-Commerce Agreement

Besides the legal recognition of digital signatures, many other legal issues would need harmonized regulations to make electronic commerce predictable, in particular across borders:

- applicable law and jurisdiction,
- export regulations for cryptographic products,
- consumer protection (in the sense of protecting weaker partners from being taken advantage of),
- privacy and data protection,
- advertising, competition, and spamming (i.e., junk mail),
- illegal content of offers and Internet pages,
- contract law (in the sense of formal requirements),
- copyright and trademark, and
- payment and taxation.

A promising solution to compensate the lack of regulation immediately is to establish model agreements to which parties voluntarily promise to adhere. Agreements have a realistic chance to be accepted by the players and approved in court if they are clear, fair, comprehensible and practicable. *SEMPER* proposes a model agreement for this purpose, called *SECA* (*SEMPER* Electronic-Commerce Agreement). An additional advantage of such an agreement is that it can enhance the awareness of users as a means to reduce risks.

3.3.1 Structure of *SECA*

SECA comprises three parts: the agreement itself that needs to be signed, a code of conduct that the signatories promise to follow, and guidelines that give advice for reducing risks due to failures and attacks and try to establish security and fairness standards for products.

Agreement. The first section of the agreement defines the scope of the agreement in terms of areas of participation and applicable transactions, and contains the obligation to follow the code of conduct. The second section regulates contracts concluded by parties having agreed to *SECA* and refers to the default values defined in the code of conduct like the applicable law and jurisdiction. This section also includes provisions for conflicts of *SECA* with other regulations the parties wish to establish. The third section regulates the liability for digital signatures as explained above. The fourth section addresses the case of parties not adhering to the agreement although they agreed to it, including revocation and blacklisting. The fifth section contains general provisions, e.g., for the modification of *SECA* and cases of inapplicability.

Code of conduct. The code of conduct is designed to ensure fairness in transactions and to facilitate cross-border commerce. It sets default values of applicable law and jurisdiction according to the relationship between two parties: private-to-private, business-to-business, or business-to-private. The interests of the consumer, as the weaker party, are favored. The code of conduct also includes regulations for fair business concerning advertising and competition, negotiation, offers and acceptances, consumer protection, content of contracts and Internet pages, and privacy and data protection. The few remaining items from the list above are better left to national law.

Guidelines. The first section of the guidelines introduces the concept of *SECA*-compliant components such as electronic-commerce software, operating systems, and secure hardware. The criteria for electronic-commerce software emphasizes user friendliness and secure visualization, and creation and handling of evidence. They are a more detailed version of the requirements "entire processes," "ensuring that users can securely manage information" and "multi-party security" listed in Section 1.5.2 as a basis for the technical development in *SEMPER*. Aiming at flexibility with respect to current and future technology, the model agreement does not try to bar other components, but recognizes *SECA* compliance as helpful for risk management.

The second section is dedicated to recommendations to users for protecting themselves. It addresses the use of fair electronic-commerce software and secure hardware and operating systems; the need of backups and secure upgrading; the generation and use of keys; liability and advice in case keys are compromised; housekeeping with respect to records created by electronic-commerce software; and recommendations for commercial parties running a server.

Certificates. An agreement like *SECA* contains a number of parameters characterizing the signatory. Hence each CA should offer several different certificates for the same key, each with a different subset of these parameters. The signatory can then choose how many parameters to show to each partner. This achieves flexible privacy of personal data or business parameters. Of course, care must be taken such that essential parameters like liability limits cannot be omitted or have a suitable default (here zero).

The full details of *SECA* can be found in Chapter 14.

3.3.2 Introducing Electronic-Commerce Agreements

A model agreement like *SECA* can easily be introduced in practice because it is only an agreement between a party and a CA. In fact, it consists of two successive unilateral statements: First the party (a person or a representative of a legal entity) declares its agreement in a traditional way to the CA; then the CA declares this fact in a certificate. *SECA* contains sufficient provision for the case where such a party does business with parties who did not sign a similar agreement. Hence it can be useful right from the start and offer a business advantage over competitors who did not sign such a clarifying agreement.

Nevertheless, an agreement is the more useful the more widely it is accepted. An obvious reason is that one also wants one's trading partner to have agreed to certain fairness rules. In addition, wide-spread use of the same agreement means that people no longer need to read the small print each time. Hence groups of CAs or Chambers of Commerce would be well advised to provide *SECA* or a similar agreement as a default. This would imply tasks like maintaining *SECA* templates, disseminating information on the legal situation in different countries, publishing key certificates of CAs supporting the agreement, and providing black lists of parties violating *SECA* rules they had agreed to.

Finally, it is useful to adapt a technical framework and a legal framework to each other as in *SEMPER* because the user's electronic-commerce tool can then securely visualize important legal aspects. For instance, the *SEMPER* TINGUIN shows at the beginning of a deal whether the partner also signed *SECA* and can zoom to certain parameters, e.g., the partner's liability limits.

3.4 Conclusions

No solution—technical, legal or organizational—can currently remove all risks in electronic commerce. Nevertheless, voluntary agreements that each party individually makes towards its CA, hopefully based on a small number of model agreements, can greatly increase legal predictability at once. We developed the model agreement *SECA* for this purpose. A particularly important aspect is the regulation of liability for digital signatures. Here, *SEMPER*'s liability limits and online Liability-Cover Service provide a good compromise for users willing to accept a certain liability. This may be a critical step to significantly increase electronic-commerce activities, including those crossing borders, while international legal frameworks are being progressed.

4. Vision of Future Products

In this chapter, we describe how the *SEMPER* framework can be used in various types of commercial products. Besides that, we believe that free distribution of a basic client version would be a useful investment in infrastructure, similar to browsers, and we describe a prototype of such a tool, the Fair Internet Trader (FIT).

4.1 Four Facets of *SEMPER* as a Product

In the course of the project, we have implemented a prototype of the *SEMPER* framework and several business applications, used them in several trials (see Chapters 7 and 8), and demonstrated it at commercial trade fairs and scientific conferences. Building upon this experience, we developed a vision of future products for secure electronic commerce based on the *SEMPER* framework. This does not mean that we propose to use precisely our prototype as a commercial product—product-quality code according to industrial standards was out of reach for us as a research project. But we do propose to implement new products within our technical and legal frameworks. Our vision of *SEMPER*-based products has four facets:

New business applications. Concrete business applications can easily and securely be implemented on top of the *SEMPER* framework. This minimizes time-to-market for new services, as well as security-related costs and technical difficulties.

Naturally all business applications at one site should use the same *SEMPER* installation. But as a strategy for introducing the framework, or in order to differentiate specific applications on the market, the framework can be bundled with the business application. For instance, we did this with the Fair Internet Trader presented in Section 4.2.2.

Facilitating the development and deployment of secure business applications has been the main motivation for *SEMPER* and will also be the main motivation for any *SEMPER*-related product. We therefore discuss this facet in more detail in Section 4.2.

New security implementations. New implementations of certain services, e.g., new payment instruments or new contract-signing tools, can easily be integrated into the framework, making them instantly accessible for all existing

G. Lacoste et al. (Eds.): SEMPER 2000, LNCS 1854, pp. 31–37, 2000.
© Springer-Verlag Berlin Heidelberg 2000

business applications (recall Section 2.2 and Figure 2.3). Moreover, developing new implementations within the framework is likely to be much easier and cheaper than developing them outside because one can build upon existing services, in particular those of the lower layers of the architecture.

The framework itself. The previous two facets presuppose that the framework itself is on the market. There are several economic ways for supporting the framework as a product:

- *Component:* The *SEMPER* framework can be offered as a new component to be integrated into existing, general merchant-server products. This allows for a gradual deployment of the *SEMPER* approach; for instance, the IBM Payment Server is based on the payment framework only (see Chapter 11).
- *Middleware:* The *SEMPER* framework can be provided as typical middleware like CORBA. As with most middleware products, the main motivation for producing it would be a general cost reduction in industry, which requires the framework to become an industry standard. The best strategy to achieve this goal would be to put a product-quality implementation into the public domain. A direct source of revenue would be the provision of technical support services.
- *Preinstalled software:* The *SEMPER* framework can be seen as an extension to a bundle of standard software initially delivered with a device. A particularly interesting market segment is mobile devices like personal digital assistants (PDAs): First, this is the most likely form factor for more secure user devices in the long run. Secondly, porting *SEMPER* to mobile devices opens up many functional options: The same security framework with a similar look-and-feel (not exactly the same because of the smaller displays) can then also be used, e.g., at Internet kiosks, at counters to buy airline tickets, at stock exchanges to take over a company, and for accessing one's private or business resources remotely when traveling.

Specific parts alone. Specific aspects of *SEMPER* can be turned into products or commercial services independently of the overall framework. The following two are the most obvious choices:

- *Exchanges:* SEMPER developed new solutions for classical problems such as fair contract signing or certified mail that are more efficient than all previously known solutions (see Chapter 10 for more details). These problems are at the core of many business processes, and anybody who designs such systems could benefit from our solutions.
- *Legal framework and certificates:* SEMPER developed new approaches to the legal problems of electronic commerce and technical solutions support these approaches by making the financial risks predictable (see Chapter 3). First, one can sell these solutions as products. Secondly, one can offer the

third-party services commercially, e.g., the certificates with liability limits and the liability-cover service, Seeing what prices certification authorities currently try to ask from clients even for certificates where the client has unlimited liability and the authority none, *SEMPER*-type certificates should be quite valuable. Moreover, they should not increase the costs or the risk for existing certification authorities if those already operate in a secure way.

4.2 *SEMPER*-based Business Applications

The rest of this chapter discusses the first, and in our opinion most important facet of our vision of future products: the development of new and attractive business applications on top of *SEMPER*. Therefore, assume for the moment that the technical and legal *SEMPER* framework were available commercially.

In the course of the project we prototyped about 10 different business applications. They fell roughly into two classes, discussed in the following two sections. We strongly believe that any similar business application and many others can be implemented with the same benefits on top of the *SEMPER* framework.

4.2.1 Secure Internet Shopping

This is the standard scenario of Internet-based electronic commerce as described in Section 1.1.1: A human buyer, sitting in front of his or her PC, browses the World-Wide Web and wishes to buy something from a remote merchant. "Something" can mean tangible goods such as books or computers, or intangible goods such as information from databases or the right to attend a certain course over the Internet.

Usually, the seller's side is fully automated and does not require any human intervention in order to perform a sale. All decisions, e.g., whether a requested good is on stock, are taken by querying the seller's back-end system.

The buyer's side is manually operated. The information-gathering phase of electronic commerce, like searching for suitable sellers and browsing catalogues, is done via the browser only. Only legally relevant actions are controlled and performed via the *SEMPER* framework. For instance, as soon as the buyer requests a binding offer, the *SEMPER* user interface is started. This happens simply by clicking on something like "yes, send me a binding offer" on the merchant's page, which links to the *SEMPER* application on the buyer's computer. All the subsequent security-relevant user interactions are done via this interface. All the necessary services are already available in the framework:

- Business documents can be signed and used later on, e.g., to justify after-sales services or as a basis for disputes at court (digital signature, non-repudiation of origin, dispute handling).
- Receipts for documents and payments are ensured: even dishonest, malicious business partners cannot get hold of documents or money without acknowledging their receipt (fair exchange, certified mail, contract signing).
- The framework does not prescribe specific implementations of these services: this can be negotiated at business time or configured per business application, partner or user. In particular, business partners can dynamically negotiate which payment instruments they want to use. New implementations can be integrated efficiently. In particular there is no need to redo the back-end integration on the merchant's side once it has been done.
- Users can act on the marketplace in confidence: documents can be encrypted so that only the intended recipient can read them. Where desired, users can even act anonymously by using pseudonyms, anonymous payment instruments, and means for anonymous communication.
- The dedicated user interface encourages users to carefully watch what is displayed and entered there. This raises the user's attention in case he or she is asked to digitally sign something, which is an advantage for all parties as users cannot claim not to have understood the action.
- The user can influence the risk he or she is taking in several ways, e.g., by referring to the *SEMPER* Electronic Commerce Agreement and setting liability limits for digital signatures.
- The overall legal context can also be determined through application of the *SEMPER* Electronic Commerce Agreement (see Chapter 3).

As this kind of business is largely standardized, it would be very simple to write business applications that can be integrated in existing merchant-server products, respectively to provide implementations of standards like OTP (OTP Consortium 1998) and OBI (OBI Consortium 1998) with *enhanced security*.

4.2.2 Person-to-Person Scenario: The Fair Internet Trader

The Fair Internet Trader (FIT) is *SEMPER*'s prototype for scenarios that require human interaction at both ends. We believe that this is an important and still neglected type of electronic commerce, in particular for small businesses offering or needing specialized services. Other areas of applicability range from transactions between private persons, like the occasional sale of used furniture or stamps, to high-value transactions like public procurement. In addition, the FIT could be used as a standardized client-side tool for typical Internet shopping as explained above, while providing more flexibility than, e.g., OBI.

The parties involved might have a pre-established business relation, like in procurement, or might meet spontaneously on the Internet just for one transaction. However, to enable certain applications, users of the FIT need to have registered with a certification authority, as explained in Chapter 3.

A typical example of a FIT application could involve a professional translator and her customer, an author of scientific books. Author and translator negotiate a commission to translate a certain book within a certain period of time. The original book is part of the contract, which is digitally signed by both parties. Thus the subject of the commission is indisputable. The translation will be fairly exchanged for a receipt, and time-stamped. This avoids disputes about whether the task was completed in time or not. The author will then want to take a look at the translation before paying. Of course, the payment or the delivery of the translation could also be done by traditional means. For their information, or in case of a dispute, the parties can review all transactions, and if necessary extract and show evidence in court. In particular, if the author does not pay, the translator can show the contract and the receipt to an arbiter. The receipt can even uniquely characterize the received information (in contrast to classical certified mail) in case there is a dispute about what translation was received.

Any FIT interaction follows a pre-defined flow with certain variants, i.e., the FIT guides both parties through a deal. Most of the interactions take place via filling in pre-defined forms on-screen and exchanging them over the Internet, *securely* and *fairly* via the *SEMPER* framework. Thus, nobody can cheat the other party without leaving a trail that can be used at court. Using pre-defined forms has several advantages:

– Forms are a familiar tool for structuring business processes and workflows in the physical world. Most users have an a-priori understanding of which fields should or must be on a form. As soon as a user knows a form like an "order," it becomes easy to verify the essential fields, like applicable law, reference to terms and conditions, delivery address, signatories, and amounts. Moreover, fields with a well-defined business semantic prevent some disputes a priori that could arise from omissions, imprecision and ambiguities which can occur with digital signatures on unstructured text such as email. Figure 4.1 shows a signed order as visualized in a business process in the prototype.

– Fields can be named and described in several languages, making National Language Support for all business partners fairly easy.

– Data of corresponding fields are automatically copied from one form to another (e.g., from "offer" to "order") as the default. Any party can then change those data that it really wants to change. The other party can have all changes highlighted by its local FIT. This makes negotiation significantly simpler and more secure.

– An "electronic auditor" can verify that the forms are filled in according to basic legal or accounting rules, e.g., that an "offer" contains a sender, a date, a description of contents, an amount, a currency, and a signature.

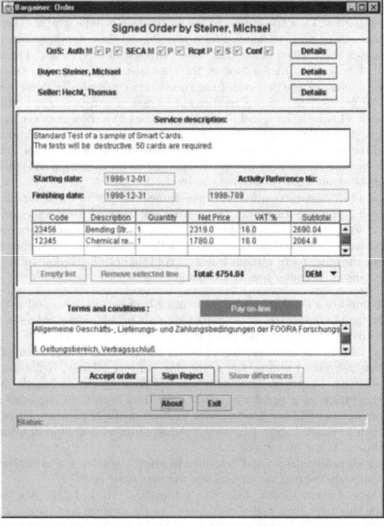

Fig. 4.1. A signed order in a business process in the FIT prototype

– Forms with fixed semantics can be imported from and exported to other programs, like accounting, fulfillment or banking programs. All transactions can be recorded, and records include signatures and receipts. Thus, arbiters can base their decisions on the evidence of these records.

Using predefined forms does not preclude fields on forms that are user-defined. The delivery of intangible goods can be done by exchanging files through the *SEMPER* framework as a kind of attachments to the forms; these files can be encrypted, signed and fairly exchanged as well.

Obviously, such a forms-based Fair Internet Trader is much more powerful than, e.g., using PGP or S/MIME to sign and encrypt standard electronic mail. On the other hand, it is more flexible and comprehensive than other proposed standards like OBI and OTP, and more worked-out than yet others like XML/EDI are so far. Nevertheless, synergy with several other standards is possible, in particular with EDI-based solutions for the standard fields on a large number of forms.

The FIT prototype provides a realistic vision of a *SEMPER*-based product for person-to-person electronic commerce. It also supports the use of *SECA* (see Section 3) and of liability limits. For more details see Chapter 8.

4.3 Outlook

We have shown that the *SEMPER* framework provides a good basis for efficient development and deployment of applications for secure electronic commerce. It offers a lot of market opportunities for the providers of both security technology and business software. Once being deployed, it will help to bring about the envisioned economic benefits of increased electronic commerce. Last but not least it has the social value of allowing anyone to make use of the benefits of the information society in a fair, secure and flexible way.

Part II

Project Achievements

Part I gave an overview of the concepts and results developed by SEMPER. Part II now goes into details. As it is impossible to present all results of a project like SEMPER in detail within one book, we had to be selective. A more complete description can be found in the public project deliverables (see http://www.semper.org).

Chapter 5 briefly describes the organizational structure of the project and general lessons we learned.

Chapter 6 gives a more detailed presentation of the technical framework and architecture than Chapter 2.

Chapters 7 and 8 report on practical experiences with the SEMPER prototype. Chapter 7 describes trials with special SEMPER-based business applications for different sellers in business-to-consumer and business-to-business scenarios. Chapter 8 describes the generic Fair Internet Trader.

Chapters 9–12 elaborate on particular aspects of the technical architecture, starting at the top. The two higher layers, the Commerce Layer and the Transfer-and-Exchange Layer, are described in Chapters 9 and 10, respectively. Chapter 11 describes how SEMPER integrates different payment systems. It also serves as an example of the internal structure of a SEMPER part. Chapter 12 describes public-key infrastructure and why local trust management for certificates is necessary in electronic commerce.

Chapters 13 and 14 describe SEMPER's proposal for fair liability distribution for digital signatures and SEMPER's legal framework in general.

Chapter 15 concludes Part II with an outlook on future directions in research, development, and legal issues in secure electronic commerce.

G. Lacoste et al. (Eds.): SEMPER 2000, LNCS 1854, p. 39, 2000.
© Springer-Verlag Berlin Heidelberg 2000

5. Organizational Overview

This chapter briefly describes the organizational structure of *SEMPER* as a distributed project and reports on some general lessons we learned in the course of it.

5.1 Structure of *SEMPER*

SEMPER was a joint research project of 20 partners from European industry and academia.[1] The consortium included partners from the banking industry (Commerzbank, Europay International), retailing (Otto Versand), consulting (EUROCOM, FOGRA), social and market research (Universität Freiburg, Institut für Informatik und Gesellschaft), and general software engineering (MARIS). All the remaining partners, at least the groups involved in the project, came from security engineering.

Between September 1995 and December 1998, about 100 persons worked on *SEMPER*, although only about 20 of them were continuously involved in the project. The project operated with a budget of about 11 million Euro. About 50% of this budget was funded by the European Union and Switzerland, within the *Advanced Communication Technologies and Services* (ACTS) research programme established by the European Commission, Directorate General XIII.

SEMPER worked in an extremely distributed environment. Among the 20 partners only very few had more than two full-time persons working on the project. In order to co-operate efficiently we implemented relatively formal communication processes, and set up a central document and code repository.

The work plan was classically scheduled, starting with an analysis of the commercial and legal requirements for secure electronic commerce, followed by the design and implementation of a prototype, a technology trial, and the evaluation of the trial results. *SEMPER* performed several trial and evaluation phases, based on different designs and prototypes.

The work was broken down into four working groups, one on requirements analysis (including the legal aspects) and the evaluation of trials; one on the security architecture, design and implementation; one on the implementation

---

[1]See the preface for a list of all partners.

G. Lacoste et al. (Eds.): SEMPER 2000, LNCS 1854, pp. 41–43, 2000.
© Springer-Verlag Berlin Heidelberg 2000

and support of demonstrations and trials; and one on project management and administration. The leaders of these four working groups plus the two technical project leaders formed the planning team of *SEMPER*.

5.2 Lessons Learned

5.2.1 Initial Education

Most team members had no prior experience in object-oriented design or general software engineering. Learning just Java was already quite time consuming for many partners, and even at the end of *SEMPER* not all of the agreed design guidelines and methodologies were consistently applied by all team members. An initial joint education effort, e.g., a joint 2-week seminar, might have speeded up design and development significantly.

5.2.2 Common Understanding

SEMPER started on the basis of a high-level project plan only. Finding an agreement on detailed technical objectives and approaches was very time consuming.

Our basic approach was to form a small architecture team that prepared all initial design decisions and produced the first complete architecture. The architecture team used the regular general project workshops to discuss their proposals with the whole team. This worked quite well in principle, but the initial knowledge advantage of the small architecture team over the rest of the consortium was too large. Ensuring a more detailed agreement *before* the project starts, e.g., in the form of an initial document of understanding, might accelerate this process.

Apart from this problem, the approach of starting with a small architecture team worked very well.

5.2.3 Teams of Individuals, not Organizations

From the very beginning we tried to structure the work such that no team member was involved in too many different tasks, and each task (e.g., the design and implementation of a service block) was handled by one or two partners only. This worked reasonably well, but next time we would apply this principle to an even greater extent.

Another aspect we learned is the importance of established sub-teams, i.e., of groups of individuals who already have some kind of successful co-operation history. Most such groups consist of members from one organization only, but we also had a few examples of established sub-teams with members from different organizations.

Finding and continuously involving such sub-teams is much more important than formal aspects like for which company a member of such a sub-team works, or whether he or she comes from industry or academia.

6. Architecture

This chapter describes the overall *SEMPER* architecture at a technical level. We assume that the reader is familiar with the overview given in Chapter 2. First, we briefly review the underlying model of deals, transfers and exchanges, and discuss security requirements and other concepts that influence the overall design. Next, we describe the layers of the service architecture in more detail by breaking each layer down into several service blocks. We then present important aspects of the implementation architecture, i.e., our general rules for realizing these blocks in software. Finally, we describe the actual Java prototype.

6.1 Important Concepts

SEMPER concentrates on the security-relevant aspects of electronic commerce. These are interactions between different business partners that create or transfer values, rights or obligations.

6.1.1 The Model of Deals, Transfers, and Exchanges

As explained in Section 2.1, the main model used in *SEMPER* is that of business processes, called deals, consisting of steps that are typically transfers or exchanges of business items. An example is shown in Figure 6.1.[1]

Where an exchange is used, it is typically required to be fair, i.e., either both items are transferred or none.

The sequence of steps in a deal, the *flow*, can be determined either directly by the user, or by a protocol for the particular kind of deal. In any case, the *SEMPER* framework keeps track of the deal, stores the security-critical information, and allows the user to review the previous steps of the deal using a deal browser.

After any step, a party might be dissatisfied with the state of affairs. For this case, exception handling must be provided and, in the worst case,

---

[1]Note that "deal" does not imply an agreement here. For example, an unsuccessful negotiation containing several legally binding offers is linked by a deal in *SEMPER*.

G. Lacoste et al. (Eds.): SEMPER 2000, LNCS 1854, pp. 45–63, 2000.

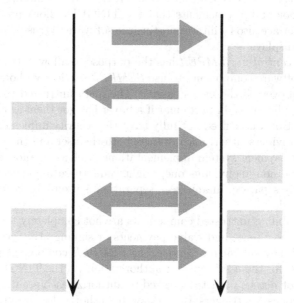

Fig. 6.1. Example of a deal consisting of three transfers and two exchanges

disputes involving outside arbiters. This may happen at different layers of the architecture (recall Figure 2.3 for an overview of the layers). Many potential problems are handled by the Transfer-and-Exchange Layer if one uses fair exchanges. Others may be excluded or at least detected by a Commerce-Layer or business-application protocol controlling the flow of the deal. For instance, the protocol can verify that the price on an invoice matches that in the offer and, if not, automatically request a new invoice. However, not everything can be verified automatically, e.g., a human arbiter might be required to decide whether the service received (e.g., the content of a report bought) matches the order. Furthermore, even if the protocol could detect all problems, the partner might simply stop answering; then outside arbitration also becomes necessary. In such a case, arbitration may need communication channels outside the network as a last resort.

6.1.2 Global Security Concepts

Several security aspects play a global role in the *SEMPER* architecture: the trustworthy graphical user interface, access control, and support for anonymity.

The purpose of the *trustworthy user interface*, called TINGUIN, is to offer a user a secure and consistent interface in a specific window. It was already described in Section 2.2. Hence all software components of *SEMPER* interact with a TINGUIN Block that provides this window, and they use common look-and-feel elements that the TINGUIN Block provides. A well-defined interface also facilitates porting the software to trusted hardware with restricted displays.

Access control in *SEMPER* has the purpose to allow untrusted (or semi-trusted) software components to use *SEMPER* services without giving them full control over all the user's assets.[2] The main untrusted components are business applications, in particular if a buyer has got them as applets from a merchant. But a user need not fully trust the security implementations from different providers either. For instance, both the user and the manufacturers of different payment system implementations, such as an anonymous one and a high-value non-anonymous one, might want these implementations to be kept strictly separate. In any case, separation is useful for keeping programming errors local.

For flexibility, untrusted components are not completely forbidden to use certain services (e.g., high-value payments or signing arbitrary documents). Instead, if they call such a service, the *SEMPER* component providing the service asks for the user's explicit authorization via the TINGUIN. However, users do not *always* want to be asked to authorize each security-critical step that an application triggers. Hence ways to authorize larger portions of a deal are needed. For instance, authorizing the purchase of an airline ticket could authorize transferring the order, the receipt, and the payment. Technically, the critical services must therefore be offered in two versions, one that does and one that does not ask the user. Access control is mainly needed for the latter services. The main challenge is to allow the user to choose which applications to allow access to the more user-friendly but more dangerous services, with very simple versions and appropriate defaults for normal users. The actual access control can then be done much like in other frameworks.

Anonymity is a global topic because any single software component involved in a deal could destroy anonymity by giving out an identity. Hence, to support anonymity, one needs a global management of names (pseudonyms) and the contexts in which they have been used (e.g., towards which business partners, or together with a shipping address, or with a certain credential). Moreover, it suggests a fairly global handling of the communication used in a deal, in contrast to leaving the communication to the components involved, in particular because most security implementations from outside providers will not know about anonymous communication by themselves.

---

[2]There is a second notion of access control, that of conditional access of people to services provided by other people. This has common aspects with access control for software components, but need not be so deeply integrated into a framework. In the *SEMPER* architecture, it is located in the Credential Block.

6.1.3 Security Attributes

Security attributes are a general way in *SEMPER* to select a certain instance of a service without having to know technical details. Security attributes can be specified for almost all services of all layers, e.g., deals, transfers, the signing of individual documents, and secure communication channels. This does not mean that the user has to input all these attributes. Many of them will be set once for each deal, and even there, they may come from preferences of the Commerce Layer. The Commerce Layer then passes them down to the lower layers. The lower layers can use either their own preferences or what is input from above; the resolution rules should also be clear from the preferences. Only if nothing at all is given they have to ask the user via the TINGUIN.

An example of a security attribute that clearly belongs to an entire deal is anonymity, and in most cases so are confidentiality and authenticity. Examples of attributes attached to individual steps are non-repudiation of origin and of receipt, in particular in a legally binding sense. For a step with this attribute, one can later convince a third party such as a court that this step took place.

6.1.4 Transactions, Sessions, Contexts

By transaction, we mean something in the computer-science sense, i.e., with atomicity. In simple words, a transaction is something where one wants a definitive output after a definitive time, like a payment or an exchange.

The steps in deals are implemented as transactions.

Related things that are long-lived and at most times only wait whether they are needed again are called sessions. For example, a deal is a session. Lower layers typically provide a sessions service as a means to keep state between several related transactions. In this sense, a secure channel defines a session, but there are also transfer sessions which contain all the negotiated attributes for several related transfers, etc.

In *SEMPER*, each transaction or session is local to one block of the architecture, but both are typically nested: The state of one of them contains (or points to) other transactions or sessions, respectively, typically from lower layers. For example, a deal typically contains a transfer session and a secure channel. A three-party deal would (at each participant) contain two transfer sessions. The state of a session is called a context from the point of view of the caller (typically in a higher layer) using this session. These contexts are not interpreted by the caller; they are simply a way to store and refer to such a session state.

6.2 Service Architecture

The *SEMPER* architecture is designed to support multi-party security in electronic commerce. As a consequence, the *SEMPER* framework, i.e., the middleware part of *SEMPER*, is symmetric instead of following the classic client-server approach: All parties have the same basic software and keep their own state. Applications, however, can be symmetric or of a client-server nature.

The *SEMPER* software is structured into so-called blocks. The main, commerce-oriented blocks correspond directly to the different concepts of the model of deals, transfers and exchanges. The overall architecture is shown in Figure 6.2. This figure refines one dimension, the layer structure, of Figure 2.3. (The other dimension is refined in Section 6.3.1.)

Actually, the blocks are the main software components in *SEMPER*. The layering is not strict: any block may use the services of all lower blocks directly (subject to access control, of course), and also of those on the same layer. For instance, a Commerce-Layer block can use local purse management, a service of the Payment Block, which has no transfer-and-exchange aspects. The fact that some Supporting Services are drawn on the left side is only an orientation for the reader: These are services like the TINGUIN that are necessarily used by all the commerce-oriented blocks. They were grouped as "local bookkeeping" in Section 2.3. The services at the bottom are primarily, but not exclusively, used by the Business-Item Layer. Two blocks each correspond to the groupings "cryptography" and "secure communication" from Section 2.3.

6.2.1 Business Applications

Business application is our name for any application that uses the services of the *SEMPER* framework, i.e., of the middleware part. Because a goal of *SEMPER* was to offer an open platform for multiple and unforeseen business scenarios, there are no restrictions, neither on the structure of such applications nor on who designs and implements them.

In spite of this openness, for normal users the *SEMPER* framework must and does come with at least one standard *SEMPER* application, which opens the TINGUIN and lets the user access local functions, e.g., browsing through deals and setting preferences. This *SEMPER* application must be equally trustworthy as the framework, i.e., the middleware part of *SEMPER*. With the Fair Internet Trader, the *SEMPER* consortium also implemented a more ambitious standard business application that carries out actual interactive electronic commerce.

In addition, *SEMPER* implemented several specific Internet shopping applications for different merchants for use in the trials, based on a common application framework.

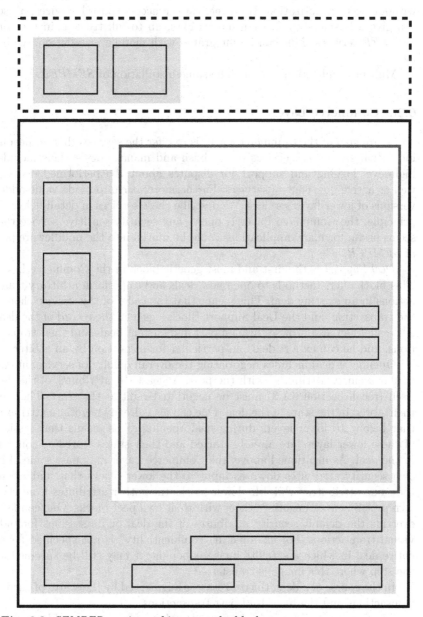

Fig. 6.2. *SEMPER* service architecture: the blocks

Because of the openness for various implementors, business applications are a priori untrusted and not allowed to perform security-critical actions without user authorization. However, via the access control services, a user can give a business application more rights, up to full trust as in the core *SEMPER* services. This can be integrated with module installation, see below.

Multiple applications can use the same installation of *SEMPER*.

6.2.2 Commerce Layer

The main goal of the Commerce Layer is to offer the services that go beyond individual steps, i.e., services to establish and manage deals. This includes high-level logging and support for disputes about the performed deals as well as active flow control services. Furthermore, it can provide value-added versions of lower-layer services. We describe these services in detail below. In principle, the Commerce Layer is open—any security-sensitive service that seems useful for many applications could be moved into the middleware part of *SEMPER*.

Deal Support is the first and most generic block in the Commerce Layer. This block offers methods to open new deals and to perform arbitrary transactions in an existing deal. This means that the caller of this service chooses the transaction, and the Deal Support Block logs it in the record of the deal. The caller can also browse through past and current deals and their transactions, and he can export deals, in particular for inspection by an arbiter.

Opening a deal includes negotiating the overall quality of service, in particular security attributes, with the peer. At least the attributes of the deal itself (recall Section 6.1.3) must be negotiated right at the start. They are then stored in the state of the deal. One can also already negotiate attributes that belong to lower layers during deal opening. This means that sessions of these lower layers are already started and their states stored as contexts in the deal. As mentioned above, the Commerce Layer may pass some of its own security attributes down as input to the lower blocks that understand the same attributes, while the lower blocks take other attributes from their own preferences or negotiate them with their own peer blocks. One can later override the default security attributes of the deal or its sessions for individual transactions. For example, if "confidentiality" is not specified for an entire deal in which a satellite image is bought, it may still be specified for the step where this image is transferred.

In the course of a deal, the deal state is augmented by the states of current transactions and the records of past transactions.

The Commerce Layer can also provide *value-added versions of lower-layer services*. The simplest case is support for *forms* for often-used business message types like "offer" and "order." Standardized forms for such messages greatly improve the security of individual users. The forms need a TINGUIN representation for the human user and an internal representation for semi-automatic processing. The challenge for this component is to make certain that the internal and external representation have the same semantics. Forms are particular kinds of statements; they are handled as such for transfer by the lower layers.

A more complicated example of a value-added service is value-added exchanges. For instance, a value-added contract signing protocol could contain a form for a contract according to a certain law, fill in certain fields automatically (like the user's own name and the current time), verify that the rest is also filled in, and then call a generic contract signing protocol (for arbitrary statements) from the Transfer-and-Exchange Layer.

Flow Control for the steps of a deal differs from Deal Support in that it actively triggers new steps, and is therefore called a different block. The simplest type is generic flow-control mechanisms, e.g., allowing the user to set a time-out for the next expected transaction in a deal (e.g., a payment or a delivery) and an alarm to be triggered if that transaction does not occur. A stronger type of flow control is that the flow is actually prescribed by a program.[3] An advantage of implementing certain flows in the Commerce Layer would be that they are then available for several business applications. Greater standardization of a flow typically also means that one can afford better security evaluation, which makes the flow more trustworthy. This holds in particular for the consumer side in the case where the business application is supplied by the merchant. Then greater trust in the flow implies that less user authorization for individual steps is necessary, which is more user friendly. Selection of a flow becomes part of the initial negotiation in a deal. Note that all flows would use the Deal Support Block for the initial negotiation and other generic aspects of the deal. All the flow control is local, i.e., the *SEMPER* Commerce Layer on one system does not trust a remote system to have the same implementation running securely. This is the same as, e.g., in any implementation of a secure payment system.

Combining flow control and forms, one can then consider complete *workflow* definitions linking different forms throughout the deal. For instance, a purchasing workflow could compare the price fields in all the forms used in a purchase.

6.2.3 Transfer-and-Exchange Layer

The Transfer-and-Exchange Layer is structured into an Exchange Block on top of a Transfer Block.

---

[3]Note that such a Flow Control Block need not and most likely cannot be comprehensive. Business applications unable to use the existing flows can define their own ones and only use the Deal Support Block. For this reason, it is important that the generic deal support is offered as separate services and not only integrated into flows.

The main service of the *Exchange Block* is to offer 2-party exchanges. Here, each party makes two main inputs:

– A business item, i.e., a description of what it is willing to send.
– An expectation, i.e., a description of a business item it expects in return.

In addition, each party may input security attributes. In particular, a fairness attribute will usually be set. Internally, an exchange starts with a negotiation where the Exchange Blocks of the two partners verify that both items offered match the expectation by the partner, and that they have a common protocol implementation that meets the requested security attributes. Fairness means that even in the case of errors or attempted fraud, either both parties will receive the respective items, or none will gain any advantage over not having started the exchange. For instance, a dishonest recipient should not even get part of a satellite image in an aborted exchange of this image for a receipt. To achieve this, the help of a third party, called notary, may be needed. *SEMPER* particularly worked out new so-called optimistic protocols where the notary is *only* needed in case of exceptions, i.e., if both parties are correct, the notary is not contacted at all. This exception handling can even be done electronically and without any involvement of a person for all items that can be compared with the expectations electronically, i.e., for payments and signatures, but not for types of information like today's newspaper or a tax-reporting software.

Typical exchanges were shown in Figure 2.1. Note that if a signed statement occurs in an exchange, the signature is the actual valuable business item, while the text is usually known in advance and belongs to the expectation. In contrast, exchange of information means that the information as such should remain secret if the exchange does not succeed. Technically, *SEMPER* does not restrict exchanges to these examples: *SEMPER* developed a general framework to exchange almost anything based on abstract exchange-enabling properties of the underlying transfers. Fair exchanges are described in more detail in Chapter 10.

A *Transfer Block* might not seem difficult at a first glance. For instance, transferring money is a payment, and transferring information means sending it. Hence essentially the lower layers should take care of it. However, this block defines generic transfer transactions with security attributes like non-repudiation of origin that can be applied to all transfers. For joint transfers of composite business items like a payment with an explanatory statement, a structure called container is defined. Particular reasons to use a container are if one desires joint non-repudiation for the container, or if the entire container is exchanged against something, or too improve the number of communication rounds needed.

Some security services related to transfers can be realized in two fairly similar ways by using security attributes on different levels. This is no problem. For example, one can give a statement a security attribute "legally binding" and then transfer it, or transfer the pure statement, but with the security attribute "non-repudiation of origin" for the transfer. The difference is usually irrelevant. However, when time-stamping is desired, a difference exists: Some documents, e.g., a will or an invention, might be signed with a time-stamp without any intention to transfer them to a recipient at this point. In other cases, e.g., a step in a legal procedure with a deadline, it is the action of transferring that needs the time-stamp. Another example is certified mail: It can be realized either as a fair exchange of two documents, or as a transfer of one document with the attribute "non-repudiation of receipt". For the latter, one must allows this attribute to be qualified by a fairness attribute, because both fair and unfair implementations of receipts exist in commerce.

6.2.4 Business-Item Layer

The Business-Item Layer contains blocks that deal with individual types of business items. It contains a Payment Block, a Statement Block, and a Credential Block. Information, which you might have expected to be a separate block considering Figure 2.1, is also handled by the Statement Block. More precisely, these blocks deal with the core security-relevant aspects of the corresponding items. Thus the statement layer does not contain editors (and even the content of forms is treated in the Commerce Layer), but only protocols to apply security attributes to statements and to implement the transfers. In contrast, the Payment Block contains all aspects of payment systems because they are closely linked. The blocks of this layer must also provide concrete implementations of the abstract concepts introduced in the Transfer-and-Exchange Layer, e.g., descriptions of business items usable as expectations in an exchange, and revocation protocols etc. for items where this is possible.

The *Payment Block* offers the generic interface by which the higher layers can make payments without needing to know any details of the actual payment system implementations used. It also offers all the related services like purse management, information about purses, and support for archiving payment records and dispute handling. The entire interface is explained in detail in Chapter 11. In the course of *SEMPER*, seven payment systems of various types, with and without secure hardware, have already been used under this interface, see Chapters 7 and 11. For cases where different payment models require this, a small number of generic subtypes of this interface are offered. So far the only necessary distinction was account-based (credit cards etc.) versus cash-like, in particular because under some circumstance (shipping of hard goods) applications using account-based systems need to authorize and capture a payment separately.

The *Statement Block* provides attribute-based security for so-called statements, which include pure information and documents. The basic goal of this block is to map the user's security requirements (specified by security attributes) to appropriate security services: Higher layers have typically no interest in the actual security mechanisms, i.e., a key handle or a crypto-graphic algorithm; what they want is, e.g., to have a statement signed or verified for a known name. Typically the Statement Block first asks the Certificate Block to find a key and then asks the Crypto Block to perform the suitable operation with the key, possibly adding appropriate fields. One important addition may be to include date, place, key and attribute certificates etc. into the signed message to make the context clear. The Statement Block may also translate between high-level terms for operations (like security envelope) and low-level terms (like encryption) such that other implementations of the high-level operations are possible in certain scenarios, e.g., usage of a specific transport medium. Furthermore, additional document-level security services like time stamping or watermarking would be provided by the Statement Block.

A *Credential Block* also belongs to this layer. By credentials we mean attribute certificates, typically corresponding to rights. In other words, a credential is a statement with the particular semantics that a certain entity (characterized by any kind of pseudonym—often a name, but also a key or an identifier that is anonymous on purpose) has a certain property or is authorized to do certain things by a certain other entity. Even obligations are possible, at least in combination with other attributes.[4] Generic functions related to the management of rights, e.g., for the evaluation of rights to grant other rights, also belong into this block. However, very little work has been done on a Credential Block in *SEMPER*.

6.2.5 Supporting Services

The Supporting Services blocks provide support to the directly commerce-oriented blocks. Except for the TINGUIN, none of them was a primary objective of *SEMPER*, but no outside services were available when we needed them. A redesign at this moment could profit more from other work. In the following, we sketch the specific aspects of the supporting blocks in the context of secure electronic commerce.

The *TINGUIN Block* provides a secure channel between the human user and the services of *SEMPER*, as described in Section 2.2. The current TIN-GUIN provides a certain amount of customization which, even on insecure hardware, makes it more difficult for other programs to produce a fake TIN-GUIN. As not everything in *SEMPER* is fully trusted, the TINGUIN has to shows the user what kind of component she currently interacts with. Apart from security issues, there are ergonomic issues like a common look-and-feel for agreeing to legally binding actions. The flow of control for what appears on the TINGUIN is of course left to the individual other blocks of *SEMPER*.

---

[4]In contrast, so far we mainly mentioned key certificates, which are handled in a block of their own among the Supporting Services. Hybrid certificates combine elements of both, typically a name, a key, and a property or right.

One of the goals of *SEMPER* was user-friendly storage and retrieval of previous transactions. This is achieved by the transaction browser, a tool accessible from the TINGUIN for looking up transactions. Transactions can be selected and browsed both deal-wise and block-wise. For instance, a user would use deal-wise browsing to find a certain payment if he wants to look up what he paid for a certain article bought from a certain business partner, while he would use block-wise browsing if he wonders why so little money is left in one of his purses.

The *Preferences Block* provides a uniform way of handling preferences for all blocks. Usually a preference denotes a preferred option, but it could also denote a forbidden options, like "never use a key below 128 bits." The user sets preferences through the TINGUIN, and the responsible block can read this choice using the Preferences Block. The blocks concerned may offer services that allow the caller to override or refine current preferences. For instance, a user might set "confidentiality" as a preference for secure communication. Later, in opening a deal with a partner in whose country confidentiality is forbidden, he might, via the TINGUIN, allow non-confidentiality for this deal. The Commerce Layer then tries to open a secure channel with this attribute. The Secure Communication Block will typically accept this in spite of the preference because it trusts the Commerce Layer to have asked the user. In contrast, if an arbitrary business application tried to open a non-confidential channel, the Secure Communication Block might reject it or ask the user for confirmation via his TINGUIN window. The exact resolution rules for such cases should be part of the preferences, with good defaults because most people do not want to be bothered.

The *Access-Control Block* provides all services needed to implement access control on the services of the various blocks of the *SEMPER* architecture. Access control ensures that potentially dangerous, compromising or undesirable operations cannot be performed by untrusted software or unauthorized other users without the user's explicit consent. Access control in *SEMPER* is capability-based. Any block may declare so-called capabilities. Then, each block can request certain capabilities for access to each of its methods; to some extent this can be done automatically using the visibility rules of the language. Parts of the capabilities may be granted in connection with the installation of the new software using the Module Installer, where certain roles can be unlocked given appropriate user authorization. This will be based on code signing, but we stress that the certificates about the code must have a clear semantics and that the final decision must lie with the user. The *SEMPER* model agreement, *SECA*, contains the notion of *SECA*-compliant software, which could be one important attribute in such certificates, besides actual evaluation of the software by a party, e.g., a consumer organization, the user trusts.

The *Module Installer Block*, apart from its role in access control, also installs the new software in the correct locations in the framework and performs *SEMPER*-internal registration for it (see Section 6.3.1).

The *Transaction Support Block* mainly defines an abstract transaction service. In object terminology, this is an abstract class or an interface that the transfer, exchange, and payment transactions implement. In the long run, a full framework would be helpful here to allow reliable canceling, recovery from crashes etc. Standard transaction support might be used, but there are specific requirements: First, *SEMPER* uses nested transactions. For instance, an exchange transaction may contain two container-transfer transactions, both containing several item-transfer transactions. Secondly, *SEMPER* needs decentralized control and trust, which is unusual for distributed-transaction managers.

The *Archive Block* provides secure storage of persistent data. Once again, security attributes like confidentiality are input. Other blocks use the archive to store objects like received signed messages, certificates, cryptographic keys, and entire transaction records. Stored objects are completely opaque and not interpreted by the archive. In the prototype, the archive is implemented using a local database and encryption. More advanced versions could additionally provide tamper-resistant memory and secret sharing. The archive also offers object-locking services for use by transactions.

The *Crypto Block* provides usual cryptographic operations; *SEMPER* did not aim at any new results in this area, but no cryptographic API or library in Java was available at the beginning of the project.

The *Certificate Block* is needed because cryptographic algorithms need keys at the lowest level, while users think in terms of names and abstract security attributes: This block provides the translation from names and attributes to keys. The actual link is typically provided by certificates (also called key certificates). In *SEMPER*, the attributes are not only simple ones like "confidentiality." In particular with non-repudiation, the different levels of liability attached to keys (more precisely to the relation between key and holder) are important, see Chapter 3. In general, an application might want to input any attribute that is known in certain certificate formats and have a key with these attributes found. Attributes may also refer to the process of certification instead of the key itself, e.g., the registration policy of the certifying authority or its liability for wrong certificates. Some attributes of a key or certification authority may be purely local, i.e., they were set by the current user of this *SEMPER* application instead of certified by others; this can be integrated as certificates by oneself. More about trust management is said in Chapter 12. Like the Payment Block, the Certificate Block contains additional management and information functionality.

The *Communication Block* supports, beyond usual communication mechanisms, multiplexing of parallel streams into a common channel and seamless integration of email.

The *Secure Communication Block* provides secure data exchange, in particular secure channels. The interfaces for opening and using secure channels are similar to the interfaces offered by the Communication Block, but now names and security attributes are input during channel establishment in addition to addresses. We use both names and addresses because we cannot assume that all certificates carry addresses, nor another general secure name-address mapping.[5] For the addresses, *SEMPER* defines an abstract interface for address objects that can be implemented both by normal kinds of addresses (mail, http addresses etc.) and by anonymous addresses. Hence the higher layers are shielded from such differences in the underlying communication.

In addition to these specific blocks from Figure 6.2, *SEMPER* contains a Utility Block with miscellaneous functionality. For instance, it contains generic logging and log filtering services for use in debugging, but also applicable for detailed audit trails. (But recall that evidence for disputes is typically collected as transaction records and accessible with the transaction browser.)

6.3 Implementation Architecture

SEMPER is implemented in Java. Many parts of *SEMPER* were modeled in UML, the Unified Modeling Language (see Fowler and Scott (1997)). One can also call this an abstract framework and regard the concrete Java version as Java bindings of it.

6.3.1 Structure of a Block: Manager-Module Concept

SEMPER's goal to provide an open security platform is achieved by allowing various implementations of each service. This was already sketched in Section 2.2. More technically, this is achieved by a manager-module concept as shown in Figure 6.3. Each block would ideally have this structure. This figure refines the second dimension of Figure 2.3, just like Figure 6.2 refined the first dimension. The exchangeable implementations from Figure 2.3 are the modules, while the rest was so far collectively called the framework of this block. In the manager-module concept, each block consists of

- abstract components, i.e., collections of interfaces and abstract classes defining the services of this block,
- modules, which are concrete components implementing these services, and

---

[5] One can offer lower-level secure channels with keys as inputs instead of our names and attributes. Our higher-level secure channels are easier to use for the commerce-oriented blocks. The Secure Communication Block uses the Certificate Block for the translation.

– a manager, which is one specific concrete component that helps managing multiple modules.

Different modules may come from different providers. Any number of them can be present in a block at any time, and they can be installed dynamically.

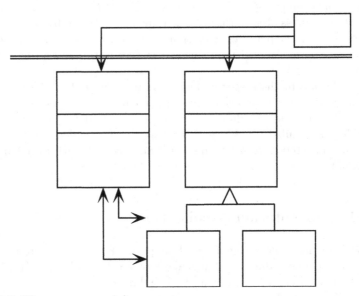

Fig. 6.3. The manager-module concept

The manager's main services are to provide information about available modules, to administer the user's preferences among them, and to assist with module selection for concrete actions. For installation of a new module, the Module Installer finds the corresponding block manager and registers the name of the new module there; then the manager can ask the module for information about itself. Module selection may be based on module names or only on certain attributes (e.g., "with anonymity" or "where I can pay € 5000"). It may involve interaction with the peer manager, i.e., the manager of the same block at the current business partner. Parts of the managers, in particular negotiation and module management, can be implemented as a common framework for the managers of all blocks.

The remaining services are offered by the individual modules, but the callers of this block handle them uniformly through the generic interfaces and do not need to know about the modules. The overall interface a caller sees is called the external interface of the block; it corresponds to an API (application programming interface). Object orientation guarantees that the manager is typically only needed once for a sequence of related actions with a module, e.g., a deal: After the initial module selection, the actual objects that the caller uses (e.g., a purse, a secure channel, or an exchange transaction) know themselves to which module they belong. The whole concept is similar to abstract factories as in Gamma, Helm, Johnson, and Vlissides (1995).

Providers of individual modules have to implement concrete classes for both the module services that are visible in the external interface and for interaction with the manager. The overall interface that the modules must have is called the internal interface; it corresponds to an SPI (service provider interface).

If certain differences between the modules need to be known to the callers, one can proved abstract subtypes of the service in the external interface. In any case, implementations from outside providers will typically need an adapter (in the usual sense; e.g., see Gamma, Helm, Johnson, and Vlissides (1995)) that at least maps the original method names to those used in *SEMPER*. Typically, the adapter will also have to provide missing functionality; if some functionality is missing for almost all outside modules, it makes sense to provide a default implementation already in the framework, i.e., in the abstract classes. For a concrete example, see Chapter 11.

6.3.2 Communication

Many blocks in *SEMPER* want to communicate with their peer blocks, if only for initial negotiation between the two managers. For consistent use of secure communication (in particular if anonymity is aimed at), it is desirable that all blocks involved in a deal communicate in a uniform way. There are essentially two ways to do this:

– Direct communication. Here, each block performs its own communication. For this, it gets a secure channel as a parameter.
– Token-based communication: Here, the actual communication is left to the caller. This means that most blocks do not actually send messages over any communication mechanism, but only return so-called tokens to their callers. The tokens are opaque objects, i.e., the caller is not supposed to interpret them. He only needs to transmit them to its own peer, who inputs them to the peer of the block who wanted to communicate.

The prototype uses direct communication. Hence different communication sessions (from different blocks and possibly even from different transactions within each block) now use the same secure channel. For this, a port-like mechanism is provided to deliver each message to the right recipient (e.g., block or transaction).

For a redesign, token-based communication seems more flexible, and the Payment Block already offers it as an alternative, see Section 11.6. This is confirmed by other developments in the field such as JCC (Sun Microsystems 1998). One advantage is that one can reduce the number of rounds of communication by assembling messages from several layers (in the highest of these layers), in particular for the use of email or via modem. Another advantage is that it decouples the blocks better, as only very few then need to know the interfaces of the Secure Communication Block. In particular, this facilitates the management of anonymity as there is a central point coordinating the communication.

6.3.3 Business Applications and Browser Integration

Technically, business applications are supported as follows: The central part of the standard application which comes with the *SEMPER* framework is called a dispatcher. It launches all the other business applications. The dispatcher can run in client or server mode; the roles could also coexist. In client mode it offers a menu where the user can select among all applications that registered with the TINGUIN during a bootstrap routine. This includes standard functions like deal browsing and purse management, the Fair Internet Trader, and other business applications loaded from outside. In server mode, the dispatcher listens for outside requests to launch business applications.

SEMPER can be integrated into an environment where electronic commerce is often started from browsers as follows: The dispatcher also provides a mode as a daemon (background process) providing an HTTP-server interface to communicate with the browser (see Hauser and Steiner (1995)). The web page of a merchant who wants the user to perform a security-critical operation has to contain a URL to the port of the *SEMPER* daemon on the user's local host.

6.4 Prototype

Most of the *SEMPER* architecture has been implemented in a prototype and used in a series of trials and demonstrators, see Chapters 7 and 8. However, the prototype deviates somewhat from the consolidated architecture described so far, and some of the following chapters report about the prototype version. The most notable differences are the following:

- The current Commerce Layer mainly offers Deal Support, i.e., the generic services needed for all deals. There are also prototypes of value-added services, called commerce transactions.
  The Fair Internet Trader, which is implemented as a business application, contains forms and a workflow with some choices for a quite generic scenario. These could be made available to more applications by moving them to the Commerce Layer.
- There is no common framework for transactions; the Payment, Transfer, and Commerce Block all define their own (though similar) notions of transactions.

- The Business-Item Layer together with the Transfer Block are called Transfer Layer.
- There is no Statement Block in the sense described above; the higher layers call the Certificate Block directly, obtain a key handle, and input that to the Crypto Block. (The functionality of the block now called Statement would be divided between Crypto and Secure Communication.)
- While anonymity was kept in mind during the overall design, almost no actual protocols supporting it were implemented.
- Not all blocks have a clear manager-module structure, in particular blocks where no implementations from other providers existed yet, and supporting blocks that were not a primary task of *SEMPER*.
- There are several names for addresses, port-like multiplexing features, and context-like objects in different blocks.

The architecture documentation (SEMPER Consortium 1999a) is publicly available from `http://www.semper.org`, including the javadoc files that describe all the interfaces of the current prototype.

6.5 Outlook

A number of other projects on secure electronic markets have been started after *SEMPER*. They fit well into our overall architecture. Here we name some where actual specifications already exist:

- Many projects aim at secure payments only, e.g., Daswani et al. (1998). As we have already integrated many different payment schemes during the project, see Section 6.2.4, we are confident that any others would also fit under our generic services without problems.
- The Java Commerce Client (Sun Microsystems 1998) mainly provides a more advanced design and implementation of our Supporting Services, in particular the gateway security model (Goldstein 1997) for access control.
- Several projects like OBI (Open Buying on the Internet), OTP (Open Trading Protocol), and also XML/EDI as far as one can see yet, mainly define forms for certain business scenarios (OBI Consortium 1998; OTP Consortium 1998; Peat and Webber 1997). They could be used as modules for the Forms Block in our Commerce Layer. OBI and OTP also contain one main workflow each, which could be offered in the Flow Block.

SEMPER was, in 1995, the first project that started to define a framework for secure electronic commerce that goes beyond individual services like secure communication, digital signatures and payment systems. To this day, no other project has an equally broad scope; in addition, multi-party security including dispute support has not been considered by any other project. We therefore believe that the *SEMPER* architecture is the right overall framework in which to bundle standardization efforts on more specific services and protocols.

7. Experiments

This chapter describes the *SEMPER* trials from user and business perspectives. The focus is on the evaluation of the trials, the feedback collected, and the lessons that were drawn. Therefore, information on trial implementation and set-up is only provided to support understanding of the evaluation results. The trials in this chapter were made with different business applications on top of *SEMPER* in both business-to-consumer and business-to-business Internet shopping scenarios.

7.1 Introduction

Live tests almost never run smoothly, but they are the best proof of concept. The *SEMPER* prototype was put to the test by conducting a series of end-user trials which began in July 1997 and continued some time after the end of the project in December 1998. With each new trial phase new business applications were added, input from the preceding trials was integrated in the user interface and additional services were offered.

Conducting trials with a prototype, rather than a product which is close to market maturity, imposes considerable restraints on the trial situation. It was necessary to adjust the trial environment on several occasions, in order to obtain a qualitative appraisal of the applicability and soundness of the security architecture and services proposed by the project, as well as an evaluation of the subset of services implemented in the software prototype. Particular challenges were posed by the complexity of the problems addressed by the research and limitations on the experience and knowledge of users.

The experiments conducted confirmed that, in spite of the rapid changes taking place in the world of electronic communication, most of the original research premises have remained valid throughout 3 years of investigation and development. Lessons learned during the prototype implementation phase also contributed to the design of the advanced prototype (described in Chapter 8) which concluded the project. User input which could no longer be implemented provides the inspiration for future research goals and product developments.

In this chapter the *SEMPER* trials with specific business applications are described and the most significant results are presented. The trial sites and

G. Lacoste et al. (Eds.): SEMPER 2000, LNCS 1854, pp. 65–93, 2000.

services are described in Section 7.2. In Section 7.3 a brief description is given of the computing platforms, hard- and software requirements and supporting third-party services used in the trials. The reactions of end users to the *SEMPER* architecture and software prototype, testing in the role of buyer, are presented in Section 7.4 and the impressions of the service providers, the sellers who provided the trial sites, are recorded in Section 7.5. The conclusion in Section 7.6 summarizes the key results and influences on the trial participants' willingness to use *SEMPER* as a tool for electronic commerce.

7.2 Trial Sites and Services

The implementation used in all trials included a basic set of security services for electronic commerce, e.g., secure identification of business partners and secure offers, orders, payment and delivery. The trials were conducted in four phases at seven sites in various business contexts. In the initial phases the prototype was tested at trial sites set up by partners of the consortium; in the final phases external trial sites were set up in Holland and France and accessed by trial participants in those countries as well as in Germany. In addition, we report on a trial in the context of another EU project.

The business contexts used for the trial scenarios included mail order, tele-training, a literature service, database access and image distribution. These will be described in more detail below. The players involved in the tests included buyers (the trial participants), sellers (the business applications implemented for the trials, e.g., a merchant server using the *SEMPER* software), a registration and certification authority (provided by the *SEMPER* partner GMD) and financial institutions (a test bank at the Universität des Saarlandes, Saarbrücken, and SET Secure Electronic Transactions payment gateways at IBM Zurich Research Laboratory and at the Commerzbank in Frankfurt).

The addition of new payment options in subsequent trial phases served to illustrate the extensibility of the *SEMPER* architecture. In the early trials a generic test purse was implemented. This was followed by the addition of a credit-card purse and stored-value payments using a chip card and, finally, by implementation of the SET payment protocol (MasterCard and Visa 1997).

During the course of the trials, more than 70 persons were able to experiment with the *SEMPER* prototype. Their comments and criticisms were collected by means of questionnaires and personal interviews. For the Phase I and Phase III trials, participants were interviewed subsequent to testing the software, whereas in the Phase II and Phase IV trials, participants were invited to the Institute for Computer Science and Social Studies in Freiburg and interviews were recorded during the trial itself. The largest hurdles which had to be overcome in the trial process were users' lack of computing confidence and their limited knowledge of the issues surrounding electronic commerce. In general, the computing skills of potential testers were too restricted for them

Trial Site	EUR	FOG	FRE Basic	OTV	ACRI	ACTI	OPL	FRE SME
Trial Phase	I	II		III				IV
Secure identification of business partner	√	√	√	√	√	√	√	√
Digitally signed offer	√	√	√	√	√	√	√	√
Digitally signed order	√	√	√	√	√	√	√	√
Generic purse (test payment system)	√	√	√	√	√	√	√	√
Digital goods delivered on-line	√	√	√		√		√	√
Real goods delivered off-line				√		√	√	√
Webpages encrypted/sent via SEMPER					√	√		√
SET payment protocol				√			√	√
Encrypted credit-card data via SEMPER					√	√	√	√
Stored value—chipcard and user device							√	√
Real credit-card payment				√			√	√

Table 7.1. Essential characteristics implemented in trials

to confidently install and configure prototype software. In spite of hotline support from project partners, nearly all unassisted trials failed.

Installing software for external testers and inviting trial participants to test pre-installed software in a supervised situation improved the test conditions, but did not resolve all of the survey problems. Testers with little personal experience of network communication, such as the members of small- to medium-sized companies who took part in the first trials in Greece, were not in a good position to evaluate measures for protecting their interests in this new commercial environment. It is interesting that even among the persons surveyed in the SME trials, who had on average 2 years of Internet experience, one of the most frequently selected responses to the question "What are the greatest threats to the security of electronic communications?" was the option "Users have too little knowledge of Internet risks." Phase II trials concentrated on in-depth interviews with expert or "power" users in an effort to obtain a more critical and qualified appraisal of the security options *SEMPER* offers. The information gained during this phase was then used to improve the interface and to prepare supporting material before launching the SME trials. For example, KPN Research, the *SEMPER* partner which supported the OPL trial, produced a CD-ROM with a presentation of issues in electronic commerce, the key aspects of security technology and an introduction to the services offered by the *SEMPER* software. In other trials the interviewer provided this background information with the assistance of illustrations.

The SME trials provided an opportunity for trial participants to visit real sites, offering real products, but obviously there were too few "semperized" websites for testers to experience routine use of the software. The trial site which could have been expected to generate repeated purchases, the mail-order scenario, was only implemented at the very end of the project. This was due to problems experienced in linking *SEMPER* into the company's fulfillment system and legal and organizational problems which resulted from the decision to have real SET certificates and payments in the test.

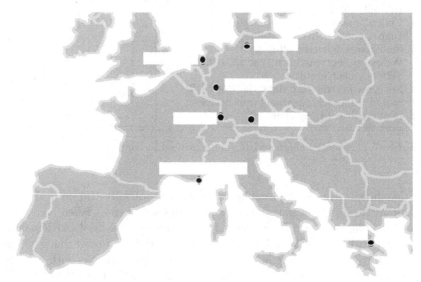

Fig. 7.1. *SEMPER* trial sites

7.2.1 Internal *SEMPER* Trials

In July 1997 the *SEMPER* prototype was tested by two service providers which are members of the consortium, EUROCOM and FOGRA. The EU-ROCOM site, located in Athens (GR), offers distance learning services. EU-ROCOM intends to use *SEMPER* to enable students to browse their offering of courses, register and pay on-line and, subsequently, gain on-line access to the selected course presentation, notes, and examinations. FOGRA, a research institute for the printing industry, located in Munich (D), offers its customers on-line ordering and delivery of documents and software. It also sees an opportunity for on-line consultancy.

The EUROCOM trials were integrated in a series of seminars for SME employees with the title "Conducting Business over the Internet." The target group was business executives with very basic, or no Internet skills. The participants were first introduced to the basic concepts of networking, such as TCP/IP, Internet protocols (telnet, ftp, http), electronic mail, web browsers, mailing lists, search engines, etc. In addition, a few more advanced concepts were also discussed, such as routing, security policies, firewalls, an introduction to cryptography, public-key cryptography, financial transactions over Internet, SET and electronic commerce in general. After a brief presentation of the *SEMPER* architecture, the participants were able to run the *SEMPER* software and to purchase a seminar from the EUROCOM electronic store. The *SEMPER* client software was pre-installed and user registration had also been performed prior to the trials. As a result, the participants experienced only the purse creation and purchasing procedures.

FOGRA demonstrated the *SEMPER* trial for three days in June 1997 at the IMPRINTA trade fair. Due to both software and access problems, this trial of the scenario was only partially successful. FOGRA remedied the problems which had occurred during the IMPRINTA tests and made additional preparations of their trial website. They also integrated a new version of the TINGUIN with some enhancements to the user interface. The installation process was repeatedly tested and modified to make it as clear as possible. In July 1997 FOGRA conducted a small external trial. Five participants from their customer base tried to run *SEMPER* and three succeeded, at least partially.

The functionality and flexibility of the *SEMPER* architecture was appreciated by the EUROCOM and FOGRA trial participants, but the state of the user interface was considered to be insufficiently developed for the ease of use to which non-specialists are accustomed. As a result, a new round of supervised trials, with participants selected on the basis of their networking experience, was conducted. FOGRA's trial site (server and business application) and the improved TINGUIN were used for these trials.

7.2.2 Freiburg Basic Trial

The *SEMPER* client software was installed at the Institute for Computer Science and Social Studies in Freiburg, Germany and tested by 12 trial participants in December 1997. Twenty hours of in-depth interview material was recorded and subsequently analyzed. A participant questionnaire was tested in preparation for the questionnaire to be used in the upcoming SME trials. All of the trial participants had extensive computing and Internet experience (on average 3 years or more) and an above average awareness of the security issues related to open networks. More than half were regular users of on-line banking, secure email, etc. They were an untypically competent and well-informed user group, but, therefore, more capable of giving the type of feedback needed for further developments of the *SEMPER* prototype.

The *SEMPER* trial software was pre-installed, but trial participants initialized it for personal use by entering a personal log-in name and password (these were freely chosen by the participant) and then completed the registration process and created one or more purses. The registration procedure was based on the participant's personal data (name, organization, city) which had been submitted to the certification authority prior to the trial in order to simulate off-line personal registration. The participant also entered a personal registration key which the CA had assigned to him/her. It was explained to the participants that, under normal conditions, in order to obtain strong certificates, they would have had to personally visit the certification authority and present proof of their identity (passport or ID card) and, in return, have received their registration key and the fingerprint of the CA for verification during the on-line registration.

Having completed these processes the trial participants used the *SEMPER* software to securely identify the FOGRA website. They then browsed the site and selected one or more digital products (abstracts from the FOGRA literature database). Once they had selected the product(s) they wanted and filled out the order form on the FOGRA website they then requested that their local *SEMPER* software process this order securely. They obtained a digitally signed on-line offer from FOGRA. They used their locally installed *SEMPER* software to send a digitally signed order to FOGRA and used the purse function of the *SEMPER* prototype to make a simulated on-line payment. The abstract(s) was delivered to the participant on-line in the Netscape browser.

During the initialization of the *SEMPER* software particular attention was paid to the participants' understanding of the actions they were taking, as well as those factors which influenced their ability to successfully complete the process. The trial was conducted at various times of the day and included the weekend, as well as working days. This ensured that the on-line registration and the use of *SEMPER* in a purchase situation were subject to the variety of conditions currently present in the Internet, e.g., varying connection speeds, loss of connectivity, etc. The business context also allowed participants to experience the flexibility which electronic commerce offers in respect of being able to conduct business at any time of day, from the office, or home.

7.2.3 SME Trials

The SME trials were conducted at four locations, primarily using "semperized" websites of companies which were not members of the consortium. The only exception to this was the Otto (mail-order) trial which was included in the SME trials because of its late start and also because it used the same improved version of the trial code.

Two SME trial sites were operated with companies in Sophia-Antipolis (F), Actimedia and ACRI, and supported by the *SEMPER* partner IBM France. Actimedia sells French-language CD-ROMs and sees potential in the WWW for reaching a customer base throughout the world. For them the Web represents a niche for selling products to the French-speaking population (and persons interested in French culture and language). This site consists of a virtual shop where CD-ROM titles can be selected, placed in a shopping cart, ordered and paid for. It is aimed at private consumers living outside France. In contrast, the second French site, ACRI, has a customer base of large organizations. The company offers on-line simulation using fluid mechanics and the capability to mark-up aerial photographs. By allowing customers to select (and pay for) a segment of a larger representation, their services become more cost-effective and, therefore, accessible to a broader customer base. For ACRI, the potential for offering their customers tailor-made solutions and distributing highly confidential information in a secure environment was the reason for participating in the *SEMPER* trials. It was particularly important to the company that they obtain evidence which could be presented at court. A respondent from ACRI described a potential conflict with the example of an oil tanker being fined for illegally releasing oil at sea on the basis of evidence gathered via a satellite picture of the incident. In this case it would be particularly important to be able to prove that the satellite picture had not been manipulated. According to him the whole value chain, from the seller of the raw satellite data up to the final picture, needs to be authenticated.

Payment on the French trial sites was possible using the generic purse and with several types of credit-card purses.

The field trial which was held in the Netherlands was supported by the *SEMPER* partner KPN Research. The party selling goods and information in the trial was Oil and Gas Product Library Ltd. (OPL). For the trial MARIS, which develops new business applications for OPL and operates their servers, became an associate partner of KPN Research. The parties buying goods in the trial were off-shore companies in the Netherlands.

The OPL shop consists of a catalogue of books, maps and CD-ROM's for the off-shore oil and gas industry. The catalogue can be searched by users and interesting items can be put into a shopping cart. In addition to the OPL shop, an on-line database was also offered for direct searching by users. The OPL database which was used contains facts and figures regarding mobile production units which are used world-wide in the production of oil and gas at sea. The database contains circa 300 records, or factsheets, related to mobile production units. The information was delivered on-line via a secure *SEMPER* channel straight from the OPL database at the server. In addition to this database, OPL has a range of comparable databases for other off-shore equipment. It is planned that these databases will subsequently be opened for users in a comparable business model.

Two purchase scenarios were supported in the OPL trial:

– *Simulated:* Users could simulate ordering products, i.e., no real payment was made and no real products were delivered. A credit-card purse (which securely transmits credit-card data from the *SEMPER* client to the *SEMPER* server), the SET payment protocol (using a payment gateway and

test bank at the IBM Zurich Research Laboratory), or a purse with stored value in a chipcard could be used for this purpose.
- *Real:* Users could order real products. In this case they indicated that their order was real and transmitted the details of their real credit card using their *SEMPER* credit-card purse. The order was followed up by real payment and real delivery of goods.

In both situations the users experienced the major part of the ordering cycle, i.e., established a secure connection first, searched in the OPL catalogue, loaded their shopping cart with goods, confirmed their orders and then transmitted their payment information. A sales ledger (database) was kept at the OPL shop server for both kinds of transactions. OPL was notified by email every time a real order was booked. This email only contained the message that an order had been received. In order to obtain further details and follow up the order, OPL had to access the sales ledger database in a secure mode.

A unique aspect of the OPL implementation of *SEMPER* was the use of the KPN Smartcard Purse, a user device with a smartcard reader, keyboard and display, which was attached to the trial participant's PC. This enabled the stored-value payments to be made securely via the *SEMPER* software. Trial participants accessing the OPL trial from Germany were also able to test this form of payment. For the trial no real money was linked to the smartcard purse, although this would have been possible. The participants received a smartcard purse which was loaded with units. Their spending was registered and deducted from their purse balance. If their balance got low they could return the purse to MARIS for reloading (which took place at KPN). Usage and purse payments were registered at the server and could be inspected by OPL in order to keep track of the business process.

About twenty-five companies in the Netherlands, most of them well-known in the oil and off-shore industry, were asked to participate in the field trial. They received a letter from OPL and were offered a small present as an incentive to participate. A total of 8 companies in the off-shore industry agreed to participate. The main reason given by companies which declined was that conducting their everyday business left them no time for taking part in tests.

As mentioned above, testing of the Otto trial site failed to meet the expectations which partners had at the onset of the project and took place only at the very end of the project. The difficulties experienced in implementing live trials in an organization with the size and structure of Otto Versand, the largest mail-order company in Germany, illustrated the complexity of implementing electronic commerce in a company with very traditional business processes. Whereas in the other trials the transition from traditional to electronic commerce functioned essentially as an extension of their existing business model, in the case of Otto Versand it reversed the trust scenario between buyer and seller. Previously the only form of payment was by bank transfer after receipt of the goods and Otto Versand had to trust that the cus-

Fig. 7.2. KPN Smartcard Purse as used in OPL trial

tomer would pay or return the goods. For the convenience of on-line shopping, e.g., being able to browse and select products on-line, check their availability before ordering, order and pay electronically, for the first time Otto customers had to trust that the company would deliver. Otto Versand envisions a mutual advantage for both buyer and seller in planned future offerings, such as on-line last minute travel bookings and software downloads, but these options were not available during the trials.

In the Otto trial there was no potential for tests using simulated purchases. It was an "all or nothing" scenario, i.e., real cash and real goods, or nothing. This meant that a real payment had to be used. The selected form of payment for the trials was credit cards using the SET payment protocol. This involved obtaining and using real SET merchant and customer certificates and having real payments cleared by a German bank which necessitated lengthy and complicated negotiations. The fact that a major revision of the SET protocol, from the draft version to the final 1.0 version, took place midway through the project also created delays. As a result, at the project's conclusion, it had only been possible to conduct a small number of tests. The lesson learned here is, perhaps, that large traditionally structured organizations are less flexible innovators in the emerging electronic marketplace than smaller organizations which perceive a niche for adding value to their existing product offering and are willing to launch small-scale experiments. On the other hand, it can be said that the Otto trial imposed realistic constraints on the trial situation, which imposed considerable delays, but were, indeed, a true test of concept. It is a credit to the determination of the *SEMPER* researchers, in particular those supporting the Otto trial, that, in spite of the official end of the project at the end of 1998, the first real SET transactions were finally made in January of 1999.

7.2.4 Freiburg SME Trial

In the trials described above the participants were customers of the companies operating the trial site and they mainly experimented with only one site. The final phase of trials, conducted at the University of Freiburg, offered participants the opportunity to use *SEMPER* from one computer to access all of the trial sites and services described above. For this trial, users with experience of using the Internet (email, WWW, etc.) but with no particular knowledge or expertise in security-related issues were selected.

7.2.5 MOMENTS Trial

The EU project MOMENTS[1] made several trials with sales of information via GSM, using a SIM purse, within their overall Access Control Demonstrator Architecture. *SEMPER* co-operated with MOMENTS. Gemplus integrated the *SEMPER* security framework with the MOMENTS business application for a laboratory trial.

7.3 Trial Implementations

The *SEMPER* prototype was implemented primarily in the Java programming language (Gosling, Joy, and Steele 1996), apart from a crypto library and some payment modules which were implemented in the programming language C and incorporated into the system using the Java Native Interface (JavaSoft 1996). In addition, it integrated to existing browsers by providing an HTTP (Berners-Lee, Fielding, Nielsen, Gettys, and Mogul 1997) server interface to communicate with the user's Internet browser. This programming approach was chosen in accordance with the aims of the project to

---

[1]The participants of the MOMENTS project were Nokia, Gemplus, E-Plus Mobilfunk, Bertelsmann, Orange Personal Communications Services, Citicorp Kartenservice, Reuters, Omnitel Pronto Italia, Zentrum für Graphische Datenverarbeitung, and DataNord Multimedia. See `http://veppi.mm.wdss.ntc.nokia.com/`.

provide a universal and extensible electronic commerce security solution. It takes into account the reality of the current situation in the Internet, where users have a variety of operating systems, such as Windows 95, Windows NT, Solaris, Unix or Linux and also use different types and versions of browser. The approach provides for generality because it runs with every browser; it provides for portability due to the fact that implementation changes are not required when changing platform; and it provides for flexibility due to the ability to pass information back to the browser.

7.3.1 Trial Services

The business applications implemented for the Phase I to IV trials (the MO-MENTS trial is described separately in Section 7.3.4) contained the following steps that were secured with *SEMPER*:

- **Registration/certification:** In the trials the Registration Authority (RA) and Certification Authority (CA) were realized by a single entity, i.e., the GMD. The trial organizer sent the RA/CA a list of trial participants and the CA then sent each of them a registration letter with the footprint of the CA's public key and their secret registration key (password). The issue of a registration for a particular trial participant followed a 'Check List Entry' policy, i.e., if there was an entry in the list delivered from the trial organizer, a customer received his/her registration. A copy of the registration was stored locally at the RA/CA, and the certification procedure was then activated automatically. The issued certificate was stored locally at the RA/CA and a copy sent to the trial participant. The participant checked the incoming certificate and stored it in his/her archive. This completed the registration/certification procedure.
- **Offer:** The offer service provided the necessary mechanisms for access of product catalogues stored either in flat files or various relational databases. In addition, specific software was provided for the access/link of legacy systems (e.g. Otto Versand's BTX system).
- **Order:** The order service provided pre-defined forms which trial participants could use to make a specific order/purchase of an item or items. These forms were designed according to the needs of the individual service providers.
- **Payment:** All trials were relying on the payment systems provided by *SEMPER*'s common payment framework. In the initial phase of the trials, we solely used the generic purse payment system, a test payment system which emulates debit and credit payments. This allowed us to get some feedback quickly and easily without the big overhead of the costs associated with setup and integration of real payment systems. With time further (real) payment instruments were integrated into the payment framework and used in the trials. In the SME trials, real credit-card payments were performed using purses implementing SET and the *SEMPER* credit-card

protocol. Stored-value payments based on the KPN Smartcard Purse were used in the OPL and Freiburg trials. Additional payment systems which were integrated and used at various occasions are digital cash (ecash), electronic cheque (MANDATE) and an off-line bill payment system (OTV purse).

7.3.2 Equipment and Set-Up

In order to participate in the trial it was necessary for users to have an Internet connection, a PC with Windows 95 or Windows NT, a browser, the *SEMPER* client and the JDK (Java Development Kit). It was possible for participants to download the *SEMPER* software from a *SEMPER* trial website. The site also provided links to the SUN website to download the JDK and a link to WinZip which was needed to unpack the *SEMPER* zip file. As mentioned in the preceding section, this procedure proved to be too complicated for most external participants.

In the EUROCOM trial, which was conducted at the EUROCOM premises, each person had access to a Pentium/100 PC, with 16 MB RAM, running MS Windows 95 with a web browser and the *SEMPER* client software installed on it.

In the first FOGRA trial at the IMPRINTA fair the *SEMPER* prototype was demonstrated using a PC with WIN95 and ISDN access to the Internet through CompuServe. The *SEMPER* prototype was pre-installed (zipfile was unpacked) and some additional scripts had been created on the desktop to enable the registration, the running of *SEMPER* and printing out of databases. For the subsequent FOGRA external trials, the participants used their own equipment and experienced considerable difficulty in installing the trial themselves.

In Freiburg, where trial participants were invited to the institute, the Basic Trial was run on WIN95 with the *SEMPER* client software pre-installed.

The SME trials were run exclusively using Windows NT. This was due to the fact that the SME trial code was implemented using a newer version of the JDK, i.e., JDK 1.1.5 (the basic trial had used JDK 1.1.1) which proved to be unstable when used with WIN95. As relatively few users have Windows NT this imposed a large constraint on trial participation. In fact, the choice of Java as the main programming language caused considerable difficulty for both development and trials over the whole duration of the project. In principle, it provided very useful platform independence, but constant changes in the language and libraries and the immaturity of the JDK code were frequently the cause of problems and delays.

In the OPL trial the trial participants also had a KPN Smartcard Purse, a smartcard reader with display and keyboard, attached to their PCs, and a smartcard. For the server side a PC running Windows NT was used. OPL queried the sales ledger by setting up a secure connection over the Internet using the SSL of the browser and server. The OPL on-line database was implemented using Visual Basic and FoxPro for Windows (via ODBC).

MARIS visited the trial participants and installed the necessary software (*SEMPER*, JDK etc.). This was done using a tape streamer connected to the parallel port of the computer. MARIS also distributed the KPN Smartcard Purse and the smartcard. After installation, MARIS helped the trial participants to register on-line at the GMD and make a first (test) purchase from the OPL shop. This support resulted in the OPL trial having the largest number of external participants of any of the trials.

7.3.3 SME Business Applications

For the Actimedia and ACRI trials *SEMPER* was integrated into the IBM merchant server net.commerce. Several unique characteristics were implemented:

- secure logos for Actimedia,
- graphical customization of offers,
- secure delivery of information to the local *SEMPER* implementation with output in the browser.

The OPL trial was partly based on this business application and some enhancements to the *SEMPER* core were provided by KPN:

- developing and adding a *SEMPER* credit-card purse that enabled secure transmission of credit-card data through *SEMPER*,
- adding the stored-value purse adapter,
- enabling encrypted file downloading for secure file transfer from the *SEMPER* server to the *SEMPER* client,
- enabling a detailed log to be kept of the queries performed by users on the OPL database as a basis for the cost calculations and purse spending.

7.3.4 MOMENTS Trial

The scenario of the EU project MOMENTS is shown in Figure 7.3.

In the MOMENTS laboratory trial a business application was built on top of the complete *SEMPER* framework. Gemplus added a payment module providing the payment services from their SIM purse.

7.4 Trial Participants' Reactions

It is possible to identify two distinct groups among the persons who experimented with *SEMPER*, what can be referred to as "basic users" and "experienced users." The evaluation of the persons falling into these two categories

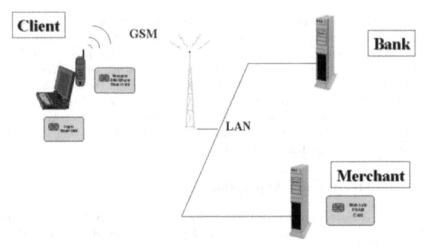

Fig. 7.3. Implementation of *SEMPER* in MOMENTS.

tended to be consistent on a number of essential points, in particular regarding the user interface, but their requirements and appraisal of the architecture as a whole were distinctly different.

In this section the trial participants' reactions are presented according to key features of the architecture which were implemented in the software prototype: personal initialization of the software (which includes local creation of signature and encryption keys, on-line registration and certification of the keys), purse creation and management and the range of payment options provided, the concept of a single trustworthy user interface (TINGUIN), and secure identification of business partners and document exchange.

7.4.1 Initializing the *SEMPER* Software

Due to the various testing environments only half of the trial participants initiated the *SEMPER* software themselves, nearly all of these with assistance. Participants who did not go through the initialization procedure were much less capable of evaluating the architecture as a whole and some were actually unaware of what was taking place during use. In addition to this, the criticisms which were made by those who did experience registration and purse creation made it clear that the installation guidelines, and the user interface in general, have not been sufficiently developed for independent use.

Two participants suggested a short tutorial which the user could go through off-line before starting the actual registration, but most felt that all the required information should form an integral part of the set-up. It was suggested that with the careful selection of texts, this could be managed efficiently during the registration without slowing down the process significantly. As the initialization process only needs to be completed once, user understanding of the process was judged to be more important than speed. An approach along the following lines was suggested:

> "All of the explanations need to be here in the TINGUIN. It needs to start with a simple picture. Here is the user and here is the CA and there are five steps, or whatever. (1) You have to log-in. (2) You need to create a password which must be kept secret. (3) You are going to create 2 key pairs, one for encryption and one for signing. (4) You will obtain a certificate from the CA. And so on, and then (5) Now you're finished. So that the user understands from the beginning what sort of stuff is in there and does not lose his orientation during the registration. Knows, for example, I have now completed step 3."

Many of the participants did not have enough background in security technologies to make informed choices. They suggested a help function, or links with supporting information, in particular, regarding the types of signature and encryption keys offered, the security importance of key length, recommendations for selecting a good password, what the seed was needed for and tips about how to enter it, etc. Participants who lacked this background knowledge invariably chose the default set-up.

> "To be honest, I don't really care which algorithm is going to be used. I mean, it's not that I don't care, I simply don't know what it's supposed to mean. I don't know why I should choose RSA or DSA. I don't understand the difference."

The biggest difference in opinion between basic users and experienced users towards the initialization process was the extent to which the user should have to, or be able to, control the process. Participants who had little previous experience with security technologies would have preferred the registration procedure to be more automated, whereas the remaining participants were of the opinion that a high degree of user intervention was essential for the user to understand the power and significance of the security architecture *SEMPER* offers. The response of the trial participants seems to indicate that there is a requirement for at least two *SEMPER* installations, what might be referred to as "*SEMPER* Basic" (a default installation) and "*SEMPER* Pro" (for the power user).

Experienced users found the fact that their signature and encryption keys were generated locally and only the public key sent over the Internet to be "a very valuable asset of the software," whereas the basic user was indifferent to this, or unaware that this was an important security feature. In addition, the more experienced users had a requirement for more information about key storage and the ability to refer to key-related information. Similar to the function in the TINGUIN which allows the user to check the status of his purses, participants wanted a means to browse the status of certificates and keys.

> "What I'm missing right now is some sort of message about my keys. Have they been generated? I want to know when I get them, where they are and I want to save them on a diskette."

> "There is nowhere where I can check my status, which keys I have, which length, that they are registered with a certain CA, that I have CA public keys lying around."

Both basic users and experienced users found it reasonable that they would need to go through a physical registration process (identifying themselves in person at a registration authority) in order to obtain a strong certificate, but only users with some prior knowledge of public-key infrastructures and developments in digital signature laws were able to comment on the type of future requirements they might have for certificate management. They suggested that the validity of certificates, both the user's own and those of his/her communication partner, should be indicated clearly in the TINGUIN and there should be an easy way of updating the certificates, without having to repeat the entire registration procedure. It was also hoped that they would be able to use an existing certificate with *SEMPER*, rather than having to obtain one specific to the software, or that cross-certification between CAs would allow them to obtain the necessary certificate with a minimum of effort. The requirement for a certificate browser had, in fact, been anticipated, but due to limited resources it was only finally implemented in the advanced prototype (FIT) which is described in Chapter 8.

7.4.2 Purse Creation and Management/Payment Options

In the early trials the full flexibility of the payment block of the *SEMPER* architecture was not well demonstrated. Participants were only able to create a generic purse and the only form of payment available was the transfer of electronic value from the trial bank. The interviewer explained the flexibility of this block, e.g., the potential for implementing different forms of payment, such as credit card payment, different currencies, etc., but the participants were not able to experiment with these options. In contrast, in the SME trials participants could test a variety of payment options and created at least one purse for each form of payment. Their requirements on the purse creation function became even more evident later in the test after they had made several transactions. Users wanted to be able to create new purses during the electronic shopping experience, when they encountered a new purchase situation, for example, a website which requested a particular currency, or a form of payment they had not thought to install when setting up their software. This requirement emphasizes the point that, due to the global nature of electronic commerce, users expect to need a broader range of payment instruments than they currently do in traditional regional markets. In this respect, the flexibility of the *SEMPER* architecture to incorporate new payment systems, as they develop or are required, was viewed very positively.

Computing experience played a very small role in the ability to evaluate the usefulness of the payment manager. The lack of a means of secure payment was viewed by nearly all trial participants as constituting a barrier to the more rapid development of electronic commerce and was most often cited by those who had never made an electronic purchase as the reason for not having done so. Users stressed that they want the same, if not more, flexibility in electronic commerce than they have in traditional markets and this includes selecting a form of payment which suits the particular purchase situation, e.g., takes into account the value of the purchase, the business partner, the form of delivery, etc. During the SME trials users consciously applied these different criteria, using the stored-value card and KPN Smartcard Purse, for example, for low-value database queries which were delivered on-line and credit-card- or account-based payment for higher-value goods which would be delivered by traditional means.

The fact that credit-card data was transmitted securely in encrypted form via the *SEMPER* software was viewed as an essential prerequisite for choosing this form of payment. Those participants who tested the SET purse found it an improvement over credit-card payments in traditional circumstances because it enabled a merchant to receive payment without necessarily obtaining the personal data of the customer. The willingness to pay electronically, however, was almost always weighed up against the advantages gained. For digital products which were received immediately there was a clear advantage to on-line payment, but there were also other situations where users would be willing to make payments on-line, in particular when time or convenience played a role, such as travel bookings, reserving theater tickets, etc.

The trial participants also viewed archiving and transaction browsing as essential components of an electronic commerce tool. The transaction archive was compared to an electronic form of bank or credit-card statement, i.e., useful for maintaining an overview, but also necessary for collecting evidence of transactions. Users with less computing experience wanted to be able to print out paper copies of the information in the transaction browser. More experienced users were content to keep the information stored on the hard drive, or possibly to back up on discs. Whether in paper or electronic form, however, all users required legally binding receipts and this was a major deficit which they identified in the prototype.

Criticisms of the information in the transaction browser focused mainly on the way the information was structured. Most essential information was recorded, e.g., business partner, time and status of transaction, but this needed to be formatted along the line of a bank statement and preferably include a description of the item purchased. The fact that the option to browse payment transactions was a separate entry in the applications list of the prototype was judged to be illogical. Most respondents expected to find the payment transaction browser under the purse management option and suggested that it be integrated there.

7.4.3 TINGUIN (Trustworthy User Interface)

The concept of having a single unified user interface where all security-relevant actions take place was viewed as an excellent approach. Trial participants generally felt that it is essential for the user to have a clearly defined area of interaction with the underlying systems and services. Nearly all trial participants would prefer to keep this interface separate from the browser and a number were in favor of emphasizing the personal link to the software more strongly by having the user's name clearly visible at all times. They felt this would increase user awareness of the significance of the actions supported by the software, e.g., digitally signing documents, or activating electronic payment, and also encourage them to protect themselves by protecting access to "their" *SEMPER* software.

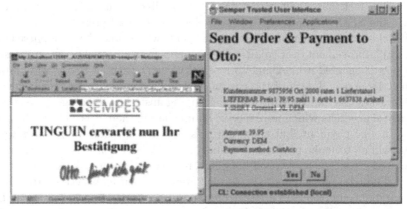

Fig. 7.4. The insecure browser window and the trustworthy TINGUIN window.

The most heavily criticized "missing feature" in the TINGUIN was the lack of a status bar, or some indication that connectivity had not been interrupted, that the system was actively doing something. Current network users are accustomed to the idiosyncrasies of network life, loss of connectivity, slow transmission speed due to an overload of traffic in the network, etc. but they need to know what is going on. Apart from this, criticisms focused more on ergonomic aspects, e.g., the failure to implement basic interface enhancements, which even relatively new network users have come to expect, than on the functionality of the TINGUIN. For example, the content of messages displayed in the TINGUIN and the format in which information is presented was not only criticized during the installation procedure described above, but also during routine use. In this respect the requirements of "basic users" and "experienced users" were somewhat different. The less experienced user wanted a fast, automated system with as little user intervention as possible.

More experienced users wanted more precise information regarding each step, e.g., "a connection request has been sent, your certificate is being checked by the Web server, your certificate has been recognized, checking server's certificate, etc." They emphasized that the content of the messages displayed must make it absolutely clear to the user what actions are being carried out, which actions have been successfully completed and which steps remain. Several persons felt that this degree of information would only be necessary during initial use and that some of the messages would no longer be required once a user had got used to the software. They suggested that the user be able to disable some messages according to his own preferences.

> "When you've understood what is going on, e.g., that the website could be a fake and that this software checks that it really is the site you think it is, you don't want to sit there every time and wait for confirmation, you just want to know that it has been done. Like with Microsoft, or Netscape, where it asks you if you want this warning or message to be displayed in the future, you should be able to disable things."

The lesson learned is that, although standard details of user interfaces may not be very innovative in a research project, they are critical if there are any end-user trials: The failure to get basic interface factors right from the start can hinder the ability of users to make an evaluation of the main aspects of the system.

The *SEMPER* software is protected by a session password, which the majority of trial participants found to be sufficient. Several users, however, who share their computer equipment with other users or considered using *SEMPER* from their office computer, wished to re-enter their password before an order could be sent. One user suggested that this could be resolved by having a *transaction PIN* in addition to the software password protection. They did not feel this would be inconvenient, but rather would offer necessary added protection and also remind the user of the significance of the action he was taking.

> "We're used to signing or confirming important things. Like at the bank to transfer money, or entering your PIN. Then you know something is being checked, or that you're doing something important. If the transactions are going to be legally binding the user has to be aware that he is doing something significant."

The more experience a trial participant had, the greater the requirement for protecting access to the system became. Two participants were in favor of storing private keys on a smartcard and one user suggested that user identification should be performed by means of biometrics (fingerprint or iris scan).

7.4.4 Secure Identification and Document Exchange

A great deal of immediate interest focused on payment, in particular in the SME trials where participants could experiment with various payment forms. In order to avoid too much emphasis on this one aspect of the architecture interviewers asked participants to imagine situations where payment would not be important, but they would still need, or want to conduct their negotiations using secure software. As the aim of *SEMPER* is to provide multi-party security, i.e., to protect the interests of buyers as well as sellers, it was important to measure the extent to which private users perceived benefits from securing the entire purchase process and not just payment.

The presence of fake websites was generally perceived among trial participants as being a greater threat to the private user than to businesses and this extended beyond the risk of credit-card data being observed, or payment being made to an impostor. The secure identification of the communication partner and the encrypted exchange of information were perceived as advantages whenever it was necessary to transmit personal data of any type. In addition, users wanted to be informed that this was taking place. Although there might be no risk of financial loss, they perceived the risk of a loss of privacy and possible annoyance, for example, unsolicited advertising.

More important advantages were seen in the ability to obtain and send digitally signed documents. In all of the examples mentioned the emphasis is on obtaining legally binding evidence that an agreement had been made and assumes that the digitally signed document could be reproduced if a dispute arose.

One participant pointed out that the ability to attach a digital signature to an order would make it much more difficult for someone to order goods and services using his personal data and, if this happened, he would be able to dispute the false order and deny payment. Another felt that the ability of buyers to make a binding order could facilitate new value-added on-line services. This applied in particular to obtaining individualized product offerings, such as a personal travel itinerary or house insurance, or any other product offering which could not be mass marketed and would result in a loss to the service provider if the customer denied having made the order. Another person suggested that it would be possible to transfer any number of documents normally sent by post more quickly and conveniently, e.g., certificates for successful completion of an on-line course, or the actual insurance policy.

Other examples included obtaining evidence that a firm offer had been made to a customer. This was applied in particular to on-line reservations. As one participant put it:

> "I don't want to take vacation from work and travel to Frankfurt Airport for a last minute flight to Spain which I booked on-line only to discover that there is no seat for me on the plane! And if it happens I want to have a legal right to claim compensation."

This was also applied to taking advantage of special offers which were restricted to a certain period of time. In this case the customer wanted proof that he had ordered within the correct period (time stamping) and that he only accepted the conditions offered for orders made during that time period. If later, when the goods were delivered, he received a bill for more than agreed he wanted to be able to dispute it. Other examples mentioned were obtaining guarantees that a task would be completed at a particular point in time, e.g., building work finished by a certain deadline, or that foreign exchange or stocks and bonds would be bought or sold at a particular time. In every case the value was linked to being able to obtain evidence for specific transactions conducted over the network. Trial participants saw potential in *SEMPER* for combining the advantages the Internet offers to react quickly to a broad range of offers with the traditional requirement for obtaining legally binding proof of these transactions.

7.5 Service Providers' Reaction

"It was a way to improve our company image and to modernize our services, especially the literature service which is now a data base which can be accessed. In the very beginning it was distributed as a print-out, then on diskettes, then CD, now the network is the clear next step. We wanted to have a chance to get a feeling of what can be done and what can be done securely. It is very important for our company image that the company is viewed as reliable."

The service providers who provided test sites for the *SEMPER* prototype were also users of *SEMPER* and they, in fact, were the most intensive "testers" of the prototype. At the conclusion of the project individual interviews with the service providers were conducted, as well as a group interview. The aim was to collect their impressions of the most important lessons learned by their companies, problems which were encountered and the impact *SEMPER* had made within their organization, as well as their views on future exploitation of the *SEMPER* architecture.

In general, the service providers felt that the willingness of their companies to participate in three years of scientific research dedicated to establishing a secure framework for doing business in the Internet clearly illustrated the importance which exploiting this new commercial environment has within their companies. The fact that their company was implementing a technology with the level of sophistication which *SEMPER* offers was viewed as a means of enhancing the image of their company as a dynamic forward-moving enterprise. In addition, they expected to gain the experience necessary to offer their customers more advanced services. For most, moving into the electronic marketplace is the logical next step in the development of their product offering.

When asked about how the achievements of the project compared to the expectations they had when they entered the project, there was general agreement that they had underestimated the complexity of the effort required to achieve the highly ambitious goals of the project. One service provider described the misunderstanding on the part of his company about what participation in the project would involve, i.e., they had expected *SEMPER* to be a complete solution which, after a year or so, they could simply plug into their system and test. They had not realized the extent to which they would be involved in defining the security services to be built. He described his company's participation as a tremendous process of learning which had enhanced the awareness within the company of the issues involved in electronic commerce and the new types of challenges it presents.

An increased awareness of electronic commerce issues and a growing understanding of the types of solutions available was cited by all service providers as a major lesson learned from their participation in the project. The project members were frequently the only member of their organization with this depth of knowledge. Management in most of the companies, for example, is only now, after three years of project participation, becoming aware of the significance of digital signatures, of a public-key infrastructure, the opportunities for electronic payment, etc.

> "*SEMPER* served as a catalyst. It started off as a research project and now Internet business is taking off. The directors have really become interested and now they want to know everything. During the last six months the question of payments and security has reached a very high level in the company."

All of the service providers had experienced some difficulty in communicating the capacity of the software to other members of their companies. As one participant pointed out, many company members simply did not have enough experience to understand the underlying concepts of the *SEMPER* architecture.

> "In order to understand the benefits of *SEMPER* you first have to have some understanding of the risks, to understand how the Internet works and where the problems with electronic commerce lie and these aspects are not well understood by most of the other people in my company."

This lack of understanding applied to the customers of the service providers as well and, coupled with their customers' relatively low level of computing skills, made it difficult for the service providers to conduct the number of external experiments which they had hoped for. The general opinion was that, in respect of the learning curve required to operate in the electronic commerce environment, it is still early days for many business users and certainly for private users. For service providers dealing with the general public there is little opportunity to support or educate their users. The opinion was that for this sector a "plug & play" solution is required. One of the service providers sees a business opportunity for his company to supply the education users will require to understand the underlying technologies of an electronic commerce tool.

"People within my company have watched the evolution of *SEMPER* very carefully. Since the company is involved in education, it intends to take advantage of the knowledge it has gained by its participation in the *SEMPER* project to assist new users. We expect a burst of interest in electronic commerce and we are preparing to be able to offer people the knowledge they will need to participate."

Where the users of the service are businesses, however, there are more opportunities to accelerate this process of learning. For example, ACRI (for trial description see Section 7.2.3), with a customer base of large important organizations and high-value digital products which require confidential access and secure on-line delivery, sees potential for integrating the *SEMPER* software into its business offering in the near future. The ACRI users have the expertise and the motivation to experiment with a prototype and ACRI is prepared to invest considerable resources in user support and also in demonstrating the software to potential users.

The sellers were asked if their experiences during the trials had altered their requirements for obtaining signed documents. An alternative would be a more simple solution, such as using SSL and, perhaps some on-line payment instruments. OPL reported a need for signed orders, due to the high value of the orders they receive, e.g., in the region of 500 Euro. ACRI's requirement for secure deliveries and evidence of these which would be suitable for presentation at court also indicates a need for signed documents. FOGRA saw a need for them in business-to-business transactions. However, the sellers did not see a need to sign every document used in electronic commerce. Otto Versand, for example, decided that signed orders were not necessary for their current business model and would, in fact, demand more commitment from customers ordering on-line than those using traditional means. (Traditional orders can be made by telephone and a signature is obtained at delivery.) If, in the future, a mass increase in fake orders via the Internet occurs, this might alter their opinion. In the MOMENTS trial, the signed order was implemented, but not the signed offer. It appears that users should be given the opportunity to choose whether they require, or are prepared to provide, signed documents depending on the particular requirements of the business context.

When asked if they had identified any services which are necessary for electronic commerce which had not been implemented, several were mentioned, e.g., a link to the accounting system of a company, the ability to forward documents from one party to another, secure email. After discussion within the group, the conclusion was that the potential for these functions is, in fact, in the *SEMPER* architecture, that they are essentially unexploited aspects of the business application (the API designed to meet the specific needs of the service provider which then accesses the various services in the *SEMPER* core). This prompted a discussion of the accessibility of the business application for application designers.

> "To build a business application you have to be a programmer in the Java world and be acquainted with *SEMPER*, so what is missing is the tools which make it easy for a programmer to write business applications. This is basically a documentation problem, a tutorial problem, it's understandable for a prototype, but a product would have to come with real documentation."

The general feeling was that additional tools need to be developed to make *SEMPER* more accessible to both business and private persons alike. All the essential pieces are there, the functionality exists, but the user interfaces need to be polished. One service provider described *SEMPER* as the "Swiss Knife for Electronic Commerce," everything is there, but the user does not yet know how to open the knife. In respect of understanding the underlying technologies used to achieve the security services provided by *SEMPER*, he made the analogy to driving a car, i.e., we all drive cars, but very few of us expect to understand the motor. In his opinion, once we begin using software like *SEMPER* in daily life, obstacles based on understanding will disappear. This produced another analogy between the TINGUIN (Trustworthy INteractive Graphical User INterface) and the dashboard of a car.

> "The TINGUIN is a very good start for a user interface and the comparison to a dashboard is good, but it needs to be researched further in respect of user understanding and requirements. The dashboard is also a product of evolution. It's a very complex thing. It has been designed to display certain functions and to hide others. I think this is a very important step which now needs to be taken."

The framework character of *SEMPER* was clearly appreciated by the sellers. Otto Versand felt it would offer significant advantages and cost reductions for adaptation to their back-end system. The company is interested in offering a variety of Internet payment systems to its customers, but is faced with the problem that it is not yet clear which payment systems will be used by customers in the future. A representative of Otto Versand described the situation as follows:

> "The costs of implementing an Internet payment system consist of (a) connecting the payment system to the Internet and (b) connecting the payment system to the back office systems and workflow. As (b) is significantly more expensive and time consuming than (a) it would definitely be helpful if dealers could use a system like *SEMPER* which only needs to be implemented once to their back office systems

and then the different payment systems can simply be added to the *SEMPER* till."

This example provides a good illustration of the economic significance an architecture such as *SEMPER* could have for parties which have to adapt their existing back-end systems to emerging security tools. According to a member of the MOMENTS project the main assets of the *SEMPER* framework are:

− Modularity: it is possible to plug in new payment modules, cryptographic modules, etc.
− Communications: it can support a variety of protocols, communication channels, etc.
− Flexibility: it offers the opportunity to design your own electronic commerce application.

These assets allow new security tools to be integrated in new business applications less expensively than if they had to be integrated on a case-by-case basis. The concept of managers and modules was viewed as useful for more than just payment instruments, for example, it could also be applied to the choice of cryptographic software and hardware. Representatives of the MOMENTS project saw *SEMPER* as a good candidate for an electronic commerce solution in UMTS (Universal Mobile Telecommunications System).

At the onset of the project the service providers had all underestimated the importance of factors related to the supporting infrastructure for electronic commerce. In this respect *SEMPER* was judged to be far ahead of the times. Non-technical obstacles to use which the service providers ran up against were the lack of a legal framework and supporting financial services. The problems experienced within the project in respect of implementing payments using real SET certificates, for example, were essentially related to the banking infrastructure and not the technology. Third-party services and a means of making legally binding contracts which would be acceptable as evidence at court still need to be established and until they are, the service providers expect continued reluctance on the part of market participants. The work within the consortium on *SECA* (Secure Electronic Commerce Agreement) was viewed as making an important contribution to overcoming this obstacle and allowing electronic commerce to take off before the supporting infrastructure has been firmly established.

On the whole, although they still perceive considerable barriers to widespread use, the service providers were impressed with the technical achievements of the project.

"*SEMPER* is the only software I have seen which organizes all the issues in electronic commerce. Other products just provide pieces, but *SEMPER* organizes them all. I've not seen any other software which can do this."

One can briefly summarize the sellers' reactions as follows:

- The fact that the infrastructure (financial/legal) to support secure electronic commerce is not yet in place inhibits users from experimenting.
- The functionality which sellers require to conduct their business electronically is in the *SEMPER* architecture, but it needs to be exploited and refined.
- Consumer education is essential.
- Businesses need an easy way to create new business applications, e.g., a "module installer."
- The framework character is expected to reduce both the costs for adaptation to back-end systems, as well as the costs for adapting crypto and payment tools to new business applications.

7.6 Conclusion

One of the most valuable aspects of the *SEMPER* architecture was seen to be the fact that it provides options, i.e., is not a static solution. This was seen to reflect the situation in traditional commerce where requirements and procedures vary from one business context to another. Factors such as the value of a purchase, whether the business partners have an established relationship or are doing business for the first time, all influence the way the business partners choose to conduct a transaction. In the trials this flexibility was mainly demonstrated by a range of payment options, but at least some of the trial participants could visualize this flexibility being transferred to other options, such as being able to accept different types of certificates, or apply different strengths of encryption depending on the business context.

Several persons, for example, made the point that they would probably impose stricter requirements at the onset of a business relationship, but would be willing to relax these as a result of positive experience. The ability to impose strict requirements could be seen to facilitate establishing business relationships in the electronic environment. In the advanced prototype, FIT, which is described in the following chapter, the user's ability to apply options has been expanded.

The main user requirements for an electronic commerce tool reported by trial participants are illustrated in the table below. Most are provided by *SEMPER*, but not yet in a sufficiently user-friendly form.

Essential in e-commerce tool	%	SEMPER
Secure payment	93	yes
Ease of installation and maintenance	85	no
Data privacy	81	yes
Ease of use	80	no
Signed offers/orders	76	yes
Encrypted data transfer	73	yes
Choice of payment options	60	yes
Record-keeping	57	yes

Table 7.2. Questionnaire Results: Eight characteristics rated essential for e-commerce tool.

In summary, the main points which the majority of testers valued were:

– the fact that all security-relevant information was presented in one window,
– the advantage of having one "security tool" to manage all electronic-commerce requirements,
– a clear separation of the secure window from the insecure browser,
– choice between a variety of payment options,

— a transaction archive and browser,
— the ability to personalize the software according to individual needs (expert users only),
— the ability to extend with use (e.g., add purses or certificate types).

The main aspects which were criticized were:

— no status bar or symbol in the TINGUIN to indicate connectivity,
— too many user confirmations required (mainly basic users),
— messages in TINGUIN not formulated clearly enough,
— lack of information about completed/uncompleted steps in process,
— information in transaction browser difficult to understand,
— no digitally signed receipts,
— not enough information about keys and key storage (mainly experienced users),
— no certificate browser (experienced users only).

Less experienced users were able to evaluate those aspects of the software which they were able to experiment with, but were less able than the more experienced user to identify missing aspects, or to suggest novel applications for use. The extent to which the user should be involved in configuring the software or in activating and deactivating security options was clearly the distinguishing point between "basic" and "experienced" users. So-called "power users" want a high level of information and control, but they are in the minority. Basic users want a patent security solution which they can trust on the basis of outside expert opinion (e.g., certification by a recognized organization, or standards body) and which requires as little personal intervention as possible.

Users who had already used public-key technologies for on-line banking or the exchange of secure email saw the advantage of *SEMPER* in the fact that the existing technologies are combined in one convenient tool which could be applied to the whole business process and would also incorporate the archiving of transactions. They also felt that a software package which combines various existing technologies, which are difficult for the non-technical user to install and manage himself, would result in increased dissemination and use of security technology, thus offering more opportunities for use.

> "The advantage of *SEMPER* is that these tools are incorporated into one tool that I can use for doing business. It's possible to assign meaningful roles to the various tools. I can say here is a database, with goods and offers in it, and I can abstract an offer from it, digitally sign it and send it over as a container and that's more than just PGP and RSA and emails."

Virtually all persons who experienced *SEMPER* felt that it would make buying and selling, doing business generally, safer in the networked environment, if and when other supporting services are in place. They are keen to take advantage of the speed and convenience of electronic commerce, but they do not want to lose the right to dispute contracts or agreements made using this medium. During the interviews, however, many felt they were being asked to evaluate hypothetical situations, which made it more difficult for them to give definitive answers. Users were, for example, able to understand and appreciate the potential of digital signatures for assuming the same significance on digital documents as hand-written signatures have on paper documents today, but they were less capable of projecting what the significance of the documents created and signed by electronic means will have in the future. The current lack of a supporting infrastructure led to answers being qualified by a number of conditions, e.g., "if appropriate cross-border agreements are reached, if digitally signed documents become valid evidence at court, if the public-key infrastructure develops in a particular way, if a large enough base of users evolves, etc., then I would...."

Essential changes to use *SEMPER*	%
Legal acceptance of digitally signed evidence	69
Used by a broad range of suppliers	64
Secure key storage	60
Electronic receipts	57

Table 7.3. Questionnaire Results: The four most important changes necessary before trial participants would use *SEMPER*.

For all of those who participated in the *SEMPER* trials, service providers as well as private users, the experience was part of a learning process which is far from being complete. It forced them to re-examine their expectations of the electronic marketplace, to re-access the technical and non-technical influences on its continued development and to define their requirements more precisely.

8. The Fair Internet Trader

This chapter presents the Fair Internet Trader (FIT) in detail. It is a new type of business application, designed for convenient and secure person-to-person electronic commerce. By this we mean electronic commerce where human interaction is needed at both ends, such as in business-to-business scenarios. We discuss our rationale, describe our prototype, and present results from interviews made during trials with this prototype.

8.1 Vision of a Person-to-Person Electronic-Commerce Tool

We already briefly introduced the Fair Internet Trader (FIT) in Section 4.2.2. Here we first show why person-to-person commerce is important and needs a tool.

8.1.1 A New Type of Electronic Commerce

Many situations in electronic business can be automated, as demonstrated by the emergence of electronic shops on the Internet. However, many cases resist automation and need human decisions and actions: At least for the time being, certain steps, such as contract negotiation or authorization of high-value transactions, are better left to human operators. We call these situations "person-to-person trade." The novelty of the FIT is to offer special support for both parties, buyers and sellers, in conducting such non-automated trade. The FIT tries to make this task as spontaneous, convenient and secure as possible. It gives easy and flexible access to services such as contract negotiation and signing, payments and delivery and makes the complete business process fair and accountable.

Person-to-person trade can involve the trade of goods, information, and services of both electronic and physical nature. It exists in the business-to-business sector as well as in the business-to-consumer market segment. It also exists in sales of used items between private persons. Here are two representative situations for person-to-person trade:

Localization of software: A US-based software company has developed a new product to be sold world-wide. In its original form, the product is only

G. Lacoste et al. (Eds.): SEMPER 2000, LNCS 1854, pp. 95–120, 2000.
© Springer-Verlag Berlin Heidelberg 2000

available in an English version. It therefore needs to be adapted to many other languages. To this end, the source code is sent to a European sub-contractor for appropriate adjustments in each European country. This work, called localization, requires prior negotiations on the specifications, the price and the deadlines, which are concluded with the establishment of a contract. While the work is in progress, it is likely that the software company and its sub-contractor will have to interact to address technical problems and to issue progress reports. These interactions will require confidentiality and authentication. Once the work is completed, the adapted software product has to be shipped back to the US software company. The sub-contractor will need a proof of delivery, time-stamped, so that it can prove that the terms and conditions of the contract were fulfilled on its part.

Sales of computer chips: For its daily production of smartcards, a smartcard manufacturer orders significant volumes of computer chips at the best price from different sources. The volume, quality, delivery dates, and prices are negotiated. As the volumes and prices vary from day to day, the smartcard manufacturer needs a binding offer that captures the results of the negotiation. Likewise, the computer chip supplier needs a binding order, should the smartcard manufacturer deny having ordered anything.

These two scenarios show that human intervention is required. The operations assume that human decisions are made as the information becomes available and cannot easily be programmed. The decisions are based on the content of information just received and the business context in which it is received. The business context includes the history of the information exchange, e.g., the certificates received from the business partner to authenticate himself and to define his liability, and the content previously received and sent. However, it also includes business knowledge and experience that has not been coded into a management tool yet.

8.1.2 The Role of a Tool

Traditional business mainly relies on the exchange of paper-based documents between the parties. One trusts the content of these documents as long as they clearly establish their origin, for example through a company letterhead and logo, and are signed. Hence, people trust that the documents represent evidence that can be used in case of disputes. Documents also frequently refer to each other as a way to trace the flow of the exchange. For example, an order will unambiguously refer to an offer or a quote, and an invoice will refer to an order and state a deadline for payment. These references are designed to ensure that the parties understand the terms of the trade and that the business flow can be reconstructed to resolve disputes.

Electronic business mimics traditional business while adding some interesting features, just like paper-based business enhanced the somewhat primitive verbal agreements that are still used in some situations. Electronic means bring the potential to assist the players in a number of verifications to be performed either before sending a document or upon receiving one. During negotiation, the differences between a proposal and its counter-proposal can be automatically identified and highlighted to the parties, an order can be quickly checked against the corresponding offer, and a payment can be matched without mistakes against an invoice. Furthermore, electronic signatures can be verified reliably, a task hard to achieve and automate for paper signatures. Electronic documents can be linked automatically with each other to reflect the business flow as it occurred and to support document retrieval. Electronic means can also assist in enforcing a minimal set of business rules, such as mentioning the terms and conditions, the country laws under which the trade is conducted, the jurisdiction concerned in case of disputes, etc. We call a tool with these functions an "electronic auditor."

While bringing these obvious benefits, electronic means modify the chain of trust that people were implicitly used to. Even with a very simple tool, users will depend on the proper visual representation of electronic documents. Hence they have to trust their hardware and software to reliably and exactly reflect the document. With a more sophisticated tool, they will also have to trust it to perform verifications reliably, enforce business rules correctly, link and archive documents correctly, and to make evidence available. Only when this trusted basis has been established, the players can make well-informed business decisions.

The *SEMPER* framework provides an ideal platform for such applications: The trustworthy user interface guarantees proper display of documents, while the support of business flows, handling of digital signatures, fair exchange protocols, and archival of documents and evidence enforce the necessary level of security. We therefore implemented a prototype of a tool that assists users in person-to-person trade as a business application on top of the *SEMPER* framework. It proposes a series of forms that the users can select to structure their communication and to ensure that basic business rules are enforced. In addition, the application implements security options that have to be supported in daily electronic commerce, such as confidentiality and on-line payment in different forms with or without receipt against payment. The application was named the Fair Internet Trader.

8.2 The FIT from a User Perspective

This section presents our prototype of the Fair Internet Trader (FIT) from the users' perspective. (This includes the underlying *SEMPER* services.) We describe the business processes and security options that are supported and how they are visualized to both participants. The software is identical at the seller's and the buyer's side, which enables users to play either role. To concentrate on essential aspects, we focused on a scenario with limited variations where a service or a product is negotiated and then sold, paid, and delivered.

8.2.1 Overview

The FIT structures business processes, deals in our terms, into three stages: negotiation, contract signing, and contract fulfillment. Each stage consists of a series of elementary steps such as request-for-offer and negotiate-offer during negotiation, or offer and order during contract signing. Critical information from each step is recorded for further reference or verification in case of dispute between the parties.

The negotiation stage begins with the negotiation of the security attributes, like authentication and confidentiality, which should apply for this deal, and the establishment of a shared security context. Then the negotiation of business matters takes place. When the negotiation stage has successfully completed, a contract in the form of a signed offer and a signed order is established. Then, the contract fulfillment stage takes place with a variety of information exchanges to transfer documents, perform payment, and provide receipts as stated in the contract. At any stage, it is possible to review the whole deal, browse though its critical steps and clarify disputes, possibly with the assistance of an arbiter.

8.2.2 Negotiation Stage

As an initial step the seller requests its FIT to listen for incoming service requests. If the buyer wants to establish a relationship with this server, he provides his own FIT with the seller's Internet address. In technical terms, a deal is then opened by the application on both sides and maintained by the Commerce Layer of the *SEMPER* framework. Each party can select the security attributes which should apply: They decide whether authentication of the counterpart is required; whether the trade has to take place within the *SEMPER* Electronic-Commerce Agreement (*SECA*) rules (recall Chapter 3); whether (non-repudiable) receipts are offered or required for payments, contracts and the delivery; and whether the communication should be confidential. The buyer's selection of security attributes is presented to the seller for acceptance, selection of further requirements, or rejection. Figure 8.1 illustrates this negotiation.

The setting of security attributes applies to the complete deal and is controlled by the *SEMPER* security services.[1] If authentication of either party is agreed, the user-relevant attributes of a key certificate of this party are presented to the other party, who may accept or reject. This is shown in Figure 8.2.

The selection of *SECA* rules implies that the certificate exchanged will be a *SECA* certificate and all signatures will be performed in the context of

---

[1] This somewhat arbitrary restriction was due to constraints in the prototype; we also experimented with a more granular setting of security attributes on a per-step basis.

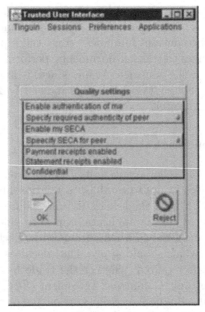

Fig. 8.1. Negotiation of security attributes: The buyer has made a proposal. The seller can now select from the unspecified attributes (pop-up menus under the boxes "specify").

SECA. If payment receipts are enabled, all payments will be exchanged with a receipt signed by the payee. This exchange is based on the fair exchange protocols described in Chapter 10. If the two parties agree upon confidentiality, all exchanges will be encrypted.

Fig. 8.2. Visualizing a certificate: As agreed on during negotiation, the business partner is authenticated. Here a *SECA* certificate is shown, in particular the liability. The user can accept and continue with trading under these conditions or reject. (The data identifying the user would be more than a name in reality)

Negotiation of the business content starts by inviting the buyer to fill in a *request-for-offer* form. The form is transferred to the seller who can provide and request clarification, hence pursuing the dialogue with the buyer. An unlimited number of exchanges between the parties may take place until negotiation reaches the point where the seller can sign a formal offer. Figure 8.3 illustrates the negotiation form.

The negotiated security attributes are briefly repeated on top of the forms, as well as the identity of the parties. This identity is extracted from the key certificate exchanged upon authentication, if agreed. Otherwise, the identity field reflects the value entered by the party. More detailed information is supplied upon request. The business content is negotiated via a free-format textual description supplemented by a tabular area to enter item references,

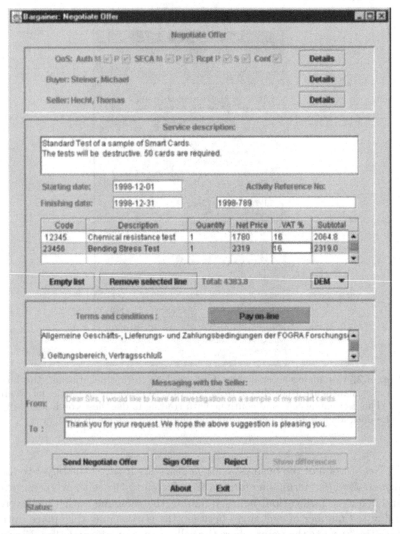

Fig. 8.3. Negotiation of business content: A Negotiate Offer form is used. The disabled button "Show differences" tells the user that his previous proposal has not been altered.

textual description, price, VAT, and automatically calculated subtotal and total prices. The forms also comprise fields to enter the currency, the terms and conditions, the applicable law, the jurisdiction, and a button to select on-line or out-of-band payment. The full interpretation of the textual fields is left to the parties, the forms being transferred without change among them. However, a display of textual differences between subsequent forms assists the players in identifying the changes made by their counterpart. Figure 8.4 shows an example of the "show-differences" functionality. (It is still in a rather primitive shape and could be integrated with the form.)

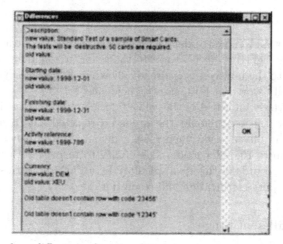

Fig. 8.4. The show-differences functionality

8.2.3 Contract Signing Stage

Assuming that negotiation has converged (otherwise, either party can abandon at any time), the seller will now make a binding offer. If that offer meets the expectations of the buyer, he can place an order on this basis. Together, the offer and the order form a contract signed by both parties.

If the seller decides to make a binding offer, the seller's FIT provides the seller with a clear point of no return: It asks the seller to explicitly authorize the signature on the offer by entering a password.

To highlight the fact that this offer is binding, the buyer's FIT renders it in a red frame with the identity of the signatory, here the seller, in the title. Figure 8.6 shows this. The form is automatically archived by *SEMPER*, both at the seller's and the buyer's side, as part of the current deal.

The buyer can only accept or reject a binding offer, but cannot modify it any more. To accept the offer, the buyer signs a corresponding *order* form.

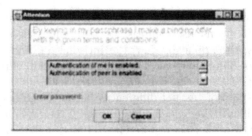

Fig. 8.5. "Point of no return:" The user has to enter his password to authorize a binding signature.

Signed offer and signed order together constitute a contract between the parties. The signed order is shown to the seller in a similar way as the offer was shown to the buyer; it was already shown in Figure 4.1. The order is also automatically stored at both sides as evidence.

The buyer is informed of the seller's decision, no matter if the order was accepted or rejected. Should the order be rejected, the commerce deal is aborted. The buyer might then raise a dispute in the belief that his order was conform to the offer made. The ability to inspect both the seller's and the buyer's records of this deal, possibly by an arbiter, forms the *SEMPER* basis for dispute clarification and resolution.

8.2.4 Fulfillment Stage

If the order was accepted, both parties have to abide by the signed contract. The seller has to supply the services or the products ordered, while the buyer may need to supply supporting information or physical material required by the seller to perform the terms of the contract. Depending on the terms agreed, the buyer may also be required to settle the contract through a specific on-line or out-of-band payment method, with payment in full or down-payment with installments, before or after delivery of the services or products.

The FIT prototype limits its ambition to a subset of these possibilities. It assumes that, if required, supporting information is provided by the buyer out of band. Delivery, however, is performed within the deal so that it is automatically recorded and linked. Furthermore, if online payment is chosen, it is assumed to be performed before delivery, while out-of-band payment is assumed to be performed after delivery.

Like any other step, invoicing is performed through a form, the *invoice* form. The FIT automatically derives the invoice from the order. The fields

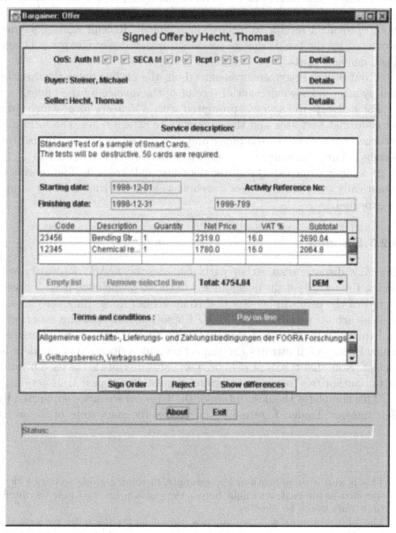

Fig. 8.6. An offer, signed by the seller, as seen by the buyer

of the invoice cannot be modified by the seller.[2] The invoice form is sent and displayed to the buyer.

Now, if on-line payment was agreed on, the payment services of *SEMPER* are triggered. They execute the payment based on any existing payment instruments—like electronic cheques, credit cards, or ecash—available at the buyer's and seller's side. If a receipt against payment was requested, the seller has to provide a receipt to receive the payment. Receipt against payment is protected by the fair exchange services; for details see Chapters 11 and 10. Then delivery starts.

If out-of-band payment was agreed on, the on-line delivery starts immediately after acknowledgment of receipt of the invoice by the buyer.[3]

For delivery, the seller is prompted with a *delivery* form which provides a free-format text area and the capability to attach a file. The form and the attached file are sent to the buyer and, if required by the security settings, a receipt is fairly exchanged.

If a file is attached, the buyer detaches and stores it. The receipt is automatically stored in the seller's archive as evidence that delivery completed as expected.[4]

8.2.5 Disputes

Should a dispute arise, either party can use the *SEMPER* deal browser to review the records of the deal and any of the steps included in it. If necessary, a copy of the deal can be exported to an arbiter for settling the claim.

The arbiter uses the same *SEMPER* software to read the exported deals and to verify the included evidence, such as contracts, receipts and certificates. Figure 8.7 illustrates the inspection and verification of the details of a receipt. Note that the same deal browser software can also be used by auditors or tax authorities to review the state and validity of past transactions.

This completes the description of the business scenarios supported by the Fair Internet Trader. Figure 8.8 summarizes the main steps of the scenario.

---

[2]This is also a simplification. For example, in some real-life scenarios the price specified in the contract might be per time unit spent, and now the number of time units would be filled in.

[3]The FIT prototype does not include provisions for the seller to state that an out-of-band payment was received. However, one could incorporate out-of-band payments in the payment framework to allow a more seamless integration.

[4]There can be two different types of receipts. The fair exchange results in a receipt which proves that the buyer has received the delivery, but not that the buyer is satisfied with the service or product. For this, the buyer could send a second receipt which states this satisfaction and allows the seller to unilaterally prove the successful completion of the trade. This is not completely implemented in the prototype.

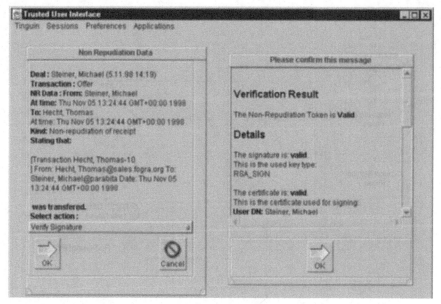

Fig. 8.7. Inspecting a receipt in the deal browser

8.3 Internal Design

We now give an overview of the internal implementation of the FIT for technically interested readers. Other readers can immediately continue with the following section on feedback.

8.3.1 Overview

The FIT is composed of three subsystems implemented by three class hierarchies: the *messages* subsystem, the *display* subsystem and the *flow* subsystem, see Figure 8.9. This separation allows simple modifications to each subsystem without affecting the others.

The *messages* subsystem is the hierarchy of the messages exchanged between the buyer and the seller. The objects of this hierarchy are derived from Commerce Layer classes and define the internal representation of the business messages.

The *display* subsystem is the hierarchy of classes that encapsulate the user interaction forms of the FIT. This is the presentation of the business messages to the user with additional tools such as "Show differences" and the visualization of the overall status such as the security settings.

The *flow* subsystem is the hierarchy of classes that implement the business logic at the buyer's and at the seller's side and enforces the consistency of

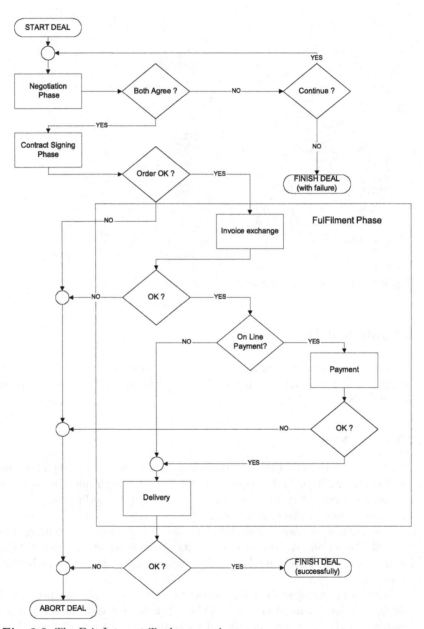

Fig. 8.8. The Fair Internet Trader scenario

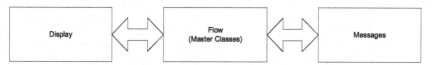

Fig. 8.9. Fair Internet Trader overall architecture

the values of the various fields. We now describe these three subsystems in detail and then the overall execution model.

8.3.2 The Messages Subsystem

The class hierarchy of the messages subsystem is depicted in Figure 8.10. These classes are derived from Commerce-Layer classes. They contain the data of the corresponding forms. For example, the **Offer** object of the messages subsystem contains the data of the corresponding offer, visualized using the offer form of the display subsystem. Their relationship with the corresponding forms of the display subsystem is determined and managed by the flow subsystem.

There are two main types of messages: The **SignedMessage** class and the **UnsignedMessage** class. The meaning of the messages is quite obvious. The contents have already been described in the form of screen shots. Which messages are signed and which are unsigned is derived from general security considerations and the given scenario.

8.3.3 The Display Subsystem

The display subsystem displays the messages and enables the user to edit the fields during the negotiation phase.

The design philosophy of the display sub-system is to split the display into two sections:

– The "form" section, which displays the forms of the deal. In other words, it is the section that displays the contents and the controls that implement the business semantics. The form section is located in the upper part of the display.
– The "control" section, which contains the contents and controls that manage the application. It is located in the lower part of the display.

For example, in Figure 8.6, the form section is the lighter part, the control section the darker part.

Some additional security-relevant functionality is integrated: showing differences, highlighting security by a red frame, inspection of the security context, etc.

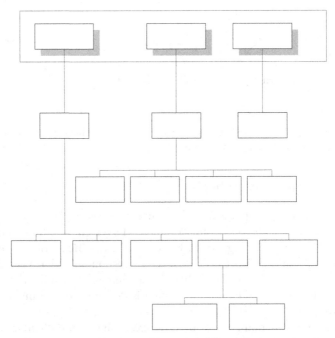

Fig. 8.10. The message subsystem hierarchy. (Note that `DeliveryReceipt` and `InvoiceReceipt` do not need to be subclasses of `SignedMessage` (as expected) as they do get signed separately as part of a non-repudiation of receipt transaction).

The show-differences functionality allows to quickly highlight the changes during negotiation and, e.g., prevents subtle changes in the Terms & Conditions from being overlooked. The show-differences button is enabled every time there is a mismatch between any of the data sent and the data received in the response form. When the enabled button is pressed, the prototype pops up a window with a report that indicates the differences as shown in Figure 8.4.

8.3.4 The Flow Subsystem

Instead of writing a thousand words, we present in Figure 8.11 the flow of the forms for the buyer and the seller. The events that trigger the creation and destruction of forms are also shown. However, for readability only a few exceptions are shown. Essentially, this is also a state transition diagram. New states are reached (and visualized) due to the arrival of a new message or due to user interaction.

The forms are represented as boxes labeled with the name of the form. The boxes also contain the buttons of the corresponding form (e.g., `RequestFor-Offer`, `Reject`) whenever they exist. The solid-line boxes represent the forms that expect a reaction from the user. User interaction is performed by pressing one of the buttons of the form (e.g., the *Request For Offer* button). The

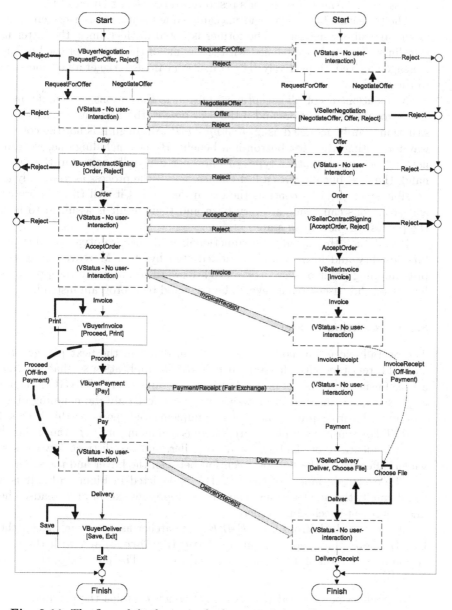

Fig. 8.11. The flow of the forms at the buyer and the seller

dashed-lined boxes represent forms that require no user interaction. These forms usually contain informational messages about the status of the deal process (e.g., "Waiting for seller's response to the recent Order...")

The transition between two forms can be due to either a user-driven event or the arrival of a message. The former is noted in thick lines, the latter in thin lines. The lines are labeled with the name of the button pressed or the message received, respectively. The transition can also trigger a new message to the other party.

As mentioned, not all exceptions are shown. Exceptions are communication errors, software errors and if the user presses the *Exit* button. All these situations can be modeled as an *improper exit*. Although it is not the correct way for exiting, the *Exit* button is a benefit. By not including one, we gain nothing because the other types of improper exit still occur. On the other hand, the *Exit* button gives a last chance to exit the process as gracefully as possible since the FIT controls the execution behind it. All these improper exit situations can occur in every form and their result is assumed to lead the process to the *Finish* state.

Recall that this is only the functionality of the prototype. Additional functionality and forms could be added step by step. Moreover, from the programming point of view it is straightforward to automate the processes by letting the "user-driven" events be triggered by a program instead.

8.3.5 Execution Model

The overall execution model is described in detail in the next paragraphs. The FIT registers with the standard *SEMPER* application so that starting a FIT business process is integrated into the same overall TINGUIN menu as purse management, deal browsing etc. Therefore only the handling of an individual business process needs to be implemented specially; this is called the FIT BA (business application). There is one main (or **Bargainer**) class,[5] which is identical for the buyer and the seller, and two distinct flow classes, which differentiate the flow of execution between the buyer and the seller.

The execution model of the FIT BA is depicted in Figure 8.12. It is a simple multi-threaded schema. The ellipses represent execution threads. The lines represent special milestones.

When launched (from the *SEMPER* dispatcher as server or client), the FIT BA starts in a separate thread (**BargainerThread**) and with the execution of a method of its "main" class **Bargainer**. The purpose of this class is:

− To create a new thread (**FlowThread**) which contains the commands to execute the business logic. Together with the **FormThread**s that it creates, it handles events in the form section of the display.

---

[5]The name "**FIT** class" would be more plausible, but "Bargainer" was the first project-internal name for the FIT.

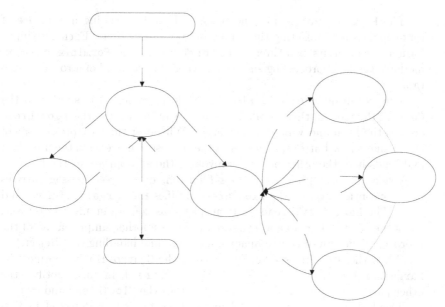

Fig. 8.12. The FIT BA logical execution model

- To create a new thread (`ControlThread`) that controls the application flow.
  It corresponds to the control section of the display.
- To wait for an event from either of the above threads.

Remember that the main class runs in its own thread (`BargainerThread`).
After creating the above threads, it sleeps waiting for an event from either
thread:

- The events from the `ControlThread` are typically the pressing of the *Exit*
  or the *About* button.
- The events from the `FlowThread` are typically "FlowFinish" or "Flow-
  Aborted" events, which represent normal and abnormal finish of the deal,
  respectively (e.g., when the business flow has finished successfully or a
  Reject message arrived in the middle of the business flow).

With this schema, it is guaranteed that the `BargainerThread` always has the
final word even in exceptional circumstances. One such example is when the
user pressed the *Exit* button while waiting for an answer from the other party.
Another benefit is that the `FlowThread` is concentrated on business-flow semantics and it does not have to care about the control of the application
(e.g., when the user presses the *About* button). This separation makes things
much simpler and clearer to administer.

There is a different `FlowThread` for the buyer and the seller. Actually,
there are two different classes: `BuyerFlowThread` and `SellerFlowThread`.
For the sake of simplicity we will call both `FlowThread`.

The `FlowThread` executes the business logic by creating a sequence of user-input forms, collecting their data and processing them. Each user-input form also runs in its own thread (the `FormThread`). The `FormThread` accommodates the local processing such as entering data removal of a row from the table.

The execution schema of `FlowThread` for user forms is similar to the `ControlThread` for the overall FIT BA. In other words, the `FlowThread` creates the form and waits for user input. Whenever the user presses one of the business flow buttons, it processes the request (e.g., collects the user data and sends it to the other party) by invoking the appropriate method.

When the user presses the *Reject* button, or a *reject* message arrives or an exception occurs, the `FlowThread` notifies the `BargainerThread` and exits. The `BargainerThread`, in turn, performs some administrative tasks, stops the ControlThread and exits too. (This is another simplification of the prototype; one can of course imagine more gradual handling of a Reject.)

When the user presses the *Exit* button, the `ControlThread` notifies the `BargainerThread` and exits. The `BargainerThread`, in turn, notifies the other party by sending a Reject message, stops the `FlowThread` and exits.

The FIT BA execution model in the time domain is depicted in Figure 8.13. The solid lines represent the flow of execution whereas the dashed lines represent waiting state.

8.4 Experiments

The following survey is based on demonstrations of the FIT prototype described above, installed on machines running Windows NT. Test users were given the opportunity to play the role of either the buyer or the seller. We assumed that the legal framework, in particular liability questions, would influence whether people would want to use electronic commerce at all for the type of business that the FIT aims at. Hence feedback on *SECA*, the *SEMPER* Electronic-Commerce Agreement, was collected at the same time. For this, the core regulations were shown and explained to the respondents. The respondents were able to choose the liability limits themselves. The in-depth interviews lasted one to two hours and in most cases were recorded on tape.[6] Twenty-one such interviews have been made by three interviewers in Austria, France, Germany and the United Kingdom. For obtaining feedback, the FIT was also presented at the *SEMPER* day in Zurich, in November 1998, and several other conferences. Further interviews took place at meetings with representatives of the EU projects WINDS, PRINT-IT and USINACTS. A simulation of the FIT was made available on the Web server of the project.[7]

---

[6]See questionnaire and more results in D12 (SEMPER Consortium 1999b).
[7]http://www.semper.org/simulator/intro.html

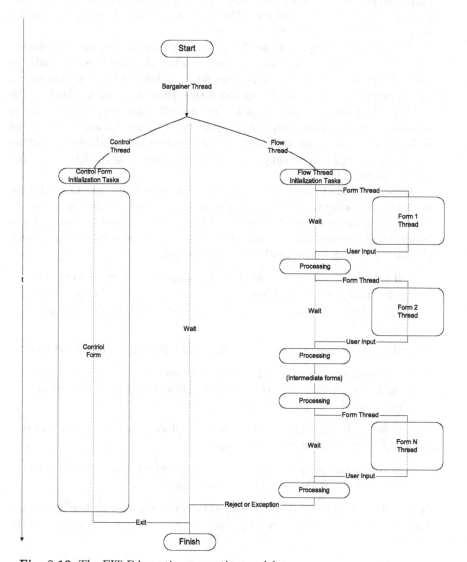

Fig. 8.13. The FIT BA runtime execution model

The respondents fall in two categories: The first were representatives of companies which plan to buy or sell on the Internet or already do so. The second were experts in related fields, such as ergonomics, law, public-key security, and certification services. Most respondents were engineers, computer scientists, economists or lawyers. The average age was 35 years; six women were among the respondents.

The general principles of the FIT were easily understood, and respondents were able to quickly imagine how and in what circumstances it could be used. They appreciated the similarities with traditional business procedures and documents. Respondents concluded that there is no similar tool on the market which would allow them to buy or sell something of their choice as securely and conveniently. They appreciated many characteristics of the FIT. These can be grouped in characteristics potentially available with secure electronic mail (if it were supported by an agreement like *SECA*), and those specific to the FIT.

Characteristics from the first group were the possibility to obtain evidence in the form of digital signatures and to achieve confidentiality. Respondents provided examples where they imagined the usage of digital signatures to be beneficial. Some saw that in transactions that are already done electronically, the issue arises of who is really at the other end:

> "If I personally know somebody I also do business with him over the phone and don't always insist on written documents. In the digital world this might not work that well: How can I identify my peer reliably?"

Also the issue of bindingness arises, e.g., when buying high-value services:

> "I outsource software development. It is very important for me that I have the system at a certain date. Otherwise I can't sell to my customers, I may go bankrupt."

Others found it particularly attractive to replace paper documents, in particular if they are inconvenient to handle:

> "If the signature is legally binding, it would eliminate the need to keep separate records—therefore save time."

Respondents concluded that the usage of digital signature technology means that it is no longer necessary to transmit one's credit-card number over the Internet:

> "Today the credit-card number is sent through the Internet. If tomorrow you could simply sign the document, this would be a benefit."

Respondents also noticed that the FIT gives them several advantages that they would not obtain with secure electronic mail:

– Usage of forms with fields:

"Nice that a part is structured, another unstructured for entering information."

"Forms are useful. Plain email would not do it."

"The 'show differences' feature is nice. It's quite important to me that such an exchange of forms takes place quickly."
- The electronic auditor:
  "I like the automatic checking of content."
- An easy way to change contents, and have the changes visualized:
  "The possibility to efficiently revise and negotiate a proposal in several rounds is very good."
- The option of on-line payment:
  "I can even at some stage receive some money through the Internet."
- Liability limits:
  "As a buyer I like to limit my liabilities to prevent getting into deep trouble if somebody steals my keys."

What would respondents do with the FIT? It turned out that the FIT is particularly suitable for certain kinds of business-to-business trade.

One is consulting, such as providing expertise or software. Such contracts are typically specific per business partner, negotiations are required, and the deliverable can easily be sent on-line. Values mentioned by the respondents range from a few thousand Euro up to the equivalent of several person-months.

"Transactions worth DM 20'000. Our company would offer the whole range of services."

Respondents of this type are in companies with less than 100 employees. Characteristics like evidential value, visualization of changes made during negotiation, receipts obtained in fair exchange, the electronic auditor, on-line payment (as with an electronic cheque), would certainly be of value to this group.

Another type of trade will be purchases of high-value hard goods. Respondents mentioned computers, machinery or telecommunication equipment and mentioned values up to millions of Euros. Naturally such contracts are frequently subject to negotiation.

"Up to DM 200,000." (for buying computers)

"For a consumer who buys a food-processor for DM 100 a Visa card is OK. But for companies, where a purchase of equipment can be worth millions, you better use digital signatures to replace the paper (contracts) used today."

In such cases, there is typically no automatic trade. Negotiations are made interactively between human beings and the number of transactions per user is relatively low. Doing private transactions, typically of medium value, such as selling one's used car as proposed by some respondents, also falls into this type of trade.

On the one hand the respondents found the FIT mostly easy to understand and use:

> "User-friendliness, simplicity and ease of use."

This also applies to the general principle of predefined forms which have to be filled in and sent back and forth, much as in today's business. On the other hand, they requested simplifications, in particular an easy-to-use standard starting screen and fewer buttons, screens and visualization of security attributes:

> "Make it more user friendly. It should look like an email program. Too many options, e.g., authentication. For normal consumers have a standard set-up, options for experts. People don't want to see messages. The demo is much too difficult to use. For instance, that you get the TINGUIN up and you enter what you want to do. Like in Word, there is a document, you can start to type."

Regarding functionality, the following changes were requested by some respondents:

– Possibility to interrupt and later resume a deal at any time.
– Selection of payment to be prior or after delivery both for on-line and out-of-band payments.
– Availability of printouts.
– Certain changes to the exact forms used, e.g., that the details about the buyer and seller and the quality-of-service attributes should be spelt out on the offer form although they had already been verified earlier and the FIT ensures that they remain the same.
– Interaction with existing backend systems, e.g., accounting software.

It was also requested that a product should require less hardware (Windows NT machines were used) and be faster. The third item and the hardware requirements are prototype-specific restrictions, and so is the first item at least if restricted to interruption between the individual steps of the deal. It would also not be a great technical problem to include more variations in the flow and modify the forms, but here the main questions are economic and ergonomic issues of flexibility versus simplicity of such a tool.

Business respondents who saw the applicability of the FIT for them expressed a certain willingness to pay for an (improved) FIT, ranging from very low amounts, much like for shareware, up to Euro 100 or 200. They considered that the FIT will bring them savings. Costs of express couriers up to Euro 500 were mentioned, and savings because they need not re-enter data. The FIT was presented as a means for valuable sales, typically not done as frequently as low-value sales, and for occasional sales. If integrated into a solution for secure daily WWW shopping, or packaged together with a WWW shop, the willingness to pay might be different. Besides, a willingness to pay for certification services was indicated for the seller and for business-to-business in general.

Respondents saw that the FIT presupposes the existence of a public-key infrastructure and that their business partners have registered and have a copy of the FIT. They saw that this "chicken-and-egg" problem needs to be solved first:

> "For non-commercial users the FIT should be for free."

> "Certification Authorities will have to give away a lot of free certificates, just to get the user base."

Regarding *SECA*, the respondents realized that it makes sense to sign such an agreement, much like they sign an agreement on their responsibilities and liabilities for their bank card:

> "*SECA* reminds me of the situation of today's credit card payments: I'm liable as long as I didn't report my card loss. This gives a clear understanding and confidence."

They also understood that they will have to bear a certain share of the damage in case of compromise. Some said they are willing to bear a loss of, e.g., Euro 1000—the highest amount mentioned was Euro 5,000. At least small companies will not wish to bear a risk of compromise in the range of Euro 100,000 or more:

> "If I'm not protected against manipulations my whole existence could go down the drain."

They assume the risk can be insured:

> "How good is the insurance? An insurance has to be part in any case."

It was also suggested that there should be a spending limit so that they cannot risk their house or company:[8]

> "I don't think that I would agree to obtain a certificate that would allow me to pay any amount of money. If this certificate is stolen then somebody can sell my house."

Respondents also remarked that limits may be impractical for business use such as in high-value procurement. Regarding *SECA*, it can be concluded that players require limits, either in the form of spending limits or in the form of liability limits for the case of compromise. The appropriate height of liability limits was subject to discussion, with proposals ranging from Euro 50 to Euro 5,000, and respondents noticed that what may be appropriate

---

[8]The Liability-Cover Service, which would achieve exactly this for general signatures, not just a payment system, was not implemented in the prototype.

for the relying party, may be painful for the signing party, and vice versa. This seems to suggest that there is also a market for more secure devices and operating systems that decrease these risks.

The feedback given by the respondents confirms that the approaches of FIT and *SECA* are worth pursuing. Some respondents from Internet service providers and certification authorities even asked the interviewers during the presentations whether they could obtain the FIT as a product for distribution by the respondent's organization.

8.5 Outlook

The Fair Internet Trader shows that an electronic-commerce tool can offer considerable support to users in business processes that are not fully standardized. The secret lies in the right combination of standardization and flexibility:

- Standardized parts can get more help from the tool. This concerns both user-friendliness (automatic copying of a field from one form to another etc.) and security (automatic verification of signatures, electronic auditor functions, consistent look-and-feel for typical data elements and events).
- Options are necessary to cover a sufficiently wide range of business processes to allow the tool to become a standard. A standard is necessary for achieving that everyone can protect himself by a trustworthy tool on his own machine.

Our prototype already gave its users a clear impression that this is possible.

The question for improvements is not so much what is technically possible —almost everything is—but what is the most appropriate choice for the users. The feedback indicates that more *business* options can easily be added without confusing the users because they know such options from conventional business. For example, more payment modalities (in particular after delivery) were desired. *Security* options, on the other hand, are less familiar and therefore tend to be more difficult to handle. They should therefore be hidden as long as possible and only be shown in situations where the user knows what they refer to, or on demand. For instance, liability questions can be deferred until the time when the user wants to make or receive a binding offer or order.

Another interesting aspect is the visualization of forms. Legal requirements and past experience in the physical and electronic world teach us what the content (data structures) of the forms has to be. However, it is much less clear what has to be shown to the user. There are two opposing requirements: On the one hand, the visualized forms should always be the same during the process and similar to paper forms to make the use familiar and intuitive. On the other hand, the visualized information should be limited to information which has to be manually verified; showing additional information which has already been verified automatically by the FIT or which has been approved manually in previous steps of the process (e.g., long and precise identity information) might only distract the user from the more security-relevant non-verified information. Finding a balance between these extremes is a delicate task and the choice whether some information is shown on the main form in full or abbreviated form, is accessible through optional secondary windows, or is hidden completely depends on the context. The current FIT is promising, but further and broader experience is needed before we can draw general conclusions on the optimal approach to visualization.

The FIT prototype is a separate application. However, another benefit of a tool combining standardization and flexibility is that integration with other systems is easier than for both a fully rigid tool supporting just one business flow and a fully flexible tool like free-format email signing. For example, the use of forms with well-known fields enables the integration into accounting systems. It also allows automation of one side in business contexts where this is possible, in particular for merchant servers, simply by adding a program that replaces the user decisions. It is even conceivable to use the FIT, for its consistent look-and-feel, in interaction with servers running various other proposed specific electronic-commerce protocols. Of course, this presupposes integration of the message formats of those systems in the lower layers of the SEMPER framework.

9. The Commerce Layer: A Framework for Commercial Transactions

This chapter presents the *SEMPER* proposal for a general framework for commercial applications. Its main concept is a commerce context called a deal, by which *SEMPER* keeps track of the flow of a business process even if that flow is controlled by an untrusted business application. The benefit of such support is that one can then allow arbitrary applications to be downloaded from business partners, thus combining the use of *SEMPER* services and the support of partner-specific business models. Hence authorization of security-critical actions triggered by the applications, the relation to access control, and downloading are also described in this chapter.

9.1 Technical Approach

9.1.1 The Challenge

For decades, a major challenge to move to computerized business has been to agree on communication formats and protocols between business organizations. Their implementation, based on different business-software products—often proprietary—, has followed the path of ad-hoc solutions: currently, more than 130 different messages are defined for EDIFACT (ISO/IEC TC154 1999). New ones are steadily appearing.

Further, digital business exchanges like EDIFACT and X.12 (ANSI Accredited Standards Committee X.12 (ASC X.12/DISA) 1992) require the establishment of bilateral agreements on the semantics of the messages before any exchange can be performed. This may, to some degree, be acceptable in a closed network of business-to-business commerce that evolves slowly over time. But even in this case, the conversion between business-internal syntax and semantics—for instance, databases, forms, software variable syntax, etc.—to EDI syntax and semantics represents a major and costly task. Of course, the converse mapping has to take place at the responding site. Legacy databases make this road even rougher.

From these observations, it is clear that a Commerce-Layer service that tries to provide common security facilities, such as secure recording of all steps, to all business applications should be independent of application syntactic and semantic definitions. In terms of the final *SEMPER* architecture,

G. Lacoste et al. (Eds.): SEMPER 2000, LNCS 1854, pp. 121–153, 2000.
© Springer-Verlag Berlin Heidelberg 2000

these services fall mostly into the Deal Support Block of the Commerce Layer. We will simply say Commerce Layer in the following according to the notation in the prototype.

In the Java environment, the issue of application syntax and semantics conversion may be partly addressed by means of the paradigm of download-able code: downloading of the client part of service-specific business applications at service-request time eliminates the need to perform any conversion between the client and the server as the client brings with it the application-specific syntax and semantics used by the server. Hence, the client behaves as the local representative of the remote organization offering the application service. To put it in simple terms, the business-application developer decides to build a service provided by a server and a downloadable client which both count in inches or centimeters, or define what the volume of a barrel is.

Obviously, the syntactic conversion and interpretation problem still exists on the client side for interacting with the customer organization-defined syntax and semantics. Normally, this conversion is acceptable to the customer. Actually, it is the de facto mode in many paper-based business transactions, where the customer is handed over a form to fill in. It is also the case with various smartcard-based customer handling systems that large organizations build and promote.

9.1.2 The Generic Deal Approach

The definition of the generic services in the *SEMPER* Commerce Layer stems from these two considerations:

- It confines itself to offering generic security services related to the flow of a business process. These services are completely independent of the business model, policies, semantics and syntax of the application exchanges.
- the client part of a business application may be downloaded at application service invocation time.

In the rest of this chapter, we assume that the client part is in fact downloaded at service invocation time. This is how the *SEMPER* trials described in Chapter 7 were implemented. Note, however, that the same services were successfully used in the Fair Internet Trader, a business application mainly intended for running locally on both sides, see Chapter 8.

This approach has implications on both the server and the client side of a business application:

- On the server side, the server part of a business application, installed statically prior to start-up, can be trusted by the service provider. Actually, it is the only place where a service provider can enforce a business policy.
- On the client side, the approach provides the following benefits, compared to a solution with a thin client where the client does not handle the business process at all:

- The client business application offloads computation power from the server, making the latter available for more service requests from customers. The client side can handle much of the formatting of Web pages, based on the raw data provided by the server. In some cases, the client might be able to serve a request without interaction with the server.
- The client business application behaves as the representative of the service provider. As such, it knows the business model and policies of the service provider. Negotiations may be partly conducted locally at the client. The server business application will eventually have to verify the validity of that negotiation, but it is a non-interactive operation.
- Even in the case of a communication failure, the client business application might be able to perform meaningful operations.

The choice of downloading client business applications also has a certain price:

- Additional *SEMPER* functionality is required for dynamic loading of business applications, and for strict secure control of their access to *SEMPER* services to protect *SEMPER* critical resources.
- Neither the service provider nor the customer can generally trust the client part of a business application: the service provider has no assurance that the client business application will behave as expected, as it executes in a foreign environment which is not under his or her control; the customer has no assurance that the client will preserve his or her interest. As regards the latter, *SEMPER* needs to include provisions to enforce the client's policy.

Based on the technical approach just described, the Commerce Layer meets a number of high-level requirements. They all stem from the general requirement to make *SEMPER* security services applicable to a broad range of business situations. These high-level requirements are outlined below.

Application downloading. The availability of *SEMPER* security services to different kinds of partner-specific business situations assumes the paradigm of client-server. One part of a business application runs at the server and the other part at the client. The client part of a business application may be dynamically downloaded from the server and installed on demand at run-time. This solution enables a customer to interact with any of the service providers who supply a client business application for downloading. There is no need of prior agreement with the service provider and no static pre-installation of a specific set of client business applications.

Business commonalities. *SEMPER* business applications can be tailored to the actual business behavior including syntax, semantics, and procedures of a particular business branch. The Commerce Layer abstracts from these specificities by offering a set of generic security services that are common to a wide range of business applications, thereby simplifying the task of application developers. The service offered by the Commerce

Layer are offered in the form of an object-oriented Application Programming Interface (API). In particular, the API provides support to manage business contexts.

Secure service access. The *SEMPER* system provides its security services to business applications through the Commerce-Layer. Client business applications may be considered trusted to some degree by some, while other applications may not be trusted at all. Commerce-Layer service access is controlled by access capabilities verified by the access-control mechanism. The distinction between non-trusted and trusted applications is enforced by the use of access capability objects presented by the actual application. For instance, the secure service access point of the Commerce Layer enforces that any security-critical action is explicitly authorized by the user.

Security policy. Client business applications request that the Commerce Layer perform security-critical actions, either on behalf of the local user or by requesting him or her to validate the action. Only those actions that are in agreement with the user's policy should be performed. They must be authorized by the user, through either an explicit user's confirmation or rights granted to business applications for performing a limited set of actions that are consistent with the user's preferences. *SEMPER* ensures conformance of business application actions to the user's security policy.

Quality of Service. Part of the user's policy is the requirements for security, reliability, and speed. The needs for security are generally specific to business situations. The Commerce Layer is meant to support several kinds of *commerce quality*. Parameters of security, reliability, and speed are associated to the business context.

9.2 Concepts and Architecture

The Commerce Layer design introduces two novel concepts: commerce transaction and commerce deal. Commerce transactions are generic commercial steps performed by participants in electronic commerce. Examples of commerce transactions include price-quotation, offer, order, contract agreement, procurement, payment, shipping and delivery, to name a few. Commerce deals represent the Commerce-Layer mechanism by which the business context established by the client and server can be maintained and persist. A commerce transaction happens within the context of a commerce deal.

9.2.1 The Commerce-Transaction Service Model

The service offered by the Commerce Layer to business applications is called the commerce-transaction service. It defines a set of commerce transactions that are necessary and sufficient to develop and run business applications in the framework of *SEMPER*.

We assume that a business application comprises business-application entities, one at the client and one at the server. Business application entities are the users of the commerce transaction service. A business application entity utilizes the commerce transaction service by invoking service primitives at a service access point of the commerce transaction service.

The commerce transaction service is provided by a set of commerce entities. The collection of all commerce entities form the commerce transaction service. A commerce entity offers business application entities service primitives at a service access point of the commerce transaction service. A service access point is linked to a *SEMPER* process uniquely identified by a distinguished name. To perform the service, commerce entities cooperate together. They communicate among themselves through Commerce-Layer protocols. They utilize the underlying services from the Transfer-and-Exchange Layer and the Supporting Services to exchange protocol data elements.

The commerce-transaction service is offered in the form of an Application Programming Interface (API). The Java based API is described by an example in Section 9.4.

The commerce transaction service is used by:

— business applications entities to open, suspend, and resume commerce deals and to perform commerce transactions, and
— the *SEMPER* dispatcher during initialization of business applications on the server. The commerce transaction service tells the dispatcher which type of business application must be instantiated and then started to handle the user's request.

The commerce transaction service uses:

— the access-control mechanism to discriminate trusted business applications from untrusted ones.
— the Preferences Block to draw user's security policies and negotiate on this basis the security parameters actually used in commerce transactions. The security policy determines whether implicit or explicit user's authorization should be applied.
— the *SEMPER* trustworthy user interface, TINGUIN, to display commerce deals and commerce transactions for authorization and acknowledgment by the user.
— the Transfer-and-Exchange Layer as a transport service for commerce transactions. The Transfer-and-Exchange Layer provides a uniform service interface for transferring different types of business items such as generic data and payments.
— the archive as a persistent storage of commerce deals and commerce transactions.

9.2.2 Trust Relations

Trust relations exist between the various blocks and layers of the *SEMPER* architecture and the environment. The trusted *SEMPER* services include the Commerce-Layer, the Transfer-and-Exchange Layer, the Business-Item Layer and the Supporting Services (at least the managers of the corresponding blocks).

On the client side, business applications are generally not trusted by other business applications or by *SEMPER*. Business applications may originate from many sources and might be downloaded and installed from the network. However, the trusted *SEMPER* services may consider some business applications more trusted than others, e.g., based on their certification by trusted third parties. Without suitable permissions, business applications should not be granted direct access to resources from other business applications or to security-critical or sensitive system resources. Such a business application can access these resources only indirectly through trusted *SEMPER* services moderating the access.

The trusted *SEMPER* services generally do not trust the user to be the legitimate user until he or she has been authenticated. User authentication should only be valid for a limited time. Security critical interaction with the user must use a trustworthy channel and user interface. Both the user and the business application must be able to specify minimal quality of service requirements.

The trusted *SEMPER* services do not trust the Web client either. Firstly, the *SEMPER* client cannot assume that the connection is really initiated from a local Web client. Secondly, the parameters sent by the Web client cannot be trusted since they actually originate from a Web server located somewhere in the network. Parameters are not formally identified, and they travel through the network without security.

The trusted *SEMPER* services on the client side do not trust the *SEM-PER* server: The *SEMPER* client cannot assume that the server will follow the protocols.

Trust relations internal to the trusted *SEMPER* services may also be important because design and implementation problems might introduce weaknesses in the implementation of some services. It is important to limit the damage that can be caused by such flaws. The services directly used by the business applications are probably most vulnerable to such attacks.

So far our attention has been focused on the client side. This is a reasonable approach as the server side presumably is operating in a much more uniform security environment. The *SEMPER* server follows the same layered architecture as the client, but there is one important distinction: the server part of a business application is trusted. Business applications on the server are developed and installed to handle exactly the services that the service provider wants to offer. The service provider possesses full control over the business applications that are installed.

9.2.3 Commerce Transaction

An ordinary commerce transaction consists of two service primitives: a service *request* on the requester side and a corresponding service *indication* on the responder side. This classifies as an unconfirmed service in the OSI nomenclature. Commerce transactions must be done in the context of a commerce deal (the notion of commerce deal is discussed in Section 9.2.4), where they are organized in a directed tree-structure by the commerce transaction service. By this, each commerce transaction may have a predecessor commerce transaction and a successor commerce transaction within the scope of a commerce deal.

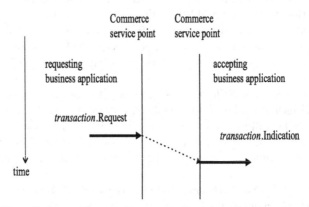

Fig. 9.1. Time diagram of an ordinary transaction with request and indication primitive types

A commerce-initiated transaction comprises indication primitives to all parts of a business application involved in the application association. This service is for reporting Commerce-Layer errors to business applications.

Commerce transactions are asynchronous: a business application can initiate multiple requests without waiting for the previous commerce transaction to complete. This model allows a much greater flexibility for the design of business applications. Also, the user is able to establish several application associations simultaneously. This provides for user-friendly operation of business applications.

9.2.4 Commerce Deal

A central concept of the service offered by the Commerce Layer is the *commerce deal*. A commerce deal encapsulates the business context on the basis of which a set of participants perform electronic commerce together. Any commerce transaction is performed within the scope of a commerce deal.

The notion of a *deal* in this respect was developed from the following metaphor:

> Whenever Alice wants a new commerce transaction to take place with Bob regarding stamp trading, she must take the shoe box labeled "Bob's stamps" off the shelf and open it. The shoe box contains her part of all outgoing and incoming transactions related to Bob and his stamps. In addition, it contains her private memos and policy with respect to doing stamp business with Bob. Symmetrically, Bob will store his shoe box relating this stamp trading with Alice. Whenever stamp trading is taking place between Alice and Bob, each pull their dedicated shoe box from the shelves, that is, get the commerce context right. The new transactions that take place are filed, and when done, the shoe boxes are put back on the shelf.

With the concept of commerce deal, the Commerce Layer does not assume anything about the semantics of the business context or the transactions that it embodies. A commerce deal can be a long lived object representing, for instance, a bank account where the commerce transactions can be deposits and withdrawals to this account, or the commerce deal can represent a single visit to an on-line store. It is up to the business application and the user to establish the meaning of a commerce deal.

A commerce deal captures the identification of the application association that links the participants, the commerce transactions that have been performed, and private data stored by each participant. A commerce deal is formally defined as a tuple of

$$(commerce\text{-}association, \{commerce\text{-} transaction\})$$

where a *commerce-association* defines the unique association list

$$((Name1, Name2, \ldots), start\text{-}time).$$

The type definition of names is left unspecified here, but should be interpreted as a distinguished name of *SEMPER* entities. In practice, the URN (Unique Resource Name) type of structure, known in the WWW, will suffice here. The *start-time* ensures the temporal uniqueness of the deal object, thereby making the *commerce-association* useful as an index field in a relational data base model.

A commerce deal is made persistent by storing it into the archive of the participant. Thus, by pulling a commerce deal out of the archive, the business context is restored. A commerce deal is created if it does not exist in the archive already, because all commerce transactions take place within the scope a commerce deal.

How can the Commerce Layer decide whether to construct a new commerce deal or to refer to an existing one? This is done in a manner similar to what is happening in a word processing tool. The user selects either to open a new commerce deal, or to search for an existing one. Opening an existing commerce deal can be done by letting the business application input the server identity. The Commerce Layer prompts the user with a list of commerce deals related to this server identity, and the user chooses which one to go ahead with.

The opening or construction of a commerce deal is a Commerce Layer confirmed service in the OSI nomenclature. The client requests the activation of a commerce deal from the server, the server receives an indication and attempts to activate the commerce deal. When successful, the server invokes a response primitive which results in a confirmation on the client side.

A commerce deal can be accessed in two main states. An *active commerce deal* establishes an application association among the participants. Performing new commerce transactions within that commerce deal updates it. All participants must be active for a commerce deal to be accessed in this state. A *suspended commerce deal* does not require the establishment of an application association. It can only be used for inspection of the business context. Any participant can access a suspended commerce deal without the cooperation of any other participant.

Business applications can access active commerce deals. This is done either by creating a new commerce deal, or by re-activating an existing one. All participants in a commerce deal must cooperate to successfully activate it. An active commerce deal supports operations for inspection and modification of private application data. Of course, participants can only access their own private data. An active commerce deal supports operations for inspecting commerce transactions already performed within it, and to achieve new commerce transactions.

SEMPER components, for instance the deal browser, can access suspended commerce deals. A commerce deal cannot be modified when in the suspended state. To modify, a commerce deal must be active as discussed previously. A suspended commerce deal can be opened independently of any other participant in the commerce deal, and without their cooperation. A suspended commerce deal supports operations for inspection of the commerce deal data and the transactions embodied in it. Commerce deals are normally kept in the *SEMPER* archive. However, it is possible to access an externally stored commerce deal in suspended state. Suspended commerce deals can also be deleted.

9.2.5 The Commerce Service API Access Control

The Commerce Layer provides a secure service access point for business applications to invoke its services. *SEMPER* defaults to the policy that users do not trust business applications to perform transactions that commit him or her in some way. An untrusted business application will use the Commerce-Layer secure service access to open a commerce deal and to perform commerce transactions in this context.

When the business application requests a transaction that will commit the user, such as a *payment* transaction or a *statement* transaction, the user must authorize the transaction before it is executed; see Section 9.2.6.

However, in some cases, the buyer may trust the business application (or the service provider) to perform certain transactions without his or her explicit authorization. In this case, the business application is given a number of privileges based on certificates attached to the business application code. The certificates support establishing trust by the buyer in the business application. These privileges can later be presented to the Commerce-Layer secure service access point to permit bypassing some of the security checks in the Commerce-Layer services. The standard *SEMPER* application, including the deal browser etc., is given privileges that grant unrestricted access. Further explanation of the mapping from certificates to access rights can be found in Section 9.3.5.

9.2.6 Authorization of Commerce Transactions

Some security-critical operations require authorization by the legitimate user. This authorization may be explicit or implicit. If explicit, it is requested by means a dialogue with the user at the trustworthy user interface. The *SEMPER* system presents information about the operation in question, for instance a payment transaction request. The user may accept or refuse the particular operation. Figure 9.2 shows an example of such a dialogue. When implicit, the authorization is performed without user interaction, based on a combination of the user's preferences and access-control privileges assigned to business applications. Such privileges are granted according to the trust level assigned to digital certificates associated with the business application, after verification of the signatures of the certificates by the downloader module.

Figure 9.3 shows the activity diagram for a transaction request. A transaction is requested by invoking the request method of the transaction object. A transaction description is then generated as described in Section 9.3.3. It is then checked whether the transaction requires explicit authorization by the user or not. If authorization is required, then a dialogue box with information about the transaction is displayed and authorization is requested.

An application-specific transaction type is constructed as a subclass of one of the predefined transaction types as shown in Figure 9.5.

In this example the **ApplicationPayment** class is derived from the **PaymentTransaction** class which itself is derived from the **Transaction** class. Each level in this class hierarchy adds some attributes to the transaction. Only the Transaction and **PaymentTransaction** classes are parts of the commerce transaction service. Thus, the commerce transaction service cannot assume anything about the semantics of the attributes added by the **ApplicationPayment** class. However, these attributes must be presented to the user in a secure way for the user to interpret these attributes in the context of the business being performed and to authorize the transaction.

Fig. 9.2. Dialogue window for authorization of transaction

To achieve this the **ApplicationPayment** class must implement the method `makeDescription` that provides a textual interpretation of the transaction. This method will be invoked from the **Transaction** class and the result stored in the description attribute. This textual description can be presented to the user for interpretation and authorization, and it is the textual description that will be signed and constitutes the "contract" between the participants of the deal. When the transaction is requested both the application data and the description are sent to the receiver. The receiver must once again perform the transformation from application data to description by invoking `makeDescription` and verify that there has been no tampering with the description or the application data. The receiver can then interpret the application data and act accordingly knowing that the peer has committed to this by signing the description.

Let's take an *order* transaction as an example of the distinction between trusted and non-trusted object structure of the commerce service. The client the business application invokes an order request to the commerce transaction service. In general, the transaction request carries two groups of parameters, as seen from the commerce transaction service. The two groups are bundled together in one unit to represent the commerce transaction content. The first group contains all the specific data structures constructed by the business ap-

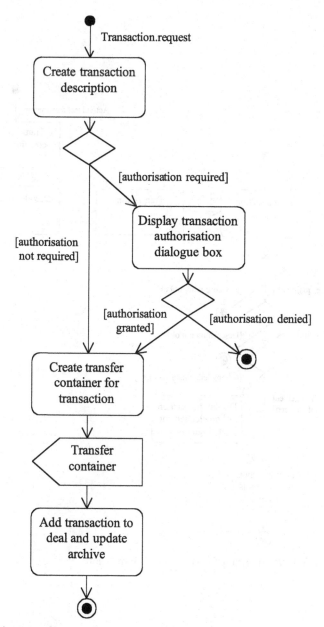

Fig. 9.3. Activity diagram for a transaction request

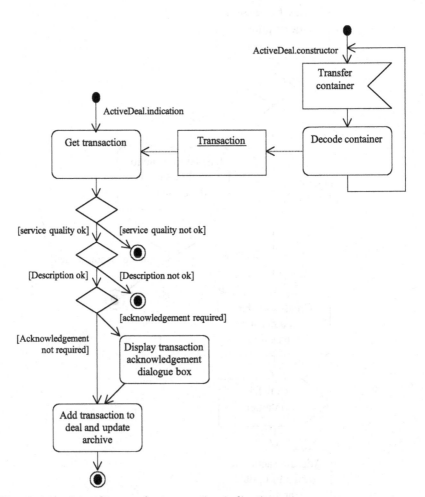

Fig. 9.4. Activity diagram for transaction indication

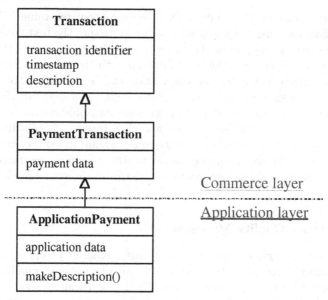

Fig. 9.5. Class diagram for application-specific transactions

plication. This first group of parameters is not used by the Commerce Layer. It is part of the application protocol among the business application entities. The second group contains some mandatory parameters—for instance, total amount and currency—whose nature is enforced by the commerce transaction service. This group of parameters also contains an HTML-formatted textual description of the content of the order, readily understandable by the person who makes the order. This textual description is generated by a method defined by the business application. The commerce transaction service will present this second group of parameters to the user at the trustworthy user interface, asking whether to accept or reject this commerce transaction. Similarly, on the responding side, the parameters can be verified and the commerce transaction authorized in person through the trustworthy user interface.

The information that the user commits to is the textual description of the commerce transaction and the parameters defined by the commerce transaction service. Business application-defined parameters are only used by business application to save on parsing the textual description to determine the exact details of the commerce transaction.

The business application cannot cheat in this scenario. All parameters are defined by the commerce transaction service and are available at the trustworthy user interface for the user to inspect. Also, by definition, it is the textual description generated by the business application together with these parameters that is signed by the user and thus are binding him.

The user cannot cheat either by altering parameter values. On the receiving side, the business application will reconstruct the textual description based on the received parameter values and verify the signature. If the signature does not verify, someone has tampered with the commerce transaction, making it rejected. The textual description can be reconstructed by an unambiguous function from the parameter values. Both that function and the parameters are part of the design of the business application.

In this scenario it is very important that business applications cannot override the methods defined by the commerce transaction service to present at the trustworthy user interface the description of commerce transactions to the user. There are different ways to ensure this in the actual implementation in Java.

9.2.7 Service Quality Management

The important service properties of security, reliability, and speed of commerce transactions are captured by the notion of commerce quality of service as presented by the Commerce-Layer API. The required service quality is associated with the specific commerce deal object in the current implementation. It might be possible that some properties could be assigned to each type or instance of the commerce transaction primitives and content. Take, for example, confidentiality. It may be sensible to make all commerce transactions of a commerce deal confidential, but for some reasons, confidentiality could only be applied to a single commerce transaction: there is no reason to make an anonymous payment if statements are signed with the user's personal signature key. This problem is part of the larger problem of how to reconcile and assign a security policy for the deal.

If security requirements were to be met by the business application, all security attributes for a commerce transaction would be specified by the business application. It would then be implied that both the customer and the service provider trust the business application, which in general cannot be the case in an open worldwide applicable system.

Security policies *SEMPER* recommends that each party specifies security attributes independently from one another: the service provider builds business applications according to his or her own security requirements. Likewise, the buyer needs to specify his or her own security attributes. In *SEMPER*, he or she does so through the preferences service and specifies a policy for assigning security attributes to commerce transactions. Exactly what preferences should be available and how they should be set are open questions, but eventually it should be possible to accommodate policies like these examples:

– All transactions should be authenticated and confidential.
– All transactions with Tina's Teddy Bear Boutique are to be conducted anonymously.
– Always use FooCard for payments to the Foo Bar.

– Transactions with Ned's News totaling less than $ 3 per day are confirmed automatically.

The commerce transaction service combines the security attributes from the business application and from the buyer to determine the actual set of security attributes to use for a commerce deal or a commerce transaction, according to a well defined policy mechanism. These security attributes used for a commerce deal result from a negotiation among the parties during the establishment phase of the commerce deal. The negotiation occurs between the client business application and the commerce transaction service acting on behalf of the user, based on the user's preferences. A transaction cannot be completed if the security attributes specified by the buyer and the service provider are mutually exclusive.

Security attributes include authentication of the participants, confidentiality of commerce transactions with respect to third parties, non-repudiation of commerce transactions, SECA requirements.

In the current FIT implementation (see also Chapter 8), the protocol for negotiation of security attributes is part of the association establishment of the Commerce-Layer entities. The protocol is a single round negotiation, where initiator sends over his requirements to the responder. The responder try to match the requirements, possibly strengthen some unassigned parameters further. The result is returned to the initiator. If the requirements does not match, the association is closed, and the outcome is reported to the user.

9.3 Design Overview

9.3.1 The Commerce-Layer Use Cases

In this section we will describe the functional and non-functional requirements to the use of the Commerce-Layer service. We use use-case modeling as defined in the UML. First we identify the different actors that are using the commerce transaction service in some way, and then we describe the various use-cases. Use-cases are summarized in Figure 9.6. Finally, we discuss non-functional requirements to the commerce transaction service.

The actors that will use the commerce transaction service are:

Business applications. Both trusted and not trusted business applications will use the commerce transaction service. Business applications will need to establish a session to their peers and to exchange commerce transactions.

Special applications. Some special applications for management of deals will exist. One example of such an application is the deal browser.

The *SEMPER* user. This is the actual person using the *SEMPER* system either as a service consumer or as a service provider. The user must have

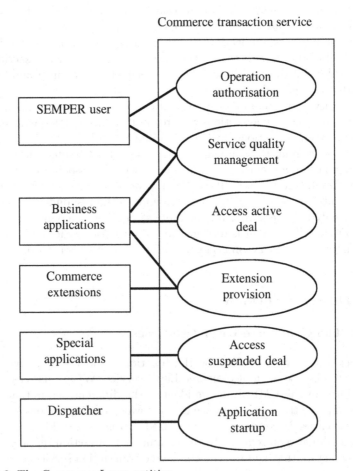

Fig. 9.6. The Commerce-Layer entities

full control of security-critical operations that is performed on behalf of the user.

Commerce extensions. It is likely that extensions to the core commerce transaction service will be developed offering services that are more oriented towards specific business scenarios and with more assumptions about the semantics of commerce transactions.

Dispatcher. The dispatcher module is responsible for accepting requests from a client side business application and starting the corresponding business application on the server side. The dispatcher interacts with the commerce transaction service to find out which business application to start.

Access to active deal. Normal business applications need access to active deals. Business applications must be able to create new active deals and to reactivate existing deals. All participants in a commerce deal must co-operate for an active deal to be successfully activated. An active deal supports operations for inspection and modification of private application data. Participants can only access their own private data. Furthermore, an active deal supports operations for inspecting the transactions in the deal and to exchange new transactions.

Access to suspended deal. Special business applications, e.g., the deal browser, need access to suspended deals. A deal cannot be modified when it is in the suspended state. To perform such operations the deal must be activated as discussed in the previous section. A suspended deal can be opened independently of any participant in the deal without the co-operation of any other participants. A suspended deal supports operations for inspection of deal data and inspection of the transactions that have been exchanged in the deal. Deals are normally kept in the *SEMPER* archive. However, it is possible to access an externally stored deal in suspended mode. Deals can also be deleted.

Service quality management. Service quality settings can be set for deals and transactions. Both the business application and the *SEMPER* user have requirements to the service quality settings, and the quality settings that are actually used are the result of a negotiation between these two actors. Service quality settings will influence authentication of participants, confidentiality of transactions with respect to third parties, non-repudiation of transactions and so on.

Operation authorization. Some security-critical operations require authorization by the *SEMPER* user. Such authorization can be given explicitly by carrying out a dialogue between the user and the *SEMPER* system. The system presents information about the operation in question, e.g., a payment transaction request, and the user authorizes or refuses the operation. Operations can also be authorized implicitly based on a combination of preferences set by the user and capabilities given to business applications based on the trust level assigned to the application.

Provision of extensions. The core *SEMPER* commerce transaction service provides only very generic transaction types with little assumption about business semantics. A framework is provided so that business applications and extensions to the core commerce services can extend this with transaction types tailored to specific business scenarios.

Application startup. The server side dispatcher accepts requests from a client to start a server side business application. Such requests are generated when the client activates a deal. The commerce transaction service provides functionality for the dispatcher to retrieve necessary information from the client about which business application to start on the server side.

Non-functional requirements. The commerce transaction service must provide a secure service access point for business applications to access the *SEMPER* services. It is particularly on the client side that the operation of the business applications must be checked. In the general case the user of the *SEMPER* system will not trust client side business applications. Such applications must be denied access to some of the services, such as inspection and deletion of random information. Other services, such as payment transactions, can be accessed after user authorization. Some business applications will be partially or fully trusted. The trust level can be based on signatures attached to business applications and user preferences. A trusted application is given capabilities to access more of the security-critical services with less user interaction.

9.3.2 Class Diagram

The realization of the commerce transaction service is based on three main class hierarchies and some additional helper classes.

Deal state. A class hierarchy for maintaining the state of a deal is provided. These classes are internal to the commerce transaction service realization and cannot be accessed directly by applications.

Deal manager. This class hierarchy provides functionality for accessing and managing deals. Deals can be managed in active or suspended mode.

Transactions. Finally, a class hierarchy representing the different types of commerce transactions is provided. The core commerce transaction service provides only very general transaction types, but business applications and extensions can provide additional transaction types tailored to specific business scenarios.

A class diagram showing the most important classes in the realization of the commerce transaction service is depicted in Figure 9.7. The hierarchy with the class **Deal** at its root constitutes the deal manager classes. A deal can be accessed in active or suspended mode by using the **ActiveDeal** or **SuspendedDeal** class respectively. An application must assume the role of initiator or respondent (client or server) when accessing an active deal. These

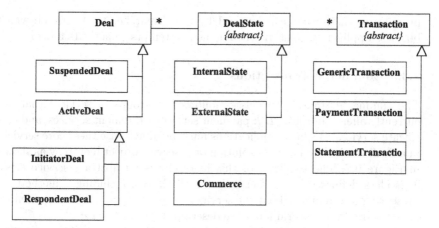

Fig. 9.7. Class diagram for the commerce transaction service

roles are represented by the classes **InitiatorDeal** and **RespondentDeal** respectively.

The class hierarchy beginning with **DealState** constitutes the classes for managing the state of a deal. These classes are invisible to applications using the commerce transaction service and can only be accessed via the deal hierarchy. A deal state can be stored internally in the *SEMPER* archive or externally as a file. These two cases are managed by the classes **InternalState** and **ExternalState** respectively.

The **Transaction** class hierarchy encapsulates commerce transactions. Three very generic transaction types are defined by the core commerce transaction service.

GenericTransaction. This transaction type can be used by applications for general data transfer between the client and server part of the application. No special processing of the data is performed by the commerce transaction service.

PaymentTransaction. This transaction type is used for performing payments from one participant to another. Payments require authorization by the user.

StatementTransaction. This transaction type is used to send a signed statement or message from one participant to another. Statements provide non-repudiation of origin. Statements require authorization by the user.

Applications or extensions to the core services can provide additional transaction types tailored to specific business scenarios. These new transaction types are subclassed from the existing transaction types.

The **Commerce** class is a static class providing some operations that do not fit naturally in any of the other classes. Some of these operations are only for internal use in the commerce transaction service, but this class also provides methods that can be used by the dispatcher to determine which business application to start when a client attempts to activate a deal.

9.3.3 Commerce Transactions

The commerce transaction classes follows the groups of services that are currently offered in *SEMPER*: payment services, statement services, and certificate services. Business applications must be able to use these core services in a flexible way. We base our solution on a service object hierarchy as shown in Figure 9.7. The top level of this hierarchy is an abstract service class. This class defines common methods for all classes, including a method for presenting information about the service in the TINGUIN. This class defines an attribute for a natural language description of the service.

At the next level we have one generic service class for each of the primitive services in *SEMPER*. These classes contain the attributes required by these services such as amount, payer, and payee for the **PaymentService** class. These classes also contain a method for displaying service attributes in the TINGUIN. At the lowest layer we envisage customized service classes that contains additional attributes describing the details of the service.

9.3.4 Representation of a Commerce Transaction

An application-specific transaction type is defined as a subclass of one of the predefined transaction types as shown in Figure 9.5. In this example the **ApplicationPayment** class is derived from the **PaymentTransaction** class which itself is derived from the **Transaction** class. Each level in this class hierarchy adds some attributes to the transaction.

As the **ApplicationPayment** class is not part of the trusted services, the class has to provide, as explained in Section 9.2.6, a method makeDescription(). This method is then used by the (trusted) **Payment-Transaction** class for user authorization.

When the transaction is requested both the application data and the description are sent to the receiver. The receiver must once again perform the transformation from application data to description by invoking makeDescription() and verify that there has been no tampering with the description or the application data. The receiver can then interpret the application data and act accordingly knowing that the peer has committed to this by signing the description.

9.3.5 The Downloader

The download service provides a framework for secure download and update of *SEMPER* components. It corresponds to the Module Installer in Chapter 6. It consists of two servers, a Download Credential Authority that associates platform-manipulation rights to parties involved in the development of *SEM-PER* software components and a News Server involved in the publication of these components to the *SEMPER* user community. Moreover, the download service consists of software components for the secure downloading and storing of new or updated software components, version management, access management directory validation, and a mechanism for the proper installation of downloaded components.

Servers.

Download Credential Authority (DCRA). The DCRA acts as a trusted third party responsible for the creation, management, and distribution of the download credentials associated with each software module.

In the following we identify three roles in the context of the download service: the role of a distributor that will act as a distribution center of the *SEMPER* software; the role of a *Mobile Code Issuer* (MCI) that is responsible for the manipulation of specific components of the *SEMPER* software and may at the same time act as a distributor; and the role of a user that will actually make use of the services provided by the downloader, e.g., download code from a distributor.

In order for someone to become an MCI, the DCRA digitally signs the manipulation rights that the MCI has on specific components and the MCI's signature certificate. This structure produced by the DCRA is called *download credentials*. It is an aggregation of the following items:

- The MCI's valid signature certificate.
- A list of files that can be manipulated by the MCI; this list may be empty.
- A list of platform directories owned by the MCI; this list may also be empty.
- A sequence number.
- The DCRA's signature on the above items.

The sequence number is useful in case of credential revocation. A download credential should be revoked by the DCRA if items contained in the structure are changed or become invalid. Typical revocation reasons are that some items in the list of files or directories have been added or dropped.

News Server. The News Server constitutes an information point for the *SEM-PER* user community. It is placed at the same location as the DCRA server, and manages information associated with new or updated software components. These software components should be modified only by the authorized MCIs. Currently, the News Server offers two services. The first one is available only to MCIs, the second one to the entire user community. These services are:

- uploading, by the MCIs, of new or modified *software component identifiers*, and
- retrieval of new or modified software component identifiers.

During the upload service invocation, the involved MCI passes a list of software component identifiers. Each of these includes the location of the updated directory and a component time-stamp associated with the last modification of this directory by the MCI. The list is signed by the MCI, so that only parties in possession of appropriate download credentials can advise the News Server. For each list of software component identifiers, the News Server also stores the exact time when it was uploaded.

The other service offered by the News Server is related to the retrieval of software component identifiers by the user community. During invocation, the user sends a previous time-stamp from the News Server to the invoked service. The News Server retrieves all those stored software component identifiers that have been registered in the News Server database at a time later than the time-stamp sent by the user. The News Server responds with a list of software component identifiers and associated retrieval information. Finally it produces a time-stamp and sends this to the user for inclusion in the next invocation of the service.

Software Design. The overall software component providing download services at each *SEMPER* user site is called the *Download Module* (DM). It consists of a set of internal modules. They are responsible for the management of the offered and downloaded software components and the execution of the protocol used for the communication with the DCRA and News Server.

The functionality provided by the DM can be split into three parts. The *basic* functionality is indented to support the *SEMPER* user community. The *extended* functionality, which extends the basic functionality, is offered to distributors and Mobile Code Issuers (MCI). Finally, the functionality that is offered only to MCIs is termed *supreme*; it inherits the extended functionality.

During initiation, the user can select to run the DM in basic or extended mode. The supreme mode is not selected, but granted by the DM, since the prerequisite for the supreme functionality is that the user selects to run the DM in the extended mode and that download credentials for the particular user exist.

Version Management Module (VMM). This module implements the functionality needed to verify the integrity and authenticity of new or updated software components during the download phase. Information that is managed by the VMM and that is essential for the whole validation procedure regarding the integrity and authentication of the stored files, located under the platform installation root, is kept in structures called *credential block(s)*.

In particular, such a block includes the download credentials possessed by an MCI, the modification state of the files concerned, and the MCI's signature on this state.

An aggregation of credential block(s) which refers to a particular directory is stored in a file named VMF. The credential blocks are sent from the distributor to the customer during the download procedure before the transmission of the updated or new files. The main responsibility of the VMM is to verify the contents of the credential blocks it receives and to verify the integrity of the updated files according the information stored in the credential blocks.

Download Control Module (DCM). It is intended to speed up the entire download decision procedure. To accomplish this task, the DCM manages information that is part of the VMFs that appears in each authenticated directory. Particularly, this module manages information contained in the DCF structure.

The DCF structure is organized in blocks. Each of these blocks refers to a single VMF. The information kept in a DCF block is the identity of the MCIs and the modification state of the files owned by a MCI. The DCF blocks that are managed by the DCM at the distributor site contain an additionally field that keeps information about the customers that have been notified about the last modification of the associated directory contents.

The DCM takes part in the entire download procedure in the sense that all the decisions regarding the new or updated software components are aided and determined by this module.

Access Management Module (AMM). The AMM is intended to offer a distributor the ability to define constraints within the offering procedure of new or updated software components. In particular, a distributor can define stored software components as public, private or protected.

If a software component is defined as public, a customer can simply download it without revealing his or her identity. A private component cannot be download by anyone via the *SEMPER* download mechanism. A protected software component is offered to a well-defined group of users. It is only sent in encrypted form, and only to users who proved their identity and their right to download this component.

Incorporation Module (IM). The IM is only available to the MCI community. This module looks for changes in the directories that are owned by a specific MCI. During the invocation of the Incorporation Module, the MCI's download credential structures are retrieved. The IM then visits each directory that appears in the MCI's download credentials structure and computes the hash values of the owned files. These hash values are compared with those stored in the VMF. If at least one file has been changed, the signature of the associated credential block is recomputed. All the updated credential blocks are saved in the VMFs located in the updated directories. Finally, if changes have been found, the IM updates the DCF structure according to the modification made in the VMF structures.

Download Server and Client Modules. These modules implement the protocol that supports the offering and downloading of new or updated software components, respectively. The Server Module runs at the distributor site.

The Client Module is invoked by the customer via the GUI Manager. The interaction between these two modules is shown in Figure 9.8.

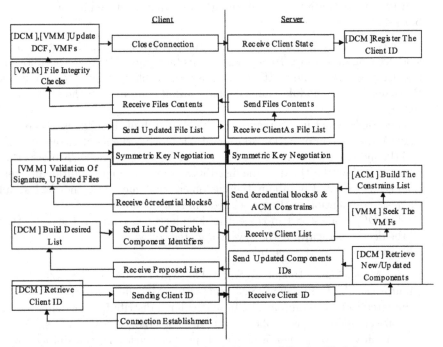

Fig. 9.8. Interactions between Download Client and Server Modules

News Management Module (NMM). The NMM is intended to support the interaction between the user community and the News Server. It offers basic functionality for the whole user community and extended functionality for MCIs. The basic functionality is the retrieval of new or updated *SEMPER* component identifiers and the IP addresses of the associated MCIs. In extended mode, the NMM grants the ability to the MCI to upload component identifiers to the News Server for registration in the News Server's database. While customer requests need not be authenticated, the News Server will verify the authenticity of requests by an MCI to upload new or updated components with respect to the MCI's credential. In the basic functionality, the NMM includes the time-stamp from its previous contact with the News Server, and the News Server only sends updates made after that time. The News Server also returns a new time-stamp, which is then stored by the NMM.

All the new or updated component identifiers are compared with those stored in the DCF structure. The NMM stores those that are new from the customer's point of view in local storage. This information can be used to advise the user to visit the appropriate MCI sites and optionally to download the new or updated components.

Credential Client Module (CCM). It manages the interaction between the DM and the DCRA. It can be called by the whole *SEMPER* user community. It handles the interaction protocol for retrieving the DCRA's trusted key, obtaining the credential revocation list, and searching for the credential structure for a specific MCI.

The list offered by the DCRA contains the revoked download credentials, and the download credential structures about the MCIs are validated according to the attached DCRA signature.

Directories Validation Module (DVM). Its main responsibility is the validation of the files that constitute the *SEMPER* platform. The validation procedure includes verifying each credential block contained in the VMF structures that are nested in every *SEMPER* directory. The DVM, in particular, validates the signature produced by the appropriate MCI and attached in every credential block.

Further, the validation procedure computes the hash value of the files contained in a *SEMPER* directory and compares it with that in the credential block.

Another essential task of the DVM is the validation of the correct placement of the downloaded software components. During this task, the DVM inspects a credential block according to the attached download credentials possessed by an MCI. If the MCI's credentials do not contain the inspected directory, or if the checked credential block has been misplaced, the DVM warns the user.

Local Installation Module (LIM). The functionality offered by the LIM is very similar to that of the Download Client Module described above. The main difference is that the LIM installs new or updated components from the local disk instead of the network.

A precondition for LIM invocation is that the user has previously obtained and stored the new or updated components from a distributor using a diskette or a file transfer protocol.

The LIM module investigates the new or updated software components which are located under a certain directory path. In particular, LIM looks for the VMF structures contained in the subdirectories and validates the signatures, the integrity of the contained files and the correct placement of the VMF structures. Then, after comparing the time-stamps in the DCF structure with those in the new VMF structures, it incorporates the new or updated files into the appropriate directories.

9.3.6 Scenarios

Opening a Commerce Deal. A business application opens a new commerce deal or re-opens an existing one. Then, it performs commerce transactions within the scope of that commerce deal. Opening an active commerce deal implies the establishment of communication between the client side and the corresponding server side of that commerce deal. The flow of events is shown in Figure 9.9. A more detailed description of these events is as follows:

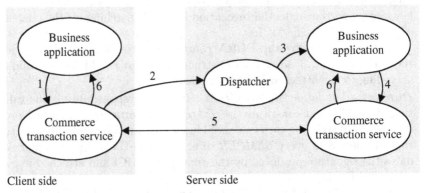

Client side   Server side

Fig. 9.9. Flow of events during the opening of a commerce deal

1. The business application requests the opening of a commerce deal by creating an object of type **InitiatorDeal**, which is defined by the commerce-transaction service.
2. The commerce transaction service establishes a connection to the dispatcher at the server. The network address of the dispatcher is one of the parameters for opening an active commerce deal.
3. The dispatcher at the server invokes the correct business application instance. If necessary, the business-application instance is created.
4. The server part of the business application opens a commerce deal by creating an object of type **RespondentDeal**, which is defined by the commerce transaction service.
5. A communication session is established between the client and server parts of the commerce deal objects. Executing a protocol between the two commerce deal objects initializes the objects.
6. The opening of the commerce deal completes both at the client and the server.

The dispatcher at the server is only responsible for the initial acceptance of the connection from the client and to invoke the proper business application instance. The business application is then responsible for completing the acceptance of the connection which involves the creation of a commerce deal object. Once the communication is established between the client and server deal objects, they exchange commerce transactions using that dedicated communication channel which involves neither dispatcher.

Invoking a Service Primitive. The following sequence takes place when a service primitive is invoked:

1. The business application entity instantiates an object of the appropriate class and assigns values to the attributes defining the service. Attributes are defined both by the generic service class and the customized service class. A textual or HTML description of the service is also generated by the business application entity by an unambiguous function of the attribute values. The finished service object is passed to the commerce transaction service.

2. The commerce transaction service invokes a method implemented by the generic service class to output a description of the service on the TIN-GUIN and get the user's authorization. This description is based on the textual description that was provided by the business application entity and any attributes defined by the generic service class. The generic service class does not know about the attributes defined by the customized service object and cannot base its description on those.

3. When the service has been authorized, it is passed to the lower layers, typically the Transfer-and-Exchange Layer, in some form. Here the attributes defined by the generic service class will define the service performed by the lower-layer service modules. The additional attributes defined by the customized service class are sent to the business application entity at the server.

4. On the server side, the business application entity receives a service object. From the attribute values, any signatures on the object can be verified and the transaction can be accepted or rejected. Only the textual description and the attributes defined by the generic service class are signed. Tampering with the additional attributes of the customized service object is detected by reconstructing the textual description from the attribute values in the received object.

Suspended Commerce Deal. A deal can be instantiated in suspended mode. This could also be denoted *local mode* because no association is made with other communicating parties. The content of the deal can only be handled in "read-only" mode. Typically, this class is instantiated by the deal browser.

9.4 Using the Commerce Transaction Service

This section contains a short description of how business applications can use the services of the commerce transaction service API. The goal is to introduce the important classes, how they are used and how they interact.

9.4.1 Case Description

We describe the use of the Commerce-Layer transaction service by using a specific case as an example. The business application will provide reservation and purchase of tickets at the imagined "Theatre Ibsen." In our example, Theatre Ibsen offers an interface where new reservations can be made and old reservations can be paid or canceled.

We define the following transactions:

Information about plays. Using this transaction the client will request information about the different plays that Theatre Ibsen accepts seat reservations for.

Information about seats. Using this transaction the client will request information about seats in different categories for a specific play, their reservation status and pricing information.

Reservation of seats. Using this transaction the client will reserve a number of seats at a specific play. The response from Theatre Ibsen is a confirmation of the reservation or a waiting list status.

Waiting list status. Using this transaction the client will inquire whether a specific reservation has been confirmed or its waiting list status is modified.

Cancellation of reservation. This transaction is used by the client to request cancellation of a reservation.

Purchase of tickets. This transaction is used by the client to purchase tickets for a confirmed reservation.

In this example, we will only elaborate on a few of these transactions.

9.4.2 Definition of Transaction Classes

The business application code must define a transaction class for each transaction that will be used. Defining a transaction class involves the following steps:

1. Based on the type of transaction, one of the Commerce-Layer classes GenericTransaction, PaymentTransaction or StatementTransaction must be chosen as the base class of the customized transaction class.
2. Any attributes describing the transaction must be defined. A number of transaction attributes are already defined by the base classes.
3. The method `makeDescription` must be implemented. This method must provide a textual description of the transaction.

Below we will show code fragments defining a few of the transaction classes required for the seat reservation business application. First we define the class **StatusRequest** to request information about the status of a particular reservation.

```
class StatusRequest extends GenericTransaction {
    public StatusRequest(
        ActiveDeal deal,
        Transaction ref)
        throws AssociationException, TransactionException
    {
        super(deal,ref);
    }

    public Description makeDescription()
    {
        return new Description("Status request transaction", ...);
    }
}
```

This class does not need any custom attributes as the class type represents the operation and any additional data is given by the transaction that this transaction references.

Any class has to provide a suitable constructor that at least passes on a set of suitable parameters to its superclass. We might also want to check that the ref parameter references a transaction of the correct type and throw an exception if this is not the case. We have omitted such error checking for brevity in the examples.

We have also defined the method `makeDescription` which is not really necessary for transactions derived from the **GenericTransaction** class as this class defines a default implementation of `makeDescription`.

We also need to define a response to the status request transaction. This transaction is a bit more complex as it is derived from **StatementTransaction**. Also, we must add some attributes to hold information about the reservation status.

```
class StatusResponse extends StatementTransaction {
    private SeatStatus[] seatStatus;

    public StatusResponse(
        ActiveDeal deal,
        Transaction ref,
        SeatStatus[] seatStatus)
        throws AssociationException, TransactionException
    {
        super(deal,ref,null);
        this.seatStatus = seatStatus;
    }

    public Description makeDescription()
    {
        // Assign to description a textual description of the
        // reservation status based on the seatStatus attribute.

        return description;
    }
}
```

9.4.3 Activation of a Deal

Activation of a deal involves the initiator and the respondent of the deal, and activation is different for the two parties. In this case the theatre guest is the initiator and Theatre Ibsen is the respondent.

Activation by the Initiator. The initiator activates a deal by creating an object of type **InitiatorDeal** defined by the Commerce Layer. This object can be used to request reactivation of a deal already started, or the creation of a new deal. In this example, Theatre Ibsen chooses to interpret a deal object as a long-term customer relationship. This implies that the theatre handles all seat reservations and ticket purchases for a given customer in a single deal instance. Thus, the Theatre Ibsen business application will always attempt to reactivate an existing deal.

```
InitiatorDeal deal;
CLAddress address = new CLAddress("Theatre Ibsen",
                               "semper.ibsen.com", "Theatre");
try {
    deal = InitiatorDeal.selectDeal(address, quality);
}
catch (AssociationException e) {
    if (e.getReason() == AssociationException.OPEN_NEW)
        deal = new InitiatorDeal(address, quality);
    else
        // handle other reasons...
}
```

The method `selectDeal` will bring up a list of all deals with Theatre Ibsen for the client to choose from. The user can also choose to start a new deal in which case the method throws an exception and a new deal has to be created. A connection will then be made to the respondent whose network address is given in the deal, and the respondent is authenticated to make sure that it is really Theatre Ibsen. The methods return when the connection has been established. If something goes wrong, an exception is thrown. Catching of other exceptions is not shown in the examples.

Activation by the Respondent. On the respondent side, things are a bit different. The respondent side dispatcher waits for an attempt by the initiator to connect to the respondent host. When such an attempt is made, the dispatcher creates an instance of the business application and invokes it. The respondent side business application must then create an object of type RespondentDeal to accept the connection attempt and activate the deal.

```
RespondentDeal deal = new RespondentDeal(session,quality);
```

The session parameter identifies the connection from the initiator. The quality parameter specifies the service provider's requirements for the deal quality. The deal will not be activated if these quality attributes are incompatible with the quality attributes specified by the initiator.

9.4.4 Inspection of a Deal

A number of methods for inspection of a deal and the transactions of a deal are defined by the classes **Deal** and **Transaction**. Deals can be inspected after they have been activated as described in the previous section, or they can be inspected in *suspended state*. A deal is accessed in the suspended state by creating an object of type **SuspendedDeal**.

Transaction instances are organized in a tree with a single virtual root transaction. Every transaction references a single other transaction, and a transaction can be referenced by many transactions. A transaction that references the virtual root transaction is said to be a top-level transaction.

The class **Deal** provides some methods for accessing transactions. The method `Deal.getTopTransactions` returns an array of all top-level transactions. The method `Deal.getTransaction` returns a single transaction object identified by its transaction identifier.

The class **Transaction** provides methods for accessing the transaction that a transaction object references or the transactions that reference a given transaction. These methods are `Transaction.getReferenced` and `Transaction.getReferencing`.

The Deal object also provides access to information about the deal itself. Methods exist for retrieving information about the quality settings in effect for the deal, a brief textual description of the deal, the peer identity, and some other parameters.

9.4.5 Commerce Transactions

A commerce transaction of some type is requested by one party and is then indicated to the peer. In this section we demonstrate how the client requests the status request transaction for a seat reservation and how Theatre Ibsen handles the indication of this transaction.

Requesting a Transaction. Requesting a transaction consists of a number of steps. First a transaction object must be created, and invoking a method of this object will then make the transaction request.

```
StatusRequest trans = new StatusRequest(deal, reservation);
trans.request(null);
```

The reservation parameter to the constructor is a reference to the transaction where the reservation was requested.

Handling a Transaction Indication. Transaction indications are queued, and the transaction queue can be inspected by invoking the indication method of the deal object. In this case, Theatre Ibsen will handle the indication by responding with a status response transaction.

```
Transaction request = deal.indication(null);
if (request instanceof StatusRequest) {
    StatusResponse rsp = new StatusResponse(deal,request,seatStatus);
    rsp.request(null);
}
else
    // Handle other transaction types here.
```

Note that the constructor creates a relation between the response and the request.

Trusted versus Untrusted Applications. Note the use of the null parameter to the `request` and `indication` methods in the examples above. We have assumed that the Theatre Ibsen application is not trusted by the theatre guest, and that it does not need any special privileges to be executed. In this case, the request method will open a TINGUIN window requesting authorization by the user before requesting a transaction that commits the user in some way. Similarly, for indications that have committed the peer a window will be opened to indicate this.

If the application is trusted then a special authorization access control capability object can be passed to the request and indication methods. This type of capability prompts the Commerce Layer to bypass the manual authorization of critical transactions. Only trusted applications will possess such powerful access control capabilities.

10. Fair Exchange: A New Paradigm for Electronic Commerce

This chapter describes the protocols and the design of the *SEMPER* Transfer-and-Exchange Layer, in particular its generic and optimistic fair exchange protocols.

The basic problem which we solved is how to provide an open and extensible solution for exchanging two arbitrary business items fairly: Up to now, specialized fair exchange protocols were developed for any combination of two goods (examples include certified mail, contract signing, and fair-purchase protocols). This leads to a rapidly growing number of different exchange protocols if new kinds of business items are installed.

Our solution to this problem is *generic* fair exchange: These protocols are based on three exchange-enabling properties that are sufficient to guarantee fairness of the exchange. In addition to reducing the number of exchange protocols needed, this enables providers of new items to enable fair exchange easily. Instead of implementing new fair exchange protocols, they just provide exchange-enabling properties for the added items.

Existing fair exchange protocols without a third party have a high error probability which is linear in the number of rounds. Since this is not acceptable in electronic commerce, we use a third party to guarantee fairness. However, our *optimistic* protocols limit the use of the third party to the cases where it is really needed. I.e., in the likely case where both exchanging parties do not try to cheat, these protocols guarantee fairness without involving the third party.

10.1 Introduction and Overview

Everywhere in electronic commerce the issue arises that two parties need to exchange two items fairly, as on a physical counter. Imagine Bob has requested consultancy services from Alice, e.g., a piece of software, a translation or a legal expertise. Alice wants to deliver to Bob a file containing the report. The file represents the work of several person-months, so Alice wants a receipt if Bob receives the file. Bob, on the other hand, only wants to issue a receipt if he received the file.

A simple protocol solving this problem would be that Alice sends the report, then Bob sends the receipt. This solution, however, does not guarantee

G. Lacoste et al. (Eds.): SEMPER 2000, LNCS 1854, pp. 155–184, 2000.

fairness: If Bob does not send the receipt, Alice sent the report while not obtaining the expected receipt. Therefore, in order to avoid such situations, we will describe protocols which *guarantee* fairness in any case, i.e., either both receive what they expect or else, no one gets even part of the expected item.

Our solution to this problem are so-called *optimistic* and *generic* fair exchange services. For a fair exchange, each party inputs what it wants to give and what it expects in exchange. For instance, Alice wants the report for a receipt whereas Bob wants a receipt for the report.

Compared to other projects, our generic and optimistic fair exchanges are not limited to particular exchanges using particular implementations of business items such as fair purchase in NetBill. Instead, our generic fair exchange protocols can be used to exchange any two business items (such as any implementation of signatures, payments, or data) fairly. Furthermore, our protocols extend the optimistic fair exchange idea (see Bürk and Pfitzmann (1990) for optimistic issuing of receipts) which means that no third party is needed to guarantee fairness if the exchanging parties are correct.

10.1.1 Why "Generic" Fair Exchange?

Besides the delivery of valuable information for a receipt (called *certified mail*) or for a payment (called *fair purchase*), there are many more types of fair exchanges. On an abstract level, any two items (e.g., signatures, data, or payments) can be exchanged for each other. This would require one fair exchange protocol for each pair of items (e.g., nine exchanges; cf. Figure 2.1 on page 16) and solutions for some of these fair-exchange problems have already been developed. So why develop *generic* fair exchange?

The reason is that this abstract view does not hold in practice: In practice, differentiating between payments, signatures, and data is too coarse since a fair exchange protocol for payment for receipt may work with one payment scheme but not with another. So instead of having nine different protocols for exchanging signatures, payments, and data, each new implementation of a business item may require new fair exchange protocols for each item which has already been installed. Furthermore, exchanging containers containing multiple business items would require specific fair exchange protocols for any fixed combination of items to be contained. Therefore, for a given number of n different modules with electronic items this leads to n^2 different fair exchange protocols if one only wants to exchange one item for another. Adding a new item to be exchanged (such as a new payment module) means adding another $n + 1$ fair exchange protocols.

The solution to this problem is to provide exchanges which are independent of the items. We discovered that fairness of an exchange can be guaranteed by exchanging transfers of business items which guarantee any of our so-called *exchange-enabling properties*.

A *transfer* sends an item from a sender to a recipient. Examples of transfers are payments (transfers value), signatures (transfers a signed document), or messages (transfers data). Furthermore, containers containing multiple business items can be transferred.

A *fair exchange* is then implemented as two virtually parallel transfers of two business items satisfying the fixed expectations of both exchanging parties. Compared to just two transfers, the focus lies on the "atomic parallelism" which is not provided by two subsequent transfers: One party (the first one to receive a complete transfer) always has an advantage if one cannot revoke a transfer of valuable information or signatures. In order to guarantee this "atomic parallelism," we interleave both transfers using the exchange-enabling properties so that the exchange-enabling properties guarantee the atomicity of the interleaving.

Unfortunately, as we will show later in Section 10.2, fairness cannot efficiently be guaranteed without a third party. For efficiency, however, we try to limit the involvement of a third party to the case of faults, i.e., if both players are correct, the third party is not actively involved.

We identified three exchange-enabling properties of transfers which are sufficient to guarantee fairness. For the generic fair exchange protocols described in this chapter, the underlying transfers of the two items to be exchanged must enable certain combinations of the following properties:

External verifiability. A third party is enabled to observe a transfer, i.e., find out whether it succeeded or not.

A simple example of providing verifiability is re-sending a signature to the third party who verifies it and forwards it.

Generatability. The parties first fix the item in a preparation protocol. If the transfer fails, the third party is enabled to "redo" the transfer using the information stored during the preparation.

A simple example of providing generatability for signatures is to authorize the third party to sign on one's behalf.

Revocability. After the item has been fixed, revocability enables the third party to revoke a transfer.

A simple example of providing revocability is to authorize the third party to revoke a credit-card payment.

Based on these properties, we are able to exchange many different pairs of items with only few different generic fair exchange protocols. With this approach exchanging containers containing multiple business items is also simplified: The transfer-based exchanges no longer differentiate between different items and containers as long as their transfers provide some exchange-enabling properties. Container transfers can be recursively based on the transfers of the contained business items so that a container provides an exchange-enabling property if all contained items do. Furthermore, adding modules for new implementations of business items is considerably easier: Now, the provider of the new module is only required to provide one or more of the exchange-enabled properties in order to enable fair exchange of the items.

In principle, our protocols for fair exchange all follow the same pattern: First, both exchanging parties sign an agreement what items will be exchanged. Then, each player transfers its items using the underlying transfer protocol. After successfully receiving the transfer from the business partner, the fair exchange protocol ends. However, if the expected item is not received, the exchanging parties may ask the third party to restore fairness. How this is done depends on the properties of the items. Some examples are:

- If one of the items is generatable and was not sent, this item is replaced by the third party.
- If one of the items is revocable and the other item was not sent, this item is revoked.

In the certified-mail example mentioned above, this means that both the sender of the valuable information and the recipient digitally sign that they want to exchange this information for a non-repudiable receipt. If these letters of understanding have been exchanged, the sender ships the information to the peer and the peer returns the receipt. However, if the sender does not receive the receipt, it contacts the third party. The third party verifies the letters of understanding provided by the sender and, if successful, generates the receipt and returns it to the sender.

10.1.2 Overview

Section 10.2 gives an overview of existing work on fair exchange. The services of transfers and fair exchanges and the exchange-enabling properties of transfers are described in more detail in Sections 10.3 and 10.4, respectively. In Section 10.5, we describe and analyze protocols which provide a generic fair exchange service based on transfers and exchange-enabling properties. Finally in Section 10.6, we describe our object-oriented design of the *SEMPER* fair-exchange framework. The framework is based on a Transfer Block which provides generic transfers of different business items and containers. Each transfer may have one or more exchange-enabling properties which are implemented as so-called security attributes. On top of the Transfer Block, the Exchange Block contains a fair-exchange manager and different fair exchange protocol plug-ins for the supported combinations of exchange-enabling properties. After the negotiation of the enabled properties, all interaction between the Exchange Block and the Transfer Block is done via the security attributes implementing the exchange-enabling properties.

10.1.3 Notation and Assumptions

A protocol takes some inputs and produces some outputs. In our interaction diagrams "command(argument list)" denotes the input of a command command with a list of arguments whereas "event: result list" denotes the output of an event together with a list of results.

In our framework, inputs will later be implemented as method invocations whereas outputs are either return values or, if the protocol runs asynchronously, protocol results which can be retrieved using specific methods.

10.2 Related Work

Before *SEMPER*, no generic fair exchange service for exchanging arbitrary items has been described in the literature. The existing work mainly deals with fair exchange of specific types of business items.

We now briefly summarize these existing concepts. For each kind of fair exchange, we describe existing concepts from the following areas:

Fair exchange with third party. These protocols include a third party that "mediates" all exchanges and guarantees fairness. The disadvantage of this approach is that the third party participates in all exchanges, which leads to performance and trust bottlenecks: Even if the participants are correct, they cause load at the third party and the third party may misbehave or infringe the exchanging parties' privacy.

Optimistic fair exchange. These protocols include a third party as well. However, this third party is not involved if both participants are correct and agree. Thus, the third party is no longer a performance and trust bottleneck while still being able to guarantee fairness in case of disagreement, misbehavior, or failure.

Note that we do not consider gradual fair exchange that does not require a third party: Unlike third-party-based exchange, it cannot produce a definite answer in a fixed time (Even and Yacobi 1980) but rather guarantees that the advantage of one party over the other can be made small (but still linear in the number of messages). For, e.g., certified mail, this means that computing the signature on the receipt requires a similar computational effort for the sender than decrypting the message for the recipient. However, we feel that such outcomes like "you have not sold your house (if your peer does not invest another 90 days of computation)" are not acceptable in practice.

10.2.1 Certified Mail

Certified mail with third party: Early work on fair exchange with in-line third party was done in Rabin (1983). Some recent proposals for different flavors of certified mail are Bahreman and Tygar (1994), Coffey and Saidha (1996), Deng et al. (1996), Micali (1997) and Zhou and Gollmann (1996).

Optimistic certified mail: Optimistic certified mail has first been described in Asokan et al. (1997) and Micali (1997). Later proposals for optimistic certified mail are Asokan et al. (1998a) and Zhou and Gollmann (1997).

Standardization: A framework for certified mail has been standardized in ISO/IEC JTC 1/SC27, N 1105 (1995). The basic evidence for sending and receiving mail is further subdivided into evidence of each step during the delivery of a message, i.e., origin, submission, transport, delivery, and receipt. The standards on certified mail are ISO/IEC JTC 1/SC27, N 1105 (1995), ISO/IEC JTC 1/SC27, N 1106 (1995) and ISO/IEC JTC 1/SC27, N 1107 (1996). The protocols proposed in these standards are similar to the protocols for certified mail with a non-optimistic third party listed above.

10.2.2 Contract Signing

Contract signing is a generalization of the fair exchange of two signatures under a contract. The term "contract signing" was first introduced in Blum (1981). In Even and Yacobi (1980), it was shown that no deterministic contract-signing scheme (called "public-key agreement system") without a third party exists if the verifier is state-less and only the two signers participate in the contract signing protocol.

Contract signing with third party: Early work on fair exchange with in-line third party was done in Rabin (1983): In this protocol, both signers send their signatures to the third party who verifies and forwards them.

Optimistic contract signing with third party: The first scheme which is somewhat optimistic[1] has been described in Even (1983). The first optimistic scheme in our sense is based on *gradual increase of privilege* (Ben-Or, Goldreich, Micali, and Rivest 1990) and may still produce some uncertainty about the outcome, e.g., "you have sold your house with 90% probability". Recent research concentrated on optimistic contract-signing schemes that avoid such uncertain situations and guarantee a *definite* decision within limited time: Asokan, Schunter, and Waidner (1997) describes a synchronous contract-signing protocol with four messages. This was improved in Asokan, Shoup, and Waidner (1998a) to a four-message protocol for asynchronous networks.

In Pfitzmann, Schunter, and Waidner (1998), these results were proven to be message-optimal for synchronous and asynchronous networks. Furthermore, the authors described provably time-optimal optimistic contract-signing schemes for synchronous and asynchronous networks.

Remark: Fair exchange of signatures[2] and *fair contract signing* are different problems since contract signing does not require a contract to be a text and two signatures. Obviously, contract signing can always be implemented based on fair exchange of signatures, but not all contract-signing schemes exchange signatures. They only guarantee non-repudiation of the agreement on a contract.

---

[1] It assumes that verification is a three-party protocol, i.e., that the contract is not valid on its own but only if a third party called "center of cancellation" does not object.

[2] Each player A receives a digital signature $\text{sign}_B(C)$ if and only if the other signer B receives $\text{sign}_A(C)$, too.

10.2.3 Fair Purchase

Fair purchase is the fair exchange of a payment for secret data to be purchased. It involves a seller and a buyer.

An inherent problem of fair purchase is that for many items, such as images, the protocol cannot guarantee that the items delivered really match the description of the buyer: Whether a program is a word-processor satisfying a set of requirements cannot be decided automatically. In those cases, the protocol can only "bind" the description to the items, i.e., produce evidence that a seller promised that the delivered items fulfill the given requirements. The dispute whether the delivered items fulfill the promised requirements then has to be resolved by a human arbiter outside the system. Naturally, the more precise this description is, the more verifications can be done inside the system and thus the stronger are the guarantees which can be given automatically. Only for machine-verifiable items, such as credentials, one can guarantee fairness automatically.

With third party: The first generic fair-purchase protocol has been proposed in Bürk and Pfitzmann (1990). In this protocol, both parties first agree on the description of the item and the amount to be paid. Then, the money is sent to the third party. After the third party acknowledges the receipt of the money to the seller, the seller sends the items to the third party. The third party forwards items and money, if the items are as agreed upon.

Optimistic fair purchase: An optimistic protocol has been proposed in Asokan, Schunter, and Waidner (1997): After the agreement, the buyer sends the money and the seller sends the items. Only if the items are not as expected, the buyer invokes the third party which verifies the items and revokes the payment if the items do not match the description. Note that this protocol only guarantees fairness if the third party is able to revoke the payment or if it knows the items to be delivered beforehand. If this is not the case, the protocol still produces evidence that the seller misbehaved, which can be used outside the system.

Producing such evidence which can be used outside the system is the aim of the generic protocol which has been proposed in Hauser and Tsudik (1996): The seller sends a signed offer. The buyer pays, the seller delivers. The buyer sends a receipt. If the seller does not send the items, the buyer raises a dispute at a court which then observes a replay of the protocol. If the seller again does not send the items, the resulting claim is settled outside the system.

Bank as third party: Most recent payment systems (Bellare et al. 2000; Cox et al. 1995; MasterCard and Visa 1997) provide a means to link a text to the payment made. This field called "merchandise description" (Bellare et al. 2000) appears on the statement of account and receipt and can be used to dispute the purchase later. However, these payment protocols do not include a reference to the items being delivered: The buyer is enabled to prove that a payment has been made to a particular seller for items matching a given description. The seller is then required to prove that it delivered items by other means.

Some payment systems also provide a real proof of the transaction, i.e., a receipt fixing the data to be delivered, the description, and the amount paid. In NetBill (Cox, Tygar, and Sirbu 1995), for example, the encrypted data is signed together with the merchandise description. The NetBill server then sends a receipt to the buyer which contains the key to decrypt the items after the payment has been made. Thus, this receipt sent to the buyer contains references to the description of the items, the encrypted items, and the key used to encrypt them. This enables the buyer to dispute the complete purchase afterwards.

A limited form of fair purchase is the exchange of *payments for receipts*. All research in this area is closely related to research in payment systems. An optimistic receipt mechanism which is independent of the payment system has first been proposed in Bürk and Pfitzmann (1989). It is similar to the generic mechanism for producing receipts described in Asokan, Schunter, and Waidner (1996).

Many payment systems, however, provide means to settle disputes about whether a payment has been made or not involving the bank as a witness (Bürk and Pfitzmann 1989; Boly et al. 1994; Bellare et al. 2000). For a survey of recent payment system see Asokan, Janson, Steiner, and Waidner (2000).

10.3 Using Transfers and Fair Exchanges

In this section, we describe our notion of "transfer" and "fair exchange" of electronic items in more detail, i.e., we describe the in- and outputs of these protocols as well as the intended behavior.

Figure 10.1 depicts the roles of transfers and fair exchanges: A transfer is executed between a sender and a recipient, whereas an exchange is initiated by an originator and answered by a responder. One of our goals is that generic exchanges are based on transfers.

Fig. 10.1. Roles for transfers and fair exchanges

10.3.1 Transfers of Basic Business Items

We assume that each type of business items, such as payments, documents, or data, defines a protocol to transfer a business item from a sender to a recipient.

To start this so-called "**transfer**" protocol, the sender inputs the item it wants to send as well as an external reference. This is a text that can be used to link the transfer into an exchange or other protocols. After successful execution of the protocol, the recipient gets the received item as an output. Furthermore, the sender may get an indication whether the transfer was successful from its point of view. The user interactions of a transfer are depicted in Figure 10.2. Note that the indication to the sender is just informational, i.e., even though a transfer may not be received, the sender may receive an acknowledgement.

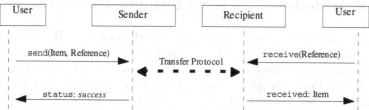

Fig. 10.2. Interactions for transferring basic business item

The security requirements on transferable items are basically that a correct recipient obtains the item if a correct sender inputs **send**. Furthermore, if the sender is correct and does not input **send**, a recipient cannot obtain the item.

10.3.2 Fair Exchange

In a fair exchange, both exchanging parties input the items they want to transfer to the peer as well as the description that the received items are expected to fulfill. Furthermore, each exchanging party inputs an external reference text for linking the exchange into other protocols (such as the deals of the *SEMPER* Commerce Layer). The interface events for a fair exchange are depicted in Figure 10.3. Note that the service is symmetric, i.e., both make similar in- and outputs.

The security requirements are that both items are transferred only if both offered items fulfill the peer's descriptions of the expected items. Else, each party cannot obtain secret information on the item input by the peer. If not, nothing happens, i.e., none of the transfers takes place. Note that an incorrect exchanging party is able to prevent successful exchange of the items in any case: It just has to input an expectation which is not fulfilled by the item input by the peer.

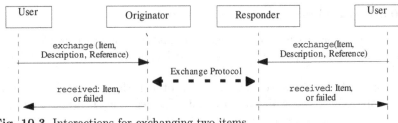

Fig. 10.3. Interactions for exchanging two items

Note that the security requirements for both roles are identical. The only difference between the originator and the responder is that the originator initiates the execution of the protocol, i.e., sends the first message of a protocol.

10.4 A Model of Transfers Enabling Fair Exchange

In our model of transfers enabling fair exchanges we will rely on specific properties of transfer protocols and employ these protocols as sub-protocols to exchange two items fairly. Note that our focus lies on defining the required properties. How these properties can be achieved is only illustrated with some examples in Section 10.4.4. For a more detailed examination, we have to refer to the related literature, in particular Asokan (1998) and Schunter (2000).

In order to build our optimistic fair exchange protocols based on transfer protocols we require that all the transfer protocols provide at least following two protocols corresponding to the phases of the exchange: The *optimistic transfer phase* tries to transfer the items without contacting the third party. After a transfer, which may have failed, the *error-recovery phase* is started if an exception, such as a wrong or missing message or a timeout, has occured. In this phase, the third party is involved and guarantees the desired property.

10.4.1 External Verifiability

External verifiability allows the third party to observe the transfer, i.e., either participate in the transfer and verify whether it was successful or not or else decide after the actual transfer based on evidence and witnesses (such as a bank) presented by the players.

An example of achieving external verifiability is to transfer the item again via the third party: The third party then verifies that this repeated transfer was really successful. Naturally, this only works if the recipient does not gain anything by receiving two identical transfers.

The interactions for external verifiability are as follows (Figure 10.4 and 10.5): The sender starts the "transfer" protocol with a command send together with the item as well as the external reference as the arguments. The recipient inputs receive, the external reference, and an input verifiable to notify the protocol that it authorizes the third party to observe this execution of the protocol. At the end, the recipient may obtain `received`: and the received item, furthermore, the protocol may signal success or failure to the sender.

If a recovery phase is required, the third party is enabled to decide whether a transfer was successful or not and what item has been transferred. It starts this verification by an input `verify` together with the external reference and the description to be verified. If an item with the input description has been transferred under the input reference, the verification outputs `verified`:*success* or `verified`:*failed*, otherwise.

The security requirements on verifiability are that the third party can correctly verify the transfer, even if the players misbehave.[3] This means that the recipient cannot deny having received an item which was successfully transferred and the sender cannot falsely claim having sent the item without sending it.

In the optimistic case, the third party does not participate in the transfer. Therefore, the third party decides based on evidence presented during the verification protocol, i.e., the sender may present evidence and witnesses that the recipient received the item or may send the item again, whereas the recipient may present evidence and witnesses to prove that it was unable to obtain the item.

A non-optimistic implementation of the verifiability property consists only of a transfer protocol where the third party verifies the received reference, description and item in-line. The verification result is then output at the end of the transfer. To adapt this implementation to our optimistic interface, the result is stored at the third party and output during verification.

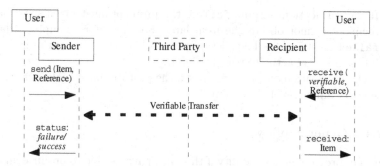

Fig. 10.4. Interactions for a transfer with external verifiability (the third party only participates if the property is non-optimistic)

---

[3]On asynchronous networks, verifiability can further be subdivided: *Sender verifiability* enables the sender to prove that a recipient was able to obtain the item, whereas *recipient verifiability* enables the recipient to prove that it was unable to obtain the item (Schunter 2000).

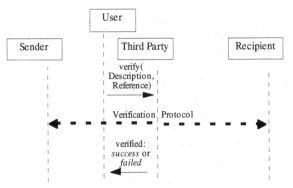

Fig. 10.5. Interactions for verifying a transfer

Most items can be adapted to provide external verifiability:

- Payment systems such as SET (MasterCard and Visa 1997) can be made externally verifiable since the third party is able to verify the signatures. For further assurance the third party can also ask the bank whether the payment was completed or not.
- Items, such as messages, where two transfers are equivalent to one transfer, can be sent again via the third party.
- Ordinary signatures as well as fail-stop signatures are externally verifiable (Pfitzmann 1996).

Another way to add external verifiability is to map existing properties, such as receipts, onto external verifiability. Still, even though external verifiability seems easy in theory, in practice, implementing it is not always trivial:

- If the verification outputs `failed`, the protocol must make sure that the recipient cannot obtain the item later. For cash, for example, a decision `failed` must include blacklisting the used coin, i.e., a coin number must be fixed before actually transferring it.
- If the verification outputs `verified`, the protocol must make sure that the sender cannot revoke the item.

10.4.2 Generatability

An item provides generatability if the third party is able to produce an equivalent replacement without cooperation of the sender. A common example is an affidavit, i.e., a replacement signature from a notary who signs on behalf of an unwilling or absent signer.

Optimistic generatability of a transferable item is provided by two additional protocols: A "prepare" protocol is used to fix and agree on the item without transferring it. The "prepare" protocol authorizes and enables the recipient to ask the third party to generate the item if the referenced exchange goes wrong. In this protocol, both input an external reference which can later be used to link the transfer into an exchange. In addition, the sender inputs the item and the recipient inputs a description of the expected item. The preparation fails if the references differ or if generatability cannot be guaranteed. After successful preparation, the usual "transfer" protocol may then be used to transfer the item. If something goes wrong, the third party may start a "generate" protocol to ensure that the recipient receives the item. To start this protocol, the third party inputs the description of the item to be generated as well as the external reference. At the end, the recipient obtains the described item.

The activities are depicted in Figure 10.6 and 10.7. Again, the third party must not participate in the "prepare" and "transfer" protocols if the implementation is optimistic.

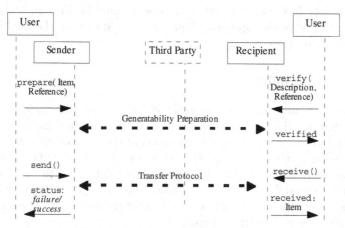

Fig. 10.6. Interactions for a transfer with generatability (the third party only participates if the protocol is non-optimistic)

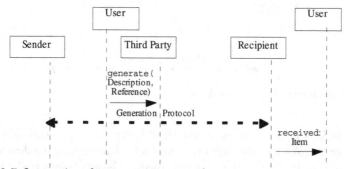

Fig. 10.7. Interactions for generating a transfer

The security requirements require that the "**prepare**" protocol outputs **verified** if and only if the input description matches the item, the input references are identical, and the item provides generatability. Furthermore, after successful preparation, the third party should be able to generate the item, i.e., the recipient will receive the described item at the end of the recovery protocol.

Note that the description and the reference input by the third party is used for verification only: If the preparation shown by the recipient contains a different description, the protocol aborts. A detailed description of adding generatability to signature and payment schemes can be found in Asokan, Shoup, and Waidner (1998b).

A non-optimistic implementation may combine the protocols "**generate**" and "**transfer**", i.e., this combined protocol guarantees to output an item if the preparation was successful. To adapt this implementation to the optimistic interface, the "**transfer**" protocol would be left empty, i.e., would always fail, while the "**generate**" protocol would execute the combined non-optimistic protocol.

10.4.3 Revocability

Revocable items can be made unusable by a third party within a certain time after a recipient has received them. Examples are delaying the deposit of an electronic coin during the execution of the "**transfer**" protocol while blacklisting it in case of revocation, or revocation of a credit-card payment.

The interactions during the transfer are identical to the interactions of external verifiability depicted in Figure 10.4, except that the recipient replaces the constant *Verifiable* with the constant *Revocable*. The interactions for recovery are depicted in Figure 10.8.

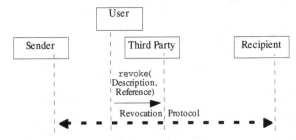

Fig. 10.8. Interactions for revoking a transfer

In order to revoke the item, the third party runs the revocation protocol on input **revoke** together with the external reference and the description.

The security requirements are that the item is only transferred if the input external references are identical and if the item can later be revoked by the third party. Furthermore, after a successful transfer, an input of **revoke** by the third party makes the item unusable.

10.4.4 Examples

We now sketch some examples of transferable items and sketch how the exchange-enabling properties can be implemented for them. Since we aim at optimistic protocols, we focus on how to provide optimistic properties.

Messages. A message is some data which is described by a predicate P. It is transferred by just sending it.

External verifiability can be provided if the sender just sends the message. Later, the sender may send the message again via the third party while the third party verifies that the message fulfills the predicate.

Optimistic generatability can be provided if the sender encrypts the message with the public-key of the third party and proves to the recipient that the encrypted message fulfills the predicate. Later, the third party may decrypt the message. Non-optimistic generatability can be provided by storing the message at the third party during the "**prepare**" protocol. Later, during "**generate**", the third party sends a copy of the message to the recipient.

Signatures. A signature is described by the message to be signed and the identity of the intended signer.

In order to enable external verifiability by a third party, the signature can be re-sent via the third party who verifies it.

Optimistic generatability for signatures can be provided if the signer signs a message authorizing the third party to sign this particular message on behalf of the intended signer. This approach provides accountability of the third party and collusions between the third party and one of the involved parties can be detected. However, a significant disadvantage of this approach is that the generated signature can be distinguished from a "real" signature. Therefore, Asokan, Shoup, and Waidner (1998b) proposed to use verifiable encryption of signatures to provide optimistic generatability: The sender encrypts the signature for the third party while proving the validity to the recipient in the "**prepare**" protocol. Later, during the "**generate**" protocol the third party may then decrypt the signature.

Signatures cannot be revoked if they shall be self-contained, i.e., if the recipient and the verifier shall be able to verify them without involving additional parties. If this is not required, the third party can keep revocation lists and the verifier has to ask the third party whether a particular signature has been revoked.

Coin Payments. An electronic coin, such as an ecash coin, is essentially a blind signature under a coin number. It is described by its currency and its denomination.

External verifiability can be provided by sending the coin via the third party. The third party then either deposits the coin on behalf of the recipient or else asks the bank blacklists a particular coin after checking whether it has been deposited before.

Generatability can be provided by using verifiable encryption: The signature corresponding to a coin can be encrypted for the third party during the "prepare" protocol in a way that the recipient still can verify its validity (Asokan, Shoup, and Waidner 1998b). Then, in the "generate" protocol, the third party decrypts the signature and sends it to the recipient who ends up with a valid coin.

Revocability can be provided in a straightforward manner if one delays the deposit of the coin while the protocol is active, e.g., by introducing a time-out: In the "transfer" protocol, the recipient is first asked to agree to the time-out and the revocation of a particular coin by the third party in case of failure. Later, during "revoke", the third party can then forward the authorization to the bank in order to prevent the deposit of this particular coin. If the bank receives this authorization within the fixed time, it blacklists the coin.

10.5 Transfer-based Generic Fair Exchange

We now describe one fair exchange protocol based on two transfers providing generatability and external verifiability, respectively. Furthermore, we sketch an exchange protocol for external verifiable and revocable transfers. Since revocability as well as generatability can be used to provide verifiability (Schunter 2000), these two protocols are sufficient to fairly exchange any two items that can be exchanged at all.

For simplicity and ease of understanding we will limit ourselves to solutions for a synchronous model (i.e., a recipient can decide whether a message is still in transit, e.g., using a time-out of the network). For protocols which work in the asynchronous model, which is more realistic but also more complicated, we refer the reader to the related literature, in particular Asokan, Shoup, and Waidner (1998a), Asokan (1998) and Schunter (2000).

10.5.1 Exchanging Externally Verifiable and Generatable Items

The following exchange protocol is similar to the protocol described in Asokan, Schunter, and Waidner (1997). It assumes that one of the items offers external verifiability[4] and the other generatability. The basic idea is as follows: The participants first prepare the generatable item sent by the originator. Then, the responder sends the externally verifiable item. Finally, the originator sends the generatable item. If the generatable item is not sent, the responder invokes the third party to generate it after verifying that the externally verifiable item was really transferred. The behavior of the scheme in the fault-less case is sketched in Figure 10.9; the recovery in Figure 10.10.

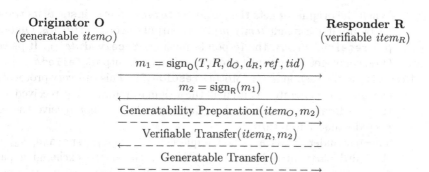

Fig. 10.9. Exchanging externally verifiable and generatable items (the first two messages are a mutual agreement on the parameters of the exchange)

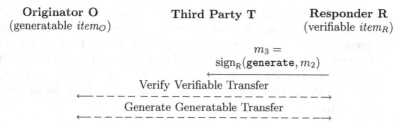

Fig. 10.10. Recovery of exchange from Figure 10.9

The fair exchange protocol consists of one main protocol called "**exchange**" and one sub-protocols for recovery by the responder. We now describe these protocols in more detail:

Optimistic exchange of two items (Protocol "**exchange**"). On start of the protocol the originator sends $m_1 = \text{sign}_O(T, R, d_O, d_R, \text{ref}, \text{tid})$ to the responder. The signed message m_1 contains the names of the third party and the responder, a description of the sent and the expected item, the external reference as well as a fresh and unique transaction identifier for this protocol run of the exchange. The responder checks whether the expectations match and then agrees by sending a message $m_2 = \text{sign}_R(m_1)$ to the originator. If the expectations do not match, the responder outputs **aborted** after sending $m_2' := \text{sign}_R(\text{abort}, m_1)$. If it receives m_2', the originator outputs **failed**. If it receives m_2, the originator starts the preparation protocol on input **prepare**(item_O, m_2), i.e., they verify that item item_O matches description d_O and provides generatability using m_2 as the external reference. If the verification is successful, i.e., outputs **verified**, the responder sends its item by inputting **send**(item_R, m_2). This transfer is then received by the originator on input **receive**(m_2).

---

[4]In this case, sender verifiability is sufficient (Schunter 2000).

When the originator gets the output received:$item_R$, it starts its transfer by inputting send($item_O, m_2$) and outputs received:$item_R$. On output received:$item_O$, the responder outputs received:$item_R$. If player O does not get an output received in time, it outputs failed.[5]

Recovery by the responder (Protocol "resolve$_R$"). This recovery protocol is executed to generate an item if the originator may have received the transfer from the responder but the responder did not receive the expected transfer in return.

The responder sends a signed request $m_3 = $ sign$_R$(generate, m_2) to the third party in order to prove the agreement the exchanging parties made. If the third party already handled a recovery for this particular m_2, it aborts. Else, the third party checks whether the responder sent its item to the recipient relying on the optimistic external verifiability, i.e., the third party inputs verify(d_O, m_2). If the verification outputs verified:$success$ to the third party, the third party generates the missing item by inputting generate(d_R, m_2) and sends a message $m_5 = $ sign$_T$(continue, m_3) to O. If the responder receives an output received:$item_O$, it outputs received:$item_O$. If the verification outputs failed to the third party, the third party sends a message $m_5 = $ sign$_T$(aborted, m_3) to the recipient and the recipient outputs failed, too.

Note that whether the resulting fair exchange protocol is optimistic depends on the implementation of the underlying properties: If the properties are implemented in an optimistic way, the resulting fair exchange protocol is optimistic. If not, the resulting exchange protocol will not be optimistic.

10.5.2 Exchanging Externally Verifiable and Revocable Items

The protocol sketched in Figures 10.11 and 10.12 exchanges a revocable and an externally verifiable[6] item. It is similar to the previously described protocol, except that recovery is done by revoking the item which was sent first.

10.5.3 Efficiency

One approach to analyze the efficiency of generic protocols is to compare the generic protocols with provably optimal protocols for particular instances of fair exchange. For contract signing, such bounds are known: In Pfitzmann, Schunter, and Waidner (1998) it was shown that message-optimal synchronous protocols require three messages in the optimistic case. For, e.g., signatures, generatability requires one message for each of the "prepare" and

---

[5]Here, we assumed that the "transfer" protocol is synchronous, i.e., if the transfer does not output received in time, it was either never started or else failed itself.

[6]In this case, recipient verifiability is sufficient (Schunter 2000).

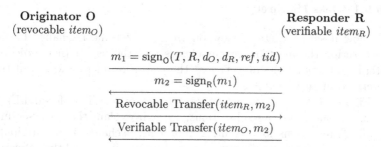

Fig. 10.11. Exchanging externally verifiable and revocable items

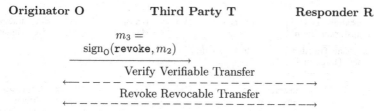

Fig. 10.12. Recovery of exchange from Figure 10.11

"`transfer`" protocols (Pfitzmann, Schunter, and Waidner 1998). Therefore, generic contract signing requires two additional messages compared to a provably optimal solution. Even though we hope that the overhead for generic exchanges is small for other instances, too, this remains to be shown.

10.6 The *SEMPER* Fair-Exchange Framework

In this section, we will give an overview of the design of the *SEMPER* fair exchange framework. This framework is built around the exchange protocols and the exchange-enabling properties described in the earlier sections.

In Section 10.6.1, we describe the static view of the exchange framework, i.e., its class hierarchy and the services of the most important classes. This includes the "wrapping" of the exchange-enabling properties (Section 10.4) and the protocols (Section 10.5) into classes. Furthermore, we recall some details of the transfer framework as described in SEMPER Consortium (1999a).

Finally, in Section 10.6.2, we describe the dynamic behavior of the transfer and fair-exchange framework. This is done in two parts: First, we describe what a running exchange looks like, i.e., which objects are instantiated and how they interact during the execution of an exchange protocol. Then, we describe the negotiation and the procedure to create such a configuration.

10.6.1 Class Hierarchy

We now describe a static view on the Transfer-and-Exchange Layer, i.e., we describe the most important classes and the use of their objects. The interaction among the objects and the execution of protocols will then be described in Section 10.6.2.

Figure 10.13 shows the topmost classes of the Transfer-and-Exchange Layer. In the following subsections, we will explain these classes in more detail: Transactions for executing protocols, exchangeability attributes for using the exchange-enabling properties, business items and their descriptions as well as managers to perform negotiations.

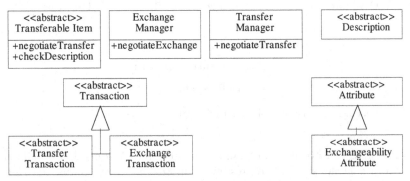

Fig. 10.13. Class hierarchy and selected methods: Transfer-and-Exchange Layer

Transactions Implementing Protocols. All protocols are provided by so-called *transaction objects*. These transactions can be exchange or transfer transactions. Each kind of transaction has one abstract subclass for each of its roles. These classes are abstract since they are only used to define the interface and some common behavior. Each actual protocol then provides one class for each role. Thus, each transaction object which can be instantiated implements one role of a particular protocol.

Note that selecting an appropriate transaction or even an appropriate role may be a complex task and need not be done by the user of the Transfer-and-Exchange Layer. The sender of a transfer transaction asks the item to be sent for an appropriate protocol, the recipient asks the so-called transfer manager, whereas exchange transactions are selected by the so-called exchange manager. So for the sequel of this subsection, we assume that the user already knows which role of which protocol to instantiate and run.

All exchange protocols provide at least two roles, namely originator and responder. In addition, each of our two exchange protocols from Section 10.5 provides an additional role named third party. The subclass originator of the "verifiable/generatable" exchange transaction, e.g., implements the left hand side of Figure 10.9. We will demonstrate how to "convert" the security protocols described in Section 10.5 into objects in more detail in Section 10.6.2.

Each transfer protocol provides at least two roles: A sender transfer transaction and a recipient transfer transaction. The actual implementors of business items then have to provide subclasses which can be instantiated (such as, e.g., a payment protocol). For more information on the transfer framework, we have to refer to SEMPER Consortium (1999a).

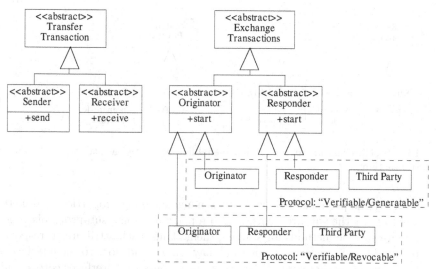

Fig. 10.14. Class hierarchy: protocols of the Transfer-and-Exchange Layer

Attributes Implementing Exchange-Enabling Properties. An attribute is an object describing required services of transactions, i.e., inputting an attribute modifies the behavior of the transaction so that the transaction guarantees the corresponding modified service defined by this attribute. An example of a transfer attribute is non-repudiation, i.e., the property that this transaction can later be proven to a judge We also designed the exchange-enabling properties of a transfer as attributes (see Figure 10.15): In order to obtain a transfer transaction satisfying a certain exchange-enabling property, the corresponding attribute is input to the negotiation.

Note that these attributes are not specific to particular kinds of items, i.e., any particular transfer transaction may provide any subset of the exchange-enabling attributes. For payments, for example, e-cash can be adapted to provide observability and generatability whereas SET provides revocability.

After negotiation by a transferable item, a transfer may provide any fixed subset of the set of possible attributes. Some attributes require a modified interface of the corresponding transfer transaction. Examples are that a non-repudiation attribute requires that the transfer transaction needs a method

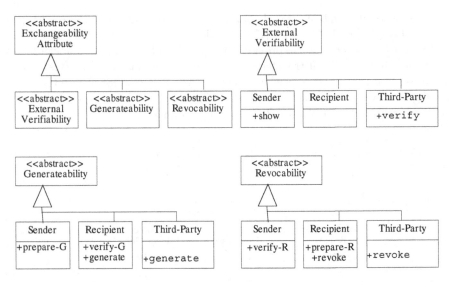

Fig. 10.15. Class hierarchy: exchange-enabling properties as attributes of transfer transactions

to verify the produced evidence, or exchange enabling properties need methods to start the sub-protocols: Each property has some sub-protocols which require specific methods for starting them. Thus, each attribute corresponds to an additional security service and may require additions to the interface of the transaction. For ease of use and security, only the interfaces corresponding to attributes which are actually provided should be visible to the user, e.g., if the transaction does not provide non-repudiation, one should not be able to show the non-existing evidence. One straightforward solution would be to add/remove interfaces of the transfer transaction dynamically at runtime depending on the input attributes. This is not possible since, in Java, each object has fixed interfaces. Another possibility is to have one transfer transaction subclass for each possible subset of the possible attributes. This, however, would lead to an exponentially growing number of different transfer transactions. Therefore, our solution is to locate the interface to the additional or modified functionality of a transaction at the attribute, i.e., only if the attribute is input, the corresponding interface is present (see Figure 10.16). Internally, however, the transaction will still need functionality and interfaces for providing all security services which are possible for this particular type of transaction. However, only the ones actually required and provided are then visible to the user. Thus, speaking in patterns (Gamma, Helm, Johnson, and Vlissides 1995), the attribute acts as a proxy to the functionality implementing the security services needed for this attribute.

Transferable Items and their Descriptions. An item is a sender's side description of a transfer protocol to be executed. A description is the re-

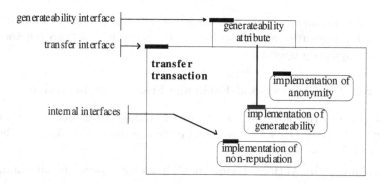

Fig. 10.16. Dynamic interfaces by means of attributes: a transfer transaction, which is in principle able to provide anonymity, non-repudiation, and generatability, currently only has an external interface for generatability

cipient's side description of a transfer. It describes the item to be received but may not be precise enough to specify the item unambiguously. Since it must be possible to describe what one expects in an exchange, each class of transferable items must provide appropriate descriptions in order to be exchangeable.

For payments, $5 from purse #3 would be an item, whereas transferring it would correspond to executing a payment protocol. The description may then be $5 from any purse.

Thus, for each kind of items to be exchanged, the appropriate item, transfer transaction, and description classes have to be implemented. Furthermore, the transfer transaction must be able to accept and guarantee one or more of the exchange-enabling attributes.

Transaction Factories for Selecting Protocols. The appropriate transactions are negotiated and selected by transaction factories (Gamma, Helm, Johnson, and Vlissides 1995): A transaction factory is able to create a transaction object and return it to the caller. The kind of transaction returned (i.e., the protocol and the role to be played) can be based on the results of a negotiation with its peer.

Transfer Transactions: The factory for sending transfer transactions of transferable items are the items itself, i.e., you may ask a transferable item to return a transfer transaction which satisfies the requested attributes. On the recipient's side of a transfer, you do not know exactly of what kind the received item will be. Therefore, you can ask the transfer manager to negotiate with the peer item and return an appropriate receiving transfer transaction satisfying the given attributes.

Exchange Transactions: The exchange transactions are produced by the exchange manager. This manager gets the transferable item to be sent as well as the description of the item to be sent as input and negotiates an appropriate exchange transaction together with its peer exchange manager.

For selecting an appropriate exchange transaction, it keeps a list of exchange-enabling properties as well as lists of exchange transactions together with their required properties.

10.6.2 The Transfer-and-Exchange Framework in Action

We now describe how the Transfer-and-Exchange Layer works. First, we describe the goal, i.e., what a running exchange protocol looks like. Then, we explain how we get there.

Exchanges in Action. Figure 10.17 shows the set-up, i.e., all instantiated objects, of one party participating in a running exchange: A running exchange transaction exchanges two transfers. It sends/receives items by calling the **send** and **receive** methods of the transfer transactions. Furthermore, it uses the property attributes for accessing the functionality of the exchange-enabling properties. Each transfer may have multiple attributes including multiple exchange-enabling attributes. However, our fair exchange protocols only use one attribute at a time.

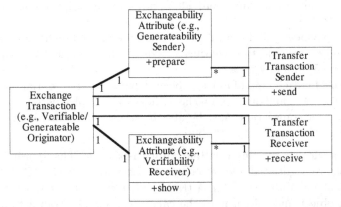

Fig. 10.17. Fair exchange in action: components and their services in an ongoing exchange

In the depicted example, the exchange transaction is an originator of a fair exchange of a verifiable for a generatable transfer (see Section 10.4). It interacts with a receiving verifiable transfer (i.e., a Receiver Transfer Transaction including a Receiver Verifiability Attribute) and a sending generatable transfer (i.e., a Sender Transfer Transaction including a Sender Generatability Attribute).

Figures 10.18, 10.19, and 10.20 provide a closer look at how the protocol is actually executed. Figure 10.18 depicts the interaction diagram for the verifiable/generatable originator exchange transaction. This exchange transaction role implements the originator's side of the security protocol depicted in Figure 10.9. The originators side of the protocol consists of the following steps:

1. After the exchange has been started by calling its `start`-method, the exchange transaction first signs an agreement with its peer. If the players disagree, the originator aborts.
2. Then, the originator's exchange transaction starts the preparation sub-protocol for enabling the responder to generate the item to be sent. This is done by calling the `prepare`-method of the generatability attribute of the sending transfer transaction.
3. Then, the originator's exchange transaction receives the transfer from the responder by calling the `receive`-method of the receiving transfer transaction.
4. Then, it sends a transfer by calling the `send`-method of the sending transfer.
5. Finally, it outputs the item which was received.

The corresponding steps for the responder are depicted in Figure 10.19. Here, the responder may have sent its item in Step 3 without receiving a transfer from the originator in Step 4. In this case, the responder starts the recovery protocol with the third party. This protocol is depicted in Figure 10.20.

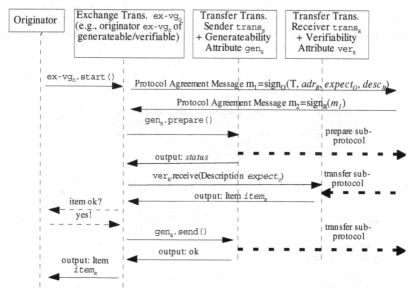

Fig. 10.18. Fair exchange: interaction diagram for the originator

The design for other exchange protocol follows the pattern described in Section 10.6.2: Again, the security protocols described in Section 10.5 are each implemented by an originator, a responder and a third party.

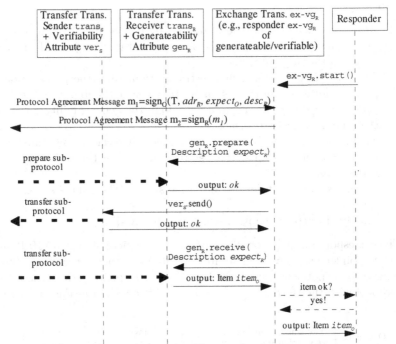

Fig. 10.19. Fair exchange: interaction diagram for the responder

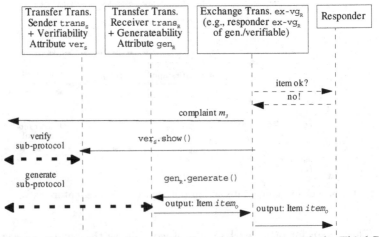

Fig. 10.20. Fair exchange: responder's view of the recovery with the Third Party

Negotiating a Transfer Protocol. For transferring an item, the sender needs the sending and the recipient the receiving transfer transaction which are able to provide the modified services corresponding to the desired attributes.

These transaction objects are the output of a negotiation between the sender and the recipient. This negotiation is performed between the item at the sender's side and the transfer manager at the recipient's side. As an additional input to the negotiation, both need the desired attributes (including exchange-enabling properties) to be fulfilled by the transfer.

Then, the negotiation of an appropriate transfer protocol is done between the item and the peer transfer manager by calling the `negotiateTransfer`-method of both of them: Given attributes, the user asks its item to negotiate with the peer transfer manager whether such a transfer is possible. If this is the case, the item returns a `Sender` transfer transaction role-object while the transfer manager returns a `Recipient` transfer transaction role-object. Note that we cannot describe this negotiation since it depends on the item to be transferred: Negotiating a payment transfer may involve selecting an appropriate purse for paying, negotiating a signature transfer may involve selecting one particular signature scheme supporting the desired attributes. For a more detailed look at general transfer negotiations, we refer to SEMPER Consortium (1999a), and a more detailed description of payment negotiation is described in Section 11.3.6.

After a successful negotiation, the transfer protocol can then be executed by calling the `send` and `receive` methods on the `Sender` and `Receiver`, respectively.

Note that this negotiation requires interaction with the peer: One may not know which payment scheme will be used, or, for containers, the enabled transfers will depend on the contained items as well as the result of the negotiations for the contained items.

Negotiating an Exchange Protocol. The fair-exchange negotiations between two fair-exchange managers get an item to be sent as well as a description of the item to be received as input and then select and return one role-object of an exchange protocol at the end.

In addition to selecting an appropriate exchange protocols and roles, it also negotiates the underlying transfers using the mechanism described above, i.e., at the end, a fixed exchange protocol together with two transfer protocols have been selected so that the transfer protocols guarantee the required exchange-enabling properties.

The negotiation is based on a list of installed fair exchange protocols and their required properties. Each role of each exchange protocol requires one exchange-enabling property attribute for the sending and the receiving transfer. During installation of a new exchange protocol class or new property attribute class, these properties and the exchanges together with the required properties are registered at the fair-exchange manager.

The negotiation is nested and works as follows (Figure 10.21):

1. The user starts the negotiation by calling the `negotiateExchange` method of the fair-exchange manager. The fair-exchange manager then retrieves the table of installed fair exchange protocols and their required exchangeability attributes.
2. The fair-exchange manager selects one exchangeability attribute for which an exchange protocol exists.
3. It asks its item to negotiate with the peer transfer manager whether such a transfer is possible.
   If this is the case, the item returns an appropriate transfer transaction. If not, it returns a failure and the fair-exchange manager selects the next attribute in Step 2. If no untried exchangeability attribute exists, the negotiation failed.
4. Given the attribute of the first transfer, the fair-exchange manager checks for what other exchangeability attributes exchange protocols exist. It selects one of them.
5. It asks its transfer manager to negotiate with the peer transferable item whether such a transfer is possible.
   If this is the case, the item returns an appropriate transfer transaction. If not, it returns a failure and the fair-exchange manager selects the next attribute in Step 4.
   If the fair-exchange manager negotiated all exchangeability attribute of the second transfer for which exchange protocols exists, it selects the next attribute for the first transfer, i.e., goes back to Step 2.
6. If both transfer negotiations have been successful so that suitable exchange protocol exists, it negotiates with the peer which player plays which role in which protocol (Note that this negotiation is only needed if the selected protocol is symmetric, i.e., employs identical properties from both exchanged transfers.).
7. Then, it instantiates an appropriate role-object of the suitable fair-exchange transaction. During this instantiation, it inputs references to both transfers, both attributes, the item, and the description into the fair exchange protocol.
8. The fair-exchange manager returns the fair-exchange transaction which is ready to run, i.e., it will execute the actual exchange after both users input the `start` command.

Note that in Steps 2, 4, and 6 the fair exchange has the choice which property or protocol to try first. Therefore, the sequence of properties and protocols can be set by the preferences input by the human user.

10.6.3 Extending the Transfer-and-Exchange Layer

Transfer Block. In order to add new transferable items, one has to implement the item, its description, and an appropriate transfer protocol. If one

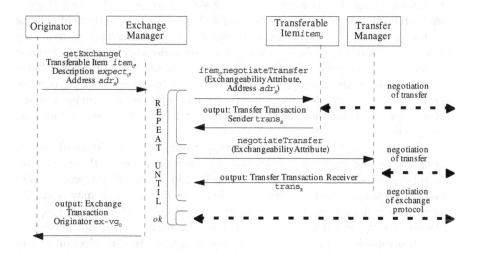

Fig. 10.21. Fair exchange: negotiating an appropriate exchange protocol

wants to exchange the item fairly, the transfer transactions implementing the sender and recipient role of the transfer protocol should be able to guarantee some of the exchange-enabling properties. For payments, for example, the implementor would be required to add a new purse, payment items, payment descriptions as well as a payment transaction which, e.g., implements generatability.

Note that providing such transfers is more easy than it seems: Given an established framework, there are usually already a variety of existing transfer transactions. Therefore, it is usually sufficient to just modify and adapt an existing transfer transaction.

Exchange Block. For the given set of properties, the current design already supplies a variety of protocols. However, it is possible to install more efficient versions of protocols for these properties. In order to do this, one may install new fair-exchange transactions for the different roles and notify the exchange manager that these protocols are available, too. In the preferences, one should tell the exchange manager to prefer this protocol compared to the old protocol. Naturally, the protocol then is only executed if the peer installed it, too.

The more interesting case is to extend the Exchange Block in a more general way. An example of such an extension would be to add gradual fair exchange protocols which do not need a third party. In the beginning we argued that these protocols are not acceptable in practice. While this is true in general there is a noteworthy exception to the rule: Purchase of streaming data such as video-on-demand. The use of micro- or tick-payments such as Pedersen (1997), Hauser et al. (1996) or Rivest and Shamir (1997) allows to continuously pay in the same rate as the stream comes in. The risk is minimal for both sides—either the value of a tick in the micro-payment scheme or the sequence in the stream, both can be made negligible—without any resort to a third party. Integration of such scenarios can be done as follows: Again, one defines new properties and implements the appropriate attributes (e.g., micro-transferable). Then, one is required to extend existing transfer transactions to provide this property. Finally, one has to provide fair exchange protocols for these new properties or a mixture between new and old properties.

Another example for such an extension would be the addition of specific contract-signing protocols. In this case, one would implement these protocols as subclasses of the exchange transaction class. Furthermore, one would either tell the exchange manager that if both items are signatures, it may select the contract-signing protocol. An alternative would be to define a new property "contractable" which is only provided by the particular inputs needed by this contract-signing protocol and which then leads to the selection of this particular exchange protocol by the exchange manager.

Note that this should not require changes to the fair-exchange manager: After installation of the new property attributes and protocols, the fair-exchange manager considers and selects them during negotiation if appropriate.

11. The Payment Framework

The core of *SEMPER* consists of several blocks. Each block is a generic and extensible framework for a particular service. This chapter describes the design of the Payment Block: the *SEMPER* generic payment service framework (GPSF).

There are a variety of different and incompatible payment systems. For business application developers this implies the need to understand the details of different systems, to adapt the code as soon as new payment systems are introduced, and also to provide a way of picking a suitable payment instrument for every transaction. GPSF is a common framework within which different payment systems can be used in a unified manner. The primary component of GPSF is a set of generic payment service application program interfaces (APIs). GPSF also provides services for transparent negotiation and selection of payment instruments. This allows applications to be developed independent of specific payment systems. GPSF was designed and prototyped during the early stages of *SEMPER*. We compare our design with more recent related designs and briefly discuss some issues which require further research.

11.1 Introduction

An important aspect of many commercial transactions is *payment*. A payment is the transfer of monetary value from one player to another. Ever since money was invented as an abstract way of representing value, systems for making payments have been in place. In the course of time, new and increasingly abstract representations of value were introduced. A corresponding progression of value-transfer systems, starting from barter, through bank notes, payment orders, cheques, and credit-cards, has finally culminated in electronic payment systems. Mapping between these abstract payments and the transfer of "real value" is still guaranteed by banks through the financial clearing systems. Several electronic payment systems have been proposed and implemented in the past few years (Asokan, Janson, Steiner, and Waidner 2000). The many different payment systems are incompatible with each other. Each individual player will have the ability to use only a subset of these payment systems. When a player wants to make a payment, he must first identify what

G. Lacoste et al. (Eds.): SEMPER 2000, LNCS 1854, pp. 185–211, 2004.
© Springer-Verlag Berlin Heidelberg 2004

payment systems he has in common with the payee, and then pick a suitable one from among them for the payment.

Ideally, a business application should be able to make use of any of the several common means of payment available to payer and payee. A unifying framework enabling business applications to use different payment systems in a transparent manner will greatly ease the task of business application developers by relieving them from having to

- make sure that the application knows how to use all the various different payment systems its users are likely to have available, and
- in case multiple payment instruments are available, provide a way of choosing one of them.

We describe the design and implementation of such a framework called the *generic payment service framework (GPSF)*. We use the term "service" as is customary in distributed systems (Linington 1983): the term "payment service" is the functionality provided by a payment system, described by specifying the interface (henceforth referred to as the *generic payment service interface*) between the system and its users. A framework is an extendable design or implementation. The primary component of GPSF is a coherent hierarchy of application programming interfaces (APIs) for the transfer of monetary value.

In addition to the unified interfaces, GPSF also provides mechanisms for automatic selection of the specific payment instrument to be used in a transaction; this will enable the business applications to be concerned just with the questions "how much to pay?" and "to whom?" but not necessarily with "what payment instrument to use?" More interestingly, these applications can specify requirements on payment instruments to be used for the requested transaction—for example, in terms of the security attributes supported by an instrument. In other words, instead of saying "pay with ABC brand electronic cash using XYZ protocol," the application can say "pay using an instrument that provides payer anonymity and non-repudiation of receipt."

This chapter is organised as follows. In Section 11.2, a simple classification of various models of electronic payment systems is presented. The design of GPSF, based on this classification, is presented in Section 11.3. Section 11.4 describes how a new payment system can be plugged into GPSF. Section 11.5 describes how a business application can use GPSF. A different, more flexible design approach (token-based) is presented in Section 11.6, and its advantages are discussed. Possible extensions to the GPSF design are discussed in Section 11.7. In Section 11.8, a brief overview of related work is presented. The chapter ends with a summary in Section 11.9.

11.2 Models of Electronic Payment Systems

In this section, we present an intuitive model of electronic payment systems as a first step in the design of GPSF. Since our motivation is to build a framework, we are interested in modeling the external behavior (i.e., how does a payment system appear to users and business applications) rather than internal details (message formats, protocol flows etc.). Further, we are interested in making a general model which is independent of specific payment systems.

First, we fix some terminology. A *payment system* is the collective name for a "way" of making a value transfer: It consists of specifications and implementations of protocols, contractual agreements, and data structures. Each participating player will have its own component of the payment system. A *payment instrument* is an instance of a player's component of a payment system.

11.2.1 Players

A basic set of players appears in all electronic payment systems. There is always a *payer* and a *payee*. The intent of the payment is to transfer monetary value from the payer to the payee. Value transfer from payer to payee also requires the participation of financial institutions which links the data exchanged in the payment protocol to transfers of monetary value. A financial institution may be a bank or a credit-card organisation which deals with monetary value represented in terms of real money; or it may be some organisation that issues and controls other forms of representation (e.g., loyalty points). Here, we use the term "bank" to mean all different types of financial institutions and the term "real money" to cover all forms of non-digital value representations used by financial institutions. Typically, banks participate in payment protocols in two roles: As *issuers* (interacting with payers) and as *acquirers* (interacting with payees). The acquirer and the issuer may be the same entity.

An *arbiter* may be involved in resolving disputes in the payment system. However, in most digital systems, the presence of the arbiter is not explicit: Even if the necessary evidence is collected, dispute handling is done outside the payment protocol and often not even specified. Usually, it is not even possible to define dispute handling solely at the protocol level since the resolution of disputes may be subject to policy decisions of the users and financial institutions (a full-fledged payment system built on top of a given payment protocol should however provide appropriate dispute-management services).

Certain payment systems might involve more players, e.g., registration and certification authorities, or other trusted third parties that provide anonymity (Low, Maxemchuk, and Paul 1994; Chaum 1981) or enforce receipts for payments (for example, using a fair exchange protocol). We limit our model to the basic set of players, shown in Figure 11.1. We focus only on

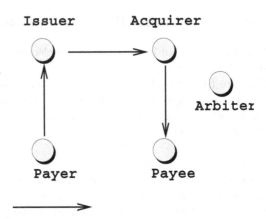

Fig. 11.1. Players of a payment system

the interactions of the payer and payee, both between themselves and with the other players. The interactions between the issuer and acquirer are out of the scope of SEMPER.

11.2.2 Payment Models

We can classify payment systems according to the flows of information between the basic set of players. Figure 11.2 lists, without claiming completeness, the four most common payment models and their information flows.

One criterion for distinction is whether the communication between the payer and the payee is *direct* or *indirect*. In the latter case, the payment operation is initiated by one player and involves only the initiator and the bank(s). The other player is notified by its bank at the completion of the transaction. An example of direct payment is paying by cash or cheque. An example of indirect payment is paying by means of a standing order or wire transfer. Most currently proposed Internet payment systems implement direct payments. Consequently, we will focus only on these systems. Indirect payment systems may fit into the GPSF without major changes to the GPSF. However, we have not verified this by adapting an actual indirect payment system into GPSF.

A second criterion is the relationship between the time the payment initiator considers the payment as finished, and the time the value is actually taken from the payer. There are three possibilities, identified by the names "pay-before," "pay-now," and "pay-later" payment systems. In pay-before payment systems, real value is removed from the payer ahead of time. This implies that some sort of electronic value token is issued to the payer at this time. These tokens are used during the electronic payment transaction. Since this is similar to cash in the physical world, we will use the term *cash-like* to describe the class of payment systems of this model.

Pay-now and pay-later payment systems are quite similar: In both cases, the user must have some sort of an "account" with the bank and a payment is always done by sending some sort of "form" from payer to payee (cheque, credit-card slip, etc.). Thus, we can treat these two cases as instances of the same model. We will use the term *cheque-like*[1] to describe the class of payment systems of this model. Similar informal models of payment systems have been used by various others (Bürk and Pfitzmann 1989; Neuman and Medvinsky 1995; Masaguer 1996). Attempts at more rigorous modeling have also been made (Pfitzmann and Waidner 1996).

Existing direct payment systems can be grouped into these two categories. Examples of cash-like payment system include ecash,[2] NetCash (Medvinsky and Neuman 1993), CAFE (Boly, Bosselaers, Cramer, Michelsen, Mjølsnes, Muller, Pedersen, Pfitzmann, de Rooij, Schoenmakers, Schunter, Vallée, and Waidner 1994) and Mondex.[3] Examples of cheque-like systems include credit-card protocols like SET (MasterCard and Visa 1997), iKP (Bellare, Garay, Hauser, Herzberg, Krawczyk, Steiner, Tsudik, Van Herreweghen, and Waidner 2000), CyberCash (Eastlake, Boesch, Crocker, and Yesil 1995) and electronic cheque schemes like FSTC (FSTC 1995).

11.3 Design of the Framework

11.3.1 Scope

The GPSF was designed to be a common framework for using payment systems belonging to various payment models as identified in Section 11.2, in particular the direct payment models. The primary component of GPSF is an API hierarchy. It consists of a base API common to all payment models, and extensions specific to each model. The GPSF specifies the services provided by a payment system to payers and payees. It further defines additional services and protocols necessary for effectively using multiple payment instruments. (An abstraction of this type of design, the manager-module concept, was already illustrated in Figure 6.3.) GPSF does not attempt to specify interactions between other players (e.g., between the acquirer and the issuer).

---

[1] In the prototype implementation, we used the term "account-based." It was somewhat confusing because certain practical implementations of cash-like payment systems, such as DigiCash's ecash also have a notion of an "account" in the bank. Thus, in the interest of avoiding confusion, we use the term "cheque-like" here.

[2] See http://www.digicash.com/ for more information.

[3] See http://www.mondex.com/ for more information.

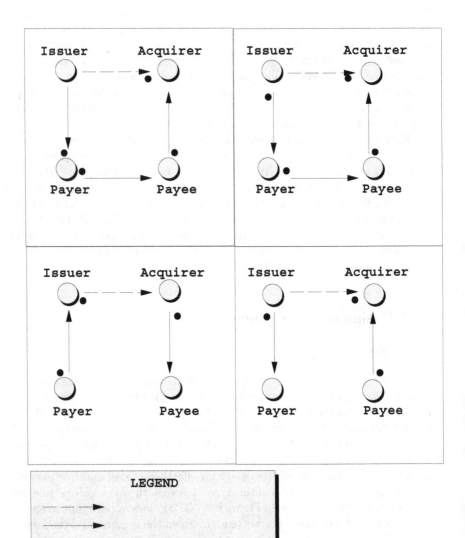

Fig. 11.2. Payment models

11.3.2 Functional Architecture

The main functionality of any payment system is to provide **value-transfer services** for moving electronic value between players. For example, moving value from a payer to a payee in the case of payment, moving it back from the payee to the payer in the case of a payment reversal, and converting electronic value into "real money" ("capture" or "deposit"). The players may specify certain security attributes for this value transfer.

In the simplest case, the transfer of value happens between two end points. Such an end point is called a *purse*.[4] A purse corresponds to a single instance of a specific payment system and contains all the user information related to that instance. For example, a user who has a credit-card account, an instance of a stored-value card and an ecash account will have three separate purses, one associated with each of the above. **Purse-management services** allow a user to set-up, configure, and delete purses.

Each value transfer in progress is embodied in a separate *transaction*. A purse may be involved in several concurrent transactions. **Transaction services** allow transactions to be queried for their status, canceled, or recovered from a crash. Before beginning a transaction, each player must choose a suitable purse. This selection may have two parts: A local decision based on preferences and requirements and a mutual decision based on negotiations. The services that enable this decision making are collectively called **purse-selection services**.

In addition to purses and transactions, a separate component called the *payment manager* manages the overall operation of the GPSF. Each player will have one active payment manager managing its purses and transactions. **Information services** enable the retrieval of information on the state of the payment manager or a specific purse, e.g., a list of previous transactions or statistics on all payments received and made in a certain period of time.

Finally, **dispute-management services** allow the user to make claims about (alleged) past transactions as well as prove or disprove them to an arbiter. None of the payment systems introduced so far has integrated dispute-handling features. Most limit themselves to the collection of evidence alone.

Figure 11.3 shows the components in the GPSF and the services they provide.[5] When a business application wants to make a value transfer, it first identifies a suitable purse, using purse-selection services. It then asks the selected purse to create a new transaction. Each transaction is associated with a transaction record where all relevant information about the transaction is maintained. Transaction records are written out to stable storage and will be available even after a system shutdown and restart.

---

[4]Sometimes, a different term—*pocket*—is used to denote the same concept.

[5]More detailed descriptions of the components in this figure appear in the subsequent sections. See Section 11.3.6 (payment manager), Section 11.3.4 (purse), Section 11.3.5 (transaction and transaction record), Section 11.5.1 (usage by business applications) and Section 11.5.2 (usage by special applications).

Note that some of the services are distributed over more than one component. For instance, information services are provided jointly by the payment manager, purses, and transaction records.

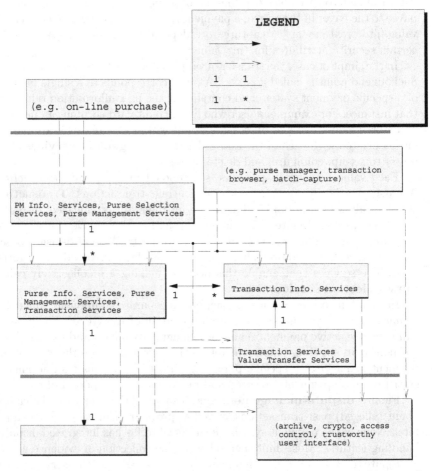

Fig. 11.3. GPSF in action: components and their services in a typical instance)

11.3.3 Design Overview

To define each of the above services more concretely, we have adopted the following approach. For a given class of services (e.g., value-transfer services):

1. First, identify the primitives for this service that are common to most payment systems. Describe these in the form of a *base* service interface.

For example, the ValueTransferServices[6] interface contains primitives like pay().

2. Then for each payment model, identify any additional primitives, not already covered in the base interface but common to all payment systems of that model. Describe these in the form of a sub-interface. For example, the sub-interface CashLikeValueTransferServices for the cash-like model defines primitives like withdraw(), that exist only in the cash-like model.

Some services, such as purse selection, are provided by GPSF itself. Other services, such as value transfer, are provided by the various payment system *modules*. To incorporate a specific payment system into GPSF, a corresponding *module* must be built. The module uses the services provided by the payment system to implement services defined in the generic payment service interface. To introduce a new model, a new (possibly empty) sub-interface will have to be defined for each service interface.

The high-level design described so far can be implemented in a variety of ways. We opted for an object-oriented approach. We describe the components of, and services required from the GPSF in terms of base classes and interfaces. The four main types of components identified in the previous section (purses, transactions, transaction records, and the payment manager) are described by four different classes. Each service interface corresponds to an interface or abstract class. Concrete implementations for the services that are independent of payment systems (such as services for purse selection) are provided by the payment manager or related classes. Modules for specific payment systems can then provide implementations for the remaining interface and abstract class methods. For example, the transaction class in a module is expected to implement the services defined in the ValueTransferServices interface as well as the TransactionServices interface. The ValueTransferServices interface has model-specific extensions. The module for a given payment system should implement the branch of the ValueTransferServices interface corresponding to the model of that payment system. Figure 11.4 illustrates the classes that constitute a module and the services they implement. In the following sections, we describe objects in the GPSF (shown in Figure 11.3) in more detail.

The users of GPSF (such as the Transfer-and-Exchange Layer) can treat the various objects (such as purses and transactions) as instantiations of the base classes. For example, an application that wants to make a payment transaction will not need to know the exact type of a purse object. It simply needs to know that the purse object is an instantiation of the abstract base class Purse (i.e., it implements the generic purse-management and purse-information services). In reality, the purse object will be an instance of a more specific purse class in a module (e.g., a SETPurse object or an ecashPurse object).

---

[6]In the prototype implementation, this hierarchy was named PurseServices. Here we opt for a more intuitive name.

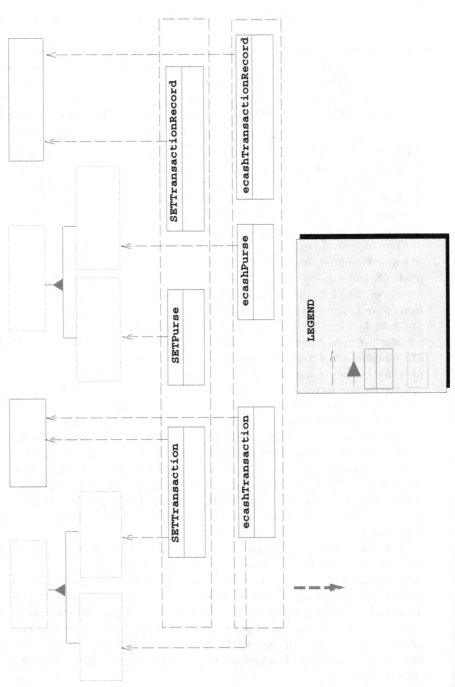

Fig. 11.4. Generic Payment Service Framework: Important classes and interfaces

As an example, the primitives of the value-transfer services interface are described briefly in Table 11.1. The complete set of primitives in GPSF API appears in Asokan (1998). Square brackets ([ ]) indicate optional parameters. Exceptions and errors are not shown. Concrete Java bindings of the service descriptions can be found in SEMPER Consortium (1999a).

Note that each transaction object knows its transaction record object, which in turn knows the purse object which created them.

Primitive	Input	Output	Description
Base Services			
pay	*payee, amount, options, ref*[a]		send a payment
receivePayment	*[options, ref.]*	*payer, amount, ref*	receive a payment
reversePayment	*transaction record*		ask/get a refund
reverseReceivedPayment	*transaction record*		make a refund
Additions for cash-like model			
withdraw	*amount, options, ref*		load money into purse
deposit	*amount, options, ref.*		unload money from purse
Additions for cheque-like model			
receiveRawPayment	*[options], [ref.]*	*payer, amount, ref.*	receive a payment (defer authorisation)
authorise			authorise a previous raw payment
capture	*[amount]*		capture a previous raw payment
multiCapture	*list of transaction records*		capture a set of previous raw payments

[a]The parameter ref (external reference) allows this payment to be tightly linked to its context, e.g., an order and its description.

Table 11.1. Generic Payment Service Framework: value-transfer services

11.3.4 Purses

A purse is an abstraction of an instance of a payment system that is available to the user. It is necessary to have services

- for creating a purse (i.e., a constructor to instantiate a purse object),
- for configuration and set-up, which will be used by purse management applications (e.g., to associate a purse with a credit card and to register with a certification authority),
- for initialisation, which are invoked during start-up to activate the purse,
- for creating transactions (see Section 11.3.5), and
- for information (e.g., answers to questions like "does this purse provide non-repudiable receipts for payments?" or, where applicable, "what amount is associated with this purse?").

These services are part of the purse-management, purse-information, and transaction services, and are implemented by the Purse class hierarchy. The base Purse class defines the aforementioned services and provides default implementations for some of them. For each payment model, the base Purse class is extended to a model-specific sub-class (e.g., ChequeLikePurse class). Module-writers are required to extend a model-specific Purse class and override/extend default implementations as necessary. For example, to adapt the SET payment system (a protocol for making credit-card transactions over the Internet (MasterCard and Visa 1997)), one can define a class SETPurse which extends ChequeLikePurse.

11.3.5 Transactions and Transaction Records

As mentioned, the base ValueTransferServices interface defines value-transfer services that are common to all payment models. Some example services defined in this interface are: pay() makes a payment from a purse to a designated recipient, receivePayment() is the counterpart of pay(); it receives an incoming payment. Model-specific sub-interfaces may define additional services. For example, the sub-interface for the cash-like model has a service to withdraw money from the bank into the purse.

Every instance of a value-transfer service is abstracted by a transaction. The base class for all transactions in GPSF is PaymentTransaction; e.g., the SETTransaction class in Figure 11.4) is based on it. Such a concrete sub-class implements all the value-transfer services described in one branch of the ValueTransferServices interface hierarchy. For instance, SETTransaction implements not only the services from the base interface ValueTransferServices but also services such as authorise() and capture() from the ChequeLikeValueTransferServices interface. Transaction objects are transient. Information associated with a transaction (both transient information such as state that is relevant only while the transaction is active and permanent information such as receipts or other evidence that is relevant long after the transaction is completed) is kept in a related PaymentTransactionRecord object. This can be used in crash recovery and dispute management as well as for informational purposes.

The base PaymentTransaction defines general transaction services such as trying to abort an on-going transaction or retrieving its current status. Each sub-class of the base class implements a leaf interface of the ValueTransferServices interface hierarchy (e.g., SETTransaction extends PaymentTransaction and implements the ChequeLikeValueTransferServices interface). Each leaf purse object serves as an abstract factory, providing a factory method called startTransaction() to create a new transaction of the appropriate type (e.g., in the SETPurse class, the startTransaction() method will instantiate a SETTransaction object).

11.3.6 Payment Manager

The payment manager provides services for purse selection as well as retrieval of management information. It keeps track of the currently available purses, known payment modules, etc. To maintain and manage this information, the payment manager provides various services such as creation, configuration, deactivation, and deletion of purses[7] and inclusion of a new modules into a user's GPSF.

Additional services are provided to make this information available to other objects and applications in a variety of useful ways. The manager is also responsible for initialising all the relevant components on start-up.

Selection of a purse to be used in a transaction is based on several factors: Requirements on the transaction (e.g., security attributes), static user preferences, negotiation with a peer payment manager, and manual selection by the user. Except negotiation, the factors are all local. The payment manager provides various services to facilitate this local selection.

Negotiation with the peer for selection of the payment instrument can be done in several ways. But all negotiation protocols consist of simple request-response exchanges. Currently, negotiation is restricted to tuples containing two parameters.

– *Payment System Name*: "payment system name" is defined as follows: Two purses that report the same payment system name can potentially engage in a payment transaction. Typically, the payment system name corresponds to a single <protocol, brandname> pair; e.g., SET:MasterCard and SET:Visa will be two different payment systems. It is up to the module to determine the payment system name associated with a purse as long as it satisfies the definition above.

– *Amount* (value and currency).

---

[7]To provide these services, the payment manager in turn relies on lower-level purse-management services provided by the purses themselves as described in Section 11.3.4.

We have designed and implemented a simple negotiation protocol which can support various negotiation policies. Two example methods, selectPayingPurse() and selectReceivingPurse() implementing a default policy, are provided: The payer is the initiator of the negotiation, and the payee is allowed to adjust the amounts in its reply (e.g., the merchant may add a surcharge for using a credit-card or give a discount for using ecash). It is also possible to enforce other negotiation policies. As an example, Figure 11.5 illustrates how selectPayingPurse() may be used.

11.4 Adapting a Payment System

In order to incorporate a new payment system into GPSF, a suitable module has to be designed; typically only an adapter for an existing implementation. (Figure 11.4 indicates what constitutes an adapter). The following steps are required in this process:

- Identify the model to which the payment system belongs (e.g., SET belongs to the cheque-like model).
- Implement a sub-class of the Purse class corresponding to the payment model identified (e.g., SETPurse extends ChequeLikePurse). This implies providing implementations for all abstract services defined in the ancestor Purse classes (e.g., Purse and ChequeLikePurse) and overriding default implementations therein where necessary. In particular, the new class must provide a proper implementation of the setup() method: This method should allow the user to carry out all configuration necessary for the payment system.
- Implement a sub-class of PaymentTransaction which implements the value-transfer services defined in the leaf of the ValueTransferServices interface hierarchy corresponding to the payment model identified (e.g., SETTransaction implements ChequeLikeValueTransferServices and inherits from PaymentTransaction).

11.5 Using the Generic Payment Service Framework

Once a user has installed one or more payment modules on her system, two types of usage are possible: making payment transactions from business applications, and using *special-purpose functionality* which allows the user to manage the configuration and operation of GPSF.

11.5.1 Payment Transactions

The primary use of the GPSF is to make payment transactions on behalf of business applications, via the commerce and transfer-exchange layers.

A user will initiate payment transactions using some sort of high-level business application. (This may be a web-browser, or a special application such as a CD-catalogue reader or the Fair Internet Trader. Within *SEMPER*, in most cases the actual caller of GPSF is the Transfer-and-Exchange Layer.) Figure 11.5 shows the object interactions that take place at the payer end during an execution of a typical payment transaction. The important things to note are:

- the user need not specify the payment instrument to use if he does not want to; the GPSF can be configured to prompt him for selection of payment instrument if it cannot do so by itself, and
- the application is not aware of the specific payment instrument being used; it deals with generic Purse and PaymentTransaction objects. If the granularity of services provided by the base interface TValueTransferServices (e.g., pay()) is sufficient for the application's purposes it need not even know the model to which the chosen purse belongs.

The sequence of events at the payee side is similar, with minor differences. The payee application may be an unattended merchant server. In that case there will be no user interaction. There may be interactions with third parties during the transaction. For example, in a cheque-like system, the payee's module may contact the acquirer for authorisation. One can also imagine a payment system where the payer's module has to obtain some sort of a credential from the issuer before each payment. All such communication with third parties are carried out within the module—the calling applications are typically unaware of them.

This example is also intended to give an idea about how the GPSF enables business application development. The primary services used by the business applications are purse selection and value transfer between payer and payee. Both of these are common to all payment systems. Thus, a large class of applications using the GPSF need not be aware of system- or model-specific details.

11.5.2 Special Application Functionality

The second category of usage is via special applications or application-parts. A base functionality is the purse-management tool.

Purse Management. Before being able to use an installed payment instrument, a purse corresponding to it must be created and configured. A special *purse-management application* is provided for this purpose. Changes to purses are written out to stable storage. Purse management is an infrequent activity (typically, once a purse is created and configured, it can be used in many subsequent payment transactions). Purse management makes use of a setup() method provided by the Purse class in a module. This method must implement all the necessary configuration for that payment system. For example,

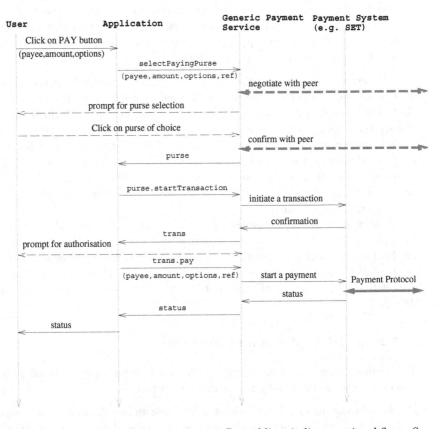

Fig. 11.5. Interactions during a payment. Dotted lines indicate optional flows. See Section 11.5.1.

the setup() method of the SETPurse allows the user to enter the credit-card information (cardholder name, brand, number, expiry date) which are then stored as part of the purse state.

Other Application Functionality. There can be a number of other special application functionalities. It is possible to seamlessly integrate them into the purse-management application. Some of the functions are model-specific. A *batch capture* function can be used by the merchant to capture a set of received payments for cheque-like purses; typically this will be used as part of end-of-day processing. The *withdrawal* functionality can be used to load money into cash-like purses. The SEMPER prototype implementation comes with a model-independent special functionality: The *transaction browser* which allows the user to browse through accumulated transaction records.

11.6 Token-based Interface Definition

In the original design, we assumed that the GPSF is responsible for all communication arising as the result of a service primitive invocation, since the first version of the SEMPER architecture did the same (SEMPER Consortium 1996). However, we have defined a *token-based* interface where the GPSF does not engage in any direct communication with the peer. Instead, the GPSF constructs the protocol messages and hands them back to the caller which is expected to take care of the communication. This is inspired by the GSS-API (Linn 1997) approach. It has two types of methods:

− one "starter" method for each different type of protocol; the starter method returns a token containing the first message of the protocol; and
− a common "processor" method; this takes a token as input, and depending on the internal state of the protocol run, may return another token as output.

A token is simply a capsule containing a protocol message. The protocol message is opaque to the caller. The GPSF is still responsible for generating and interpreting tokens, and maintaining the state of a protocol run. The initiating caller invokes an appropriate starter method in the payment service API to start a protocol. Typically, these starter methods will return a token as output. The initiating caller application is expected to communicate this token to its peer entity, the responding caller application. The latter in turn will invoke the processor method on its instance of GPSF and give the received token as input. From this point on, whenever a caller receives a token as output from the processor method, it will send the token to its peer; whenever a caller receives a token from its peer, it will invoke the processor method on its GPSF giving the received token as input.

A token-based version of value-transfer services is defined in an interface hierarchy called TValueTransferServices parallel to the ValueTransferServices

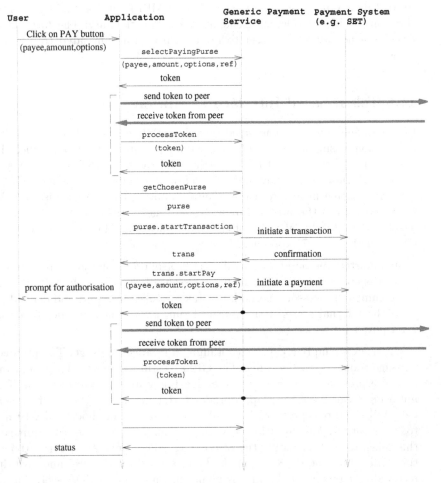

Fig. 11.6. Interactions during a payment in the token-based model. Dotted lines indicate optional flows. See Section 11.6.

interface hierarchy. For each method (e.g., pay()) in the latter, a corresponding starter method (e.g., startPay()) is defined in the former. In addition, a common processor method processToken() is defined in the TValueTransferServices interface. Figure 11.6 illustrates object interactions in the same scenario as depicted in Figure 11.5, but with a token-based interface for negotiation and value transfer.

Since there is no peer-to-peer communication taking place inside the GPSF, the caller does not have to block on service invocations waiting for communication. This allows the designer of the calling application the freedom to use an event-based implementation architecture: a thread can start a transaction, receive the first protocol message from GPSF, send it to the peer and go away; when the reply comes from the peer, a new thread is scheduled to receive and process it.

More importantly, the token-based approach easily allows an application to supplement the level of security provided by a payment system by transporting the tokens via a channel with particular security attributes. For example, even though payment protocol messages in SET are encrypted, an eavesdropper may be able to determine and link the identity of the payer and payee by watching the network addresses in the payment messages. With a token-based interface, if the applications were able to establish an untraceable communication channel between them, they can extend the untraceability to SET payments as well.

In the current implementation, the interface TValueTransferServices is optionally implemented by sub-classes of the PaymentTransaction class. Since the token-based version is more general than the synchronous version, it deserves to be the default value-transfer services interface.

11.7 Extending the Design

A prototype of the design described so far has been implemented and used in various SEMPER trials. We have also investigated extending the design by adding functionality, and by revising some aspects by using better techniques. In this section, we describe these extensions.

11.7.1 Dispute Management

Support for handling disputes is a crucial aspect of any system providing accountability. However, many payment systems limit themselves to the generation and collection of evidence. It is assumed that such evidence can be used in some dispute resolution procedure external to the system. Such procedures are usually left unspecified.

In this section, we investigate how the GPSF can be extended to provide dispute services, while retaining its generality: to the extent possible, we want to allow users and applications to initiate or respond to payment disputes in a payment-system independent manner.

We begin by viewing evidence tokens as essentially part of the internal structure of the system; their structure and raw contents are not relevant outside the system. For instance, a payment receipt in the form of a digital signature is outwardly just a string of bits. Even if the receipt is in a format which allows anyone to securely verify who signed it, and when it was sent or received, the semantics of the evidence has to be provided by the system itself. Outside the system (that is, from the point of view of the user of a system), what is necessary is to know what the evidence *means*, and how it can be *used* in disputes.

In a dispute, there is a set of (one or more) players called *initiators* who start the dispute and another set of players called *responders* who participate in it. A special player called the *verifier* or *arbiter* makes, or helps making, the final decision regarding disputes, according to some well-defined procedures which can be verified by anyone. The initiator(s) try to convince the verifier of a *claim*. Initiators may support their claims by producing evidence or engaging in some sort of a proof protocol. Responders may attempt to disprove the claims. The verifier analyses the claims made and the evidence presented. This analysis may lead to a judgment as to whether a dispute claim is valid or not.

Completely automated dispute resolution may not always be feasible or even desirable. Our dispute-management service should instead be used as a tool in human-driven dispute resolution. For example, it can be used by an expert witness in court in order to support his testimony. Or, it can be used by an entity like the Online Ombuds Service (Katsch 1996) which is not a legally competent authority but helps players resolve their disputes. In these cases, the verifier does not make a final decision. Instead, it presents an analysis of the evidence to a human judge. The verifier may even be one of the players themselves, trying to settle a dispute in a friendly way without going to court, or trying to convince itself of which disputes it can win.

As we saw earlier, a payer makes a payment by telling a payment instrument (a) who the payee is, (b) what amount is to be transferred, and (c) certain other parameters. For example, Figure 11.7 illustrates the interface events during a payment transaction from a customer Alice to an airline BobAir:

– pay $200 to BobAir ("#434: For flight 822 on Jan 19").

Let us attempt to get an idea of the kinds of claims that need to be expressed. What sorts of disputes, related to the above value transfer, does the payer (Alice) expect to be able to initiate and win? For example, Alice may want to claim that

– she paid $200 to BobAir (perhaps because BobAir refused to send the tickets claiming no payment was made), or

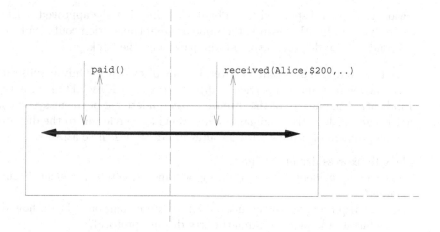

Fig. 11.7. An example payment transaction

– her payment was made before Jan 12 (perhaps because there was a deadline).

Some disputes may be about negative claims: For example, BobAir may want to prove that

– BobAir did **not** receive $200 from Alice.

In other words, dispute claims are statements about the characteristics of value transfer. These characteristics are determined by the service primitives used, together with their parameters, and additional contextual information (such as the time of value transfer).

As we saw in Section 11.2.1, in addition to the payer and payee, a financial organization may be involved in value-transfer transactions. Thus the value transfer may involve two or more sub-protocols involving different pairs of players. For example, in the cheque-like model, the payer sends a "form" (e.g., a cheque or a credit-card slip) to the payee using a payment protocol and the payee may use a deposit or capture protocol to claim the real money. This leads to two other types of dispute claims.

– Suppose BobAir makes an offer to Alice for a cheap ticket if she makes the payment before Jan 12. Alice goes through the steps of the payment protocol (e.g., sending a credit-card slip). However, BobAir changes his mind after receiving the credit-card slip—he does not "capture" Alice's payment. Alice of course cannot prove that the value transfer took place. But if she has a signed acknowledgement from BobAir, she can prove that the value transfer *could* have taken place without further help from Alice, if BobAir had wanted.
– Suppose Alice pays $200 to BobAir using a debit card. Later, she finds an entry in her monthly statement indicating a debit of $300. Alice may now

want to start a dispute with the bank claiming that she approved a debit of only $200. In other words, the same original transaction could lead to a second type of dispute, involving the payer and the bank.

A transaction may result in several items of evidence. Only a subset of these may be relevant to a particular dispute. Hence, it is useful to have a way of indicating the nature of the dispute to the underlying payment system so that it can produce the minimal amount of evidence relevant to the dispute.

The problem of dealing with disputes in GPSF has three aspects:

– how to express dispute claims?
– how to map evidence collected during a transaction to subsequent dispute claims?
– since a dispute involves the interaction of more than one player, how do we define and implement a multi-party dispute protocol?

In general, dispute claims can be expressed in terms of *statements* about a (possibly alleged) transaction. The terms of these statements correspond to the parameters of the methods in the ValueTransferServices interface hierarchy and a finite set of other "environmental" terms (such as the time of transaction). In Asokan, Herreweghen, and Steiner (1998), we presented the grammar for a language to express dispute claims in GPSF.

The dispute-management interface provides services to construct dispute claims and prove them to an arbiter.

In the simplest case, it is enough to extract the right pieces of evidence (such as receipts) and present them to the verifier. In other cases, it may be necessary to interact with the verifier using a complex proof protocol. The Purse sub-classes in the modules can be required to implement the dispute-management interface.

Typically, disputes are about payment transactions. These disputes will be started by the applications that initiated the payment in the first place (e.g., a web browser on the payer's side and a merchant server on the payee's side). Disputes between a user and the bank (e.g., wrong entry in a bank statement) will require special bank-specific applications to drive the dispute.

Designing a full-fledged framework for handling disputes in electronic payment systems is a complex task. In addition to the technical aspects, various legal and business practice aspects must be taken into account. This remains an open research issue.

11.7.2 Payment Security Policies

Limits on Value Transfer. A user of GPSF may wish to associate several types of limits to the purses available, e.g., to implement policies on who is allowed to spend how much in a company. Some examples of the types of limits are:

- Total payments from all purses taken together should not exceed 1000 CHF in any 24-hour period.
- Total payments from all purses should not exceed 10,000 CHF in a given calendar month.
- Each payment from a specified purse should not exceed 100 CHF.
- Payments below 10 CHF do not need explicit user authorisation.
- No more than 4 payments without explicit user authorisation in any 24-hour period.
- If a payment will bring the balance in a specified purse (say P2) below 200 CHF, it must be explicitly authorised by the user.

Clearly, the limits may involve complex computations and may require several different pieces of information during the computation.

Access Control. Access control is a critical functionality of a payment system. We note the following in order to motivate our design:

- Access control is required in the following cases:
  - Access to secret information required to use the underlying payment system (e.g., PINs, passphrases, credit-card numbers, etc.). There may be several different pieces of such information.
  - Access to purse operations.
- Even for the same purse operation, it may be necessary to control access differently depending on the parameters. For example, a user may decide to have no access control for payments of small amounts or have a different passphrase to authorise high-value payments. The underlying payment instrument may or may not support such granularity.

A Common Solution: Policy Framework. We have taken a common approach to address both limits and access-control requirements by using the notion of **policy objects**. A purse can associate one policy object with each service it provides. Whenever a service is requested from a purse, the corresponding policy object will be queried to determine authorisation for the service (Figure 11.8). All policy objects provide ways to check for the current availability of a service (the isAllowed() method), and to indicate that an authorised service is being provided (the update() method) so the policy object can change any relevant internal state parameters (note that several policies in the examples above are stateful).

These methods can be used by purse services (such as the pay() and receivePayment() methods) to manage authorisation. A reference to the transaction record is provided as an argument to the isAllowed() and update() methods. Through the transaction record, it is possible to access the purse(s) involved in an operation. Thus, different implementations of these methods can access all the information they need in order to make the policy decisions.

Extracts from the Policy class hierarchy are shown in Figure 11.9. A policy may be simple or aggregate. Simple policy objects are self-contained

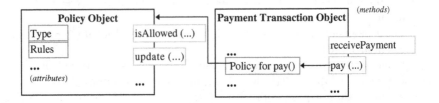

Fig. 11.8. Incorporating policy in a purse

and make their decisions independently of other policy objects. There may be several kinds of simple policy objects. Some examples are:

- *AskUser* policy class displays relevant information about the transaction to the user and asks for her approval,
- *MinBalance* policy class makes sure that the minimum balance is above a specified value, and
- *TimebasedLimit policy* class provides a way to set simple time-based limits.

Aggregate policy objects have a list of constituent policy objects. The policy decision of the aggregate object is a function of the policy decisions of its constituent objects. Some examples are the *OR* policy, which allows the service if any of its constituent policies do so, and the *AND* policy, which allows the service if all of its constituent policies do so. With these two policies we can

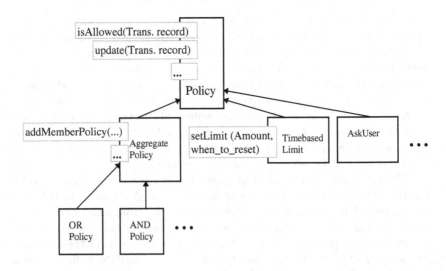

Fig. 11.9. Partial view of the class hierarchy for policy objects

express complex policies. For example the policy "if the amount is less than CHF 10 and the balance afterwards is going to be above CHF 200, allow the payment, otherwise ask the user" corresponds to the policy-object network shown in Figure 11.10. If a policy object has constituent policy objects, a top-to-bottom evaluation order is assumed.

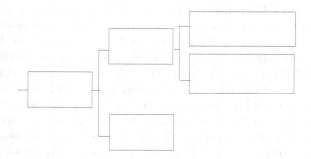

Fig. 11.10. An example policy

Additional policy classes may be defined and incorporated into this hierarchy. Users of policies (e.g., the pay() and receivePayment() methods) will have a single access point. Notice that policy objects are intended as a mechanism to express policies. The enforcement of these policies is up to the implementations of the services: For example, as shown in Figure 11.8, the pay method in the transaction class of a module must query the payment policy object in its purse before proceeding with the payment.

Clearly, there are several issues to be resolved. We require a language to express policies and efficient techniques for evaluating and updating policies. A similar approach is given by the PolicyMaker framework (Blaze, Feigenbaum, and Lacy 1996). However, in PolicyMaker policies cannot be defined in terms of pure contextual information such as the total amount spent from a purse.

The description here is intended only to give a flavour of the issues involved. More research is needed to address these issues in depth.

11.8 Related Work

U-PAI (Ketchpel, Garcia-Molina, Paepcke, Hassan, and Cousins 1996) is being developed as part of the Stanford Digital Libraries project.[8] Their focus is on providing a unified interface to payment services. They do not address negotiation of parameters before a payment transaction begins; nor do they explicitly address issues like refunds. They also assume a distributed

---

[8]See http://www-diglib.stanford.edu for more information.

object infrastructure such as CORBA and do not have a very clear security and trust model.

The Joint Electronic Payments Initiative (JEPI) of the W3C Consortium focussed only on defining the protocol for the negotiation of various payment-related parameters such as the payment system. The scope of our work roughly corresponds to the scope of these two projects taken together.

Sun's **Java Commerce Client (JCC)**[9] is a major on-going effort in building an extensible framework for enabling electronic commerce. In scope, JCC is comparable to SEMPER as a whole. Thus some of the following observations are not limited to the GPSF, but are equally applicable to the other SEMPER blocks. The payment service portion of JCC differs from the GPSF in several respects. JCC is concerned only with the payer side. The payee (assuming it is acting as a server) is required only to know how to construct messages to the client according to a specific format (Java Commerce Messages). The JCC model also distinguishes between a payment *instrument* and a payment *protocol*. In GPSF, these correspond to the Purse and Transaction classes, respectively. However, in GPSF, there is a tight binding between the two. In the JCC model an instrument can, in principle, be used with multiple protocols. This separation is elegant although it is not clear if it makes much of a difference in the end given that most protocol-instrument relationships are one-to-one. The separation also raises several other issues. First, the instrument must keep any protocol-specific information (e.g., SET certificates in a credit-card instrument). Second, the instrument class and its API may need to be extended each time support for a new protocol is added. The protocol-instrument separation may be more intuitive to the user; for example, the user probably wants to select the instrument by name (e.g., "My XYZ credit card"), but the protocol by abstract security services (e.g., "pay with a credit-card, while getting a receipt fairly").

The **E-CO System project** (Bahreman 1996) had roughly the same scope as our work although their main focus, until the project was discontinued, was on establishing APIs and mechanisms for payment negotiation (Bahreman and Narayanaswamy 1996).

The design of the **IBM Payment Server** in the IBM Payment Suite is similar to ours. Its initial design was in fact based on GPSF.

Our work differs from the related work described so far in two important ways. First, GPSF is the only framework to specify a fine-grained, and yet extensible, interface for value-transfer services. Second, to our knowledge, no one else has started addressing the problem of handling disputes in a generic manner.

---

[9]See http://www.javasoft.com/commerce for more information.

11.9 Summary

In this chapter, we have described the design and implementation of a **generic payment service framework**, which includes the definition of a common application programming interface for payment systems. The main advantages of GPSF are generality, transparency and abstraction. It is general because any payment system can be incorporated into the framework. The unified service definition hides the details of particular payment systems from business applications, allowing them to be implemented independently of payment systems. Developers of these applications do not have to know about details of particular payment systems. Finally, they can specify abstract requirements on the payment instrument to be used for their value-transfer transactions.

Complete Java bindings of the payment service interfaces can be found on the web page of the SEMPER deliverables at `http://www.semper.org/info/index.html#D10`. A prototype of GPSF with all the basic functionality has been implemented. This work served as a basis for the design of the IBM Payment Server in the IBM Payment Suite. Adapters for a variety of other payment systems, including SET, ecash, a stored-value card system called Chipper,[10] and an electronic cheque system called MANDATE (MANDATE II Consortium 1998), have been developed by various partners in the SEMPER consortium.

---

[10]See `http://www.chipper.com/` for more information. The Chipper integration in *SEMPER* is called KPN Smartcard Purse and was a basis for standardization of TeleChipper by Chipper NV.

12. Trust Management in the Certificate Block

This chapter describes the trust management in the *SEMPER* Certificate Block. First, we briefly outline the use of public-key cryptography and public-key infrastructures (PKI), mainly focusing on certificates and certificate authorities (CAs). The existence of several CAs offering services of different quality and certificates with different semantics is one of the main reason why trust management is needed. More precisely, trust management provides the means for enabling:

- the user to specify the policies for the use and acceptance of certificates and CAs, and
- the application to select and use the appropriate ones.

We define the necessary information that should be maintained for a policy; it comprises the business situation and quality requirements on the CA that has issued the certificates. Both the user and his business application

Finally, we briefly describe the actual PKI and trust management that has been implemented and demonstrated as part of the *SEMPER* prototype.

12.1 Public-Key Infrastructure

Public-key cryptography can be used to provide confidentiality as well as authentication (e.g., identification and digital signatures). In a public-key cryptosystem the user has a key pair consisting of a private key known only to himself, and a public key which may be publicly announced. The public key and the algorithms, usually standardized algorithms such as DSA (U. S. National Institute of Standards and Technology NIST 1994a) for digital signatures and RSA (Rivest, Shamir, and Adleman 1978) for both confidentiality and signatures, must be known to all other parties that want to communicate securely with the user in question.

Consider a party, A, having a key pair (s, p), where s is the private key and p the public one. Other parties can send information *confidentially* to A by encrypting the data under A's public key. A can retrieve the original information by deciphering the ciphertext using the private key s. As only A knows this key, A is the only person who can retrieve the encrypted information.

G. Lacoste et al. (Eds.): SEMPER 2000, LNCS 1854, pp. 213–232, 2004.
© Springer-Verlag Berlin Heidelberg 2004

Due to efficiency reasons asymmetric algorithms are not to be used in cases where large amounts of data are encrypted. For that reason, public-key cryptography is often used to negotiate other (symmetric) keys, which are then used to encrypt information, potentially several times during a session. This is often referred to as *key exchange*.

With the same setting as above, A can digitally sign a message using his private key s. This results in a *digital signature* which can be verified by anyone using A's public key p. The verification process ensures that only someone knowing the private key corresponding to the public verification key (here A) could have produced the signature. We note here that digital signatures can be used to achieve a number of fundamentally different goals such as the following:

- Identification of A.
- Authentication of a document (the recipient recognizes that the signed document comes from A, but cannot prove later that the document originated from A and that A committed himself to the content of the document).
- Non-repudiation (the recipient recognizes that the signed document comes from A and binds A to promises in the content, and can later prove this fact to third parties).

Although the digital signature from a technical point of view is the same in all cases, the last application differs significantly from a legal point of view.

In the above applications of public-key cryptography, it was tacitly assumed that other people could recognize A's public key. Without this essential property, it would be easy to forge A's signatures by generating a new key pair and pretending that the public key belongs to A. Assuming that the attacker knows (in fact has generated) the private key, it is a simple task to make a signature which anyone, believing that the public key belongs to A, would accept as A's signature.

In practice, this problem is solved using *public-key certificates*. A certificate is, as mentioned in Section 1.3.3, an electronic message stating that a given public key belongs to a given person. A certificate is issued and digitally signed by a third party called a *certification authority* or just CA. Thus everybody knowing the public key of the CA can verify certificates issued by that CA and hence use the public keys in these certificates. Two certificate standards are given in ISO/IEC (1990) and ISO/IEC TC154 (1999) Note that another type of certificates is attribute certificates, see Section 6.2.4.

While the CA is central for establishing a *public-key infrastructure* (PKI), two other third parties are often involved:

- A *registration authority* (RA) which verifies information about the user (in particular the identity of the user) and links the public key to the user. In some applications a number of local RAs are required where users must show up in person before getting a certificate.

– A *directory authority* (DA) which maintains a register of public information about users and certificates. Certificates can be published in and retrieved from a directory.

The user first registers at the registration authority and then obtains a certificate from the certification authority. Later the certificate can be used either by including the certificate in the electronic messages or by letting the counterpart obtain the certificate from the directory authority. The public key can subsequently be used by anyone believing that the information in the certificate is correct.

Since the purpose of a certificate is to link together a person and a public key, it is important that the identification of that person as well as the verification of the correctness of the key are done thoroughly; it must be ensured that the name of the person is correct and that the person acknowledges that the certified public key belongs to him. (More details on the notion of "belonging" for signature keys, in particular to what extent it can and should imply liability, are discussed in Chapters 3, 13 and 14.)

However, no matter how many resources are put into the verification of the information in certificates when they are issued, the PKI must support means for revoking certificates. Most noteworthy, this will happen if the certified key pair is (suspected to be) compromised, but it could also be necessary in less dramatic circumstances (e.g., if information in the certificate is out-dated as a result of the owner changing affiliation). If a certificate is revoked, the PKI must make sure that the change of status is announced properly. This could for example be through announcements of certificate revocation lists, or by providing an on-line directory service which can always give the correct status of any given certificate.

The correctness of the information in a certificate depends heavily on the services offered by all parties involved in the PKI to which the CA belongs, in particular the associated RAs. Thus, a user should only accept certificates from a given CA if he trusts (has satisfying guarantee) that the entire PKI associated to this CA provides reliable services. In the following, when we say that a user trusts or accepts a CA we therefore mean that the entire PKI is trusted or acceptable, respectively.

The group of parties trusting a CA constitutes the *trust domain* of that CA. A trust domain is defined by a unique key pair used by the CA to issue certificates. Thus all parties in the same trust domain can communicate with each other in a secure manner by relying on the certificates issued by the corresponding CA (and which can be verified against the public key of the CA). If a CA certifies other CAs, and is also trusted for this, the trust domain of that CA encompasses a number of subdomains corresponding to the trust domains of the certified CAs.

12.2 The Need for Trust Management

Managing certificates and CAs would be very simple if a CA that issued certificates acceptable to all users in all business sessions were established. However, such a situation is extremely unlikely to occur as a number of organizations issue certificates and some applications may require their own PKI. For example, the SET protocol for credit-card payments requires an independent hierarchy of CAs issuing certificates that may only be used in SET, see MasterCard and Visa (1997).

Thus a number of CAs are available, and a given user may only want to use certificates issued by some of these. Obviously, there can be a number of subjective reasons for the selection of acceptable CAs (e.g., a European user may only want to use European CAs). The choice may also depend on the services offered by the corresponding PKIs. Different CAs may offer PKI services of a different quality and a single CA may offer various classes of certificates corresponding to services of different quality. The quality of a PKI depends on a number of issues such as the following:

- Accessibility of information about the status of certificates.
- The level of verification of the information in the certificate.
- Additional services.

We will discuss the first two issues in more detail because the additional services of a CA often depend on the intended use of the certificates.

As mentioned above, a certificate may be revoked and after that it should no longer be used for some purposes. In certain (typically high-value) transactions, it is important that information about revoked certificates is published as fast and reliably as possible. Other applications may be less vulnerable if a revoked certificate is used. The former is for example often the case in business sessions. A CA may, as an additional service, have an insurance covering losses due to the use of revoked certificates in the period from revocation to announcement of the revocation.

When issuing a certificate, it must be ensured that the owner is correctly identified and that he accepts to be the owner of the public key. Several levels of identification are currently used. At one level the identification of the user could be simple verification of an email address, while at another extreme, the certified user would have to visit a local RA and present a passport in order to identify himself. Obviously, the latter type of registration results in more reliable certificates, and that level may be necessary in critical applications. However, as this leads to a heavy registration procedure a simpler, but less secure, procedure is often followed (e.g., see Section 12.4.1 and IETF Working Group ()).

To enhance security, it must be ensured during certificate issuance that the user requesting a certificate really accepts the public key as his own. If no such proof is available, the user may subsequently deny having made a signature by simply claiming that the public key in the certificate belongs to someone else. Again different levels of guarantee can be offered by the PKI. For example, to solve such disputes the user may, during registration, have to sign by hand a contract explicitly stating that he is the "owner" of the given public key.

When it comes to non-repudiation issues (compared to the use of certificates only for authentication and encryption), the PKI quality depends on additional services. To ensure non-repudiation, legal requirements must be taken into consideration and certain restrictions and liability are posed on the user and the CA. Most noteworthy, the certificate should be backed by a hand-signed contract containing (a digest of) the public key and defining the liability and obligations of user and CA. This binds the user to a signature made with a specific key, so that the recipient recognizes that it comes from him and is able to prove this fact later to third parties in the case of dispute. This binding can be made more or less explicit.

In general, from a security point of view, high-quality PKI services seem to be advantageous, but they are not always required. As such services typically are more expensive than low-quality ones, a price-security trade-off will often lead to applications using PKI services with non-optimal security.

Thus we have a picture consisting of many CAs, each of which may issue certificates of different quality; each user will have several certificates with different properties from one or more of these CAs. It must be possible to select certificates *automatically* in a business session and it must be possible to decide whether or not to accept a new certificate from a user. The objective of trust management is to provide means allowing a user to specify the *policy* for the following actions:

- The use of his own certificates. For each certificate, the user must be able to specify under which circumstances that certificate can be used, e.g., a user might want to stay anonymous when buying video films and will allow only anonymous pseudonyms[1] in such contexts. Obviously "always" could be an option.
- The use of certificates received from other users. During a business session, the user may have received a certificate on a signature key from another user. It could then be desirable to specify the business situations where that certificate can be used, as this will allow use of the certificate in other sessions *without negotiation* with the peer (see Section 12.2.2).
- Accepting new certificates. This basically means that it must be possible to specify when CAs are trusted, so that new certificates can be accepted.

Local trust management must make sure that these choices are respected in business sessions when selecting certificates for a user and when receiving certificates from peers. In the following, we take a closer look at the possibilities

---

[1]Note that anonymity towards a business partner and non-repudiation are not mutually exclusive. The real identity might be known by the CA and could be revealed in the case of disputes.

and requirements for specifying these choices and using them when selecting certificates.

12.2.1 Specifying Trusted CAs and Acceptable Certificates

In an application, a user may at a certain point have a number of certified keys and have received a number of certificates from other users. In order to use these certificates as well as to accept new certificates from other users, it is necessary to lay out rules, known as policies.

Specifying the policy for new certificates from a CA (when they can be used) involves two things. First, the user must describe the *situations* in which certificates from a given CA can be accepted and, second, as a CA may issue certificates of different quality, *quality requirements* must be set. Thus, it must be possible to specify the "business situation" as well as the "quality of a PKI."

What does it mean to specify a business situation? We cannot give a definitive answer to this question as it depends on the environment where trust management is used. However, one parameter which has turned out to be useful is the name of a particular business application (e.g., "buying flight tickets") or the name of a group of business applications (e.g., "shopping"). A user can specify that a given certificate can be used in the application for buying flight tickets. Another parameter describing a business situation could be the name of the communicating entity (peer). For example, a user may have a certificate that he only wants to use for shopping at a few businesses. If the name "Otto Versand" is added to the specification of the situation, then the certificates can only be used in shopping applications with Otto Versand.

Obviously, for certificates received from others it does not make sense to specify the name of the peer since that name is already included in the certificate. This suggests that it must be possible to specify a situation differently depending on whether the user wants to define a policy for accepting CAs or for using his own or received certificates.

The parameters describing the quality of the PKI services depend on the CA, as there is no standardized definition of the various levels of quality of a PKI service. If the CA provides no options, there is no need to specify the quality. If, on the other hand, the CA supports different quality levels, the CA must supply a description of these, so that the user is able to define the required level of quality for each business situation.

For already known certificates, be it the user's own certificates or certificates from other parties, it only makes sense to specify the business situations where each certificate may be used, as the quality is usually pre-determined.

12.2.2 Selecting Certificates Automatically in a Business Session

Determining the certificates to be used in a given business session involves

– selecting the user's own certificates and
– selecting certificates of the peer.

In order to perform this, trust management clearly needs a description of the actual situation. This could be the name of the business application, and the required pseudonyms or credentials of the peer entities. (Note that users may have different names in different certificates, e.g., they can be named according to their function in a company, according to their real name or with a completely anonymous pseudonym.) Of course, anonymity could be a requirement as well. A shop may, for example, request that a registered customer uses a particular name, while an individual user may want to remain anonymous. In the latter case, the trust management must select a certificate that protects the privacy of the user.

Afterwards, the level of quality defined for this situation can be found. From the full description of the requirements and according to the policy specified by the user, potential trusted CAs can be determined. Among already known certificates, the ones issued by a potential trusted CA, and whose policy satisfies the requirements (situation and quality), are selected.

However, in practice, it turns out that selecting and accepting certificates based on this will be insufficient, as it only takes into account the requirements of the user. It is very likely that the caller of the service, i.e., higher layers of the framework or the business application, has additional requirements on the certificates that can be used, which the user may not be aware of. An obvious requirement could again be the quality of the PKI (e.g., an application involving expensive goods may require very high certainty that a certificate is not revoked). Furthermore, the caller may require that certain attributes are present in the certificates. For instance, it may require that

– the key pair used to sign an order was backed by a by hand-signed agreement (like the *SEMPER* Electronic-Commerce Agreement, *SECA*, see Chapters 3 and 14), or
– that the postal address of the user can be retrieved from the certificate.

Thus, automatic selection of a certificate must also take into account requirements due to the nature of the application, apart from the actual situation and the policy specified by the user.

The process of selecting certificates can either be *interactive* or *noninteractive*. In the latter case a user selects his own certificate according to the requirements and policies just mentioned. In the interactive selection case, a negotiation between the parties takes place and each user must select certificates based on his own requirements as well as the requirements received from the peer.

12.3 Design of Policy Management

Trust management must provide means for defining a trust policy and maintaining information about the policy of a user, as well as methods for selecting and accepting certificates according to the policy. This section suggests a design for handling trust management efficiently.

12.3.1 Maintaining Information about Policies

In order to maintain the information about the policy, three objects are necessary. One describes the policy for accepting (certificates from) CAs, one describes the policy for the use of the user's own certificates and one describes the policy for the use of certificates previously received from other parties.

Let `Situation` be a class that describes the situation in which a given certificate or CA can be used. Then the policy for the use of a particular certificate (be it the user's own certificate or one received from another party) can be represented as a list of `Situation` objects. `Situation` is defined as an abstract class, which must be subclassed as needed, to cover the description of policies for the user's own certificates and the ones received by other parties (as discussed above).

Similarly, the policy for accepting a CA (in particular the certificates issued by this CA) can be described as a list of objects consisting of a `Situation` object and a `QualityRequirement` object. Each pair describes that a certificate from the CA can be used in business sessions matching both the `Situation` object and the quality requirements described by the `QualityRequirement` object. Again the `Situation` object is actually an object of a suitable subclass of `Situation`.

Since there is no standardized definition of "quality of a PKI," the `QualityRequirement` class should be subclassed according to the quality levels offered by a given CA. Given a certificate it must be possible to decide if a given `QualityRequirement` is fulfilled. This can, for example, easily be done if the certificate describes its quality in an attribute (extension), which can then be compared with the given `QualityRequirement`.

We do not go further into the actual representation of lists corresponding to policies, but it must be possible to retrieve the certificates and CAs (including quality requirements) that are allowed for a given actual situation, as well as the entire policy for a given certificate or CA. The former is clearly necessary in the selection process, where certificates and CAs allowed in the actual situation must be retrieved, while the latter is necessary in order to easily display the policy for a given certificate or CA (see also Section 12.4.2).

12.3.2 Using Policies

Policies for certificates and CAs are used to automatically select and accept certificates. Certificates can be selected either non-interactively or interactively through negotiation with the communicating peer.

Selecting certificates requires a description of the actual situation in order to find CAs or certificates that the user is willing to accept in this situation. The class describing the actual situation is called `SituationDescription`. Given the `SituationDescription`, a `Situation` object must be able to decide if it is satisfied by the `SituationDescription` or not. If it is satisfied, a certificate can be chosen among those that can be used in the situation described by the `Situation` object. In other words, our abstract class `Situation` must define an operation

`Boolean` satisfy(`SituationDescription` situationDescription)

From `SituationDescription` and `Situation`, it is thus possible to identify certificates and CAs matching the policies of the user. As explained above, the service in which the certificates are going to be used may have additional requirements on the chosen certificates. We distinguish two types of requirements:

— mandatory requirements, which must be defined in any case, and
— optional or extensible requirements corresponding to additional specific requirements.

In order to impose as few demands as possible on the caller, the number of mandatory requirements should not be high, and we have, in fact, identified only one such requirement: the use of the certified key. Whenever a caller requests certificates, it should specify the intended usage of the key. This could be expressed very simply by a request for a signature or encryption key, but in general, there may be more cases.

We do not have a full picture of the possible parameters which may go into the optional requirements, and it does not seem possible to make a fixed standardized set of such requirements used when selecting certificates. However, we suggest to group these requirements as follows:

— Requirements on values of certificate attributes, including extensions in X.509v3 certificates. One example, used in *SEMPER*, is the requirement that the use of the certified key is backed by *SECA*.
— Requirements on the quality of the PKI. The `QualityRequirement` object (e.g., support for revocation, the class of the certificate, etc.) corresponds to this.

`SelectionRequirement` is the base class that describes the optional requirements posed by the caller. Requirements not already supported in the base class `SelectionRequirement` can be described in a suitable subclass. In order to enable the selection of certificates, the class `SelectionRequirement` must supply methods that determine whether a given CA or certificate satisfies the selection requirement.

Note that the mandatory requirement on specifying the use of the key could be expressed also as a part of the `SelectionRequirement` class (e.g., in X.509v3, a `keyUsage` extension has been defined). We suggest, however, to treat this requirement separately in order to enforce that the caller must always make clear what the key should be used for. Hence, in *SEMPER*, we keep this requirement separate from the optional ones.

With the above setup, trust management can now select a suitable certificate among the user's available certificates. This is done as follows:

- The caller (the entity using trust management) defines the requirements to the user's certificates. These include a description of the use of the key as well as the optional requirements described by a `SelectionRequirement` object.
- The caller constructs a appropriate `SituationDescription` object to describe the business session.
- Based on the `SituationDescription` the certificates allowed to be used in this situation are retrieved (by using the satisfy method on `Situation` objects).
- Among these certificates, one matching the mandatory and optional requirements from the caller is selected.

In a similar way, an appropriate certificate for the peer can be selected among those certificates already received from the peer.

12.3.3 Negotiation of Certificates

In the following we consider how the above procedure can be extended to allow interactive selection of certificates based on negotiation with the communicating peer, where two parties want to agree on a single certificate from each. In order to achieve this, each entity using the trust management functionality (i.e., at both sides of the negotiation) must describe:

- the business scenario (a `SituationDescription` object);
- the required `keyUsage` and a `SelectionRequirement` object of the user's own certificate; and
- the required `keyUsage` and a `SelectionRequirement` object for the certificate of the peer.

If more certificates are negotiated, the two entities must prepare the requirements for each certificate. Given this information, two trust management entities A and B are now ready to *interactively* agree on certificates. This can in principle be done in many ways, but we suggest to do it in a way that reveals as little information as possible about those certificates that are not chosen and the policies of a user. Assuming that A is the party initiating the negotiation, one way to do this is the following:

1. Based on A's policy, potential CAs are selected matching the input (`SituationDescription`, `keyUsage`, and possible quality requirements in `SelectionRequirement`).

2. *A* sends the list of acceptable CAs to *B*, including the requirements defined by *A*'s policy, plus the `keyUsage` requirement and `SelectionRequirement` related to *B*'s certificate.
3. *B* selects all possible certificates matching his own policy based on the requirements on his own side (as described in the preceding section). Among these certificates, one is selected that also matches the requirements received from the peer (quality requirements as well as key usage).
4. *B* then sends back the chosen certificate and:
   - the list of CAs that *B* accepts in the given situation plus the quality requirement,
   - the requirement on key usage, and
   - possible optional requirements given by a `SelectionRequirement` object.
5. *A* can now select a certificate as *B* did, and send the certificate back to *B*.

12.4 Prototype Implementation

12.4.1 Public-Key Infrastructure in the *SEMPER* Trials

No infrastructure of local RAs that the users could visit in person was available for the *SEMPER* trials. Furthermore, we could not assume that the users would be willing to bear the same registration overhead for a mere trial as they would before really entering a wide range of electronic commerce with the corresponding risks. Nevertheless we wanted to give the users an idea that registration is a security-critical and somewhat involved procedure. The following compromise procedure was used:

Establishing certificates in *SEMPER* involved in addition to an RA and a CA (see Section 12.1) the following two kinds of players:

- A *service provider* was the organization which provided the online services. See Chapter 7 for more details.
- A *user* was anyone who applied for a certificate at the registration or certification authority, respectively.

Thus a participant such as Otto-Versand acted as a service provider towards the customers and as a user when getting a certificate from the CA.

In *SEMPER* the certification authority was located at and operated by GMD, the German National Research Center for Information Technology. The registration authority was split between the service providers, which acquired the trial participants and acted as the RA's "front desk," and GMD, which coordinated and managed the registration information. This does not completely reflect the real world, where the service providers in most cases would not be involved in the registration process. The users would go personally to a separate registration authority and get registered after filling in the registration form there.

The following steps had to be performed in order to get registered and to obtain a user certificate for the *SEMPER* trials:

1. *Pre-arrangement between service providers and certification authority:* Through a secure channel (e.g., personal messengers, closed secure private network, secure mail, etc.) every service provider in *SEMPER* received a letter from the certification authority. This letter contained, among other things, the fingerprint of the public key of the certification authority running at GMD.

2. *Pre-arrangement between service providers and users:* Users who intended to deploy the *SEMPER* software contacted their service provider(s). The service provider collected the users' data and sent it electronically over a secure channel to GMD, the CA. The CA maintained all the information of these pre-registered users in a pre-registration database.

   In the trial with Otto-Versand, this phase also involved a registration with the Otto Customer service.

3. *Pre-registration phase:* Each user now received a registration letter and the *SEMPER* software. The registration letter contained, besides the terms & conditions and some information on the trial, a unique and secret registration key (i.e., a text string) and the fingerprint of the public key of the certification authority.

4. *SECA contract signing, optional:* If a user wished to obtain a *SECA* certificate (see Chapter 3), he had to sign a *SECA* contract. To this end a stand-alone application was provided which allowed the user to select the *SECA* attributes, such as liability limits, and to produce a *SECA* contract. After signing the *SECA* contract, the *SECA* contract was sent to the RA/CA on paper.

5. *Registration phase:* The user established a secure connection to the registration authority via SEMPER and requested an online registration form. The registration form was filled out by the user and sent back to the registration authority via this channel. The registration authority verified all information supplied by the user. Based on the user information in the registration form, the registration authority issued the digital user registration. A copy of the registration was sent to the certification authority.

6. *Certification phase:* The user sent a message to the certification authority requesting a certificate. The certification authority issued certificates for the user corresponding to the user registration that was sent by the registration authority in the previous step. After that, the certificate was sent to the user.

7. *Obtaining SECA certificates, optional:* The user could now request his *SECA* certificate. If the CA had received the corresponding *SECA* contract, a *SECA* certificate was issued containing the *SECA* attributes contained in the *SECA* contract as extension attributes.

As mentioned in Section 12.3, the allowed usage of the certified keys was indicated in the certificate.

During the registration and certification process, the mutual authentication of user and RA/CA had to be guaranteed: the user must be assured that he contacts the right RA/CA, and the RA/CA must be able to check that the user who requests the registration and certification is indeed the right, pre-registered user.

– *Client authentication:* In the certificate and registration request, the user had to send his confidential registration key as part of the registration form to the RA/CA (in this case, GMD) along with some personal information. Using the pre-registration database the RA/CA was able to check the authenticity of the request on-line, register the user and issue certificates for him thereafter.

– *CA authentication:* It is extremely important for users to know that the certification authority is authentic. Not only might somebody else steal the registration key to masquerade the user, but the whole security of the PKI in future transactions will tumble if a bogus public key of the CA is accepted, because wrong certificates from others would be accepted. In other words, the certification authority should authenticate itself to the users. As mentioned before, the users received a hard copy of the fingerprint of the certification authority's public key in a registration letter. In addition the user received the electronic copy of that public key during the registration procedure. The fingerprint of the received public key was computed locally at the user side and presented to the user through the TINGUIN. The user had to compare the two fingerprints, one on the TINGUIN display and one in the hardcopy form. If the user accepted the fingerprint of the public key as equal, the authenticity of the public key could be assured and the *SEMPER* software ensured that all further communication with the CA was performed over a secure and authentic channel.

Every user owned at least two key pairs in the *SEMPER* trials, one for signature and one for encryption purposes. Both public keys had to be certified. Thus, the certification phase had to be executed twice, first for the signature key and then for the encryption key. If a user required a *SECA* certificate, this certificate was issued in an optional third run.

12.4.2 Trust Management

The trust-management design described previously follows the one used in the *SEMPER* prototype, but includes a few improvements based on the experiences gained. In the following, we briefly outline implementation aspects and point out the differences from the design described in Section 12.3. In the *SEMPER* implementation, a class called `CertBag` is used to maintain the policy for certificates, while a class `AcceptPolicy` is used to maintain the policy for the use of CAs. Two subclasses of `Situation` (somewhat misleading) called `PolicyId` and `GeneralPolicyId` are used, and a class `CertRequirement` is used to express the requirements on CAs that issue certificates.

See Figure 12.1 for an overview (actually, `Situation` is an interface in *SEMPER* and `GeneralPolicyId` is a superclass of `PolicyId` implementing this interface). `GeneralPolicyId` allows to describe a `Situation` by defining only the name of the business application, while `PolicyId` extends this by adding the name of the peer. `GeneralPolicyId` is used to specify business situations where CAs and received certificates can be used, while `PolicyId` is used to specify the situations where the user's own certificates can be used.

Situation
<<Interface>>

GeneralPolicyId

PolicyId

Fig. 12.1. Situation hierarchy in the *SEMPER* prototype.

`AcceptPolicy` maintains information about the policy for using a given CA. This object maintains for each CA a list of `GeneralPolicyId` objects, each describing the business applications in which the user wants to accept certificates from the given CA. Each CA is described by an object that defines requirements on names for that CA. These requirements must be satisfied in order to accept certificates from that CA,[2] and are introduced in `NameRequirement` objects that can express two things:

Registration level It describes the level of certainty with which the user is identified during the certification process.

---

[2]Due to the experiences gained in *SEMPER*, the design in Section 12.3 differs from this.

Identification level It describes the amount of information about the user in the certificate.

Possible identification and registration levels will depend on the module and the registration procedures supported by the whole PKI, part of which is the CA.

The `NameRequirement` is not used in the certificate selection in *SEMPER*, and we remark that this class should have been a subclass of the `SelectionRequirement` class mentioned in Section 12.3. This subclass could also have been used to express requirements on *SECA* certificates. In the implementation of the *SEMPER* prototype, these requirements on *SECA* certificates are squeezed into the `SituationDescription` class as discussed below.

The assignment of policies (list of `Situation` objects) to CAs, and certificates, is supported through two applications using the TINGUIN. Figure 12.2 depicts some of the screens that the user sees when defining his policy.

In the *SEMPER* prototype, the business situations are described either by the name of the business application (`GeneralPolicyId`) or by both the name of the business application and the name of the peer. Figure 12.3 illustrates policies (lists of `PolicyId` objects) for the user's own certificates.

The chosen certificates are maintained in `CertificateContext` objects. *SEMPER* distinguishes between certified keys used for signatures and certified keys used for encryption. A `CertificateContext` object can be prepared to hold an encryption or a signature certificate for a particular user or both, to force the caller to specify which type of key is needed. Normally, two such objects are required—one holding certificates of the user and the other holding the certificates of the peer. A `CertificateContext` can be established when negotiating the certificates with the peer, as well as when retrieving certificates non-interactively (establishing a context for the peer non-interactively requires that the user has already received certificates in a previous negotiation with the peer). The negotiation takes place as described in Section 12.3.3, except that no `SelectionRequirement` objects are used as mentioned above.

A simple `SituationDescription` class has been implemented, describing the actual situation with the use of the following parameters:

- Preferred pseudonym of the user.
- Preferred pseudonym of the peer.
- Name of the business application in which the certificates are to be used.
- Requirements on *SECA*. Using this attribute it is possible to require a *SECA* certificate as well as to specify the values of the *SECA* attributes.

Note here that according to the design in Section 12.3, the requirements on *SECA* should have been in a separate `SelectionRequirement` class. But, as mentioned previously, this class is not supported in the prototype. One price

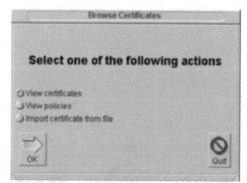

(a) The start-up of the trust management functions;

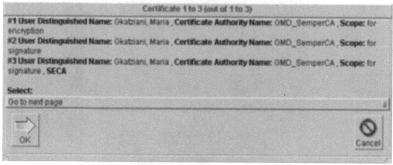

(b) the available certificates;

(c) the available CAs.

Fig. 12.2. Assigning policies to CAs and certificates (1).

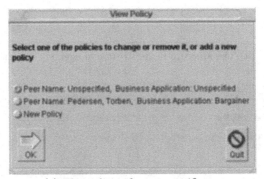

(a) The policies for one certificate;

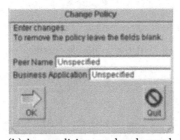

(b) how policies can be changed.

Fig. 12.3. Assigning policies to CAs and certificates. (2)

we had to pay for that is that during the negotiation it is not possible to have different *SECA* requirements for the user himself and the peer.

The SituationDescription class contains the parameters for the creation of PolicyId and GeneralPolicyId objects. Thus it is straightforward to see if an object of one of these two classes is satisfied by the actual situation. The preferred pseudonym of the user is included, as a user may have different names in different certificates. This allows the (user through the) calling service to specify that a particular pseudonym should be used.

It is worth mentioning how the validity of the selected certificates is handled in the *SEMPER* prototype. Unfortunately there is no provision for on-line verification of certificates and no support for certificates revocation lists. The trust-management functionality requires that the user has the root certificate of the CA that signed the certificates stored in his archive. Chosen certificates are then validated locally and are rejected unless they can be correctly verified.

12.5 Related Work

Trust management is to some extent available in most Internet browsers, in which it is possible to install certificates of peers and CAs. In the following, the trust management in Netscape Communicator as well as in Microsoft Internet Explorer is discussed. Other browsers are likely to offer similar services.

Apart from Internet browsers, which are implemented systems on the application level, PolicyMaker (Blaze, Feigenbaum, and Lacy 1996), the best-known proposal for addressing the decentralized trust management problem, is described. PolicyMaker can be built into an application (as a library) or run as a daemon process.

12.5.1 Netscape Communicator

For the user's own certificates it is possible to designate one certificate as the default one to be used for encryption and signing when sending e-mail. Moreover, when a user has to be identified to a web site he can specify whether he prefers to be asked every time for a certificate, or to choose a certificate automatically, or to designate a particular certificate for identification to any web site.

For certificates received from CAs it is possible to specify that the given CA is trusted in different situations:

- for certifying network sites,
- for certifying e-mail users, and
- for certifying software developers.

This resembles to some extent the *SEMPER* proposal, except that *SEMPER* allows more flexibility by letting the user specify the situations where a CA or certificate can be trusted, corresponding to the wider range of possible situations in electronic commerce.

More elaborate trust management is provided for handling signed code (e.g., signed Java applets and JavaScript scripts) and the certificates of the signers. (In the *SEMPER* architecture, these aspects do not belong to the Certificate Block described here, but to the Module Installer and the Access Control Block.) Here it is possible to grant privileges to the certificates of the signers. In that way different levels of access can be given for instance to signed applets depending on who signed the applet. For example the user can view the certificate with which the JavaScript script or Java applet has been signed, and then he can grant or deny access for reading files from his computer, which is considered a high-risk privilege.

Trust management is easy to handle using Netscape Communicator. The certificates are classified in categories and the possible applications are listed so that the user can specify at any time when a certificate can be used.

12.5.2 Microsoft Internet Explorer

Microsoft Internet Explorer handles the user's own certificates in the same way as Netscape Communicator: It is possible to specify a certificate to be used for encrypting and signing when sending e-mail.

For the certificates received from other users, a trust status indicates whether the user trusts the individual, group or corporation to whom the certificate was issued. According to the trust status, the certificate can then be used for the specified purposes such as trusting a web site or sending and receiving e-mail.

There are three options for the trust granted. The user can select either to have the same level of trust as the one specified for the CA that issued the certificate, or trust the certificate irrespectively of whether he trusts the issuer. It is also possible to explicitly distrust the certificate or the person or company it is associated with.

When the user receives a certificate from a CA, he can place it in his list of trusted issuers by enabling it. Different uses for the certificate can be specified:

– network client authentication,
– network server authentication,
– secure e-mail, and
– network publishing.

However, there is a disadvantage in the way Internet Explorer handles the trust put in a CA's certificate: Once the user has specified for what the certificate is trusted, he cannot change it any more.

The way Internet Explorer handles trust management seems rather complicated. The certificates can be viewed by using the Address Book as a part of the personal details of a user. There is no clear distinction of certificates, and a CA certificate can be displayed only by selecting to edit the issuer's certificate of a person's certificate.

12.5.3 PolicyMaker

PolicyMaker (Blaze, Feigenbaum, and Lacy 1996) is a prototype for a trust management system which claims to be efficient and sufficiently reliable for electronic-commerce applications. It comes in response to deficiencies of PGP (its reliability may suffice only for personal communication) and the X.509 authentication framework that assumes a global tree structure of CAs.

PolicyMaker resembles a database query tool. It gets as input a collection of local policy statements, a set of credentials and a description of the proposed action, and allows or disallows the proposed action if the evaluation procedure returned a yes or no reply. (In the *SEMPER* architecture, this corresponds primarily to the Credentials Block, not to the Certificate Block.) It distinguishes between restrictions provided locally and application-specific ones. In order to decide if an action is allowed or not, the PolicyMaker binds public keys to predicates that describe the actions they are trusted to sign for, rather than to the names of the key owners. In that way, applications can also include anonymity as a security requirement. For trusted CAs no assumption of a global tree structure is made. The user specifies whether he trusts a CA or not in certain circumstances or proposed actions, according to the reliability he requests and the quality services the CA may offer.

The PolicyMaker prototype resembles the trust management system of *SEMPER*. A major difference is that PolicyMaker makes no attempt to define policies. In *SEMPER* we have tried to add semantics that can describe the information maintained for policies, whereas in PolicyMaker there is no such suggestion. It is left to each application to define a set of application-specific policies. Another difference is that PolicyMaker does not validate the signatures on the certificates used in the processed queries. An external program instead should verify them, whereas in *SEMPER* this is a part of the trust-management functionality.

13. Limiting Liability in Electronic Commerce

Digital signatures are supposed to ensure non-repudiation. However, depending on the environment, attacks might obtain signatures in an underhanded way. This implies conflicting interests: The key holder does not want to be held liable for signatures he has not made. The relying party wants to rely on a digital signature and be able to enforce it in a law court. This chapter tries to find an acceptable compromise. It introduces the necessity for limiting liability for digitally signed transactions, presents the Commitment Service and shows how it can be used as Liability-Cover Service to limit the key holder's overall liability for digitally signed messages. The main principle is a separation between deniable signatures and undeniable commitments.

13.1 Introduction

13.1.1 Necessity to Limit Liability

Digital signatures (Diffie and Hellman 1976; Menezes, van Oorschot, and Vanstone 1997) are currently not established to be used as equivalents to "handwritten" signatures. A uniform legal framework has not yet been built to recognize digital signatures in the same manner as handwritten signatures (compare Chapters 3 and 14). The EU Directive on "Electronic Signatures" (European Union 2000) is a considerable step in that direction, at least for electronic commerce within the European member states and others that will apply the Directive. However, none of the existing approaches is able to solve all problems which could and should be solved. The main reason is that they do not cover the entire system environment at the key holder's side.

In spite of sufficiently secure existing signing algorithms, the technical possibility of obtaining signatures in an underhanded way, aided by such mechanisms as Trojan horse attacks, cannot be ignored. Such attacks might result in an unpredictably high damage for the key holder, especially if he cannot prove that an attack has happened. Hundreds or thousands of transactions can be made within a short time by an attack.

To protect the key holder as well as the relying party, we recommend to implement digital signature laws based on the emerging EU Directive (see

G. Lacoste et al. (Eds.): SEMPER 2000, LNCS 1854, pp. 233–255, 2000.
© Springer-Verlag Berlin Heidelberg 2000

also Chapter 14) only in combination with Commitment Service developed by *SEMPER* as presented in this chapter.

Trojan-Horse Attacks. Trojan horses would not affect the signing algorithms themselves. They could manipulate the information to be signed without being noticed by the key holder. Even when smartcards are used for storing keys and performing the signing algorithm, passphrases might be captured. Even for very sophisticated secure smartcard solutions, Trojan horse attacks might choose another malicious strategy: they could pop up a window which looks exactly like the window the key holder expects and which contains the information he or she intends to sign, but then inject—unnoticed by the key holder—completely different information which would actually be signed. For software-only equipment, attacks can be performed even more easily by capturing passphrases or even the signing key itself.

Trojan horses, no matter for which configuration or environment they have been designed, might typically be part of a program different from the one to be attacked (e.g., an electronic-commerce program). They might be located on the same machine or network and thus be executed by the machine which runs the program to be attacked. The latter itself might even have been designed absolutely correct, or at least, might have been designed correctly under the assumption that the operation system does exactly what its specification says and nothing else. Most programs today are designed based on this assumption, and especially for software-only solutions, there is no real chance to design a program which is able to prevent other programs from affecting it. This means: A software solution for digital signatures might be completely correct and nevertheless cannot prevent malicious Trojan horse attacks. This situation will persist as long as no really provably secure operating systems exists which can prevent applications from affecting each other. A good protection, in terms of attack detection, can be provided by so-called "secure devices" which are tamper-resistant, store the secret key and perform the signature without leaving the device, and have a display to show the user exactly what he signs.

Other Attacks. There are other kinds of attacks which have to be mentioned here, too. For those attacks, as well as for the malicious Trojan horse attacks, we want to reduce the key holder's potential damage. The Commitment Service presented in this chapter will be the vehicle to achieve this.

Let us start with some attacks which can easily be avoided by the user himself, and increase the seriousness along the considered attacks.

- This "attack" is performed by the user himself. It can be seen as any disruptive element which leads to an unintended signature of the user. It might be caused by the user himself.
- The attacker uses the user's passphrase which he finds written near the user's computer.
- The attacker continues the user's session and makes a signed transaction while the user left his computer for a moment.

– The attacker makes a signed transaction based on the knowledge he has received directly or indirectly from the user (e.g., via a secretary who once made a signature on behalf of the user).

Just some discipline is needed to avoid those attacks. Our solution will additionally restrict potential damage even for those simple attacks. There are further attacks which our solution makes less damaging for the user:

– The attacker forces the user to sign some information, aided by brute force or other means.
– The attacker breaks the signing function of the key holder and produces signed transactions.
– The attacker knows the hole in the user's bad or malicious signing software and exploits it.
– The attacker lets a self-produced key be certified as being the key of the user and creates signed transactions on behalf of the user.

The latter attack should be prevented by a proper identity check of the user by the certification authority before certifying his public key. To be complete, we also list here the Trojan horse attacks mentioned above:

– The attacker makes the user load a program which is able to inject some information the signing program will sign (and send), without being noticed by the user.

The Commitment Service to be presented in this chapter will limit the user's damage for all these kinds of attacks. This holds for software-only solutions as well as for smartcard solutions.

Consequences of the Existence of Attacks. Without the existence of any attacks, handling digital signatures would be much easier. Each digital signature could serve as the proof that the key holder has signed a certain message. The key holder would not have any possibility to deny having signed. Within a legal framework, this would mean that the apparent signatory might be forced to fulfil what he signed—provided he agreed initially to be bound to the technical signature considered.

A legal framework, if appropriate for general electronic commerce over the Internet involving private, non-technical users, should take into account that average Internet users, in particular those who do not want to accept restrictions of their freedom in downloading and installing any programs from the Internet, will not be able to avoid or exclude such Trojan horse attacks. In most cases, they even do not know the risks and often are convinced by mistake of using a secure operating system. Therefore, approaches which put the full responsibility of avoiding Trojan horse attacks on the users are not appropriate. Probably most of the users would commit to keep their passphrases secret. Probably many of them would be willing to commit to be responsible for their own equipment and to keep it free from malicious software, maybe just based on the conviction that they are the only person using their PC. However, most of them will not commit to never download or install any additional software, after installing the electronic-commerce software, and to delete all the previously installed software once downloaded from the web or installed from disks or CDs received via advertising mails. Anyway, it cannot even be assumed that the software coming from well-known manufacturers is always 100% free of viruses and Trojan horses, or that virus protection programs will find the Trojan horses contained. Thus, the typical private Internet user cannot really control his environment entirely to ensure that he will never fall victim to an attack. Nor can many commercial players, either.

In this chapter, we do not consider techniques to prevent such attacks—for this we refer to Chapter 14. On the contrary, we propose a solution which enables users to live with the possibility and occurrence of Trojan horses, even while using software-only signature functionality and downloaded software. Our solution restricts the potential damage to an a-priori limit which can be chosen by the key holder himself. A further advantage of our solution is that this limit even includes damage by extortion.

Further measures for protection against damage by Trojan horses are recommended because they will bring the risk of the actual liability closer to zero.

Potential Damage to Involved Players in the Case of Attacks. We assume that the considered digital signatures are legally binding, and that attacks might not be able to be proven, e.g., because Trojan horses can destroy themselves after a successful attack. Furthermore, we assume that the law court—based on insufficient evidence to decide whether or not the signature was actually attacked—might take the wrong decision.

Potential damage to the key holder. The damage to the key holder in the case of attacks might be high without prior limit:

Assume an attack which produces several orders, e.g., for wagons of fresh fruit or fresh meat, to different providers. The faked orders make it plausible to each of the providers that the high quantity of food in this single order is needed, e.g., for a big conference. The attack could intend to damage the apparent signer: Either he takes all the food and pays the money, or he withdraws the orders and pays a high compensation to the suppliers, or he makes himself untrustworthy to other parties (e.g., the suppliers of food) by denying the orders on the grounds that he had fallen victim to a Trojan horse attack.

The amount of one single order could be much lower, and at the same time the number of orders and of recipients of the orders could be much higher. This shows that in the case of an attack, the damage of the key holder can be unpredictably high if the court decides in favour of the relying parties.

Potential damage to the relying party. The relying parties might suffer the same damage as with fulfilled orders without getting paid.

Assume a similar attack as described above: The court could decide, this time, in favour of the attacked key holder, which could mean that the relying parties, i.e., the providers of fresh fruit or fresh meat, would have to take the damage themselves.

Another kind of attack might be that a Trojan horse within some program is downloaded by several people (e.g., customers of a certain service) from a fake server which pretends to be the one of their common service provider. That Trojan horse might aim at damaging another service provider, e.g., a supplier of fresh fruit. That supplier would get numerous orders for high quantities of fresh fruit, and based on those orders, would in his turn order fresh fruit which he would have to pay. However, all the apparent signers would claim not to have signed, and—due to the occurrence of so many denied orders by independent players—the court might believe the attack. The court might even suspect the merchant himself of having produced the Trojan horse to increase his earnings.

Even without a Trojan horse the merchant might be damaged: In a situation looking very similar to a law court, the conspiring signers might lie in claiming that they haven't signed. They might try to damage the supplier and just try out (with an acceptable low risk for each of them, but with a high risk for the attacked supplier) if the court will believe that all orders were faked—they will succeed to find expert witnesses who will confirm that such Trojan horses can exist. How should the court be able to decide "correctly"?

This shows at least that the merchant might run the risk of accepting a high amount of orders without getting paid after fulfilling them.

13.1.2 Separation Between Digital Signature and Undeniable Commitment

In most of the current approaches for applications using digital signatures, two aspects of a digitally signed transaction are mixed together: The digital signature bound to an entity, and the legally binding commitment, given by the transaction. A user's digital signature is usually meant as a proof that the user has signed a certain transaction. The signature is intended to serve as a guarantee to the recipient, which can be enforced in court. The examples above show that those approaches have several disadvantages, especially in environments and scenarios prone to certain attacks.

For our solution we aim at a separation between the following two aspects:

- A digital signature for identity authentication and message authentication which mostly will work but can be denied in certain cases (e.g., when provided under extortion, or in the case of an attack, but also if the signer lies).
- A binding commitment, witnessed and provided by a third party, as a means of trust on which the recipient can rely in case the digital signature

is denied. This binding commitment cannot be denied, not even in the case of attacks. Hence we call it an *undeniable commitment*.

The necessity of this separation depends, of course, on the intended use of the digital signature as well as on the environment where it is used.

In which cases is a separation not needed?. Not separating deniable signature and binding commitment from each other so strictly can, of course, be justified in many applications and environments:

- When legal binding is no issue at all, e.g., if the digital signature is used for plausibility reasons without any further consequences if the signature is denied, e.g., in many informal transactions including secure email (e.g., within closed user groups like companies, consortia, government, business), many voting, some bidding applications, even contract signing if it is clear between the parties that any denied signature (which might be considered unlikely) will make the parties conclude the contract by other means.
- If the environment is closed and the occurrence of attacks is highly improbable, e.g., in many medical applications, or in cases where the damage would be relatively small, e.g., for buying bus tickets etc.
- If secure hardware is used which can safely be trusted and includes secure I/O so that the signer always sees what he actually signs—a good possibility for all areas including high-value electronic commerce over the Internet.
- If the digital signature is used in applications where the relying party is prepared to take the risk that the apparent signer might claim not having made a certain signature, e.g., in some bank applications for electronic funds transfer, or if the relying party anyway uses additional means to reduce the risk for high-value or other critical transactions, e.g., by calling back the apparent signer.

In which situations is a separation recommended?. In all scenarios we are considering in *SEMPER*, e.g., in open electronic commerce over the Internet involving non-technical and private players, a separation between signature and undeniable commitment is highly recommended. Otherwise, the key holder might have to suffer damage to an extent which he would probably not have accepted if he had had the choice. Similarly, the relying party might suffer damage from denied transactions.

Especially, a separation is highly recommended if

- digital signatures are legally binding, and the use of the digital signature is not limited (e.g., by the volume of transactions per month) *and*
- applications using digital signatures are established in a way that attacks might be profitable, *and*
- the environment enables transactions, e.g., over the Internet, so that Trojan horse attacks might become active, *and*
- no secure hardware is used for the signing functionality, *and*

– there is no party which takes all the liability a priori (e.g., the seller or the bank).

In the remainder of this chapter, we assume this scenario because it is considered typical for the increasing electronic marketplace on the Internet.

13.1.3 Principles and Achievements of the Solution Proposed

We propose the Commitment Service which, on the one hand, allows the potential damage for the key holder to be limited, and, on the other hand, provides undeniable commitments for the relying party.

Principles. The Commitment Service is based on the following principles:

– Key holders can provide undeniable commitments: A commitment certification authority issues those guarantees on behalf of the key holder, but only up to a key holder pre-defined limit (e.g., per month).
– Key holders generally have to keep to what they signed using their digital signatures, without restriction or limit. In this respect, the digital signature has similarity to the handwritten signature which can be used without restriction or limit and might be denied if the apparent signer claims forgery.
– If a key holder claims a compromised key, then this is "believed", in the first place. However, if the transaction includes an undeniable commitment, the key holder must fulfill it, independently of whether it was obtained based on an attack or not.
– Blacklists can be used to warn users of other users who claimed a compromised key—be it justified or not.[1]

In this way, key holders do not have to fear too much liability caused by compromised keys or signatures received in an underhanded way, even in cases where the attack cannot be proven. Their obligations in the case of attacks (or pretended attacks) will never exceed the user-predefined limit for issued commitments.

On the other hand, the verifiers, i.e., the relying parties, do not necessarily have to fear damage by the apparent signer's claim that his signature on a certain transaction message (e.g., an order) was compromised—provided they always require an undeniable commitment covering the damage expected if the signature is denied.

For the risk to be taken by the key holder, the following holds:

– The more flexibility he wants, the higher the risk he has to take. This corresponds to the amount for which the commitment certification authority can issue undeniable commitments.
– The better he protects himself from attacks by additional means and discipline, the less probable will be any actual damage due to the risk taken.

---

[1]This is only possible if accepted by data-protection laws. For instance, blacklists would not be acceptable in Germany.

Achievements of the Commitment Service. The Commitment Service will be presented in more detail in Section 13.2. However, its main achievements are already summarized here:

1. It enables a *separation* between signatures which can be denied in the compromised case, and undeniable commitments.
2. It enables the *key holder to limit his risk* in case of compromised signatures. The key holder can choose his own limit.
3. It enables the *relying party to request undeniable commitments* of any meaningful amount.
4. If the undeniable commitment is related to the signing key used for transactions, the *relying party need not consult the certificate revocation list (CRL)* for the corresponding public key, as the issued commitment confirms that the key was not revoked. It only needs to check that the commitment certification authority's key was not revoked (which is less likely, hopefully).
5. It can *perform time-stamping* for the transaction at least in the way that the transaction cannot be backdated. If the commitment certificate is issued before the key was revoked, and used after the key was revoked, it will stay valid nevertheless. What exactly will be time-stamped beyond a unique transaction context ID can be chosen by the players. Also the complete content of a transaction can be time-stamped if the signer wishes.
6. It can be performed in a way that *the transaction and the relying party are not revealed* to the commitment certification authority. Only a unique ID of the former and a hash of the latter need to be revealed to the commitment certification authority.
7. It can be used in a *most flexible way* to allow the user to specify any undeniable commitments, even other than covering amounts of money, and conditions which must be fulfilled to make a commitment valid.
8. It does not have to wait for a harmonization of the legal situation nationally or internationally. It can be built and used right now.

13.2 Description of the Commitment Service

The Commitment Service has some similarities to credit-card systems where the bank checks some limit before issuing the "authorization response" to the merchant.

In a similar way, the so-called *commitment certification authority, CCA,* controls the issued undeniable commitments of a subscriber so that those commitments cannot exceed a certain volume, e.g., per month. Exactly this limits the damage for the subscriber in case of attacks.

However, there are essential differences to credit-card systems:

1. A Commitment Service is not a payment system. Binding commitments can be made independently of a payment (the latter might be performed at a later stage). The commitment is bound to a unique transaction context and to the beneficiary.
2. The subscriber of a Commitment Service can define his (e.g., monthly) limits himself. A credit limit for a credit-card system however is usually defined by the bank and influenced by the status of the bank account.
3. The subscriber of a Commitment Service defines the amount of an issued undeniable commitment himself, unlike with credit-card payments where the merchant's authorization request can include an amount lower or higher than the amount processed in the transaction itself, unnoticed by the customer (typically done for rented cars or hotel reservations).
4. A compromised signature can be denied in the case of an attack, if it is associated with a Commitment Service. The undeniable commitments involved determine the obligations of the apparent signer. However, if a bank issues an "authorization response," this does not necessarily mean an obligation to pay, especially not if an attack had happened.

13.2.1 What Exactly is an Undeniable Commitment?

Saying "undeniable commitment," we mean a legally binding commitment which can be enforced in court. If the commitment is associated with a condition, the commitment has to be fulfilled if the condition is satisfied. The condition can itself consist of a logic expression of several conditions.

We use the following trick: The subscriber has to initially commit himself, per contract with the CCA, to fulfil all commitments issued by the CCA, up to a certain limit (e.g., per month). We call this the *initial commitment* of the subscriber. On the other hand, the CCA commits not to issue undeniable commitments which exceed the limit, and only to issue commitments which have apparently been authorized by the subscriber (e.g., were signed with the subscriber's key which has not been revoked). This means that the subscriber initially commits to fulfill commitments issued by the CCA *before* he knows if and how many commitments will be authorized later. At the same time, this means that the subscriber has to fulfill all commitments—up to a certain limit—which are issued by the CCA but the authorization of which was obtained by an attack. Exactly this is what makes the undeniable commitment very valuable for the relying party: Commitments are to be fulfilled by the subscriber even in the case of claimed attacks.

At a first glance, the process might look as if the subscriber gave blank cheques to the CCA to be filled in and issued by the CCA—hopefully in most cases after an authorization by the subscriber. However, even in the case of attacks, the subscriber is protected as far as he does not have to fulfil commitments which exceed his pre-defined limits.

13.2.2 Initialization of the Subscriber

Registration. At the beginning, the subscriber and his key are registered at the CCA (or any local commitment registration authority, CRA). The CCA is responsible and liable for the fact that the correct entity is registered—a crucial requirement since binding commitments will be assigned to the registered entity.

Set of commitments. The subscriber defines his set of commitments (or limits for amounts, respectively) to be controlled by the CCA. This set can refer to a certain month, to each month, or be a total amount. Different sets can be defined for different periods. Examples of commitments might be a certain amount of money (e.g., Euro 2000), but also goods or services. This includes the possibility of having different limits for different purposes or for different types of authorization.

Validity conditions. At the same time, the subscriber defines, separately for each set of commitments, the conditions under which the commitments shall be valid. The following examples suggest that there is a wide range of possibilities, also for combinations.

1. Valid if and only if the digital signature of the related transaction was claimed compromised.
2. Valid if and only if the subscriber withdraws the related transaction, this being accepted by the relying party.
3. Valid if and only if the relying party shows information X signed with the secret key belonging to the public key pk (this can even be another undeniable commitment).
4. Valid under a certain condition being defined by the subscriber later when authorizing the commitment.

The validity of subscriber-defined conditions only concerns the subscriber and the relying party; they do not have to be checked by the CCA. They can be "blindly" confirmed by the CCA, in the same way as the special commitments. They do not even have to be understood by the CCA. In dispute cases, however, they might be checked by a law court.

However, for some types of CCA, certain conditions might be fixed: For instance the first condition (see above) will be fixed for the special service (the Liability-Cover Service) we have in mind to realize a separation between deniable digital signature and undeniable commitment.

Modifying the set of commitments. The way of "refreshing" or modifying the set of commitments in an authenticated way is agreed between subscriber and CCA. This might require personal presence of the subscriber at the CCA, or a written or digitally signed electronic notice including some one-time password. Even smartcards might be issued by the CCA for this purpose. Modifying the set of Commitments has to be handled with the same care for security as the initial commitment itself.

Contract between subscriber and CCA. A contract between subscriber and CCA has to be signed by both parties by handwritten signatures. It defines or includes, respectively:

1. The subscriber's initial commitment to be legally bound to all digital signatures he actually made with the registered key.
2. The subscriber's initial commitment to fulfill all valid commitments issued by the CCA, also in the case of attacks, provided they do not exceed the predefined limits and the authorization key has not already been revoked, and the CCA has not acted negligently.
3. The type of the service, including the ways of authentication of the subscriber's requests, the responsibility and reliability for the authentication, and the costs. For instance, a service type "N" (normal) would be the usual one which would require a request for an undeniable commitment just signed by the subscriber. In another type "H" (high security), the CCA would have to check the authenticity of the request by other, additional means. Different service types can be combined, e.g., depending on the value or frequency.
4. The commitment of the CCA not to issue commitments if they have not been authorized or exceed a pre-defined limit, and to take the liability for its failures otherwise.

13.2.3 Key Certificate

The CCA initially issues a key certificate for the subscriber's public key to inform the relying party that the corresponding signature key is only valid within the scope of the Commitment Service. For the special type of service we have in mind, this includes the information that the signature key can be denied by the subscriber in the case of attacks, even if the attack cannot be proven.

The Commitment Service can also allow subscribers to use a signing key for the requests to the CCA which is different from the signing key used in normal transactions by the key holder. Both keys might be certified and included in the initial commitment. As these keys have completely different functionalities (signing the request to the CCA, and signing a transaction containing a commitment), they might use different technology, e.g., a very secure one for the requests and a weaker one for the transactions. Even completely different non-electronical means to send the request can be agreed initially between key holder and CCA. However, in the context of this chapter, and for the sake of simplicity, we treat both keys as identical.

The key certificate might refer to a blacklist containing users (or pseudonyms) which had claimed compromised signatures within a certain period. This is not meant as discrimination of the subscribers who might indeed have been attacked, but shall make the relying parties careful when doing business with entities who might be prone to attacks (or pretend attacks). As a consequence, the relying parties might negotiate to get commitments of a sufficiently high amount to cover potential damage due to a denial (within the scope of their own risk management)—as they should do anyway. As a side effect, of course, it aims at educating subscribers to protect their own environment as far as possible, and not to claim compromised signatures without justification. In some countries, e.g., in Germany, such blacklists might not be allowed, for reasons of data protection. We would like to emphasize that we do not recommend to use blacklists—but at least this might be a possibility for service providers who consider it useful.

Generally, key certificates can be issued for pseudonyms while the correct name might only be revealed in a dispute case if necessary.

13.2.4 Key Revocation

Like all certification authorities, the CCA must enable key revocation of lost or compromised keys within short time. The CCA must enable relying parties to check the revocation information (e.g., aided by a certificate revocation list). If the CCA has issued an undeniable commitment and the subscriber uses the key registered at this service for making the transaction with the relying party, the relying party can conclude from the issued commitment that the key was not revoked at an earlier time.

After a key was revoked, the CCA must not accept requests for commitments signed with that key. Depending on the policy, a new initialization using a new key might be required.

13.2.5 Commitment Request and Response

If a transaction made by the subscriber involves an undeniable commitment for the relying party, the subscriber sends a *commitment request* to the CCA. The subscriber authenticates this request in the way agreed initially, i.e., usually signs it digitally with the key registered in association with the Commitment Service.

The request should contain the following information:

− Service ID of subscriber.
− A unique subscriber identification in the way it shall be shown to, and understood by, the relying party. (A certified pseudonym might be sufficient.)
− Either the following mandatory information, or a hash value of it so that the commitment certification authority is not able to read it:
  1. Unique context ID, specified by the subscriber for the considered context within the considered transaction, so that the relying party can check it.
  2. Unique ID identifying the relying party (also via pseudonym) so that in a dispute case, neither an intruder nor the subscriber can claim that another party was meant.

- Commitments which the subscriber intends to commit to (e.g., Euro 500), together with additional conditions per commitment if any (e.g., "only if signature is claimed compromised") and with validity expiring dates each.
- Further transaction information (encrypted or clear) to be time-stamped by the CCA in connection with the transaction.
- The subscriber's digital signature on all this information.

The CCA performs the agreed authentication, e.g., checks the digital signature and its revocation status, and if the requested commitments exceed any of the pre-defined limits. The request is rejected completely if the latter is the case. It also checks if, for this transaction context and this relying party (or for this hash including both), a commitment certificate has already been issued earlier. If yes, no new commitment certificate is issued, just the old one is repeated as a copy, if needed. If all checks were successful, the CCA issues the commitment certificate and updates the information on the set of commitments which still can be issued within the considered period (e.g., decreases the limit by Euro 500).

The response, i.e., the issued undeniable commitment, which we will call *commitment certificate*, should contain the following information:

1. Serial number of issued commitment certificate.
2. Subscriber identification (see request) in the way it shall be shown to, and understood by, the relying party.
3. The public part of the subscriber's key used to sign the transaction, or a reference to the corresponding key certificate.
4. Either the following mandatory information, or a hash value of it so that the commitment certification authority is not able to read it (see request):
   a) Unique context ID, see request.
   b) Unique ID identifying the relying party, see request.
5. Commitments which the subscriber intends to commit to (e.g., Euro 500), together with additional conditions per commitment if any (e.g., "only if signature is claimed compromised", "but not exceeding the relying party's actual damage") and with validity expiring dates each, see request.
6. Further transaction information (encrypted or clear) to be time-stamped by the CCA in connection with the transaction (see request).
7. Date, time, validity.
8. Confirmation that the listed key of the subscriber has not been revoked.
9. Pointer to policy and scope of the subscriber's digital signature.
10. Signature of CCA on all the information, and additional information so that the relying party is able to check the trust path for the CCA.

The usual message flow is that the CCA sends this commitment certificate (i.e., the undeniable commitment being witnessed by the CCA) to the subscriber, who may forward it to the relying party, related to the transaction referred to in the commitment certificate. The subscriber can check that the commitment certificate was issued properly before forwarding it. After receipt, the relying party can check all details of the commitment certificate and, if successful, knows that it can rely on it. The relying party does not have to consult the revocation information for the subscriber's key as the commitment certificate confirms that it was valid when the commitment was issued. If it was revoked later, the subscriber is nevertheless bound to this commitment.

Sending a commitment certificate might also be the only action of a transaction. It does not have to be related to any other super-context beyond just sending the commitment. For instance, the commitment certificate might be a voucher as a present, and the condition could just be "valid at your next birthday anniversary."

On the other hand, the commitment certificate might be part of a transaction the outcome of which is not clear at that point of time. For instance, the commitment certificate might include a certain price which is only due under the condition "if the services have been performed appropriately," although the contract has not been concluded so far. If, however, the relying party performs the service, the price is due and might be enforced in a law court.

13.2.6 Validity of the Commitment Certificates

It is highly recommended to generally restrict the validity of issued commitment certificates to a short time, i.e., for instance to one or two months. This information must be visible in the key certificate. This will reduce the possibility of an attacker to misuse the key over a longer period, e.g., while the key holder is in vacation or hospital, and presenting all claims for fulfilling the commitments after his return.

As a good possibility to protect the relying party, the CCA might be used as a witness and time-stamping service that the claims (i.e., that the commitment included should be fulfilled) have actually been sent to the key holder. This would prevent key holders from denying to have received the claim within the validity period.

13.2.7 Using the Commitment Service as Liability-Cover Service

The *Liability-Cover Service* (for short: *LCS*) presented here is a special simplified type of the Commitment Service which we believe is the minimum service that should be implemented for practical use. It is intended to specify and commit a liability for a digital signature within a transaction, exclusively under the only possible condition that the signature is claimed compromised. The fact that we call the commitment "liability" induces an additional semantics for the commitment.

There is only one type of commitment: Amounts of money, up to a certain pre-defined limit, or, if possible, several pre-defined limits depending on the requested amount or the type of authentication of the request etc.

The commitment itself is a statement on a liability taken, covering the relying party's damage, up to a limit specified in that statement, but not exceeding the relyling party's damage. Without this restriction, the commitment would not depend on that damage and thus always be paid fully.

Of course, such LCC should not be requested by the relying party in cases where a consumer protection law allows the signer to withdraw the order without compensation anyway. Such commitments might not be enforceable in those cases.

13.2.8 Integration in a Legal Framework

In Chapter 14, the Liability-Cover Service will be integrated into a legal framework, especially into *SECA*, the *SEMPER* Electronic-Commerce Agreement. The main aspects specific to the Commitment Service, especially the Liability-Cover Service, will be summarized already here.

1. The basis of this service is a contract between subscriber and CCA.
2. This contract regulates and restricts the scope of the digital signature key registered for this service. The relying party is referred to this policy by the key certificate as well as by the commitment certificate.
3. The contract restricts legal binding of a transaction signed using the signing key corresponding to the registered public key. One restriction is that the signature is valid if and only if it has not been claimed compromised.
4. The undeniable commitment issued by the CCA cannot be denied, not even in the case of attacks. In cases of CCA's negligence the CCA is liable. This allows the relying party to trust in the commitment. At least, it can be enforced in a law court.
5. The subscriber's pre-defined limit is defined by the subscriber himself, as well as the commitments to be issued for a transaction. The CCA has to monitor the limits.
6. The relying party is supposed to know that signatures can be denied in the case of attacks, and that they should require commitment certificates (or Liability-Cover Certificates) covering the damage expected in case of withdrawal, to limit their own potential damage.
7. The CCA is responsible and liable for commitments issued without justification and for insufficient identity authentication during registration.

13.3 Possible Variants and Supplements

Several modifications and additional features of the Commitment Service are possible. Some of them are presented here.

13.3.1 Limits

In all variants, the CCA can handle any additional limits which it is able to control. Natural limits presented so far are related to the set of commitments to be issued, e.g., Euro 2000 per month as a limit for the amount of commitments, or a special set of additional commitments like "120 hours consulting work," "50 hours maintenance," etc. Any combinations of this can be meaningful. Issued undeniable commitments can contain any subset, e.g., "Euro 200 plus 5 hours consulting work."

However, additional limits to be checked can be defined by the subscriber and be controlled by the CCA. The following points are just examples:

- The total number of issued commitments per month can be fixed, e.g., to 20 commitment certificates.
- The limits can depend on the time of day, day of week, the number of previously issued commitments within a certain period (e.g., each transaction beyond the 5th per day might decrease the limits for issuable commitments by 3 times the amount), or even on the particular relying party.
- The limits can depend on the kind of authentication of the request. There might even exist a low limit (e.g., Euro 200 per month) for which commitments can be issued although the authentication is done without any digital signature. The risk is at the subscriber, of course. A very high limit can be agreed for an authentication with digital signature and additional means, e.g., calling back or using a secure device with a limited number and amount of commitments, especially if the CCA takes the responsibility and liability for the authentication of the request (type "H," see above). This would result in a more expensive type of service since the CCA should take out a third-party liability insurance.
- The limits themselves can be increased by the subscriber, e.g., if they have exceeded unexpectedly early, or if the subscriber prefers low initial limits. Additional ways of a highly secure authentication method are needed here to prevent attackers from increasing and exploiting the subscriber's limits.

13.3.2 Message Flow

In one variant, the request can be sent to the CCA by the relying party, but must of course be authorized by the subscriber, especially the contained commitments. In this case, the issued commitment certificate can be sent directly to the relying party. Messages are not saved this way, even less as additionally a copy of the commitment certificate should be sent to the subscriber, so that he knows whether the CCA actually issued the commitment certificate and reduced the available amount of commitments. With this message flow, the service has more similarities to credit-card systems. However, we think that it is more natural and in the interest of the subscriber if he has the control over sending the requests to the CCA. In any case, it will probably be in the interest of the relying party not to have to send the request (authorized by the subscriber) to the CCA and to wait for an answer. It is more convenient to get the commitment certificate already together with the transaction message.

Another reasonable variant would be that the request to the CCA is sent by the subscriber (e.g., also including the order or other transaction message), but the CCA sends the response directly to the relying party (including the order). Without further messages, this also reduces the subscriber's control; however it might make sense in cases where the subscriber cannot wait for the CCA's response.

Both possibilities will reveal the business partner (or its pseudonym) to the CCA, which is an additional disadvantage.

13.3.3 Combination with "Solvency Service"

The commitment certificate confirms the subscriber's obligation to pay if the associated conditions are fulfilled. However, it does not give any information on whether the subscriber will be able to pay. On the other hand, in credit-card systems, the bank gives information in the authorization response confirming that the key holder is able to pay—we might call this "Solvency Service" to distinguish it from the "Commitment Service." However, this does not say anything about the key holder's obligation to pay, e.g., if he fell victim to an attack.

Both kinds of information, the obligation to pay as well as the ability to pay, can be combined in one service. The semantics of the Commitment Service just has to be modified so that the CCA does not only confirm that the subscriber committed to fulfill his obligations, but also confirms that he will be able to do so. For this purpose, the Commitment Service should be performed by a bank, or by any party which controls a sufficient deposit of money for the subscriber. This would include that this party could transfer this money to the relying party, at least in dispute cases if the subscriber refuses to do so without justification. To transfer money could also be a replacement for performing committed services in certain cases. The service would have to issue a policy for this, so that the relying parties can be aware of the conditions.

13.3.4 Recharging Liabilities

If the Commitment Service is used primarily as a Liability-Cover Service, then the following situation will happen frequently: The subscriber sends an order to the relying party, e.g., on an amount of Euro 1000, together with a commitment certificate covering, e.g., Euro 250. In the usual case, the order is processed, the goods are shipped or the service is performed and paid by the subscriber. In this case, the Commitment certificate is completely irrelevant after a successfully performed transaction since the condition of the commitment is valid only if the subscriber claims a compromised key. However, the limit for further commitments was decreased by Euro 250, although the risk has not changed.

One can argue that those Euro 250 can be "recharged" to increase the limit again, if it turns out that the transaction has been performed successfully and the relying party will never claim that the commitment must be fulfilled. So, "recharging of liabilities" can be included in the Commitment Service in the way that the relying party sends the Commitment certificate back to the CCA, together with the confirmation that it will not claim its fulfillment anymore. The Commitment Service must have enough information (which might reduce the level of anonymity) to verify this statement. If successful, the limit of the user can be increased again by the commitments contained in the commitment certificates.

However, especially for software-only solutions we recommend that recharging should not be allowed. One problem is that the relying party does not know whether the signature will be claimed compromised later, even after a successful-looking business transaction. Another reason is that the relying party itself might be attacked: the confirmation that it will not claim the fulfillment of the commitment might have been compromised.

A third reason is that a new kind of attack will become possible: The attacker succeeds in placing a Trojan horse on the subscriber's machine. The Trojan horse affects the transactions made as well as the subscriber's electronic payment system, e.g., SET. Now, the attack may result in several orders to the merchant, for several goods to be sent to a certain delivery address (unknown to the subscriber). The attack includes request and response of the Commitment certificate. The Trojan horse also performs the payment properly. This means that for the relying party the issued commitment certificates are not relevant any more, and they can be recharged. However, the limit will not decrease in this way, and many purchases of this kind can be made by the attacker without any involvement of the subscriber (who might be on vacation). This contradicts the aim of the Commitment Service to protect the subscriber from attacks.

This example shows that certificates should at least not be recharged before the subscriber might recognize the damage and can try to withdraw the order as well as the payment, based on the fact that he has become the victim of an attack. Furthermore, the recharging should include the approval of the subscriber himself, to give him the chance to recognize attacks. This approval must be given outside of the system which can be attacked (so that this approval cannot be faked).

13.3.5 Several Relying Parties or Beneficiaries

If a transaction requires commitments to more than one relying party, or commitments whose beneficiary (or beneficiaries) is not identical with the relying party verifying the commitment certificate, all this can be included into the same commitment.

A more general structure can be considered here: The paths over which the commitments are forwarded might have the shape of a tree. The relying party, i.e., the first recipient of the commitment certificate, is the root of the tree. It checks and splits the information for its direct children and forwards the resulting packages to the respective children. These children perform the same procedures for their children, and so on. The results of the checks include all results of all children and must be transferred in the reverse direction.

In this way, it is even possible to encrypt or decrypt information for each parent-child pair, so that the upper nodes do not get information on which commitments are needed by which entities. The request must be performed in the reverse way, including encryption for only those recipients who should read or encrypt the data again.

This includes complex procedures but enables flexibility and a high degree of anonymity for rather complex transactions.

13.3.6 Other Kinds of Authorization and Issuance of Commitment Certificates

Request as well as issuance of commitment certificates could also be done outside the Internet. Of course, the permitted procedures must be determined a priori in the contract between subscriber and CCA.

We already mentioned that the digital signature key used for the transaction need not be identical with the one registered for the Commitment Service. This has some disadvantages, e.g., if a digital signature is used with less protection for the subscriber, though, the subscriber is allowed to do so. Of course, both keys or even more can be registered at the CCA, with the corresponding policy.

Here are some examples of other possibilities to send the request for a commitment certificate.

1. We assume that neither the subscriber nor the relying party necessarily have an Internet connection. The relying party, a merchant, requires a trustworthy fax. Note that a handwritten signature on a fax order might not be secure enough because it might be provided by cut-and-paste by an attacker.

   In this example, the subscriber might want to order fresh food for a big party. The problem of the relying party might be that such orders can be denied if done by phone or fax, and the damage would be high since the food might get spoilt soon. Thus, the relying party requires a commitment certificate on Euro 500. The subscriber requests the corresponding commitment certificate by phone including voice recognition, or by fax, or even both, at the CCA. The CCA checks the authenticity of the request and the limits and, if successful, produces the commitment certificate which is sent per fax to the subscriber. Now, the subscriber is able to include this certificate into his own fax containing his order to the relying party, which can read and check it using a scanner and a PC. In this way, this fax order is much more trustworthy for the relying party than one with a handwritten signature. Of course, the authentication of the request must be secured properly, to protect the subscriber. Similarly, the subscriber is recommended to check the received commitment certificate using scanner and a PC as well, but he might also trust the CCA instead, knowing that he is protected by his upper limit.

2. Similarly, a phone order to the merchant can be secured additionally by making the CCA send him a commitment certificate electronically (assuming that he can receive it) or by fax. This can make sense for orders like flowers to be sent to a remote person.

These sketches of use cases show that the Commitment Service can be run in ways useful for any persons even without Internet connection, to increase the trustworthiness of their transactions towards relying parties.

13.4 Who is Liable for Failures at the CCA?

It is obvious that the Commitment Service provides optimal benefit only if the CCA takes responsibility and liability for commitments issued without justification. This does not include the case that the subscriber has been attacked, unless the contract between CCA and subscriber fixes responsibility and liability for authenticating the subscriber's request at the CCA so that only the subscriber and no attacker can have made the request. Without this special type of contract, the risk of attacks always is at the subscriber. However, it is obvious that not the subscriber should be forced to take the liability for mistakes at the CCA, since the aim of the Commitment Service is to limit the obligations of the user to a user-defined limit, and exactly this will motivate users to become subscribers. Vice versa, the risk of having to take more liability will prevent them from subscribing.

A requirement is that the CCA must be able to prove that it has been acting properly. The processes to be defined here must also take into account insider criminality which should not be able to remain undiscovered in a dispute case. Such insider attacks might create unjustified commitments within the limits, thereby claiming that the subscriber requested them.

Accreditation procedures for CCAs are recommended here.

A CCA might not be able to provide compensation to a high degree. Realistically, compensation will anyway be reduced to the values contained in the issued commitment certificates. In the worst case, the CCA might go bankrupt before having satisfied all claims. As such a situation is not satisfactory for its subscribers nor the corresponding relying parties, it should be backed up by an unlimited third-party liability insurance. An alternative would be a fond provided and managed by the Chambers of Commerce and supported by the merchants.

13.5 Conclusions

The Commitment Service is a third-party service to enable a subscriber to provide an undeniable commitment to the relying party. "Undeniable" means that it is not deniable even in the case of attacks, and for this reason it can be considered trustworthy by the beneficiary.

Providing undeniable commitments to other parties enables those parties, on the other hand, to accept transactions which are signed using a digital signature which is deniable in the case of attacks, even if the attack cannot be proven. The Commitment Service combines registration and certification of keys under this policy, in additional to its "normal" task to control user pre-defined limits on commitments which can be issued within a certain time period.

We summarize the benefits of this service (already given in Section 13.1.3) by answering the question who might be interested to use this service and why.

13.5.1 Reasons for Merchants to Use the Commitment Service

It is obvious that especially the merchants on the Internet will be profiting from the Commitment Service. They can use part of the advantages of having digital signatures and public-key infrastructure, i.e., being able to identify the other party as far as necessary, or at least its public key. This is a big step compared with the current situation where phone orders or postcards, maybe with forged addresses and signatures, do not necessarily provide a link to any registered person.

The fact that digital signatures can be denied due to attacks might provide the merchants more customers who are willing to use such a digital signature. More and more people are becoming aware of security weaknesses of software-only configurations. If asked if they were willing to use a digital signature on their PC, without smartcard or secure device, they might answer that they would not accept to use it, because they would have to sign statements which will make their legal situation worse than it was without any digital signatures at all.

The other advantage for the merchant is that he can require undeniable commitments over an amount which covers the potential damage which he might suffer if the apparent signer withdraws his transaction due to an attack. Due to the generality of the Commitment Service, the commitments can be defined to be valid even if the signer withdraws the order without an attack. This might facilitate withdrawals of orders in general, though they always will be annoying.

Furthermore, the merchant does not have to consult key revocation directories if he requires and gets a commitment certificate. It is only necessary to check the certificate and the trust path of the CCA. This should be done anyway for digital signatures in general.

Thus, apart from the overhead to require, receive and process commitment certificates, there is no disadvantage for the merchant which could not be avoided. The solution is better than one using digital signature increasing the risk for the customers, and much better than a solution without digital signatures at all. A precondition is, of course, that the liability for any failures of the CCA is not solely at the merchant.

13.5.2 Chambers of Commerce to Provide the Commitment Service?

Since the Chambers of Commerce represent the interests of the merchants, it seems obvious that they might be interested to provide the Commitment Service, in connection with, or performed by, already existing CAs. It should be possible to run a profitable service, by charging for commitment certificates. To afford a third-party liability insurance, the fees will be the higher the more critical the action, e.g., in the special service type where the CCA is responsible and liable for the authentication of the request.

If the buyers are charged, this should result in reduced prices at the merchants since the latter get some means of trust in exchange. In a probably better model, the merchants as a community of interests might fund the service. This, again, might be organized by the Chambers of Commerce.

13.5.3 Reasons for Buyers to Use the Commitment Service

For the buyers, the situation seems different. They might not find an obvious advantage in subscribing to a service which, in the worst case, obliges them to pay for commitments which they, in the case of attacks, did not authorize.

However, the only secure alternative for the buyer is using no digital signature at all. This is the only way not to run the risk to be bound to orders by email, phone or fax because they can deny all of them and probably would win a law suit.

However, if digital signatures become legally binding and backed by digital signature laws and, on the other hand, are required by the merchants, buyers might lose flexibility and the possibility to buy over the Internet under favorable conditions if they refuse to use digital signatures. Assuming that they choose to use digital signatures, it is clear that using them under the conditions of a Commitment Service implies a much lower risk than under a different policy which might not allow to deny signatures in the case of attacks. With a Commitment Service, their risk is limited to a known limit. Without a Commitment Service, there is no such limit.

Furthermore, the buyer is able to provide means of trust, i.e., undeniable commitments to the merchant. This might give him better conditions for negotiation. Of course, this will impose a certain risk in the case of attacks, but—in contrast to undeniable digital signatures—this risk is limited. The buyer can even define the limit himself.

A non-provable attack on an undeniable digital signature, however, may result in an unpredictable and unacceptable high damage for the key holder. The same attack, using the Commitment Service, will result in a damage not exceeding the user pre-defined limit.

The principle of splitting usual digital signatures into

1. a deniable signature, and
2. an undeniable commitment

should be used as long as subscribers cannot protect themselves from attacks reasonably, i.e., as long as no secure operating systems for signing devices are available. Even when devices with secure operating systems are available, problems will be left which can cause impersonating attacks, e.g., in the process where the key holders identify themselves towards their devices and in cases of extortion. For all such cases, the Commitment Service will reduce and limit the potential damage to the key holder.

All parties will benefit from reduced risk and from the means of trust enabled by the Commitment Service.

14. Legal Aspects

In this chapter, we first discuss legal aspects in electronic commerce in general. Next, we analyze current approaches at legal frameworks. We show that all of them are insufficient with respect to the protection of the key holder against compromised signatures through realistic attacks. The liability is at the key holder in most approaches. On the other hand, it is obvious that the relying party must be protected against signed transactions claimed compromised.

An approach is presented which reduces the risk of all parties to a level which can be handled much better: In *SECA*, the *SEMPER* Electronic-Commerce Agreement, signatures are deniable, but users have to take a certain limited liability. Additionally, they can use the Commitment Service presented in the previous chapter to reduce the risk of the relying parties.

SECA enforces secure and fair commerce among all players having signed this agreement at certification authorities supporting *SECA*. It includes the Agreement, a Code of Conduct, and Guidelines. The Code of Conduct provides, in particular, regulations with respect to defaults for applicable law to facilitate cross-boarder commerce, and regulations to enforce fairness, privacy and data protection and consumer protection, including aspects like advertising and negotiation. The Guidelines define "*SECA*-compliant components" to protect their users, and give information to the users on how they can reduce their exposure to damage due to failures and attacks.

14.1 Introduction

When transactions are performed electronically, new legal issues arise, additionally to those which we already know from the non-electronic world. As *SEMPER* aims at a *secure* electronic marketplace, this chapter will concentrate on security-specific aspects, in particular the use of digital signatures based on a local or global public-key infrastructure. Issues like content and performance of a contract are not specific for electronic transactions; hence we will leave them mostly outside of the scope of this chapter. Liability for products, network performance, crashes, acts of God, etc. are not discussed either. Those issues can be considered separately, without questioning or affecting the results and considerations specific for *SEMPER*.

G. Lacoste et al. (Eds.): SEMPER 2000, LNCS 1854, pp. 257–303, 2000.

We will concentrate on legal aspects which concern the actions of the players involved in a secure electronic transaction, especially liability regarding
the legally binding character of electronic transactions. This also involves the
certification authorities (CAs) as supporting parties. The main result of this
chapter is *SECA*, the *SEMPER* Electronic-Commerce Agreement, which is
presented in Section 14.4. We will show how *SECA* can be used to provide a
legal basis for all players participating in *SECA* and to reduce their risks with
respect to attacks. To motivate the development of *SECA* in *SEMPER*, we
will consider the requirements on a legal framework and investigate existing
approaches (Section 14.3). We will see that none of the approaches is able
to provide a comprehensive legal solution acceptable for *all* players. We will
show how some of the main problems are solved by *SECA* which can serve
as a starting point to experiment on, and further develop, agreements as the
legal basis for secure electronic commerce with a risk which can be limited
for all parties. As another advantage of *SECA*, it can be deployed right now,
without waiting for a harmonized legal regulation.

To give a complete picture, in Section 14.2 we start by discussing general
legal issues that arise when doing business via open networks like the Internet.

14.2 Legal Issues in Electronic Commerce

In this chapter, we will provide a general outline of the legal aspects of
electronic commerce, describe them and summarize the latest developments.
Most of these issues also exist in the non-electronic world, but some get more
complicated in the electronic world as certain characteristics of the world
of open networks like the Internet do not fit into traditional laws and regulations. Laws mostly run behind the technique because any elaboration of
legal regulations takes a long time until it can be applied, and because it is
very difficult for lawmakers to draw up accurate and suitable regulations on
techniques that live in a steady development.

The various legal aspects that are affected by electronic commerce are:

− applicable law and jurisdiction,
− validity and proof of digital signatures,
− export regulations for cryptographic products,
− consumer-protection laws,
− privacy and data protection,
− advertising, competition and spamming,
− content of contracts and Internet pages,
− copyright and trademark law,
− different payment systems, and
− tax law.

The questions of applicable law and jurisdiction are answered entirely by *SECA*, whereas the questions of consumer protection, privacy, data protection, advertising, competition and content of Internet pages are partly regulated in the Code of Conduct. Aspects like export regulations, copyright law, contract law, payments and taxation are not regulated at all for several reasons that are explained in the corresponding sections.

14.2.1 Applicable Law and Jurisdiction

Probably some of the most important questions for any person doing electronic commerce are, "Which regulations are applicable to this contract, about which law do I have to be concerned and where do I have to go to court if a dispute should arise from this contract?"

For cross-border electronic commerce the applicable law will be determined either by the players or by standard regulations. Participants will not move into a "legal vacuum" or into a situation where two different laws are applicable at the same time to one specific transaction or contract. This holds even if they have not agreed on any jurisdiction. A contract is assigned to a certain jurisdiction (in doubt a judge will decide) but the players can always agree explicitly on a deviating regulation if they want to.

The law that regulates the applicable law and the place of jurisdiction, called "law of conflict of laws" or "Private International Law," is regulated differently in different countries: some states have a closed system of regulations concerning the conflict of laws, others have single regulations embedded in existing laws and others have customary law on these issues, thus no special regulations. It statutes the applicable law, the place of jurisdiction and the recognition and enforcement of foreign decisions when dealing with a scenario that is multi-national in respect to the nationality and the domicile of the players. Since almost each country of the world has its own national law and since there are a lot of different jurisdictions, it is important that the players know that in electronic commerce all involved jurisdictions might be affected. The Private International Law of a country (as a law or as regulation within the existing regulations) determines, for example, the applicable law for a contract of sale or a service contract between two parties whose domiciles are located in different countries and it determines also the place of jurisdiction for this concrete transaction. Other examples of the importance of the Private International Law are the contracts closed between merchants and consumers. There are some compulsory regulations concerning applicable law that have to be considered.

In *SECA*, regulations on the applicable law are set in the *SECA* defaults (Section 14.5.2) that have to be applied if a *SECA* player uses his *SECA* key for electronic transactions.

14.2.2 Electronic Authentication—Validity of Digital Signatures

A contract can be closed electronically in the same way as it can be closed orally as far as formal requirements do not hinder the validity. The legal issues related to digital signatures are the different or also unpredictable treatment of digitally signed documents as a means of proof in court. Especially in countries where the principle of freedom of proof does not exist, digital signatures are mostly not recognized for evidential purposes yet. The approaches at building a legal framework for the use of digital signatures generally treat the first point when stating "electronic signature shall not be denied legal effect, validity or enforceability solely on the grounds that it is in electronic form" but they leave the second aspect, i.e., the validity of a digital signature as a means of proof up to the national legislation.

Approaches at building a legal framework are discussed in Section 14.3.

14.2.3 Proof of Digital Signatures

In general, contracts are legally binding if there are no requirements on formalization (e.g., handwritten signature, public deed, witness) that cannot be fulfilled by digital signatures. If they are supported by a consideration in the common law countries, e.g., Anglo-American legal systems (England, Canada, USA, Australia, New Zealand and the British Empire States), or a corresponding manifestation of intention in the civil law countries, e.g., German, Roman and Nordic Legal Systems, contracts can be closed informally. The list of contracts that have to be in writing in order to be valid or enforceable can usually be found in the corresponding codes or in statutes in the civil law countries .

The fact that leads to problems in a dispute case is that the party claiming to get something from the other party has to prove that claim. This means that in a law suit a party always has to carry either the burden of proof or the burden of counter-evidence. It is either the proof of the existence of a valid and enforceable contract or the proof that the claimed contract is not valid or enforceable.

Consequently, there are three important aspects related to proving digitally signed transactions:

- The legal recognition of digital signatures for evidential purposes in general.
- The proof that the transaction was signed digitally by a certain person.
- The consequences of the non-provability of not having signed the transaction digitally.

The first aspect should not be mixed up with the pure possibility to close a contract. It rather is the general legal recognition of digital signatures for evidential purposes within national law. There are very few states that explicitly accept digital signatures and documents for purposes of evidence

(Russia, South Korea, Italy within its digital signature law no. Law 59 of 15 March 1997) but most states do accept digital signatures and electronic documents implicitly with some restrictions, e.g., formal restrictions (University of Leuven 1998).

The second aspect is the likelihood of proving that a message was signed digitally by a specific person. During a law suit the party who is claiming that a certain message was signed digitally by the other party has to prove the existence of the claimed digitally signed message. Usually, the plausible justification of this fact is sufficient for a refutable presumption and therefore, a reversal of the burden of proof. This means that the defendant who denies the presumed fact now has to persuade the court of not having signed the questionable document. No law-suit case exists so far. However, it can be assumed that the defendant will continue justifying his position with the consequence that the further decision will be in the discretion of the court. This is the way it could happen in the German legal system; the situation could vary in different legal systems but the general tendency is likely to be the same.

The third aspect follows the second since it explains the consequences of the non-provability of not having signed digitally and the problems related to the aspect.

First, it has to be recognized that it is hardly possible to prove that a message signed with the digital signature of a certain person was not signed by this specific person although the digital signature might be assigned to the person with whose private key the signature was created.

Since the recognition of digital signatures for evidential purposes can only be enforced if there are certain technical requirements on digital signatures, certificates and keys set up, it becomes a very difficult endeavor for the victimized key holder to prove that she has not signed a certain message digitally. This is the problem of the Utah Digital Signature Act (see Section 14.3.4) where "in adjudicating a dispute involving a digital signature, a court of this state shall presume that: [...] (3) if a digital signature is verified by the public key listed in a valid certificate issued by a licensed certification authority: (a) that the digital signature is the digital signature of the subscriber listed in that certificate; (b) that the digital signature was affixed by the signer with the intention of signing the message; and (c) the recipient of that digital signature has no knowledge or notice that the signer: (i) breached a duty as a subscriber; or (ii) does not rightfully hold the private key used to affix the digital signature; and [...]." For the defrauded signer this means that she has to produce prima facie evidence to rebut the presumption and to persuade the finder of fact that the presumed facts are not true (Biddle 1996). This leads to a paradox: The higher the technical standards for the security of digital signatures are set, the more drastic the consequences for victimized key holders might be as it might become more unlikely that they can prove that they have not signed a message digitally.

These consequences for victimized key holders have to be taken into account when elaborating regulations on the evidential means of digital signatures. In *SECA*, the proof of having signed or not is not regulated. *SECA*, though, provides a general solution to this problem: The *SECA* liability limit for claimed compromised keys and the optional use of the Liability-Cover Service (Section 13.2.7) and partner-specific limits. The *SECA* liability limit is assigned to a specific *SECA* certificate and therefore, a defrauded signer is only liable up to the total of the *SECA* limit per month.

14.2.4 Regulations for Use and Export of Dual-Use Goods

Digital signature (authentication) and encryption (confidentiality) in electronic transactions require the availability and interoperability of products providing cryptography.

In almost every country the export of cryptographic products or products that can be used for creating cryptographic products is at least controlled. Cryptographic products are considered "dual-use goods," i.e., products that can serve both, civilian and military purposes. Dual-use goods underlie certain restrictions according to laws or arrangements that regulate import, export, and use of arms. One of these arrangements is the Wassenaar Arrangement(The Wassenaar Arrangement 1996) (former COCOM) that regulates the control and the information flow between the participating countries related to exports of dual-use goods. The EC Dual-Use regulation (European Union 1994) is modeled on the Wassenaar Arrangement and has a similar purpose, but its aim is also a harmonization of the regulations and facilitated export within the European Union. Recent developments indicate that cryptographic products will be transferable without major obstacles within the European Union.

Usually, the controls or restrictions concern cryptography that is used for encryption, i.e., to ensure confidentiality of messages. Since a government could hardly justify any restriction on the use of cryptography for authentication, this kind of cryptography should not underlie any controls or restrictions on the one hand. On the other hand, cryptography that is used for authentication can be modified in many cases so that it can be used for confidentiality purposes. Therefore, most governments control or restrict software or products that are used for any of these purposes.

In general, the export of "weak" cryptography (e.g., with a certain maximum key length) and so-called "mass market software" is not restricted. Another means of control performed or demanded by governments is key escrow of encryption keys; a measure that might contradict, in our view, the fundamental right of privacy in a modern constitutional state if used to control the content of communication over open networks. For economic concerns with respect to the difficulty of implementing efficient key escrow, and to the reluctance of the industry to allow others than the involved parties to get access, we refer to the results of the EU project KRISIS (Key

Recovery in Secure Information Systems) (KRISIS Consortium 1998). Other arguments against key escrow or key recovery are that people can use non-recoverable systems to encrypt their messages and then encrypt them again with recoverable systems. Even if this was forbidden, criminals could hide their (encrypted) messages in pictures using steganographic products, which can be downloaded from the Internet today. Another problem might be the trustworthiness of third parties who would be able to recover the messages.

The consequences of these restrictions for players doing electronic commerce are not that drastic for most countries because they have export controls rather than restrictions of domestic use. Import restrictions play a minor role. The use of cryptographic products is free in most countries, at least within Europe and North America. The only exception within Europe was France. In spring 1999 France liberalized its import restrictions and moved from an authorization system to a declaration system.

14.2.5 Consumer-Protection Laws

As consumers become essential participants in electronic commerce, regulations of traditional commerce that aim at protecting consumers—as the economically weaker and less experienced party in business—have to be adapted or modified for electronic commerce. In traditional commerce they are spread over various fields, but they can also be applied to electronic commerce. Depending on the juridical system, formal requirements on certain contract types like land sale, surety, installment credits, insurances, certain long-term contracts, leasing, sales of goods that exceed a certain value or bail are laid down when involving consumers. To protect consumers from being sued abroad or having to charge the vendor abroad, some mandatory regulations of the Private International Law state that the applicable law and the jurisdiction is always the one of the consumer. Other rules explicitly stated in favor of consumers are the right of withdrawal without penalty and without giving any reasons as, for example, stated in the EC Directive on Consumer Protection (European Union 1997b), consumer protection in the indication of the prices of non-food products or rules on unfair terms according to the Council Directive on Unfair Terms in Consumer Contracts (European Union 1993). The conditions used in the Commitment Service (Section 13.2.7) might have to be adapted accordingly.

Some of these aspects are covered by the Code of Conduct in *SECA* (Section 14.5.2). The Guidelines (Section 14.5.3) also aim at enforcing consumers' interests.

14.2.6 Privacy and Data Protection

In a system where personal data from individuals flow to merchants, CAs, banks and other individuals and where data bases are a common means for simplifying administration, it is highly important that the rights of individuals are respected. No personal data of any player should be used for actions which could violate the freedom or the right of personality of individuals and personal data should be collected and used only for purposes that are relevant to the business using the data. Players who gather data from their customers must respect these principles.

The EU Directive on Data Procession Protection (European Union 1995), which became effective end of October 1998, is a good example of an extensive data-protection regulation. A principle of the Directive is regulated in point 28 (that refers to article 6 of the Directive) of the recital: "[...] any processing of personal data must be lawful and fair to the individuals concerned; [...], in particular, the data must be adequate, relevant and not excessive in relation to the purposes for which they are processed; [...] such purposes must be explicit and legitimate and must be determined at the time of collection of the data; [...]the purposes of processing further to collection, shall not be incompatible with the purposes as they were originally specified."

Privacy and data protection are issues that do not only concern governments. There exist a lot of private initiatives from banks, industrial companies or consumer-protection groups (for the United States, see the Better Business Bureau, the Electronic Frontier Foundation or the Internet Content Coalition). Those initiatives aim at protecting privacy of individuals (e.g., consumers on the Internet) and protecting them from being personally profiled without their knowledge, or at generally ensuring privacy of the consumers on the Internet. Because this issue is very delicate and because we think that there must be some general rules of conduct, it is also a concern of *SECA*. Although *SECA* cannot provide a complete solution on how to handle personal data and how not to violate the rights of individuals, there is a *SECA* default regulation reflecting this issue and some regulations on privacy and data protection in the Code of Conduct (Section 14.5.2).

14.2.7 Advertising, Competition, Spamming

The growth expected from advertising varies from source to source but the tendency is obvious: Internet advertisement will grow. The revenues from Internet advertising are reported not to be overwhelming yet but a leap is expected.

Most of the EU member states (and also others) have compulsory advertisement restrictions. The goal is to protect the consumers. One of these regulations is the EU Directive 97/55/EC on misleading advertising which also defines the requirements on comparative advertising (European Union 1997a). In some countries advertising for certain professions, e.g., lawyers, medical persons, or clerics, is prohibited by law or the advertising for certain goods is restricted, e.g., tobacco, alcohol, or medicine, or for certain services. These compulsory rules have to be respected in order to comply with the law. Companies that are involved in electronic commerce have to check the legal regulations on advertising of all those countries where they want to obtain a market effect of the advertisements. Additionally, a careful clarification of the legal regulations is necessary for those states where the enterprise has relevant interests in expanding or market opening (Widmer and Bähler 1997), especially if they want to establish a server in those countries.

Sending unsolicited commercial emails or advertising emails to users or newsgroups, so-called "spamming," or sending emails with fake return address, a practice called "spoofing," is combated, especially in North America. California, Washington and Nevada have already enacted antispam bills where junk emailers can be fined up to several thousand dollars.

Because a lot of advertisement actions that take place on the Internet are not illegal but very annoying for many players, groups of certain business sections elaborated some Internet advertising policies; the same was done by the U.S. Federal Trade Commission and by the International Chamber of Commerce.[1]

There are several Internet pages that maintain blacklists of companies or privates who send inappropriate commercials, "inappropriate" in the meaning of sending to newsgroups or groups that explicitly do not tolerate commercials, or blacklists of email spammers.

SECA regulates parts of these points in the Code of Conduct (Section 14.5.2).

14.2.8 Content of Contracts and Internet Pages

The Internet is a channel for information transport that can become very influential. Reliable numbers about the quantity of Internet users are not available and the statistics vary, but the tendency and the prospects are clear: The Internet is in some sectors already or will definitely become a major channel for publication and procurement of information as well as for electronic commerce for everyone. A medium like the Internet can be misused for the distribution of illegal or harmful messages, products or services. Thus, conflicts with criminal laws or rights of personality of individuals are expected or already happening. There are a lot of approaches by governments, international organizations and the private sector to take action against the authors of such publications or defaming messages. These rules are optional codes of conduct rather than laws, since the national penal laws seem to be able to combat illegal content of Internet pages, messages or offers. The

---

[1]Advertising Standard Canada (private): http://www.screen.com/mnet/eng/indus/advert/Caf.htm

Federal Trade Commission: Advertising and Marketing on the Internet: The Rules of the Road http://www.ftc.gov/bcp/conline/pubs/buspubs/ruleroad.htm

International Chamber of Commerce: Guidelines on Interactive Marketing Communications, June 1996: http://www.iccwbo.org/Comm/html/Internet_Guidelines.html

problem is the difficulty of prosecuting the authors and publishers. In order to avoid these difficulties, the Bavarian authorities charged and convicted a former manager of an Internet Service Provider (ISP) of spreading illegal (pornographic) contents on an Internet page, which was operated by the ISP. The Somm judgement[2] caused quite a stir and it should not serve as a good example. It caused uncertainty among the users, ISPs and participants of the Internet and electronic commerce, as it is well-known to be impossible for ISPs to have full control over the content their customers publish or the links put on their customers' pages. Finally, this judgement was revised, based on the realization that the provider could not be made responsible for illegal content published by his customers.

The European Committee released a Communication on Illegal and Harmful Content on the Internet (European Union 1996) with the following core policies:

- Co-operation between the member states with a view to exchange information and to define minimum European standards on criminal content.
- Clarification of the administrative rules and regulations which apply to access providers and host service providers.
- Encouragement for self regulation.
- Support for the use of filtering software and rating systems.
- Organization of conferences and information exchange with international organizations.
- Establishment of an initiative that will support national awareness actions for parents and teachers.
- Various support actions.

SECA regulates some general principles of the issue in the Code of Conduct, with respect to self-regulation.

14.2.9 Contract Law

The core of almost every electronic-commerce relationship is the intended contract. In general, a contract can be concluded without any formal requirements, but in most jurisdictions, formal requirements for specific types of contracts can hinder the validity of such contracts or their enforceability (United States). Hence the players have to check and follow the requirements in order to settle contracts unhindered. In general, donations, contracts on land sale or bails require a certain form or a formalization. Additionally, there are some consumer-protection regulations that require certain forms, i.e., written contracts or handwritten signatures. Electronic commerce cannot fulfil the requirement of writing as long as the definition of "signature"—as this is the case in the civil law systems—is made by law mostly as a connection between ink and paper. In contrast, in the common law countries

---

[2]Decision of 28 May 1998 – 8340 Ds 465 Js 173158/95 – "CompuServe"

a signature is defined according to its function, i.e., evidence, caution, deterrence, channeling. Therefore, it can be assumed that a digital signature will be treated equal to paper-based signatures in the common law countries. A digital signature can legally not replace a "paper-based signature" as long as the "paper-based signature" is defined in relation to paper and pen. *SECA* cannot ignore these requirements because differing regulations would not be valid in countries where the definition is as strict as mentioned above. Nevertheless, in *SECA*, the players commit not to deny the validity of a signature solely on the ground that it is in electronic form. Hence contracts can be closed with digital signatures (unless the contract requires written form, handwritten signature or attestation by notaries). The EU Directive (see Section 14.3.2) includes an "advanced electronic signature" which will have to be implemented by the law of the member states by 2001 to be legally equivalent to the handwritten signature, additionally to paper and pen.

The content of contracts and the performance of the promises are not subject of *SECA*, but have to be handled according to the applicable law.

14.2.10 Copyright and Trademark

The development of new media technology on the one hand, and the decreasing costs of computers, storage media and usage of the network for consumers on the other hand enable attractive and efficient possibilities to distribute and sell digital goods like images, videos, software, books, newspapers, encyclopedias etc. over the Internet or other open networks (e.g., ISDN over phone lines). The advantages for the market are obvious, as well as the risks of suffering damage by piracy. Especially when links are provided to other Internet pages or frames where downloading is possible, the question of authorship and legal use arises. If protected material is made digitally accessible on an Internet page, it is much easier to violate copyrights and, at the same time, much more difficult to prosecute the violators.

Technical means for copyright protection are upcoming. Some of these enable the customer to consume the information only a restricted number of times or for a certain time along with charging. Others do not technically prevent the customer from consuming or distributing the information, but enable the detection of distribution (e.g., watermarking). Objections and discussions on this can be found in Kahin (1994). In addition to any technical measures, copyright protection must be regulated by law or international treaties. Therefore, initiatives from international organizations like the WIPO (World Intellectual Property Organization) released treaties to enforce international copyright protection on the Internet in 1996 (WIPO 1996). Based on the WIPO treaties, the European Commission released a proposal for a "Directive on Copyright and Related Rights in the Information Society" in December 1997 whose key regulation is stated as follows: "In particular, the proposal would grant authors, performers, phonogram and film producers and

broadcasting organizations an exclusive right to authorize or prohibit repro-
ductions (an equivalent exclusive reproduction right for authors of computer
programs and databases and for some other rightholders is already provided
by various Directives (European Union 1997d)). The harmonized definition
of the reproduction right would cover all relevant acts of direct or indirect reproduction, temporary or permanent, whether on-line or off-line, in material
or immaterial form."[3]

The Directive will regulate the following issues:

- The reproduction right by defining who has the right to do a certain kind
  of reproduction.
- Exceptions: "use for the sole purpose of illustration for teaching and scientific research, non-commercial uses for the benefit of visually-impaired or
  hearing-impaired people, use of excerpts in connection with the reporting
  of current events, quotations for criticism or review, use for the purposes
  of public security or proper performance of an administrative or judicial
  procedure."
- The distribution right, which is limited to the "right of the originator that
  shall be exhausted within the Union with the first sale or other transfer of
  ownership of the original of their works or tangible copies of them by the
  rightholder or with his consent."
- "Regulations on the obligations due to technical measures and on protection against persons who remove copyright related information without
  authorization."

Although criticized as being overprotective by voices from North America,
the prospective Directive has a real chance to be implemented by the member
states of the European Union. The proposal is planned to be adopted by the
European Parliament and Council by the end of June 2000.

Trademark is a concern when used for Internet domain names. Network
Solutions, Inc. (NSI), the entity that registers *.com domain names, published
a "Domain Name Dispute Policy"[4] aiming at encouraging disputing parties
to settle their differences without involving NSI (Ford and Baum 1997). Since
the decisions of the courts have not been consolidated yet neither in the USA
nor in Europe, the recommendation by Ford and Baum (1997) for participants
in electronic commerce can be passed on: register appropriate domain names
promptly and consult with counsel regarding strategies for enforcement of
your intellectual property rights in cyberspace (Ford and Baum 1997). Basically the tendency is that the allocation of domain names for the purpose of
later sale to the "appropriate" company is not protected by courts yet.

Copyright and trademark issues are not covered by SECA due to the
fact that they are already regulated either by national laws or international
treaties and recommendations. Nevertheless, it is very important that the

---

[3] http://europa.eu.int/comm/dg15/en/intprop/intprop/1100.htm
[4] http://rs.internic.net/help/policy.html

players doing electronic commerce know about the existence of these regulations and are familiar with the basic principles of copyright and trademark law.

14.2.11 Payment

In electronic commerce, payment can be performed conventionally or electronically. If performed conventionally, the legal requirements are the same as in the non-electronic world: There is an order, the delivery, the invoice and maybe a payment or prepayment before shipping the goods. For electronic payment, systems like SET, MANDATE and ecash are provided and controlled by financial institutions.

The terms and conditions for the legally binding character and liability of digital signatures when paying electronically are determined by the financial institutions. Customers usually cannot change or negotiate the conditions. As financial transactions are rather sensitive, financial institutions aim at providing their customers with smartcards, wallets or at least provide the software for key creation and signature. According to what Visa and Master-Card announced some months ago on the Visa homepage for their joint use of SET, customers would have to take the full liability for all transactions, even if they claimed that their key was compromised. Similar regulation seem to hold for some SET applications (e.g., by some banks in Switzerland). The possibility of software attacks is not considered at all. It is very likely that regulations like this will not be acknowledged as "state of the art" by courts, and several banks do not consider this meaningful, either. We expect that this view cannot be kept without damaging the reputation of financial institutions. There is no reason for treating the customers differently in SET or ecash concerning liability than in conventional credit card systems, where— e.g., according to the Visa Switzerland general conditions for the use of the Visa card—"for damages arising from misuse of the card since its loss until this time [notification], the cardholder who has exercised due diligence to the full extent shall be liable for a maximum of CHF 100.- per card." (The same user-friendly approach is followed with the *SECA* liability for general signatures rather than for payments.)

Not only with payments, also in all other areas of electronic commerce, the users should always have a liability limit for authorized transactions in total, at least as long as certain malicious attacks cannot be excluded technically.

SECA does not regulate the legal aspects of payments, as the general terms and conditions of the provider of the payment systems are set by the financial institutes providing the systems. However, *SECA* would be able to also handle the digital signatures used for payments.

14.2.12 Taxation

The regulation of taxes is not in the scope of *SECA*. Setting up regulations on taxes is an exclusive competence of the governments. Nevertheless, the current tax situation is summarized.

Trades made through the Internet are currently taxed like all other trades: If a service or a product is provided via the Internet, e.g., a consultation or a computer program, it generally has to be taxed as if it were ordered by letter or phone and provided non-electronically. Therefore, the medium Internet does not help to avoid paying taxes.

Discussions are going on about the sense and the likelihood of the acceptance of a "Cybertax" or a "bit tax," terms that are not used homogeneously, here in the meaning of special taxation for Internet transmissions. In Europe, this idea was refused broadly and in the United States, the House of Representatives passed an "Internet Tax Freedom Act".[5] The World Trade Organization (WTO) agreed on continuing the moratorium on tax-free Internet business, goods or services ordered electronically but delivered non-electronically.[6] Provisionally, the discussions are theoretical rather than practical, as the ideas are not convincingly presented and therefore meet with disapproval. Furthermore, governments are afraid of discouraging people from using the Internet by imposing new taxes.

14.2.13 Conclusions

There are various legal issues a person has to be aware of when being involved in electronic commerce. Most of these issues are regulated by national laws and hence do not have to or cannot be regulated differently by *SECA*. Topics like applicable law, privacy, consumer protection or copyright might have an influence on the rights of the players and therefore are partly regulated by *SECA*, because *SECA* aims at enforcing fair electronic commerce.

14.3 Selected Approaches at Legal Frameworks

Current and emerging approaches at legal frameworks for electronic commerce or digital signatures deal with parts of the legal aspects described in Section 14.2. We will describe the most important and most-discussed proposals and point out in which respect we consider them insufficient, so that the need for a new approach that deals with the most serious lacks can be understood. This is the aim of the *SEMPER* Electronic-Commerce Agreement (*SECA*), which will be described in Section 14.4.

---

[5]http://thomas.loc.gov/cgi-bin/query/z?c105:H.R.1054:
[6]http://www.wto.org

14.3.1 UNCITRAL Model Law on Electronic Commerce

The United Nations Commission on International Trade (UNCITRAL) elaborated a Model Law on Electronic Commerce in 1996.[7]

As stated in the Guide to Enactment, "The purpose of the Model Law is to offer national legislators a set of internationally acceptable rules as to how a number of such legal obstacles may be removed, and how a more secure legal environment may be created for what has become known as 'electronic commerce'." The UNCITRAL approach is a good basis for further national regulations, provided that the states do transfer these provisions into national law. Because no direct obligations for players are set in the Model Law, nothing will change for the players in relation to the uncertain legal situation in electronic commerce until the states transfer the principles of the Model Law uniformly into their own law. So far, there are only a few national approaches that are based (although partially) on the UNCITRAL Model Law, e.g., in Australia, Singapore and Columbia.

The Model Law suggests a solution to remedy the legal difficulties caused by certain requirements in some legal systems for writing, handwritten signature and original of documents. The main principles of the Model Law are the following:

- "No denial of legal effect, validity or enforceability of an electronic signature solely on the grounds that it is in the form of a data message."
- The requirement of "writing" is fulfilled with a data message under certain circumstances.
- "Where the law requires a signature of a person, that requirement is met in relation to a data message if: "(a) a method is used to identify that person and to indicate that person's approval of the information contained in the data message; and (b) that method is as reliable as was appropriate for the purpose for which the data message was generated or communicated, in the light of all the circumstances, including any relevant agreement."
- Where the law requires information to be presented or retained in its original form, that requirement is met by a data message if: (a) there exists a reliable assurance as to the integrity of the information from the time when it was first generated in its final form, as a data message or otherwise; and (b) where it is required that information be presented, that information is capable of being displayed to the person to whom it is to be presented."

Obviously, these principles neither state any regulations concerning liability for digital signatures, certificates or the issuance of certificates, nor do they contain any provisions concerning jurisdiction or applicable law, nor any provisions about the recognition of foreign certificates. One obvious point is that the Model Law does not require mechanisms for non-repudiation, i.e., it

---

[7]http://www.un.or.at/uncitral/english/texts/electcom/ml-ec.htm

could be fulfilled even when using mechanisms based on symmetric cryptography only for message integrity and authentication based on a shared secret (also sometimes called "digital signature," but without justification from our point of view). As with symmetric cryptography, both sender and recipient can have produced the message, non-repudiation cannot be provided by such mechanisms. This would not impact the legal effect of the message itself, but it would affect its evidential value in a dispute case. Another problem is the fact that the message cannot be transferred to others with the same legal effect, without also transferring the shared secret. The management of such keys is rather inefficient compared with keys based on asymmetric cryptography.

Compared to *SECA*, an agreement between players, the Model Law is much more abstract and it does not address the players directly, with the consequence that the concerns of the players are not fully taken into account. *SECA* is an agreement that was built in order to diminish the legal uncertainty of the players and that can be signed and applied directly by the players. In *SECA*, the players can rely on the signed provisions which provide mutual protection since all *SECA* players sign basically the same agreement.

The UNCITRAL Working Group on Electronic Commerce released "Draft Uniform Rules on Electronic Signatures"[8] on November 23, 1998, which should either constitute a separate legal instrument or be incorporated in an extended version of the Model Law. The final proposal is anticipated to be released in summer 2000. The purpose of the Uniform Rules is "to promote the efficient utilization of digital communication by establishing a security framework and by giving written and digital messages equal status as regards their legal effect." The principles are mainly the same as stated in the Model Law but always extended to an enhanced secure electronic signature, i.e., a signature that "can be verified through the application of security procedures." Additionally, the Uniform Rules state some regulations about the liability for enhanced secure electronic signatures, about digital signatures supported by certificates, and about duties and liability of certification authorities. Unfortunately, the regulation of the liability for electronic signatures is not satisfactory at all. They propose in variant A "Where the use of a[n] [enhanced][secure] electronic signature was unauthorized and the purported signer did not exercise reasonable care to avoid the unauthorized use of its signature and to prevent the addressee from relying on such a signature, Variant X: the signature is nevertheless regarded as authorized, unless the relying party knew or should have known that the signature was not authorized. Variant Y: the purported signer may be held liable only for the cost of restoring the parties to their position before the unauthorized use of the signature, unless the relying party knew or should have known that the signature was not that of the purported signer. Variant Z: the purported signer is liable [to pay damages to compensate the relying party] for harm caused,

---

[8]http://www.un.or.at/uncitral/english/sessions/wg_ec/wp-73.htm

unless the relying party knew or should have known that the signature was not that of the purported signer." However, there is no regulation for the case that the purported signer did exercise reasonable care to avoid the unauthorized use of its signature but nevertheless fell victim to an attack. In *SECA* this case is solved with the *SECA* limit (as described in Section 14.4.5) and the Liability-Cover Service (Chapter 13).

14.3.2 Approach of the Commission of the European Community (CEC)

We consider here the EU Directive on "Electronic Signatures" (European Union 2000) which is to be implemented by 2001 by the member states. We also take into account earlier discussions with the EU Commission, and the final report of the European Electronic Signature Standardization Initiative (EESSI) (Nilsson, Van Eecke, Medina, Pinkas, and Pope 1999).

The purpose of the Directive on a "community framework for electronic signatures" is to "facilitate the use of electronic signatures and to contribute to their legal recognition." The aim is to establish "a legal framework for electronic signatures and certain certification services in order to ensure the proper functioning of the internal market."

The Directive introduces two classes of "electronic signatures," the "electronic signature" and the "advanced electronic signature."

The "electronic signature" is defined as "data in electronic form which are attached to or logically associated with other electronic data and which serve as a method of authentication." This means a very broad class, including digital signatures, but also message authentication codes (MAC) which are only based on symmetric cryptography and thus do not provide non-repudiation. In the EESSI report, it is emphasized that this definition "does even not exclude the typed name at the bottom of an email or the attachment of a scanned signature to a document." For this kind of signatures, the Directive states that the member states shall ensure that it is "not denied legal effectiveness and admissibility as evidence in legal proceedings solely on grounds that it is in electronic form ..." or that it does not fulfil the criteria of the "advanced electronic signature" described below. In contrast to verbal orders (which today have legal effect as well) for which verbal recording is not admissible as evidence in some countries, because it is easy to manipulate, email orders without digital signature will be admitted as evidence. We expect that the conclusiveness of such evidence will be handled in court correspondingly.

In the Directive, the "advanced electronic signature" is defined as an "electronic signature" which meets the following requirements:

1. it is uniquely linked to the signatory;
2. it is capable of identifying the signatory;
3. it is created using means that the signatory can maintain under his sole control; and

4. it is linked to the data to which it relates in such a manner that any subsequent change of the data is detectable.

According to the Directive, the member states must ensure that "Advanced electronic signatures" can be treated similarly to handwritten signatures if they have been created by a secure signature-creation device as defined in Annex III, and if they are based on a "qualified certificate" which also includes certain requirements on the trustworthiness of the CA and its procedures (defined in Annex II of the Directive). According to Annex III, such signature-creation devices must ensure that the signature-creation-data used for signature generation can practically occur only once, that their secrecy is "reasonably assured," that they "cannot, with reasonable assurance, be derived and the signature is protected against forgery using currently available technology," and that they "can be reliably protected by the legitimate signatory against the use of others." These are requirements against the direct use of the key by others—however these clauses, in the whole context of the Directive, do not mean protection from others who inject a Trojan horse in a PC (see Weber (1998)), which forges the data before they are transferred to a secure signature-creation device where they are signed.

A further requirement is that such secure signature-creation devices "must not alter the data to be signed or prevent such data from being presented to the signatory prior to the signature process." This does not imply that data to be signed must be protected from Trojan horse attacks operating outside the device.

That Annex III does not exclude Trojan horse impersonating attacks becomes clear by the Clause 15 at the beginning of the Directive: "whereas ... Annex III covers requirements for secure signature-creation devices to ensure the functionality of advanced electronic signatures; whereas it *does not cover the entire system environment in which such devices operate.*" This restriction contradicts a suggestive interpretation of the definition of the "advanced electronic signature" (see the list above): One would think that the "means" which the signatory "can maintain under his sole control" should include everything on the path from the display, where the signatory sees data that he believes he signs, to the actual signing. However, following Annex III and Clause (15), this interpretation seems to be correct at least if this entire path is on the signature-creation device, but not necessarily correct otherwise.

Another issue which should have been included implicitly or explicitly is provisions so that the format, including the fonts (to avoid malicious fonts with changed digits), has to be signed together with the information, to avoid different interpretations of the same bit string when using different systems (Fox 1998).

"Qualified certificates," according to the Directive, must be able to include limits for the value of transactions". However, a total limit is not mentioned. The CAs have to take liability for accurate information in the qualified certificates they issue, including that "at the time of the issuance of the certificate, the signatory identified in the qualified certificate held the signature-creation data corresponding to the signature-verification data given or identified in the certificate." The liability of the key holder is not regulated.

We must state clearly that the regulations in this Directive are not sufficient to protect the signatory from impersonating attacks: Undetected forgery of data before they are signed must be prevented, and for this, secure operating systems have to be developed. Current operating systems cannot perfectly protect sensitive applications from being affected by bad applications.

The "advanced electronic signature", to be handled in the same manner as a handwritten signature, is generally not supposed to become the usual kind of signature for electronic commerce. The "electronic signature" is expected to suffice here, which binds the user but should not be enforceable if an attack was plausible.

For practical use, as Trojan horse impersonating attacks cannot be excluded for both kinds of "electronic signatures", it would have been wise to include at least the optional use of Commitment Services as proposed in the previous chapter, and to fix the overall liability per key in the compromised case to an a-priori known amount, as proposed in *SECA* in this chapter. *SECA* may be handled as a "closed system" with respect to the Directive, which means that the regulations in *SECA* are not affected by the regulations of the Directive.

14.3.3 OECD Guidelines

The OECD Guidelines for the Security of Information Systems (European Union 1992) and the OECD Cryptography Policy Guidelines (European Union 1997f) are papers that point out the advantages and the vulnerability of information systems and cryptography. They recognize certain principles and give respective recommendations to the governments. "The objective of security of information systems is the protection of the interests of those relying on information systems from harm resulting from failures of availability, confidentiality, and integrity," as stated in the Guidelines for the Security of Information Systems. Thus, an issue of these Guidelines is liability. This is not usual for frameworks of this kind. However, the treatment of liability is limited to the recommendation that appropriate policies, laws, decrees etc. have to be adopted which include provisions for the allocation of risks and liability for failures of the security of information systems. Although addressed to the public and the private sector, the Guidelines do not provide any regulations or concrete proposals; they leave the translation into formulations to the member countries. Nevertheless, it has to be recognized that the Guidelines were published in 1992 and for that time they showed unmistakably what the private and the public sector would have to be prepared for.

The better-known Cryptography Policies focused on the use and promotion of cryptography without publishing any provisions concerning key escrow or key recovery. They are a catalogue of general recommendations addressed to the governments. *SECA* goes further: *SECA* provides the concrete regulations on liability, and *SECA* makes the players aware of the threats, risks and the means for repulsing the threats and reducing the risks. *SECA* can be seen as the completion of the Guidelines' recommendations that are related to electronic commerce; it is not a catalogue of principles but rather a synopsis of a code of conduct accompanied by recommendations that contain some regulations mentioned in the OECD Guidelines.

According to the official conclusion and action plan for electronic commerce of the OECD Ministerial Conference held in Ottawa in October 1998 and its follow-up conference in Paris in October 1999 and updated on a regular basis, the OECD is planning the elaboration of further policies on the protection of privacy on global networks, consumer protection, authentication and taxation. In December 1999, the Council of the OECD approved the "Guidelines for Consumer Protection in the Context of Electronic Commerce",[9] which are "designed to help ensure that consumers are no less protected when shopping online than they are when they buy from their local store or order from a catalogue."

14.3.4 Utah Digital Signature Act (1996)

The Utah Digital Signature Act was enacted in 1996 and it was the first act of this kind (State of Utah 1996). It sets up regulations for the building of a CA, its duties, regulations for the subscriber and repositories (meaning certificate databases) and regulations on the legal effect of digital signatures. It also includes regulations on the validity of digital signatures and some regulations on liability and duties of subscribers. Several bills have been enacted in the meantime that amend the Digital Signature Act. However, the principles as outlined below have not materially changed.[10]

It is very progressive to unite all these aspects under one law, but unfortunately the subscribers are put into a very unfavorable position concerning liability: It describes the subscribers' duties concerning their private keys in article 46-3-305 as follows: "By accepting a certificate issued by a licensed certification authority, the subscriber identified in the certificate assumes a duty to exercise reasonable care to retain control of the private key and prevent its disclosure to any person not authorized to create the subscriber's digital signature." It is likely that the term "exercise reasonable care" has to be defined by a judge and it is not clear at all if securing his own equipment should be included in the reasonable care. Furthermore, the Utah Act states in article 46-3-401 that a digital signature is deemed to satisfy legal signature requirements under certain circumstances that are named in the cited article. Therefore, players are liable for the messages signed digitally

---

[9]http://www.oecd.org/dsti/sti/it/consumer/prod/CPGuidelines_final.pdf
[10]http://www.le.state.ut.us/~1999/htmdoc/hbillhtm/HB0246.htm,
    http://www.le.state.ut.us/~1999/htmdoc/sbillhtm/SB0075.htm

with their private key, unless they can assert the invalidity of this acknowledgment, because digitally signed documents are considered acknowledged documents under the Act (Biddle 1996). For a victimized subscriber the unpleasant consequence is that if there is a message or a transaction or anything that was signed with his private key, he is liable for the legal consequences of that message unless he can prove that he took reasonable care and that his key was compromised. As it is might be impossible to prove that a key was compromised, the subscriber has to take the burden of the acknowledgment of digital signatures, because the burden of proof has to be carried by the victimized subscriber. This is the main disadvantage of the Digital Signature Act, and we agree to the critique of Bidder when writing: "The allocation of liability and evidentiary burdens imposed by the Utah Act put users of digital signatures who are victimized by fraud in a position that is disadvantageous compared to several analogous situations."

Unlike in *SECA*, the regulation of the Utah Act is not consumer-friendly at all. In *SECA*, subscriber (consumers included) are liable up to their *SECA* limit and additionally to other liability limits they can choose. This is a major advantage of *SECA* compared to the Utah Act.

14.3.5 German Digital Signature Act (1997)

Article 3 of the Information and Communication Services Act is the Digital Signature Act that was enacted on July 1st 1997. Its purpose is stated in paragraph 1: to establish general conditions under which digital signatures are deemed secure and forgeries of digital signatures or manipulation of signed data can be reliably ascertained (German Government 1997). The act is accompanied by an ordinance and a catalogue of measures ("Massnahmenkatalog") where the implementation of the act and details of principles described in it are regulated very extensively. The act is an infrastructure act, i.e., it sets out the qualifications for establishing a CA and for obtaining a license from the state. Furthermore, it describes the requirements for issuing and revoking certificates, for the content of certificates, for technical components and the administration of a CA. The Digital Signature Act does not include any regulations concerning liability. The legal recognition of digital signatures and the admissibility of digital signatures as evidence are not issues of this act nor of the ordinance and are therefore not regulated. The act requires a very high security standard for CAs and certificates. One could say that the name "Digital Signature Act" is a bit misleading because it only regulates one aspect of digital signatures, their technical and organizational environment. It neither regulates the consequences of using digital signatures, e.g., liability for issuing certificates, nor the liability for compromised signatures or keys.

The act addresses prospective CAs rather than participants of electronic commerce like sellers, buyers or banks. The act's target group and the purposes of the act are not the same as in *SECA*. An advanced point of the

Digital Signature Act, at least in its motivations, is the realization that without secure hardware devices including secure I/O, the signature cannot be really secure, and the resulting regulations on the technical components for creating digital signatures. In the history of its development, threats of impersonation have been discussed, as well as secure user I/O as some means of protection. Thus this approach tries to take these threats into account, at least to some extent. In *SECA*, different levels of signing equipment including software-only solutions are possible, but this is compensated by the possibility of additionally providing undeniable commitments to the relying party as introduced in Section 13.2.1. Thus, *SECA* does not primarily aim at an equivalence between handwritten and digital signature, which, however, is intended to be one of the future achievements based on the German Digital Signature Act.

There are currently discussions going on about the replacement of the Digital Signature Act by a new Act which would be called "Framework Regulations for Electronic Signatures". The draft framework aims at reflecting the European Directive on Electronic Signatures. The main changes that are planned can be summarized as follows: Introduction of "qualified electronic signatures" and "qualified certificates", adjustment of security requirements to the EU Directive, accreditation model for CAs dropped, introduction of regulation about the liability of certification authorities, extension of current data protection regulations. The draft is planned to pass the parliament in fall 2000 and to be in force on 1 January 2001. In addition to this draft Framework there are currently discussions going on about the inclusion of the electronic form using a signature according to the Digital Signature Act in the Civil Code (Bürgerliches Gesetzbuch, BGB) so that the electronic form becomes an equivalent to the written form as defined in the Code.

14.3.6 Electronic Data Interchange Agreements

The term EDI (Electronic Data Interchange) stands for the area and for the standards for electronic data interchange between business partners, based on certain message structures defined in commonly known code tables. UN/EDIFACT (ISO/IEC TC154 1999) is a well-known example of an EDI message standard. SNA, X.400, and increasingly TCP/IP (e.g., over the Internet) are used for transferring EDI messages. EDI primarily aims at commerce between commercial business partners who have a well-established and frequently used business relationship a priori. Multilateral agreements developed for this area are based on the assumption that each business partner can provide security and care for its own functional environment. Thus, compromised signatures are not an issue. Service providers as third parties are supposed to provide network and value added services and therefore are also included in the agreements. Only messages, including receipts and acknowledgments, are considered, rather than complete business applications which consist of complex protocols and which include more than two parties in general, as assumed in *SEMPER*.

The UN Model Interchange Agreement as well as the similar European Model EDI Agreement (Knott and Stemerding 1996) are model agreements which can be used between business partners. They regulate basic rules for business-to-business commerce: the responsibility of the parties for securing their own procedures and equipment, the interoperability based on agreed parameters, the legal compliance of their messages, and confidentiality. They regulate the legal effect of messages with or without receipts and acknowledgments and in case of technical errors, as well as the time point a contract is closed. The business partners have to commit, e.g., not to challenge the admissibility as evidence of EDI messages and records in court.

In the meanwhile, many organizations have provided their own Interchange Agreements, based on those models, to be signed by their business partners. They contain similar basics, but some are much more detailed and have many additions. Many of them can be found on the Internet (e.g., a very detailed version of Texas Instruments).

In contrast to the conditions assumed for electronic commerce in the EDI field, *SEMPER*, as well as *SECA*, takes into account that electronic commerce—especially over the Internet—is not limited to closed business-to-business user groups. With open networks like the Internet, everyone including private persons, can participate without establishing business relationships a priori. Thus, the approach of the UN Model Interchange Agreement is not sufficient to be adopted for our purposes as it does not take into account the requirements of all, private, business and non-technical players.

14.3.7 Conclusions

One of the main differences between *SECA* and the current approaches, and our main motivation to develop *SECA*, is the missing liability limit for signatures in case of malicious attacks getting signatures in an underhanded way. The equipment of an average private Internet user does not prevent such attacks. The situation is equal or similar for many small companies (SMEs). None of the present approaches provides sufficient protection to the key holder.

14.4 The *SEMPER* Electronic-Commerce Agreement

14.4.1 General

SECA, the *SEMPER* Electronic-Commerce Agreement, is an agreement to be signed in writing by any participants of electronic commerce who want to use *SECA* as a legal basis.

SECA is built for a global network. It includes players that do not have mutual trust relationships a priori. Not only business-to-business transactions are captured in *SECA*, but also private-to-business and even private-to-private transactions.

SECA can exist independent of *SEMPER*, though the technical recommendations in the *SECA* Guidelines (Section 14.5.3) contain the definition of "*SECA*-compliant" components and electronic-commerce software which have been elaborated according to the main principles of *SEMPER*.

SECA addresses the *SECA* players and obliges them to act according to the Code of Conduct (Section 14.5.2). Some further recommendations are given in the Guidelines, but the individual contractual relations are not regulated. Thus, *SECA* does not lay down the duties of the individual players in every phase of an electronic-commerce scenario. The principle of "freedom of contracts" remains with *SECA*. Nevertheless, *SECA* takes into account some mandatory existing rules in trade like distance-selling regulations, consumer-protection laws and privacy laws.

SECA is neither new law nor a new international treaty. It is a contract between *SECA* players and their certification authorities (CAs) with effect on contractual relationships between the players.

SECA claims to be fair considering liability. The regulation of liability for certificates and digital signatures of players, third parties and certification authorities is compulsory within *SECA*. The provisions set in the Agreement can be enforced in court and might also lead to an exclusion from *SECA*. We think that with *SECA*, a good compromise has been found that contains very few strict rules with much effect on the practicability, fairness and risk reduction of electronic commerce within *SECA*.

14.4.2 *SECA* CAs

CAs participating in *SECA* are called "*SECA* CAs." *SECA* CAs are regular CAs that additionally offer to register and certify natural persons or legal entities under the *SECA* regulations. It makes much sense if they also provide a Commitment Service (Section 13.2) or Liability-Cover Service (Section 13.2.7), but these services can also be used if the CAs providing them are not identical.

For the purpose of simplicity, we do not differentiate between registration authorities and certification authorities in the remainder of this chapter. The reader, however, should be aware that these functionalities can be provided by different services. For instance, the registration might be delegated to local registration offices, post offices or banks, provided that a correct identity authentication can be performed.

Each *SECA* CA is assumed to be trusted to some extent, by the subscriber as well as (indirectly) by the relying party. This can be supported by a hierarchy of CAs or by cross-certification, or any hybrid public-key infrastructure which enables checking each other's certificates along a "trust path." Here

is no difference to "usual" CAs within a "usual" public-key infrastructure
(PKI).

In analogy to Section 13.5.2, we recommend that *SECA* CAs might be
handled, e.g., by Chambers of Commerce in different countries.

14.4.3 *SECA* Legal Body

To complete our model, we also include one or several "*SECA* legal bodies",
which have the task

– to maintain and publish *SECA*, i.e., the agreement templates,
– to collect all jurisdictions with respect to *SECA* and provide appropriate
  updates,
– to provide information which should be found at one point, e.g., public-key
  certificates of *SECA* CAs and root CAs if existing,
– to publish blacklists of users and CAs failing seriously, and lists of entities
  having been excluded from *SECA*, provided such lists are required and
  allowed,
– to publish information about the legal situation in different countries with
  respect to electronic commerce and encryption.
– to publish information about up-to-date crypto algorithms, key lengths
  and the expected period they will be safe (Lenstra and Verheul 1999).

The *SECA* players will not have to interoperate with the *SECA* legal
body directly, apart from retrieving information. Depending on the demand,
a *SECA* legal body might exist on each continent, in each country, or wherever
needed. They are supposed to co-operate.

14.4.4 Joining *SECA*

The procedure for registering a subscriber for *SECA* must enable the *SECA*
CA to ensure that the right person is registered with the right initial public
key. This includes that the *SECA* CA has to check that the registered person
has the secret key and strongly advise that person to keep it (and all later
keys) secret. The *SECA* CA can define appropriate processes which might
also include notary services in certain cases. The responsibility and liability
for proper identity authentication is at the *SECA* CA.

One possible procedure is described in the following:

The player generates a key pair (which might also be on a smartcard or
secure device, in which case the key creation should at least be influenced
by the user if possible) and self-signs the public key together with his name,
passport, a unique ID (e.g., social security card number, identity-card number, maybe later also biometrics), the intended role(s) in *SECA*, the name
of the *SECA* CA, and the date. Then he visits the *SECA* CA bringing these
data with him, e.g., saved on a disk or on a laptop.

The public key will be registered and certified as the *SECA* key after the player has signed the *SECA* agreement, which does not need to include the key.[11] The player will later use the private key to "sign with her *SECA* key" when doing electronic commerce.

The *SECA* CA must perform personal identification including checking the passport or any other valid means proving the identity. The player has to provide all requested information: roles in *SECA*, domicile address, birthday (passport), fingerprint of key. Then he has to determine all the options, and sign the commitments belonging to his role—not including the initial key— with his handwritten signature.

The player might also answer a certain choice of control questions (different for each player) from his personal surroundings, which he could answer again later for authentication purposes towards the *SECA* CA, e.g., when terminating or modifying his commitments in *SECA*.

The *SECA* CA verifies all information and checks if the player was once excluded from *SECA*. Thereby it also checks the self-signed information—if there were any doubts, the player would have to additionally sign a challenge using the private key. If there are no inconsistencies, it issues several certificates: a long certificate containing all the information including the public *SECA* key, a *SECA* birthday attribute certificate (for a private player) containing at least the date of birth of the key holder and his public *SECA* key, and several short certificates (on special request) with restricted information, e.g., including a pseudonym instead of a full name for the key; the full name would have to be revealed in a dispute case if necessary.

For key updates later, the *SECA* CA provides secret challenge data which the subscriber has to sign. This can be done remotely if there exists an older key with valid *SECA* certificate; in this case the result is additionally signed with the older key to prove that the player actually owns the key and is identical with the alleged player.[12]

Remark: Different key pairs can be created and the public parts of them registered and certified, each for a special purpose, e.g., different limits. Remote updates of such keys would have to be signed with the corresponding old key. For simplicity, we do not consider this possibility in more detail in the remainder of the chapter.

14.4.5 Liability Limits in *SECA*

Three different types of limiting the liability for digital signatures are used within *SECA*. The first (the fixed *SECA* limit) is mandatory, the second (the Liability-Cover Service, see Section 13.2.7) is optional but recommended, and

---

[11]Of course, policies may be defined such that each key or its fingerprint must be signed on paper by the key holder. This increases the overhead but reduces the necessary trust in the CA.

[12]I.e., the signed data cannot have been sent by an attacker trying to provide a wrong key connected to the right name.

the third (the partner-specific limits) is optional and recommended only for specific situations. All three of them can be combined arbitrarily.

All three limits are based on the fact that the *SECA* digital signature can be denied by the subscriber in the case of attacks, even if the attack cannot be proven. These are the same provisions as for the Commitment Service presented in Section 13.2.

We consider the use of the Liability-Cover Service rather than the more general Commitment Service in the remainder of this chapter, since it simplifies our considerations. However, a general Commitment Service can be used instead.

SECA Limit. The *SECA* liability limit *SECA_Limit* is fixed and mandatory. It is the limited liability which the subscriber must take if his key was compromised. This limit is specific for the key and due only once, i.e., if the subscriber claims this key compromised. In this case, he might have to satisfy claims of damaged relying parties. Those claims might cover a high amount; however, the subscriber will have to satisfy them only up to the amount *SECA_Limit*. The question in which order the claims have to be satisfied is not considered here. We suppose all players know the risk of accepting signed transactions without requiring any further guarantees like a liability-cover certificate (see Section 13.2.7). So we do not bother to provide particularly fair solutions to satisfy relying parties that did not ask for additional undeniable commitments.

The fixed value of *SECA_Limit* might depend on the role or business of the player, on the trust he wants others to have in him (this turned out to be an issue for commercial players, from the surveys made by *SEMPER*), and on the equipment used for digital signatures (see also Section 14.4.7). Correspondingly, the *SECA* certificates should show a certain liability level taken (e.g., Euro 500, Euro 50.000, Euro 5.000.000). Although a relying party cannot conclude from that level that it would get any compensation (since it is unclear how many relying parties would claim for compensation, especially in the case of multiple attacks), the difference between those levels is significant.

Liability-Cover Service in SECA. The second kind of limits is provided by the Commitment Service (Section 13.2) or Liability-Cover Service (LCS, Section 13.2.7), which the subscriber uses in connection with or independent of *SECA*. It should be the *SECA* key which has additionally been registered for the Commitment Service or LCS. Both services can be used independently, but here they are considered as combined.

While the *SECA* digital signature for signing transactions is deniable in case of attacks, at least all provided commitment certificates or liability-cover certificates must be fulfilled in the case of an attack, up to the (e.g., monthly) limit *LCS_Limit*.

To encourage the user to use the LCS without increasing their liability too much regarding the additional *SECA* liability limit *SECA_Limit* (see Section 14.4.5), we will count all fulfilled liability-cover certificates as fulfilling also the *SECA* liability limit. Hence, if the *SECA* liability limit is exceeded by fulfilling liability-cover certificates after a key was claimed compromised, no additional claims have to be fulfilled due to the *SECA* liability limit. Vice versa, however, it is different: Even if the *SECA* limit is exceeded, all liability-cover certificates have to be fulfilled. The resulting worst-case liability is max(*SECA_Limit, LCS_Limit*).

Partner-Specific Limits in *SECA*. The third kind of limits for a subscriber is specific for some of his business partners with whom he does business regularly. For such business partners, it may make sense to define separate partner-specific limits), leaving the use of the LCS to more spontaneous business with other partners.

With different partners P, the subscriber might agree different limited liabilities *P_Limit*. The liability *P_Limit* for one partner P means that, if a signature was compromised which concerns a transaction with this business partner P, the subscriber is nevertheless liable up to a total limit of *P_Limit* for all compromised signatures towards P.

P itself can check whether outstanding transactions would exceed the limit *P_Limit* he had agreed with the subscriber, and be careful if this is the case, i.e., ask for liability-cover certificates or ask the subscriber to increase *P_Limit*.

These limits make sense for the subscriber and his business partners if they do business frequently and if they do not want to use the LCS (with appropriately high limits) for some reason. Subscribers should be aware of the fact that the worst-case liability given above increases by the total of all partner-specific limits P_i_*Limit* for all i partners.

14.4.6 Blacklists of Players Claiming Compromised Keys and Signatures

As the regulations of *SECA* require limiting the liability for compromised signatures, it will happen that in certain cases, where a player claims a compromised signature, the resulting damage will have to be taken by the damaged business partner himself as the player's limits have already been exceeded. Although *SECA* gives useful recommendations how those business partners can protect themselves from these events, these business partners are free to take that risk. (*SECA* does not forbid players to do it with software-only signatures without any further means.)

However, we also want to protect potential business partners from such damage as far as possible. Furthermore, we want to protect the *SECA* community from subscribers claiming compromised signatures without justification. For this purpose, players who claim a compromised signature and thereby damage any business partner might be put onto a publicly accessible blacklist, in principle, for the following reasons:

- Before doing business with a player, the business partner shall have the opportunity to check the blacklist for the name or pseudonym of this player. If the player is on the list, there is usually no reason at all to stop doing business with this player. The business partner should just make sure that he is protected in this business transaction, e.g., by requiring liability-cover certificates or a partner-specific limit.
- Each player can become the victim of an attack. However, the better the player protects himself against such attacks, e.g., by never downloading uncertified or unknown software from the Internet or installing programs from other suspicious sources (e.g., advertising mail), the better he will be protected against such attacks. The blacklist should at least be a motivation to protect oneself better from such attacks.
- The blacklist shall prevent people from wrongly claiming compromised signatures (which in most cases will not be provable). If a player does so and some business partner suffers damage, he is put onto the blacklist. After this, the other business partners (who check this blacklist) will not take this risk again. They will require guarantees next time.

The business partner who was financially harmed will inform the *SECA* CA and show the signature which was claimed to have been compromised. The *SECA* CA will check with the charged player. If the charged player denies having claimed the signature compromised, then the *SECA* CA will inform the business partner that the player will stand by his signature. If the charged player admits having claimed his signature compromised, then his user identity and all his pseudonyms (without links among each other) are put onto a blacklist. The player has to revoke the compromised key and all its certificates immediately. The user's identity and his pseudonyms will stay on the list for a certain period (e.g., 6 months or 1 year), and all new pseudonyms created during this period will also be added. All of them will be deleted after that period. The period can increase per subscriber in the case of repetition and depending on the amount of the damage for the relying parties.

Notice that certificate revocation lists and blacklists are not related to each other. Revoked certificates are not published via the blacklists.

Blacklists might also be handled for players failing otherwise (e.g., acting in a way conflicting to *SECA*) or having been excluded, for example for failing third parties and manufacturers of *SECA*-compliant components (see Section 14.5.3).

Note that the use of blacklist might not be allowed in certain countries for reasons of data protection. Since blacklists are not a basic part of *SECA*, as they just increase awareness of the risks, they can be omitted.

14.4.7 Levels of Equipment

The security of digital signatures against malicious attacks (see Section 13.1.1) depends on several factors which determine the so-called *equipment level*. The following classification should only serve as an example which would have to be refined.

Source of Software.

1. Any software from any sources was and will be installed (e.g., downloaded software or from CDs in advertising mail).
2. Only software is used which has been signed by the manufacturer and where a certificate has been verified, so that the originator is known.
3. Only software is used which has been certified according to standards guaranteeing that the software is secure and fair (standards to be developed).

Signing Component.

1. The signature is computed using a software-only solution, i.e., a normal user PC without additional secure hardware.
2. The signing key is stored on a smartcard or PCMCIA card and will never leave this device. The digital signature is computed on that device.
3. A "secure hardware device" is used which includes producing the signature (while the key never leaves this device) and showing to the user what will be signed.

Operating System.

1. The operating system underlying the process performing the digital signature allows other applications to affect that process, e.g., to capture passphrases or inject other values to be signed, without being noticed by the user.
2. The operating system underlying the process performing the digital signature does not allow other applications to affect that process.

We highly recommend to specify appropriate protection profiles (see Section 14.5.3) for evaluation, e.g., according to ITSEC, Common Criteria, or FIPS respectively.

A possible modification of *SECA* would allow the equipment level to be included into *SECA*, so that the business partner can estimate the probability of compromised signatures, and to oblige the players not to use any lower level. Consequently, the players would be responsible and liable for damages if they use lower levels—or at least they would be added onto another blacklist. There are arguments which would require all commercial players to show their equipment level while this would be voluntary to private players. However, we leave such regulations to those who will employ and refine *SECA*.

14.5 The Content of *SECA*

SECA consists of 3 parts:

1. The *Agreement* itself which has to be signed with a handwritten signature by the *SECA* player at his *SECA* CA. Its wording is given in Section 14.5.1.
2. The *Code of Conduct* to which the *SECA* player commits when signing the Agreement. It is given in Section 14.5.2.
3. The *Guidelines* which define "*SECA*-compliant components" to protect their users, and give information to the users on how they can reduce their exposure to damage due to failures and attacks. It is given in Section 14.5.3.

14.5.1 The Agreement

The Agreement

The *SEMPER* ELECTRONIC-COMMERCE AGREEMENT ("***SECA***") is entered into force as of .... [date], by and between the *SECA* certification authority ("***SECA* CA**") ...., with its principal place of business at .... [place] and .... ("***SECA* player**") with its domicile or principal place of business at .... [place].

It is an agreement between these two parties that statutes some provisions with effect on third parties.

Section I: Scope

§1 Definitions

In the purpose of this Agreement and the referring Code of Conduct,

- "player" shall mean a natural person or legal entity that is doing electronic commerce;
- "Contract" shall mean the relation between the players that is based on the manifestation of a mutual assent;
- "*SECA*" (*SEMPER* Electronic-Commerce Agreement) shall mean the Agreement itself, the Code of Conduct and the Guidelines;
- "The Agreement" shall mean the first part of *SECA* that has to be signed by the players when joining *SECA*;
- "The Code of Conduct" shall mean the second part of *SECA* which reflects also the principles of the Agreement and sets some general provisions that enable fair electronic commerce; the players commit to the observance of the Code of Conduct by signing the Agreement;

- "The Guidelines" shall mean the third part of *SECA* where recommendations relating to security are given;
- "*SECA* player" shall mean a player who signed *SECA* and appears on the electronic-commerce platform with a *SECA* certificate;
- "*SECA* key" shall mean the key whose public part is registered and certified after the Agreement was signed. The private part of this key is intended to be used for digital signatures within scope and policy of *SECA*;
- "*SECA* CA" shall mean a certification authority that participates in *SECA*;
- "party" shall mean any party to a contract;
- "relying party" shall mean any party who depends on a received digitally signed message;
- "business" shall mean any player being merchant, i.e., a person who deals in goods or services of the kind or otherwise by his occupation holds himself out as having knowledge or skill peculiar to the practices, services or goods involved in the transaction or to whom such knowledge or skill may be attributed by his employment of an agent or broker or other intermediary who by his occupation holds himself out as having such knowledge or skill;
- "commercial" shall be a synonym for business;
- "private" shall mean any player but business;
- "consumer" shall mean any natural person who purchases goods or services only for private use, i.e., does not use them for producing other goods that are sold to make a living with it;
- "signer" shall mean any player who puts his signature under a paper or digital document either by pen or digitally; a digital signing process can be delegated to a machine;
- "CRL" shall mean Certificate Revocation List;
- "CPS" shall mean Certification Practice Statement.

§2 Area of Participation

The *SECA* player is obliged to act under the *SECA* rules wherever he uses or offers to use his *SECA* key for doing business.

SECA players can do electronic commerce with other *SECA* players and with non-*SECA* players. If either party is a *SECA* player, the *SECA* defaults are applicable for either player and either player must observe *SECA*. If a *SECA* player uses his *SECA* key when doing electronic commerce with a non-*SECA* player, the *SECA* player is obliged to show the *SECA* certificate for this key to the non-*SECA* player. If the other player disagrees explicitly to applying the *SECA* principles, the *SECA* player must not continue doing electronic business using the *SECA* key with this player.

§3 Area of Applicable Transactions

SECA applies to any business relation, between merchants and privates, between merchants , and between privates, including, but not limited to sale and exchange of goods, services, construction of works, lease, factoring, carriage of goods and persons, insurances, financial transaction contracts, and industrial or business cooperations.

SECA is applicable for any bilateral or multilateral relation that is not bound to any formal restrictions.

§4 Obligation of the *SECA* Player

The *SECA* player and the *SECA* CA shall act according to the Code of Conduct.

Section II: Formation and Validity of Contracts

§5 *SECA* Defaults

The *SECA* defaults are defined in the Code of Conduct. A *SECA* player shall have a link to the *SECA* defaults put on all his certificates. A *SECA* player shall have the *SECA* defaults applied if he signs with a *SECA* key unless the parties explicitly agree otherwise.

§6 Negotiation

The *SECA* player shall use the *SECA* defaults as a starting point for negotiation.

§7 Collision of Regulations

In the event that any provision of a player's general terms and conditions or any contractual regulations contradict the *SECA* defaults or their agreed modifications set by the players or any *SECA* regulations, the regulation of the *SECA* default or their agreed modifications or the *SECA* regulations, respectively, shall have priority.

§8 Validity of Contracts

The *SECA* player shall not deny any legal effect of a contract or any transaction on the sole ground that it is in electronic form, that it was signed with a digital signature or that it was negotiated and closed via open networks like the Internet.

§9 Assent of Digital Signatures

The *SECA* player and the *SECA* CA receiving a message signed digitally with a non-revoked *SECA* key assent to the legal validity of the digital signature.

§10 *SECA* CA

The *SECA* CA shall store the signed Agreements and be the administrative body. The *SECA* CA shall hand out its CPS to the *SECA* player latest at registration.

In the event that any provision of a *SECA* CA's CPS do no correspond to the provisions set in the Agreement, the provisions of the Agreement shall have priority.

The regulations for operating a *SECA* CA shall be governed by the laws of the domicile of the *SECA* CA.

Section III: Liability

§11 Liability for Digitally Signed Messages

A *SECA* player shall be liable for the messages signed himself with his *SECA* key. If a *SECA* player claims that his digital signature was compromised, he is liable for the obligation resulting from the digitally signed messages made with his *SECA* key, prior to its revocation, up to the **SECA limit of** .... **EURO.**

If a partner-specific liability limit is specified for the relying party, this partner-specific liability limit replaces the *SECA* limit in this case.

The following partner-specific limits are specified: ....

The liability resulting from liability-cover certificates (see respective contract, if existing) is not affected by the *SECA* limit or by the partner-specific liability limit.

The liability resulting from liability-cover certificates in the case of a compromised signature will reduce the respective partner-specific limit or the *SECA* limit.

No *SECA* player shall hold another *SECA* player liable for an amount that exceeds the *SECA* liability limit or the partner-specific limit, respectively, unless it results from obligations caused by liability-cover certificates. Failure of this provision leads to an exclusion of *SECA*.

§12 Revocation of Claimed Compromised Key

After having claimed his key compromised, the *SECA* player shall revoke his public key and all its certificates at the *SECA* CA immediately by phone, fax, or email, the latter by signing the revocation request with the key to be revoked, if available. The *SECA* CA shall provide a signed statement that the public key has been revoked.

The *SECA* CA shall ask some control questions if such had been agreed upon during registration, and notice whether or not the player was able to answer, but immediately mark key and certificates as revoked. It may later clarify the authenticity of the revocation. This is not necessary if the revocation request was signed with the key to be revoked.

The *SECA* CA has to provide and manage an appropriate, well-known and well-accessible mechanism for dealing with revocation and providing players access to the status of certificates which must always be kept up to date.

§13 Liability of Manufacturers

A manufacturer who produces *SECA*-compliant software or hardware components shall declare software or hardware components "*SECA*-compliant" only if they fulfil the requirements defined in the Guidelines.[13]

The manufacturer shall be liable for damage caused by relying on claimed but not fulfilled *SECA* compliance of components.

Section IV: Breach of Contract

§14 Exclusion from *SECA*

The *SECA* player who is convicted of breaching this Agreement or who tries to enforce any provisions contradicting this Agreement, shall be excluded from *SECA* and shall not be able to join *SECA* again. All *SECA* certificates of this player will be revoked.

The *SECA* CA convicted of breaching this Agreement shall be excluded from *SECA*. The title "*SECA* CA" will be withdrawn. The failing *SECA* CA is obliged to carefully transfer all information concerning its actions as a *SECA* CA to another CA.

§15 Blacklists[14]

Any *SECA* player who is excluded from *SECA* or who claims that his signature was compromised will be put on a blacklist. These blacklists are publicly accessible and can be found on .... and always are signed by .... The corresponding certificates can be retrieved from ....

The time to deletion from the blacklists depends on the seriousness of the failure and will be determined by ....[15]

---

[13]These should be replaced by exact criteria, e.g., exact protection profiles.

[14]The *SECA* CA issuing this Agreement must omit this paragraph if it contradicts applicable law.

[15]*SECA* CA or *SECA* legal body, depending on the overall organization of those bodies.

Section V: General Provisions

§16 Entire Agreement

SECA may not be modified except that partner-specific liability-limit commitments can be added or removed. The modification has to be in writing and signed by the *SECA* player and *SECA* CA.

§17 Severability

In the event that any provision of *SECA* shall be unenforceable or invalid under the applicable law, such unenforceability or invalidity shall not render *SECA* unenforceable or invalid as a whole, and, in such event, such provision shall be changed and interpreted so as to best accomplish the objectives of such provisions.

§18 Termination

The *SECA* player may terminate *SECA* upon a digitally signed notice to the *SECA* CA. The *SECA* CA will check the identity of the *SECA* player and ask some control questions and revoke all *SECA* certificates of the *SECA* player. The termination must be confirmed in paper-based writing by the *SECA* player.

The *SECA* CA may terminate *SECA* if a *SECA* player does not act according to this Agreement.

§19 Governing Law

This Agreement shall be governed by the law of .... The provisions regarding the establishment of a CA shall be governed by the laws of the corporate domicile of the *SECA* CA.

§20 Place of Jurisdiction

Place of jurisdiction is ....
    Place/Date: .... *SECA* CA: ....
    Place/Date: .... Player: ....

14.5.2 The Code of Conduct

SECA Defaults. The following rules hold per default, if not explicitly agreed otherwise by all involved and concerned business partners of a transaction for any contract concluded within this transaction:

– For a private-to-private relation:
  The contract shall be governed by and construed in accordance with the internal laws of the private offeree's domicile country. Place of venue is the private offeree's domicile.
– For a business-to-business relation:
  The contract shall be governed by and construed in accordance with the internal laws of the offeror's principal place of business or domicile country. Place of venue is the offeror's principal place of business or domicile.
– For a business-to-consumer relation:
  The contract shall be governed by and construed in accordance with the internal laws of the consumer's domicile country. Place of venue is the consumer's domicile.
– The contract shall come into force when the acceptance reaches the offeror or when a consideration is made.
– Personal data or confidential information collected will be used only for purposes that are relevant to the business using the data.

Comportment Related to Business.

Advertising and Competition. Any *SECA* player is obliged to

– exclude or restrict the validity of the offers on her Internet page for countries where the offer should not have any effect,
– not put any deceptive marketing or disparagement on her Internet page nor disclose any trade values of others with the advertising on her Internet page,
– not send any unsolicited advertisements to persons who have stipulated that they do not want to receive any advertisements,
– have put on her *SECA* certificate if she does not want to receive any unsolicited advertisement,
– indicate the correct price and taxes for her products or services,
– not use unfair terms that may mislead other players.

Negotiation. Any *SECA* player is obliged to

– negotiate seriously and to act according to good faith and loyalty,
– provide a *SECA* certificate upon request.

Offers and Acceptances. Any *SECA* player is obliged to

– sign her offers, acceptances, calls for offers digitally with her *SECA* key if one of the other *SECA* players involved asks for it,
– sign her public pages which are marked as being provided to *SECA* players, using her *SECA* key,[16]
– indicate her particulars or to submit a certificate with her offer or with her acceptance,

---

[16]This is to protect herself and her *SECA* business partners from spoofing attacks.

– put digitally signed general terms and conditions (GTC) to the offers. The GTC must be clearly visible, clearly understandable, concise, and of reasonable length compared to the value of the offered good. Their link must be marked separately if the full text of the GTC is not visible on the screen. A reference without the full text of the GTC is not valid. Modified GTC are considered as offers from the modifying party.

Consumer-Protection Issues. Any commercial *SECA* player is obliged to

– offer the consumers a right to withdraw the contract and to send back the goods, e.g., within x working days after delivery, if this is required by the applicable law. Such withdrawal does not fulfil the validity condition[17] of a liability-cover certificate of a Liability-Cover Service. Liability-cover certificates whose validity condition includes "withdrawal" are not due in this case. Commitment certificates which are not liability-cover certificates might not be due, either, depending on the applicable law.
– inform the consumers about formal requirements on certain contracts, e.g., sales contracts that exceed a certain value or sales on credit.

Content of Contracts and Internet Pages. Any *SECA* player is obliged to

– not offer any goods or services that violate the fundamental principles of law.

Privacy and Data Protection. Any *SECA* player is obliged to

– not collect any personal data for other than just internal processing and archiving reasons or for reasons that are not related to the business the player received the information for without the prior written or digitally signed consent of that specific player,
– hand out any information about stored personal data of any customers upon the request of the specific customer,
– not disclose the information about personal data he gets about his customers except if the customers agree to this explicitly,
– treat the personal data confidentially,
– store the personal data of customers that are needed for tax and other reasons, prescribed by the applicable law, reliably; and not to provide any unauthorized third parties with information about these personal data.

14.5.3 The Guidelines

The *SECA* Guidelines given here complement the *SECA* Agreement and the *SECA* Code of Conduct. They define "*SECA*-compliant components" to protect their users, and give information to the users on how they can reduce their exposure to damage due to failures and attacks.

---

[17]see Section 13.2.2

SECA **Compliance of Components.** Components must only be declared to be *SECA compliant* if they enable safe, secure and fair electronic commerce, according to the *SECA* Guidelines given below. The label '*SECA* compliant' is valid only if it was signed by a manufacturer's *SECA* key and is accompanied by the manufacturer's *SECA* certificate.[18]

Electronic-Commerce Application. Here, an electronic-commerce application is considered including the supporting software needed (e.g., the crypto software to perform and check electronic signatures). The criteria are independent of the platform or configuration (secure device, smartcard or software-only for the signing procedure). This means that the criteria must be fulfilled under the assumption that the operating system was working securely (which will usually not be the case).

An electronic-commerce application is allowed to be declared *SECA compliant* by the manufacturer if all of the following conditions are fulfilled:

- It *identifies* the user properly before performing any critical transaction or operation which might legally bind (e.g., digital signature) or potentially damage (e.g., delete stored information) the user.
- The *default timeout* of the signing facility after user identification is short. The user must be made aware, when modifying timeouts, that he might unintentionally enable others to make use of his signing functionality.
- It is *well documented and comprehensive* with respect to all functionalities, in particular for non-technical users.
- It provides means to easily maintain, administer and *retrieve evidence,* to be used, e.g., in dispute cases. Tools must exist independently of the user's system which can be used in court and which can evaluate the evidence provided by the user's system. Evidence is, e.g., signed offers, signed orders, certificates.
- It explains the options to the user and shows how to modify them. It reminds the user to check her options regularly.
- It shows the critical content of transaction information (business partner offers, orders, etc.) received, and the user is alerted to check all details.
- It shows clearly the *point of no return* in a transaction, i.e., a) that the user is going to sign in the next step b) exactly what the user is going to sign, and requests user confirmation and performs user identification before actually a signature is computed. Thus, confusing buttons like "signature" are not included, as they do not tell clearly whether pressing this button will already sign, or only lead to a preparation for the signature.
- It verifies signatures, certificates and CRLs, and alerts the user if the checks were not successful.

---

[18]We give here the criteria as developed in *SEMPER.* However, it is clear that Protection Profiles for "*SECA* compliance" will have to be elaborated which would allow a formal evaluation and certification.

- It enables the user to negotiate business parameters (including applicable law and place of venue), goods, quantity, means of payment while simultaneously looking for better offers of competing business partners, without being forced to make a decision earlier than intended.
- It supports fair exchange protocols.
- It allows the user to specify preferences for her transaction which are partly negotiated with the business partner and partly enforced by the own application, such as:
  - Business partner has to identify himself using identity / pseudonym / other.
  - Business partner has to show a certain certificate (e.g., a *SECA* certificate) with certain options to be specified by the user.
  - All messages have to be digitally signed.
  - Fair exchange protocols shall be used.
  - Anonymity towards which player / untraceability / unobservability.
  - A *SECA* certificate of the other party must be shown and the *SECA* key must be used.
  - The birthday certificate of the other party must be shown.
- It shows at least the following information before a transaction is signed (at most after one mouse click forth and back each):
  - Identity of the business partner if required (e.g., by pseudonym plus certificate), result of the identity authentication (e.g., "success"). Availability, and the content, of the business partner's *SECA* certificate, if required by the user's preferences. Clear messages if some of the required information is not available.
  - Own role: private player, commercial player, consumer (additionally).
  - Parameters that are relevant for place of venue and applicable law and have been negotiated before: Domiciles, role of business partner, own role, agreed place of venue, agreed applicable law.
  - Description of the good that is going to be ordered / offered (incl. quantity).
  - Price of the goods.
  - Conditions in general.
  - Place of delivery (if involved).
  - Whether or not a fair exchange protocol is used for this transaction.
  - Payment conditions (including the player's account number and the information whose account number it is, in the non-anonymous case), if involved.
  - Type of transaction to be signed (e.g., offer, order, invoice, contract).
  - Equipment level of the business partner if required and available.
  - Own equipment level for the signature key to be used, on request, if available.
  - All involved CAs and other Third Parties, together with the indication if they are trusted by the user.

- Use of own full name or pseudonym in this transaction, on request.
- Relevant certificates shown in this transaction (e.g., a certain short certificate, birthday certificate), validity, result of checks.
- Validity and content of certificates of business partners, checking result, on request.
- Own trust parameters, related to this transaction.
- Business options, related to this transaction.
- Own liability-cover certificate coverage for this transaction, and remaining limit, on request.
- Business partner's liability-cover certificate coverage for this transaction.
- The software provides *information on how to protect keys* against misuse and loss.
- The software provides *information* on how to improve the security level of the equipment.
- Contained *crypto software* is secure, according to state of the art. This means that no weak cryptography must be used for the signing functionality, and the signing key must not be allowed to be escrowed at others or in any other way be made recoverable by others. (Encrypted backups are allowed.) Additionally, the crypto algorithms and key lenghts must be declared so that the user can identify them easily and compare with recommendations. An estimation must be added for each algorithm until when it will be safe, e.g., according to Lenstra and Verheul (1999).
- It can *support secure hardware configurations,* e.g., smartcards storing the secret key and performing the signing procedure, or electronic wallets doing the same and also providing input and output. Alternatively, it should at least be able to work together with a Commitment service.
- It enables the user to perform *housekeeping,* i.e., to easily check her state of current transactions, of money in all her electronic purses, available credentials and vouchers, etc., and of all previous transactions performed. Deletion of old transactions, old purses, credentials, vouchers, etc., keys, certificates and crypto tools, etc. is not performed unless the user explicitly wishes to do so, and not without prior warning. In the case of a lack of disk space, the user is advised in time how to make external backups (e.g., which files have to be saved on another disk).
- It provides means to initialize or enter *dispute procedures.*
- The application is designed in a way that it can *recover* from recovery points.
- It stores backup states between the individual transactions, and provides means to recover from these states after a crash.
- It shows information to *make the user aware of necessary actions* for maintenance and backup of data.
- *Upgrading software* is provided in a secure way. Means have to be provided to the user to securely upgrade software: The upgrades are signed.

SECA compliance is defined locally for the part of a business application belonging to a specific user roles. It does not have to be fulfilled for the software for the other roles of the business application. Thus, it is not excluded that the *SECA*-compliant business-application part of one user (e.g., a private buyer) works well together with the corresponding part for another user (e.g., a merchant), while the latter is not *SECA* compliant.

The complete business application including all roles of business partners can be declared *multi-party SECA compliant* if the software parts are *SECA* compliant for all roles.

Operating System. Manufacturers are allowed to declare operating systems *SECA compliant* if they fulfil the following requirements.

- The operating system does not allow any application (or applet, or cookie) on the same machine, or received from outside, to observe, influence, or impersonate any other application which is on the machine, running or not running, or to modify any data on disk or memory belonging to a different application, without knowledge and approval of the user.
- Certificates of software are checked before software is loaded.
- The operating system protects itself securely against unauthorized modifications, aided by some kernel stored in hardware (assuming that the hardware is secure). Sufficient checks are performed to exclude unauthorized modifications.
- The handbook for the operating system provides comprehensive information on the risks and recommendations on how to proceed in the case that one application asks to access any critical data of another, including in the installation process.
- The operating system has been evaluated successfully with respect to the given criteria. The identity of the evaluator is public.

Secure Hardware Device. To provide diversity in development of components and to avoid malicious effects of Trojan horses in any other than the electronic-commerce program, a *secure hardware device* should be chosen by the user, independent of his PC, and used to perform digital signatures, at least as long no secure, *SECA*-compliant, operating systems for PCs are available.

The important point is that the processor of a secure hardware device cannot be controlled by the potentially insecure computer. Unfortunately, such solutions on a hardware device integrated in the business or verification processes are not state of the art yet.

Manufacturers are allowed to declare a user device *SECA compliant* if the corresponding component

- is designed to perform, on the device and controlled by the device,
  - user's input (keyboard, microphone, scanner, etc.) for critical data (passphrases, biometrics, data to be signed, seed, etc.),

- output (display, voice, printer, etc.) for critical data (data to be signed, data having been checked, checking results, content and validity of checked certificates, etc.),
- and to support critical protocol steps, in connection with the electronic-commerce application, in order to let the user see and sign the intended payment, order etc., showing also the information that it is a payment of which amount to whom, order to whom for what, etc., checking which critical data with which check result, etc., in a comprehensive and unique way for each kind of application and transaction, and according to standards as soon as such exist.
- is tamper-evident as a whole,
- has special tamper-resistant storage for the user's keys,
- prevents tampering the data transferred between memory and processor on the hardware device,
- has a tamper-evident kernel for secure booting,
- is resistant against any attacks while the device is in use (including also all kinds of unusual operations of the device),
- has itself a small *SECA*-compliant secure operating system,
- can be used for all user-representing functionalities for secure transactions, in particular for performing the user's digital signatures including showing the content to be signed to the user,
- contains one or more processors which perform the key creation, the signature algorithms, the verification algorithms (and optionally encryption and decryption for confidentiality),
- requires for key creation random sources of enough entropy to seed cryptographic function which can come from any combination of user input, unguessable system data and physical (e.g., thermal) noise,
- has been designed in an open way so that any independent evaluator can check the design,
- has been evaluated successfully, according to these criteria, by an independent evaluator whose identity is public.

Recommendations for the Users. This section is intended to serve as Guidelines for the *SECA* user to protect herself from damage as far as possible.[19]

Recommendation to Use Secure Hardware and Secure Operating Systems. It is highly recommended to use a secure hardware device for producing digital signatures, which shows the critical actions of the electronic-commerce software and cannot be tampered with—however, such devices are currently not available yet. There are several initiatives to develop such devices, and it can

---

[19]Readers of the book who have already read the first part of the Guidelines describing the requirements on components may skip this section. It provides similar procedures, described from the point of view of the user. Since it is part of *SECA*, however, we decided to include it.

be expected that in a few years, they will be available. The same holds for secure operating systems which would not allow applications to affect other critical applications.

Without secure devices and secure operating systems, attackers might impersonate the user without being detected, even if the electronic-commerce components are 100% correct. Using smartcards for the signing functionality provides already a good protection against many impersonating attacks.

Players should be aware of their equipment level regarding protection against attacks.

Maintenance and Error Recovery. The users are responsible for maintaining their software and data. Backups of all critical parts shall be made regularly. It is recommended to use only commerce software which additionally provides means to store recovery points so as to be able to start from a consistent state after a crash.

Upgrading software should be checked for correct signature and 'SECA compliant' label in the same way as installation of the original software.

The user shall make herself familiar with how to maintain software and make backups.

Care for Keys. To be on the safe side, the user should create a key pair herself. She should make sure that the key cannot be replaced by another before it is certified.

If a key pair is used for signature, it shall not be used for encryption, and vice versa. The user shall not use any of these keys for authentication purposes that do not involve the user's own actions (e.g., for SSL or TLS on the session level).

The user shall use appropriate algorithms and key lengths for all purposes to enable the intended security, as far as this is not restricted by the applicable law. The applied algorithms, key lengths and security period (depending on, e.g., for how long encrypted or signed data are intended to be stored and expected to be unforgeable) should be compared with recommendations retrieved from the *SECA* legal body.

The user shall not give access to her private keys to any other persons. She shall not document how to access her private keys in any way that other persons gaining access to the computer (e.g., by brute force) could get this information.

What to Do if the Key was Compromised. Each signer who has the impression that his key might have been compromised has to do the following:

– revoke the key and all the *SECA* certificates on it immediately,
– revoke the key at the Liability-Cover Service, if any, if the Liability-Cover Service is not performed by the same CA as the *SECA* CA,
– re-organize his own key management to prevent any access to passphrases etc. by others,
– re-organize his equipment,

- upgrade to a higher level of equipment, if possible,
- create a new key pair and register the public key at the *SECA* CA, in the same way as the first time.

Liability for Compromised Signatures. It is very important that the players understand the importance of liability for signed transactions. Therefore, they have to be aware of the possible consequences of not treating information, software, hardware or keys securely.

The player has to be aware of the following facts:

- If a court rules that a claimed compromised key (i.e. a non-*SECA* key) was not compromised, she might have to take the full responsibility for the occurred damages. This applies also for signatures on transactions which look different than what the player thought he would sign (e.g., if a Trojan horse showed a fake window pretending to be an expected window). Such a judgment is more likely for signature keys beyond *SECA*, as in *SECA* it is explicitly possible to deny the signature. Therefore, players can only be protected against unforeseeable damage if they do not use any other signature keys without liability limit.
- The existence or non-existence of Trojan horses can hardly be proven.
- If the user denies a signature and damage is left to be taken by relying parties, she will be put on a blacklist.
- In the case of a compromised signature, a certain liability must be taken. The worst-case liability can be influenced by the user herself. It is the total of all partner-specific limits plus the LCS limit, or *SECA* limit, respectively, depending on which one has the higher value.

Thus, it is recommended

- for the signer
  - to take care of keys, software and hardware in order to avoid that her key will be compromised, e.g., by installing software only from trustworthy sources,
  - not to use any other signing key whose liability is not limited,
  - to find a good balance, depending on the own practice to make electronic commerce, between using the Liability-Cover Service and establishing partner-specific limited liabilities;
- for the relying party, in order to limit the risk of financial loss caused due to claimed compromised signatures:
  - to require liability-cover certificates from the signer, on an amount which would provide sufficient compensation in case the signer claims a compromised key. Alternatively, to require a sufficient specific liability for oneself (assigned to the name of the relying party itself) to be shown in the signer's certificate. The amount of it should cover the worst-case damage expected for every point of time. In the latter case, each signed

transaction of the signer must be checked if a denial could exceed this amount (taking into account all pending transactions with this signer).

Housekeeping. The user is responsible for performing housekeeping: she should know how to check the state of current transactions, of the amounts of money in all her electronic purses, available credentials and vouchers, etc., and of previous transactions performed.

Each deletion of old transactions, old purses, credentials, vouchers, etc., keys, certificates and crypto tools, etc. should be made carefully.

In the case of a lack of disk space, the user must make external backups in time (e.g., save files on disk).

Evidence. The user shall be aware that her electronic-commerce application may create evidence to be used in dispute cases. The user shall make herself familiar with how to maintain, administrate and retrieve evidences. If the software does not contain the functionality of an archive where evidence is stored automatically, she should store copies of all signed statements she has sent or received.

Fair Business. To make sure that the business will be fair, the user should

- ensure that the electronic-commerce software is recommended by consumer organizations (for the buyer), Chambers of Commerce (for the seller), or labeled as *SECA* compliant, software and label being signed by a manufacturer which is not on the blacklist. Check the signature.
- be especially careful if the business partner can be found on a blacklist, e.g., for compromised signatures. Liability-cover certificates should be requested in this case.

Awareness of Performed Transaction. The user should carefully read the alerts presented by the software. She should be aware of the current state of the transaction. She should carefully study the results of checks of certificates. She should check all values carefully before signing the transaction.

Recommendations for Commercial Players Running a Server. Commercial players are expected to take responsibility and care for their hardware, software and transactions on their own. *SECA* does not provide special guidelines or criteria for this.

The commercial player is expected to use facilities in a manner that his digital signatures cannot be compromised, e.g., employing good firewall concepts and organizational means to prevent insider criminality, misuse and accidental access, best aided by professional support. The commercial player is expected to be liable (reflected by a sufficiently high *SECA* liability) and responsible for other players' damage due in the case his key was compromised.

14.6 Conclusions

SECA as a legal framework can be used already now. Players do not have to wait for regulations, they can join *SECA* which is an agreement valid within the *SECA* community, and towards users outside the community who accept the *SECA* rules when accepting a digital signature together with a *SECA* certificate. *SECA* itself can be handled as a "closed system" with respect to the EU Directive on "Electronic Signatures", which means that the regulations in *SECA* are not affected by the regulations of the Directive.

We expect that *SECA* enables self-regulation with respect to the following aspects:

- Buyers will want to use *SECA* keys rather than other signature keys, to limit their own liability in the case of attacks. Compared to the current situation, they might be willing to use signatures at all if the liability is limited.
- Compared to the current situation (at the time of writing this), sellers would be glad to get any signatures with a binding character. Compared with a situation where even signatures obtained by an attack would bind the apparent signer (e.g., for signatures according to the EU Directive on "Electronic Signatures"), sellers will more and more be forced to accept transactions signed using *SECA* keys because the customers will become reluctant to take the risk of losing money due to attacks when using signatures without *SECA*. In return, they will require undeniable commitments (e.g., liability-cover certificates or partner-specific limited liabilities) in order to reduce their own risk in case the signer claims a compromised signature.
- Thus, players will increasingly use the Liability-Cover Service to fulfil the requirements of their business partners.
- Blacklists will prevent players from claiming compromised keys without justification.
- Players who had fallen victim to an attack will aim at improving their equipment. They will increasingly require smartcards, secure devices and secure operating systems. They will prefer the use of *SECA*-compliant components.
- Manufacturers will be required to provide *SECA*-compliant components. Security evaluation criteria will be developed for security standards, e.g., Common Criteria and FIPS. The current "criteria for *SECA* compliance" can be replaced by well-established and approved criteria fulfilling the requirements identified in *SEMPER*, as soon as such criteria exist.
- People will more and more overcome their inhibitions to start or extend doing electronic commerce since, using *SECA*, the legal situation is safe, and the user herself can reduce her risk of unforeseeable damage.

15. Future Directions in Secure Electronic Commerce

The previous chapters presented results of *SEMPER*. In this last chapter, we step back and review issues that we encountered in *SEMPER* where more work—research, development or deployment—is necessary in the future. We do not aim at reviewing the state of the art, but rather present the open problems and the directions the work should take.

We start with purely non-technical issues, such as insufficient user education and the impact of crypto regulations. Next we discuss global issues related to architecture, then issues related to services and protocols, and finally implementation issues.

15.1 Non-technical Issues

Security in electronic commerce is never a purely technical issue. Technology can offer building blocks of various quality at various costs, but finally everything depends on how well these building blocks are integrated into economic and social structures.

15.1.1 Security Awareness

Most opinion surveys list "insecurity of financial transactions" and "loss of privacy" among the major impediments to electronic commerce. But in fact most users only have vague ideas about the threats and risks, and a very limited understanding of the technical and legal options for minimizing their risk. As a result, many misperceptions exist. For instance, the card holder's risk in sending his or her credit card number over the Internet in the clear is typically *overestimated*. At present, such payments are treated like mail-order/telephone-order (MOTO) transactions, which means that in principle the card holder is not liable at all (cf. Section 1.1.1). All the risk is with the merchant. But the risk in sending sensitive data in an electronic mail is typically *underestimated*. Probably most users of email know the mere facts: neither confidentiality nor integrity nor availability are guaranteed. Nevertheless many users do not hesitate to send all kinds of personal or business data to their friends or colleagues without protection.

Education and creating awareness has to achieve the following goals:

G. Lacoste et al. (Eds.): SEMPER 2000, LNCS 1854, pp. 305–323, 2000.
© Springer-Verlag Berlin Heidelberg 2000

- Users have to learn and internalize the concept of *multi-party security*. They need to understand their own security requirements. They also must become aware that *they* themselves have to decide whom they can reasonably trust for specific requirements, and that they want to be able to hold these parties *accountable* if this trust is abused. The users have to learn to distinguish between solutions that support their requirements and trust assumptions, and solutions that violate them.
- Until better abstractions of security services and properties are available (see Section 15.2.7) this requires learning the basics of security technology. For instance: What are "passphrases" and how must they be handled? What is a "digital signature?" What is the consequence of "entering a PIN?" What does "public-key certification" mean, and what are the implied trust and liability assumptions? What is "encryption?" What is a "trusted path from the user to the system?"
- Users have to understand the *limitations* of existing or proposed solutions. They have to learn that a certain level of security requires a certain level of complexity and investment, i.e., that security is not for free and that they have to make a risk management decision. This means they have to understand and choose which risks they can prevent, which risks they are willing to tolerate, and which services they rather do not use at all.

Security awareness is not only a problem on the consumer side. Many decision-makers in business and politics are faced with security-related decisions without fully knowing the threats and risks. For instance, many problems with public-key infrastructures, see Section 15.3.2, are not really technical, but due to misunderstandings and unharmonized terminology. There is also a lack of awareness among developers, e.g., of the fact that legal certainty cannot be provided by transparent security approaches, i.e., by approaches that do not involve the user at all. Another problem with developers is ignorance of common and easily exploitable bugs like buffer overflows.

15.1.2 Crypto Regulations

Several countries regulate the deployment of strong encryption technology by law, see Chapter 14. As discussed there, it is questionable whether *any* regulation of encryption technology can be effective in fighting organized crime. Moreover, if "Trusted Third Parties" are introduced that obtain or can recover secret keys, it is an open issue how these "single points of failure" can be sufficiently protected (Abelson et al. 1997).

Many types of commercial transactions require strong confidentiality, which cannot be satisfied in some countries or across some borders. For instance, consider two large companies preparing a merger. Clearly their negotiations require top confidentiality. Even the fact that they are preparing the merger, i.e., that they are communicating intensively, will be extremely sensitive. This requires services not only for confidential, but for anonymous communication.

Political regulations are not subject to security research. But we clearly see the need for an international agreement on a liberal and consistent regulation of cryptography. Electronic commerce demands strong confidentiality, which can only be implemented by strong encryption schemes.

15.1.3 Legal Issues

The two most important legal issues at present are fair assignment of liability for digital signatures and international harmonization. Both were important issues for *SEMPER*, and our proposals are described in detail in Chapters 3, 13 and 14. Such solutions need to be taken up by certification authorities, and the players that benefit most have to provide the financial incentives as sketched in Section 3.2.3. This would bring about immediate clarity. Nevertheless, some issues need national and international regulation, and it should also be clarified that certain other, highly unfair solutions are invalid.

15.2 Global Technical Issues

In this section, we discuss future directions in global issues concerning security architectures. They elaborate on or extend Sections 2.1, 2.2 and Section 6.1 where we explained the model and global concerns underlying the *SEMPER* technical framework.

15.2.1 Process Orientation

Most of the existing research in security for electronic commerce concentrated on building blocks like electronic payment systems or digital signatures. *SEMPER* stressed that what is actually needed is comprehensive secure *processes*, not just secure *steps*. Some of the reasons were:

- Even if the individual steps of a process (offer, order, payment, etc.) are selected and authorized by the user, secure references between them are needed for the evidence.
- Some security requirements, like anonymity, can only be satisfied if they are consistently applied throughout a process.
- Process support can greatly increase user friendliness: The user's electronic-commerce tool can perform a lot of standard consistency checks for the user and transfer common data from one step to the next.
- The user may also wish to authorize entire processes, instead of each single step in them.

SEMPER took steps in this direction, but a lot of territory remains to be explored. The consolidated Commerce-Layer design in Section 6.2 shows landmarks, but the prototype only contained a subset of the services we envision. Future directions are:

- Implementing a useful set of value-added lower-layer services, i.e., primitives enriched with business semantics.
- If possible, agreeing on a simple language with which concrete processes can easily be built from such primitives (compare the service providers' feedback in Chapter 7).
- Extending the approach of the Fair Internet Trader, which was to build a general-purpose tool for person-to-person purchase processes, to person-to-machine purchases, in particular standard types of Internet shopping. Here the challenge is to identify a set of processes that is
  - large and flexible enough to cover the majority of potential applications, yet
  - small enough so that the options remain easily understandable by the users, and so that it can be evaluated carefully. Evaluation implies that the processes can then be considered equally trustworthy as the other services of the framework and users can in fact safely leave routine work to them.

Note that if this approach does not work, the approach where consumers get a suitable business application from each merchant, e.g., as an applet, does not work either, at least not in the sense that the user can leave security issues to this application if certain certificates are offered: If almost all merchants need their own business applications, it is not possible to carefully evaluate and certify them. Hence the user may use them for informative actions like browsing and shopping carts, but cannot trust most of them any further.

15.2.2 Dispute Handling

Systems for electronic commerce have to be prepared for the case of disputes among the parties. First, the protocols must generate and store all the necessary evidence, typically in the form of digitally signed documents and receipts. Secondly, the system must be able to *evaluate* this evidence, i.e., there must be protocols for proving certain facts about transactions to a third party, e.g., a court. Thirdly, there should be a way to express dispute claims that does not depend on the specific protocol, i.e., a generic dispute language. It will have a really generic part for all services, which contains temporal and logical connectives, and use the interface primitives of individual services as elements.

This does not mean that an electronic-commerce system must enable automatic resolution of disputes. Ultimately, legal disputes will have to be resolved by human judges. But the system must prevent unnecessary disputes (e.g., by enabling the parties to verify that they have sufficient evidence to prove a certain claim) and assist human expert witnesses in their analysis of certain transactions or business processes.

SEMPER did some work on this topic, in particular for electronic payment systems (see Section 11.7.1 and Asokan, Herreweghen, and Steiner (1998)). But there is still some way to go before one can describe and resolve dispute claims generally, for all kinds of commerce services.

An additional practical problem is to add disputability to existing standard protocols or implementations, e.g., to existing payment systems: Although many electronic-commerce protocols create all necessary evidence, almost none of them supports storage, retrieval, and evaluation of this evidence. To understand the size of the problem, imagine the following paper scenario: Consider a company that cuts off all signatures from all letters, contracts, cheques, etc. that it receives and throws them in the wastebasket. Nobody would expect this company to convince a court of anything in the case of a dispute. But this is pretty close to what happens in many security systems. For instance, SET does not cut off all signatures, but current implementations do not offer any way to get them back once stored, i.e., they are as useless as they would be in the wastebasket.

15.2.3 Access Control

If we want openness for new business applications without making lengthy evaluation processes for them mandatory, there must be notions of more and less trusted applications. Trust is closely linked to access control: More trusted applications should have more rights. Basic mechanisms for granting (delegating) and revoking such rights have been known for a long time in the operating-system and database communities, e.g., Harrison, Ruzzo, and Ullman (1976), and basic mechanisms for process-based access control are also known, e.g., Clark and Wilson (1987), Biskup and Eckert (1994) and Atluri and Huang (1996). The challenge lies in finding an appropriate mix of mechanisms that is simple and business-oriented enough to be understandable by the user.

Most current approaches simply delegate the access-control decisions to outside authorities: Code signing is used, and either a signed application gets full rights, or fixed rights prescribed by the signer, or, as the most flexible solution, it gets a set of rights to any other available software component that the author of this component has prescribed in certain roles.

None of this is exactly what is needed in secure electronic commerce. A major reason is that different users have widely varying preferences between security and user-friendliness.

One idea in *SEMPER* was to separate services into those with and without user authorization. This yields a simple strategy with two classes of application components: trusted ones that can do everything alone, and less trusted ones that have to ask the user to authorize every security-critical step.[1] In the long run, however, users will want an application to buy a newspaper every morning or to make micro-payments for non-gratuitous web pages up to a certain amount (chosen by the user), etc. This means a flexible, business-oriented concept of roles that can be instantiated in the user's preferences. The policy objects in the payment framework, see Section 11.7.2, are a start in this direction.

The same considerations as for business applications hold for individual modules (security implementations) as soon as such modules are aware of the framework they come into and therefore want to use other services from the framework. (A stand-alone module like an existing payment system implementation can, instead, run in a kind of sandbox.)

All these concepts also need a code-signing mechanism. However, for openness we stress that the infrastructure must be flexible and not controlled by the first provider of the software. In this respect, the PICS system for content labeling (Resnick and Miller 1996) can serve as an example. Even more clearly, the keys and certificates used in the context of code signing must, in contrast to some other code-signing proposals, be distinct from the key certificates of the software designers and also from attribute certificates with other semantics, e.g., certificates that state that someone is a known merchant. Otherwise one is back to the situation where any merchant can simply take money out of the buyers' purses, and most other security measures could be omitted.

15.2.4 Pervasive Anonymity

Real marketplaces allow users to act *anonymously* in many situations. For instance, there is no need to identify yourself in order to browse in a mail-order catalogue or to buy a book in a bookstore (at least not if you pay cash). "Loss of privacy" is often mentioned as a serious concern by Internet users. Thus one can assume that most users would also sometimes like to act anonymously on electronic marketplaces.

The technical approach to anonymity is to let people act under *pseudonyms* that do not reveal their real-world names or locations.[2] Optimally, each pseudonym is only used for one transaction or deal (*transaction pseudonym*). This is called unlinkability of the different actions. If a pseudonym is used in too many situations, information accumulates and reidentification often becomes possible.

---

[1]This is quite similar to the original Java security concepts, but in SEMPER commerce-oriented services are protected instead of or in addition to operating-system services like opening files and network connections.

[2]In some cases, identification might be required, primarily for dispute handling (as in the German signature law). But in many cases even a dispute can technically be resolved anonymously (Pfitzmann, Waidner, and Pfitzmann 1987).

Protocols for several types of anonymous transactions are known. One type is *anonymous communication*; it is essential for any real anonymity in higher layers. The solutions include the addressing of holders of pseudonyms. Pfitzmann and Waidner (1987) is still a valid overview of the basic concepts. There are also various proposals for anonymous payment systems, ranging from the commercially available ecash over research prototypes such as CAFE (Boly et al. 1994) to a large number of scientific papers (see Asokan et al. (2000) and Jakobsson et al. (1999) for some surveys).

SEMPER did some work on integrating such primitives: We integrated ecash and a protocol for untraceable communication (Fritsch 1998; SEMPER Consortium 1999a), based on the concept of mixes (Chaum 1981).

Several problems are still open, in particular that of *pervasive anonymity*: A system like *SEMPER* has to offer a consistent and enforceable abstraction of anonymity, both to developers and to users. The basic concepts are there in *SEMPER* with the security attributes that should be enforced across entire deals, but anonymity is not supported by all blocks in the prototype and thus the enforcement is not actually done. Another issue not worked out is degrees of anonymity: Full unlinkability is easy to enforce consistently: all steps in a deal must use a transaction pseudonym not used in any other deal; however this is not always desired from a business-process point of view. Similarly, very weak anonymity is easy: all steps must not use a real name. Intermediate types where some steps use longer-lived pseudonyms are more difficult because appropriate pseudonyms must be selected (from preferences or with the help of the user), and the electronic-commerce tool must warn the user if a deal links pseudonyms that were so far not linkable.

There are also open problems with the individual primitives. While untraceable payment systems are already sufficiently secure and efficient, in particular for the typical online scenario of electronic commerce, two other main classes of primitives are not, anonymous communication and *unlinkable credentials*.

None of the current protocols for anonymous communication is *both* suitable for all facets of Internet communication *and* offers a predictably high degree of anonymity. For instance, classical mixes (Chaum 1981; Abe 1998; Jakobsson 1998) are limited to store-and-forward communication such as email. Simply extending mixes to connection-oriented services gives rise to timing patterns (Pfitzmann, Pfitzmann, and Waidner 1991) and thus an unpredictable degree of anonymity; this is a disadvantage of real applications like Reed, Syverson, and Goldschlag (1998) and also the non-mix approach in Reiter and Rubin (1998). The extension of connection-oriented mixes to hide timing patterns in Pfitzmann et al. (1991) and Jerichow et al. (1998) needs significantly more bandwidth and doesn't seem to scale beyond local area networks if perfect hiding is desired. Even more resources are needed by the perfect solution of DC networks (Chaum 1998).

Unlinkable credentials are a technique to adapt attribute certificates to anonymous scenarios. As already said, the basic approach to anonymity is to use pseudonyms instead of names. Technically one can identify a pseudonym with the capability to digitally sign statements under it, i.e., a public key. A credential simply becomes a statement about a certain pseudonym (typically about rights or properties of its holder), signed under some other pseudonym (Pfitzmann, Waidner, and Pfitzmann 1987). When users start using several different pseudonyms, the need arises to transfer credentials issued on one pseudonym of a user to another pseudonym, without revealing to the business partners that these pseudonyms belong to the same person (Chaum 1985). Credentials allowing this are called *unlinkable*. There are efficient basic constructions (starting with Chaum (1985)), but the construction of semantically rich or personal credentials and the integration into complex policies are still open issues.

15.2.5 Web Tracking, Personalized Accounts, and Directed Marketing

One of the real differences between conventional and electronic commerce is the cost effectiveness of *personalization* of marketing information and intangible goods (Bakos 1998). For instance, several search engines determine which advertisement to show by analyzing the current request: the search result for "Switzerland" is likely to be accompanied by an advertisement from a travel agency. Other examples include customized stock quotes, or book recommendations based on prior purchases at an Internet bookstore. Another example is spam mails, which are often caused by previous requests to servers.

Certain types of such directed marketing are obviously advantageous for everybody, in particular those that are fully controlled by the customers. Others can easily become a privacy nightmare, in particular if the collected customer data are sold and accumulated. Hence, the main security aspect of this topic is its relation to anonymity, i.e., how one can actually implement the local control of the personalization at the customer side. *SEMPER* did not address this problem at all, but some research is going on (Cranor and LaMacchia 1998; Gabber et al. 1997; Bleichenbacher et al. 1998). This issue and anonymity together can be seen as a whole new supporting block "name and personality management" in the *SEMPER* architecture, as a large extension of the Certificate Block and the Credentials Block, which only address certain aspects of the relations of names and rights or properties.

15.2.6 Multi-party Protocols

Most tasks in electronic commerce involve only two users, besides a number of enabling parties (like banks, directories, certification authorities). Some tasks, however, naturally generalize to an arbitrary number of parties, for instance, *auctions* (Turban 1997), *public procurement* and *voting*.[3]

SEMPER did not work on such n-party protocols. They would naturally fit into the overall architecture, but not into the prototype because some simplifications for the two-party case were made. For most tasks mentioned above no efficient *and* multi-party secure solutions are known yet (see Franklin and Reiter (1995) and Schoenmakers (1999) for state-of-the-art protocols). Most practically deployed solutions are not multi-party secure, as they are based on a central, trusted party, like an auctioneer or a tally center. A problem with the secure protocols is that they typically assume secure consistent broadcast, which is an expensive primitive in practice.

15.2.7 Visualization of Security

From the point of view of an ordinary user, the concepts and options of most security systems look very complex, and they are in fact difficult to understand. Even most computer scientists outside the area of computer security and cryptography have difficulties in understanding all the possibilities of trust management, and even more the concepts and options in an overall system like *SEMPER*.[4] Nevertheless one needs to interface with the user, showing him security-relevant information and getting his input with respect to functional and security options and, most importantly, his agreement or disagreement with security-critical steps (such as authorizing a payment, or approving that a certain piece of confidential data is sent to someone). At least three problems have to be solved for this.

Simple Abstractions. The technicalities of how security works are far too complex for ordinary users; thus a simple abstraction is needed. For instance, the intuitive model of a car most drivers have is very different from the model an engineer would use, but still it suffices to operate and use the car safely. Something like this is also needed for security.

The basic approach in *SEMPER* was to channel all communication between the user and the security system through a single window, the TINGUIN (Trustworthy INteractive Graphical User INterface), and to tell the user that exactly what is communicated through this channel is trustworthy.

---

[3] Voting might not be commerce in the usual sense, but it shares many global security issues with electronic commerce and can share many supporting services. However, some aspects are different, e.g., the compromise of a user's signature keys cannot be handled by liability limits and might not even be noticed. Hence we strongly warn against implementing important elections on current user equipment of at most PCs and smartcards. Another problem is pressure on voters, which is much reduced by real voting booths.

[4] This is not a specific problem of *SEMPER*—if another electronic-commerce toolbox offers fewer services, understanding the overall security including the now external services will be even harder.

Nothing else, in particular nothing that is shown on a browser window. This allowed us to present a consistent look-and-feel for all components.

The security of actions was characterized by letting the user require certain *generic security attributes*, like "confidentiality" or "authentication."

The feedback on the prototype showed that channeling everything through one single window was easy to understand and greatly increased security awareness. But our concept of generic security attributes was still too technical, too far away from the ordinary user's world. Analogies from the paper-based world may be helpful. Additionaly, deciding only between "trusted" and "untrusted" windows is too simplistic if one considers semi-trusted business applications; finer-grained abstractions must be developed.

Minimizing User Interaction. Given a certain user-comprehensible model of the system, one has to design the dynamics of the user-system interaction. From a security point of view the most important points are the following:

- Most business processes have a few *points of no return,* i.e., steps that if taken cannot be reversed locally. Each such step needs to be authorized by the user. Examples are sending a binding order or concluding a payment. Such points must be clearly indicated and explained. In *SEMPER* we tried to keep the appearance of these points uniform across different applications, thereby teaching the user to be alerted whenever such a point is reached.
- Obviously the power to authorize a point of no return must always be with the user. But users must not be asked to authorize steps too often, as they might then do it without thinking. Thus there must be ways to pre-authorize certain steps, e.g., by deducing authorization from already authorized steps (like 'if the order is authorized then payment is automatically authorized as well'), or from policies ('for the next 30 minutes all payments up to a total of 10€ are automatically authorized'), or from preferences ('always send my certificate to merchants who can show a certificate issued by XYZ'). In general context-based, intuitive authorization systems are needed (see also Section 11.7.2).
- Users might be able to maneuver their system into obviously dangerous states, like authorizing a priori all payments. The system should not necessarily prevent this completely, but should alert the user and possibly reset the system automatically to a somewhat safer state after a while. The most popular example is to automatically close a user session that has been inactive for a certain time.

Actual Visualization. Finally, one has to map everything to a real user interface. The only security-related difficulty we considered in this area was support for "small" displays: Ideally, security systems should be implemented on trustworthy systems. These are likely to be physically rather small (see also Section 15.4.1), like a personal digital assistant (PDA) or mobile phone.

We took this into account by keeping the actual design of the TINGUIN small and simple, i.e., it would fit on the screen of standard PDAs. We also considered the idea of a *split TINGUIN*, which means to split the output of the security system into "critical output" and "fyi output" ("for your information"). The critical output must be displayed on a trustworthy display. If that display is powerful enough, the fyi output is displayed on it as well, but otherwise a less trustworthy output channel is used.

The size and quality of the output channel of the trusted device has further implications; see Pfitzmann, Pfitzmann, Schunter, and Waidner (1997).

15.3 Services and Protocols

We now address open issues that correspond to individual services and protocols, i.e., issues that can be assigned to individual blocks in our architecture. Issues regarding the two highest layers were already discussed under the global heading "process orientation" in Section 15.2.1. The Transfer-and-Exchange Layer, a novel aspect of *SEMPER*, is clearly just a start and will evolve in the future. We now concentrate on the lower layers with the more well-known services.

15.3.1 Business-Item Layer

Electronic Payment Systems. Electronic payment systems have been the prime target of research in electronic commerce for over two decades, and most of the basic concepts are quite old. If one looks for open issues, it is appropriate to distinguish between anonymous (or untraceable) and traceable payment systems. For traceable systems essentially all known research questions are solved. The big open issues are standardization of payment and negotiation protocols and integration in applications. Using a generic framework like *SEMPER* greatly eases the technical integration, but legal issues of liability and cross-border payments are also serious impediments. Anonymous payment systems exist, too, e.g., ecash and CAFE. The main problem with such systems is political acceptance. The often discussed risk of money laundering exists, but is generally overestimated: The main issue is to prevent the systems from being more extensively used than cash today, for instance by limiting the maximum amount of payments and the amounts that each user can withdraw per month. Most systems are actually less anonymous than normal cash (unless bank notes were routinely traced) because payees are not anonymous and money must be deposited in a non-anonymous bank account between any two transfers. Some technical questions are also still open. The main one is to design an efficient system that is provably secure under standard cryptographic assumptions; Pointcheval (1998) was a step in this direction (random oracle model) after the inefficient Pfitzmann and Waidner (1992).

We already mentioned the issue of dispute handling in payment systems.

Notary Services for Documents. Traditionally, the term "electronic notary" means all technical services that simulate services provided by existing, real-life notaries. Technically, fair exchanges are at the core of many notary services, e.g., certified mail and contract signing. Those have been treated in the work on the Transfer-and-Exchange Layer in *SEMPER*. However, notary services can also refer to a document, i.e., a statement, independent of a transfer. Examples are notarization of a signature (see Adams and Zuccherato (1997) for a standardization attempt), time stamping (Haber and Stornetta 1991; Bayer et al. 1993; Buldas et al. 1998; Adams et al. 1999), and secure archiving of documents (Nilsson and Pinkas 1999; Bertsch 1999).[5] Some notary services are already commercially available,[6] but in general such services are not well-known and well-used.

Intellectual Property Rights. The protection of intellectual property rights (IPR), often abbreviated as copyright protection, on the Internet is an area with a lot of open problems. *SEMPER* did not work on this topic because it was the subject of several other EU projects. We do not discuss detailed questions here because we have not even introduced the terminology.

Credentials. As already mentioned, *SEMPER* did not really work on the Credentials Block, i.e., on the use of attribute certificates in electronic commerce. The most complicated aspect, both cryptographically and for user-friendly design, is the combination with anonymity as discussed in Sections 15.2.4 and 15.2.5. However, even without anonymity, some work remains to be done.

One aspect is the inclusion of attribute certificates, which vary widely, into standard business flows. For example, given the virtuality of electronic commerce, buyers might more than ever require merchants to show certain quality certificates issued by trade or consumer-protection organizations. This ranges from attributes on fair trade, such as agreement to the *SECA* code of conduct, which might be included into the key certificates, to business-oriented attributes like product quality (e.g., "authentic antiques" or "up-to-date on-line information"). Credentials concerning individual products might also be integrated into catalogue browsing; then the services of a tool like *SEMPER* would be used outside a typical purchase flow. Buyers also sometimes need credentials, e.g., credit rating or the proxy right for a certain company.

If attribute certificates attesting fine-grained rights (e.g., subscriptions and vouchers) become common, support for retrieving and showing the appropriate rights is needed. Then the concept of a Commerce-Layer context, which is currently only used for one deal in the sense of, e.g., one purchase,

---

[5]The main issues here are *availability* of the stored data for a very long time and optionally *confidentiality* of the stored data. Note that many cryptographic keys have a lifetime of a few years only.

[6]Examples are time-stamping by *Surety Technologies, Inc.*, http://www.surety.com, and certified mail by *e-Parcel, LLC,* http://www.e-parcel.com.

will be extended to at least a tree structure: There will be overall contexts for certain business partners, and derived contexts for individual deals. This is already partially provided in the *SEMPER* prototype.

The set of necessary credentials might be clear to the requester a priori, but in the general case it is negotiated between both parties and it might involve more parties, e.g., in the case of mandatory online verification. Another aspect is under which circumstances a party is willing to give out credentials about itself.

Often several credentials are needed. In particular, there may be meta-rights allowing certain parties to grant other rights. Some of these are centralized, e.g., the right to give licenses to be a bank or a doctor. Others are local, e.g., the trust in a consumer organization that tests product quality. Management of combinations of credentials is often collectively called *trust management*. Advanced techniques to express access control policies in operating systems and databases already addressed the same problem. Some sophisticated proposals already exist (Blaze et al. 1996; Blaze et al. 1999; Herzberg et al. 2000), but still many practical problems are unsolved, or at least the proposed general frameworks have to be instantiated with appropriate and user-friendly application-specific elements. Application-specific first means specific to certain blocks of the architecture (key certificates, access control, etc.) and secondly specific to certain business domains. It is still contested whether it is really worth while to provide an application-independent mechanism for access control decisions (Feigenbaum 1998); the alternative is to support only retrieval and verification of credentials, and to let each application implement the connectives it needs as a normal part of its program. In addition, most of the proposed applications for trust management assume a cross-organizational, role-based model. So far there are not many examples of such models.

15.3.2 Supporting Services

Atomic Secure Transactions. Currently, there are on the one hand electronic-commerce systems without particular care for security. They often use standard transaction processing to make commercial transactions atomic and to allow recovery from crashes, i.e., transactions either complete successfully or are completely undone. On the other hand, there are security-specific protocols, but those often neglect crash resistance as an implementation detail. One might hope that one could also simply plug a transaction-processing system underneath these protocols, but such an approach does not easily provide the required multi-party security because it usually assumes a *centralized* trust model. (Sometimes this entity is hidden in primitives like a "secure bulletin board".)

Actually, Bürk and Pfitzmann (1989) already describe how to achieve atomicity in payment systems in a multi-party secure way. The paper is primarily about different types of anonymous systems, but solutions for non-anonymous systems can be derived as subsets. They also demonstrate that in some cases pure atomicity is unachievable and dispute handling must come to the rescue.

SEMPER did some research in this area by its work on fair exchanges. In this context one might interpret fair contract signing as a multi-party secure and verifiable version of distributed commit. But more work is needed on more general solutions combining both worlds and dealing with nested transactions.

Public-Key Infrastructure. Open electronic commerce needs a public-key infrastructure (PKI) for secure user registration, public-key certification, and directory services (see Chapter 12). Like payment systems, this has been an area of research and development for over two decades and the basic solutions are very old. Nevertheless, there are problems with the development and use of PKIs. The most important one of these was a solution for liability for digital signatures that is both reasonable for users that have at most PCs and smartcards, and for relying parties. We believe that *SEMPER* has found the right suite of fair solutions to this problem, see Chapters 3, 13 and 14.

Several other problems concern awareness, terminology and choosing the right solution for the right purpose.

One such issue is that there are somehow two camps discussing "the semantics of certificates". One camp argues that a certificate should be interpreted as a statement saying that a certain key belongs to a certain name. The other camp argues that names are not appropriate, and that a certificate should be a statement saying that the owner of a certain key has a certain *right*. The former are often proponents of the X.509 standard and the IETF PKIX working group, the latter of the IETF SPKI working group. (Of course, not everybody supporting these groups belongs to such a camp.) The solution is simply that there are key certificates and attribute certificates, and both have their uses and should be distinguished in the formats. (The fact that X.509 was only a format standard, with originally a minimalistic set of fields and no attached semantics, was one reason for such discussions starting at the wrong end.) Important uses for key certificates are wherever a real-world entity has to take liability for digitally signed statements, or where a-priori trust in a real-world entity is deferred to the electronic world. Hence key certificates and thus non-electronic registration are needed in particular in secure banking and in electronic offers and orders binding real-world entities, and also in secure email at least while conventional names are still prevalent. Important uses for attribute certificates are in access control for software and as credentials in electronic commerce. Moreover, even in certificate chains for key certificates, all the certificates of CAs are not only statements about keys, but about the fact that an entity is a CA, and thus attribute certificates.

Often even the basic semantics of each class of certificates is not clear. For instance, many people believe that an ordinary key certificate *creates* liability for the party who owns the corresponding secret key. But a user has to explicitly *agree* on taking such liability during registration, and if a certification authority claims liability for the user otherwise, this is likely to be legally meaningless. Also the "rights" in attribute certificates are sometimes taken to always mean an expression of trust by the certifier, whereas, e.g., the right to use the money on a certain account is simply a matter of correct handling of ownership.

A more technical problem is how to *revoke* public keys. The safest approach is to require online verification of all certificates, but this is not always feasible. Alternatives like certificate revocation lists are costly and introduce a certain delay until they become effective. There have been several recent proposal for efficient and secure updates of lists of still-valid certificates, e.g., Aiello, Lodha, and Ostrovsky (1998). An often overlooked problem with revocation of signature keys is that it requires secure *time stamping* of all signatures (Bertsch 1999; Nilsson and Pinkas 1999). Otherwise one could use a revoked key forever simply by backdating signatures (and making them promise something for the future).[7] Another nasty and not really well-solved problem is how to proceed if a PKI has a root key and that becomes compromised (see MasterCard and Visa (1997) for a discussion and a first, pragmatic solution).

Cryptographic Primitives. All cryptographic primitives needed for typical electronic commerce exist in some way. The main open questions are in the areas of security proofs and secure implementations:

- Development of *efficient* and *provably secure* cryptographic primitives. Today most systems are not both efficient and provably secure (under standard assumptions). Using provably secure systems reduces the overall risk of failure, and allows one to make clear statements about the security of the system, e.g., Cramer and Damgård (1996) and Cramer and Shoup (1998).
- *Secure initialization* of cryptographic primitives, which means primarily the secure generation of secret keys. Many systems using cryptography were broken because the vindexrandom number generators used were predictable; see Eastlake et al. (1994) and Jakobsson et al. (1998).[8]
- *Variants secure against non-functional attacks.* This means variants that do not leak information on secret keys via hidden channels. Such hidden channels can be created by an attacker (Trojan horse attacks) or might exist, e.g., because the computing time or the power consumption depends on the secret key (Kocher 1996; Kocher et al. 1999; Chari et al. 1999). Some hidden channels can be exploited only in the case of a failure, as the attack depends on how the implementation reacts on a failed computation. This

---

[7] As a side effect this would be solved by the Liability-Cover Service, see Chapter 13.

[8] It is advisable to combine *several* sources of randomness. In particular the system should involve the user into the generation of one source, e.g., by measuring the time between key strokes.

includes fault-based cryptanalysis (Anderson and Kuhn 1996; Boneh et al. 1997) as well as the usual problems with non-encrypted backup tapes. An alternative to providing robust algorithms is to destroy the hidden channels in the implementation of the computing base (see Section 15.4.1), but this is often more difficult.

15.4 Implementation

In this section, we discuss open issues and future directions related to the implementation architecture and actual implementations.

15.4.1 Trusted Computing Base

The most fundamental problem in security is to find a (trustworthy) trusted computing base (TCB). In electronic commerce (in contrast to traditional centralized security systems), this is particularly important for the end users' devices because anything a user can do online, a successful attacker against these devices can also do.

Today most electronic-commerce systems depend on standard PC operating systems and web browsers, maybe using scripting languages. All such systems are notoriously insecure. This is in particular true for operating systems that do not support any separation between different processes, which is true for most of the popular ones. In such systems any malicious program can completely corrupt any security system, without giving the user a chance to recognize the problem easily. As explained in Section 1.2.3, such malicious programs can come in different disguises. Anti-virus tools cannot detect them unless the manufacturers of these tools have recognized them, and intrusion-detection software is also not perfect and typically not used on end user devices.

With Java, attempts have been made to replace parts of the missing operating system security in a programming language. Combined with a browser allowing applets only in this language one certainly gets a much smaller risk than without such an approach. Still, on the one hand, not all malicious programs come via the browser. On the other hand, some flaws in the Java Virtual Machine have also been found already, and to some extent Java shares the problem of current operating systems that they are too big and without clear semantics.

There have been experimental highly secure operating systems in the past, but none has reached the mass market. One reason may be that they tried too much: a general purpose operating system will get large, and it is hard to compete with mainstream operating systems, i.e., a system without a large base of standard applications seems unmarketable. Some efforts are under way to construct more secure versions of standard systems, but there is always a tradeoff between somewhat restricting the rights of applications, but still not to disallow most of the existing ones. One approach that we advocate to try is to use a very small security kernel, to run a standard operating system as one application, and a much smaller self-made operating system specifically tailored to critical aspects of electronic commerce. A first prototype of such an approach was constructed in Stüble (2000). Combining safe languages with marketable systems at this layer is also still a challenge.

Even if there were a sufficiently secure operating system, there would be the problem of distinguishing between authentic systems and rogue systems, see Pfitzmann, Pfitzmann, Schunter, and Waidner (1997).

For the protection of secrets after theft, one has to assume that certain pieces of hardware resist all physical attacks, i.e., that they are tamper-resistant. Others need to be at least tamper-evident, i.e., an attacker cannot make invisible successful alterations of the functionality.[9]

A lot of research has been done in this area, but only little has been published. Hence the general public has only very limited knowledge about the physical security of devices. The main standard in this area (U. S. National Institute of Standards and Technology NIST 1994b) only considers restricted classes of attacks. Stronger public standards are needed.

One result of this lack of knowledge is the perception of smartcards as tamper-resistant. Recent experiments have confirmed suspicions that most smartcards offer only poor security against moderately skilled and funded attackers (Anderson and Kuhn 1996; Kocher 1996). Better solutions exist.[10] Moreover, the path to the user must be trustworthy, i.e., a smartcard-like device alone cannot play the role of the secure end-user device.

15.4.2 Dependable Third-Party Implementations

Notary services have occurred several times so far, e.g., in fair exchanges and notarized transfers, as services for individual documents, and as arbiters in dispute handling. (The standard, but somewhat misleading term is Trusted Third Parties; we will use "dependable third parties" as a compromise.) Before any of these services can be used in practice, the notary side must be implemented in a way that is both sufficiently trustworthy and sufficiently efficient and scalable.

There are three approaches to achieve the trustworthiness; they are best combined:

– *Minimization of trust.* We have stressed in *SEMPER* that one has to *minimize* the required trust in any other parties; this is the basic concept

---

[9]Even stronger tamper resistance is needed if other parties have to trust the integrity of the user devices. However, for standard Internet commerce services like signatures and online payment this is not necessary.

[10]For instance there are tamper-resistant PC cards. The main reason why they offer better security is their improved coating and their ability to erase their volatile memory in the case of an attack, thanks to an onboard battery.

of *multi-party security*. One flavor of this is *accountability*, i.e., to ensure that if a somewhat trusted party misbehaves (including negligence that allows employees or even outsiders to carry out the actual misbehavior), this is detectable and provable to other parties. One should also maximize the misbehaving party's risk in this case (liability for damages, additional punishment) and minimize the potential gain.

This was an approach via protocols and the legal framework. However, it does not solve the problem completely and must therefore be complemented by implementation measures. For instance, the users still need trust in cases where damages are immaterial and cannot be repaired. Or the damages might exceed the amount for which the notary has reserves and insurances. Or the other parties to whom misbehaviour of an arbiter is proven might use the same corrupted software.

– *Distribution of trust.* One can design systems such that trust is *distributed*. Basically, this means that there is no single point of failure in the trust assumptions. For instance, if a certain signature is valid only if the holder can show n certificates, then no single certificate authority can cheat the user by issuing a wrong certificate: at least n CAs would have to co-operate to achieve this fraud. To balance security and availability, one can often design k-out-of-n systems, i.e., there are n specific parties, and the system is secure as long as at least k of them are honest. Efficiency and scalability of such solutions has not been fully explored yet.

A weaker way to distribute trust is to offer at least a certain choice of parties to trust (as in real life everybody can choose among many different banks the one that looks most trustworthy—as far as one can judge that).

– *Establishment of trust.* One needs to establish some original trust. This may come from prior experience, but may be improved upon by public control of the respective parties and opening the design of their computer systems to public scrutiny. Once original trust is there, it may be transferred to other parties by recommendations, i.e., credentials and trust management.

All these concepts are well-known in the theory of security systems, but not much use is made of them in practice yet.

15.4.3 Assurance

For all parts of a security framework and business applications that must be trusted by at least one party, security evaluation is necessary.

What is missing most are general protection profiles for formal certification, e.g., according to the Common Criteria (Common Criteria Project Sponsoring Organisations 1999). *SEMPER* did some work in this direction. In particular, the high-level criteria for *SEMPER* compliance of different parts of a system are meant as the basis for such profiles. In practice, so far at most small parts of electronic commerce systems, e.g., the smartcard part of a signature application, seem to have been certified, and the profiles used are not even public. We believe that there is still quite a challenge in developing comprehensive criteria for entire business processes, in particular for those aspects that concern the user.

Even for individual services, e.g., a payment system and without the user-interface aspects, there are no comprehensive models yet, nor are there comprehensive definitions in the security community. For example, dispute handling is typically not considered. Not only could therefore the dispute handling procedures be insecure, but some security properties of systems can *only* be formalized by including the dispute handling, see Pfitzmann and Waidner (1996).

The field for research into definitions and proofs of security systems becomes even wider if one wants the proofs to be in a formal language and with the support of verification tools.

For systems that need to be trusted by the general public, public availability of the evaluation is essential so that any expert can verify the quality. Security by obscurity has far too often lead to insecure systems.

References

Abad-Peiro, J. L., N. Asokan, M. Steiner, and M. Waidner (1998). Designing a generic payment service. *IBM Systems Journal 37*(1), 72–88.

Abe, M. (1998). Universally verifiable mix-net with verification work independent of the number of mix-servers. See IACR (1998b), pp. 437–447.

Abelson, H., R. Anderson, S. M. Bellovin, J. Benaloh, M. Blaze, W. Diffie, J. Gilmore, P. G. Neumann, R. L. Rivest, J. I. Schiller, and B. Schneier (1997). The risk of key recovery, key escrow, and trusted third-party encryption. *The World Wide Web Journal 2*(3), 241–257.

Adams, C., P. Cain, D. Pinkas, and R. Zuccherato (1999, June). Internet X.509 public key infrastructure time stamp protocol (TSP). Internet Draft. draft-ietf-pkix-time-stamp-02.txt.

Adams, C. and R. Zuccherato (1997, February). Notary protocols. Internet Draft. draft-adams-notary-01.txt.

Aiello, W., S. Lodha, and R. Ostrovsky (1998). Fast digital identity revocation. See IACR (1998a), pp. 137–152.

Anderson, R. and M. Kuhn (1996). Tamper resistance — A cautionary note. See USENIX (1996), pp. 1–12.

ANSI Accredited Standards Committee X.12 (ASC X.12/DISA) (1992). X12 standard, version 3. American National Standards (ANS).

Asokan, N. (1998, May). *Fairness in Electronic Commerce*. Ph. D. thesis, University of Waterloo.

Asokan, N., E. V. Herreweghen, and M. Steiner (1998). Towards a framework for handling disputes in payment systems. See USENIX (1998), pp. 187–202.

Asokan, N., P. Janson, M. Steiner, and M. Waidner (1997, September). State of the art in electronic payment systems. *IEEE Computer 30*(9), 28–35.

Asokan, N., P. Janson, M. Steiner, and M. Waidner (2000, March). State of the art in electronic payment systems. In M. V. Zelkowitz (Ed.), *Advances in Computers*, Volume 53. Academic Press. This is an extended and revised version of (Asokan, Janson, Steiner, and Waidner 1997).

Asokan, N., M. Schunter, and M. Waidner (1996, November). Optimistic protocols for multi-party fair exchange. Technical Report RZ 2892, IBM Zürich Research Laboratory.

Asokan, N., M. Schunter, and M. Waidner (1997). Optimistic protocols for fair exchange. In *4th ACM Conference on Computer and Communications Security*, Zürich, pp. 6–17. ACM Press.

Asokan, N., V. Shoup, and M. Waidner (1998a). Asynchronous protocols for optimistic fair exchange. In *Proceedings of the IEEE Symposium on Research in Security and Privacy*, Oakland, CA, pp. 86–99. IEEE TC S&P: IEEE Computer Society Press.

Asokan, N., V. Shoup, and M. Waidner (1998b). Optimistic fair exchange of digital signatures. See IACR (1998b), pp. 591–606.

Atkinson, R. (1995). Security architecture for the Internet Protocol. Internet Request for Comment (RFC) 1825, IETF.

Atluri, V. and W.-K. Huang (1996). An authorization model for workflows. In E. Bertino, H. Kurth, G. Martella, and E. Montolivo (Eds.), *Proceedings of the Fourth European Symposium on Research in Computer Security (ESORICS)*, Number 1146 in Lecture Notes in Computer Science, Rome, Italy, pp. 44–64. Springer-Verlag, Berlin Germany.

Bahreman, A. (1996). Generic electronic payment services: Framework and functional specification. See USENIX (1996), pp. 87–103.

Bahreman, A. and R. Narayanaswamy (1996). Payment method negotiation service. See USENIX (1996), pp. 299–314.

Bahreman, A. and D. Tygar (1994). Certified electronic mail. In *1994 Symposium on Network and Distributed Systems Security (NDSS 94)*. Internet Society: IEEE Press.

Bakos, Y. (1998). The emerging role of electronic marketplaces on the Internet. *Communications of the ACM 41*(8), 35–42.

Bayer, D., S. Haber, and W. S. Stornetta (1993). Improving the efficiency and reliability of digital time-stamping. In *Sequences II: Methods in Communication, Security, and Computer Science*, Berlin, pp. 329–334. Springer-Verlag.

Bellare, M., J. Garay, R. Hauser, A. Herzberg, H. Krawczyk, M. Steiner, G. Tsudik, E. Van Herreweghen, and M. Waidner (2000, April). Design, implementation and deployment of the iKP secure electronic payment system. *IEEE Journal on Selected Areas in Communications 18*(4), 611–627.

Ben-Or, M., O. Goldreich, S. Micali, and R. L. Rivest (1990). A fair protocol for signing contracts. *IEEE Transactions on Information Theory 36*(1), 40–46.

Berners-Lee, T., R. T. Fielding, H. F. Nielsen, J. Gettys, and J. Mogul (1997). Hypertext transfer protocol — HTTP/1.1. Internet Request for Comment (RFC) 2068, IETF.

Bertsch, A. (1999). On sustainable digital signatures. In G. Müller and K. Rannenberg (Eds.), *Multilateral Security in Communications, Vol. 3*, pp. 269–282. München, Germany: Addison-Wesley.

Biddle, C. B. (1996, November). Comment: Misplaced priorities: The Utah digital signature act and liability allocation in a public key infrastructure. *San Diego Law Review 33*, 1143–1193. Available from http://www.acusd.edu/~biddle/.

Biskup, J. and C. Eckert (1994). About the enforcement of state dependent security specifications. In *Database Security VII: Status and Prospects*, pp. 3–17. North Holland.

Blaze, M., J. Feigenbaum, and J. Lacy (1996). Decentralized trust management. See IEEE TC S&P (1996), pp. 164–173.

Blaze, M., J. Feigenbaum, and A. D. Leromytis (1999). Keynote: Trust management for public-key infrastructures. In B. Christianson, B. Crispo, W. S. Harbison, and M. Roe (Eds.), *Security Protocols—6th International Workshop*, Volume 1550 of *Lecture Notes in Computer Science*, Cambridge, United Kingdom, pp. 59–66. Springer-Verlag, Berlin Germany.

Bleichenbacher, D., E. Gabber, P. B. Gibbons, Y. Matias, and A. Mayer (1998). On secure and pseudonymous client-relationships with multiple servers. See USENIX (1998), pp. 99–108.

Blum, M. (1981). Three applications of the oblivious transfer. Technical Report Version 2, University of California at Berkeley.

Boly, J.-P., A. Bosselaers, R. Cramer, R. Michelsen, S. Mjølsnes, F. Muller, T. Pedersen, B. Pfitzmann, P. de Rooij, B. Schoenmakers, M. Schunter, L. Vallée, and M. Waidner (1994). The ESPRIT project CAFE — High security digital payment systems. In D. Gollmann (Ed.), *Proceedings of the Third European Symposium on Research in Computer Security (ESORICS)*, Number 875 in Lecture Notes in Computer Science, Brighton, UK, pp. 217–230. Springer-Verlag, Berlin Germany.

Boneh, D., R. A. DeMillo, and R. J. Lipton (1997). On the importance of checking cryptographic protocols for faults. In *Advances in Cryptology — Eurocrypt '97*, Number 1233 in Lecture Notes in Computer Science, pp. 37–51. IACR: Springer-Verlag, Berlin Germany.

Buldas, A., P. Laud, H. Lipmaa, and J. Villemson (1998). Time-stamping with binary linking schemes. See IACR (1998a), pp. 486–501.

Bürk, H. and A. Pfitzmann (1989, August). Digital payment systems enabling security and unobservability. *Computers & Security 8*(5), 399–416.

Bürk, H. and A. Pfitzmann (1990). Value exchange systems enabling security and unobservability. *Computers & Security 9*(8), 715–721.

Chari, S., C. Jutla, J. R. Rao, and P. Rohatgi (1999). Towards sound approaches to counteract power-analysis attacks. See IACR (1999), pp. 398–412.

Chaum, D. (1998). The dining cryptographers problem: Unconditional sender and recipient untraceability. *Journal of Cryptology 1*(1), 65–75.

Chaum, D. L. (1981, February). Untraceable electronic mail, return addresses, and digital pseudonyms. *Communications of the ACM 24*(2), 84–88.

Chaum, D. L. (1985). Security without identification: Transaction systems to make big brother obsolete. *Communications of the ACM 28*(10), 1030–1044.

Clark, D. D. and D. R. Wilson (1987). A comparison of commercial and military computer security policies. In *Proceedings of the IEEE Symposium on Research in Security and Privacy*, Oakland, CA, pp. 184–194. IEEE TC S&P: IEEE Computer Society Press.

Coffey, T. and P. Saidha (1996). Non-repudiation with mandatory proof of receipt. *Computer Communication Review 26*(1), 6–17.

Common Criteria Project Sponsoring Organisations (1999, August). *Common Criteria for Information Technology Security Evaluation*. Common Criteria Project Sponsoring Organisations. Version 2.1, adopted by ISO/IEC as ISO/IEC International Standard (IS) 15408 1-3. Available from http://csrc.ncsl.nist.gov/cc/ccv20/ccv2list.htm.

Cox, B., D. Tygar, and M. Sirbu (1995). Netbill security and transaction protocol. See USENIX (1995), pp. 77–88.

Cramer, R. and I. Damgård (1996). New generation of secure and practical rsa-based signatures. See IACR (1996), pp. 173–185.

Cramer, R. and V. Shoup (1998). A practical public key cryptosystem provably secure against adaptive chosen ciphertext attack. See IACR (1998a), pp. 13–25.

Cranor, L. F. and B. A. LaMacchia (1998). Spam! *Communications of the ACM 41*(8), 74–83.

Daswani, N., D. Boneh, H. Garcia-Molina, S. Ketchpel, and A. Paepcke (1998). A generalized digital wallet architecture. Technical report, Stanford University, Computer Science Department.

Dean, D., E. W. Felten, and D. S. Wallach (1996). Java security: From HotJava to Netscape and beyond. See IEEE TC S&P (1996), pp. 190–200.

Dean, D., E. W. Felten, D. S. Wallach, and D. Balfanz (1998). Java security: Web browsers and beyond. See Denning and Denning (1998), pp. 241–269.

Deng, R. H., L. Gong, A. A. Lazar, and W. Wang (1996). Practical protocols for certified electronic mail. *Journal of Network and Systems Management 4*(3), 279–297.

Denning, D. E. and P. J. Denning (Eds.) (1998). *Internet Besieged: Countering Cyberspace Scofflaws*. New York: ACM Press / Addison-Wesley.

Denning, P. J. (1990). *Computers under Attack - Intruders, Worms and Viruses*. New York: ACM Press.

Diffie, W. and M. E. Hellman (1976). New directions in cryptography. *IEEE Transactions on Information Theory 22*(6), 644–654.

Eastlake, D. E. (1999). Domain name system security extensions. Internet Request for Comment (RFC) 2535, IETF.

Eastlake, D. E., B. Boesch, S. Crocker, and M. Yesil (1995, July). CyberCash credit card protocol version 0.8. Internet Draft. draft-eastlake-cybercash-v08-00.txt.

Eastlake, D. E., S. D. Crocker, and J. I. Schiller (1994). Randomness requirements for security. Internet Request for Comment (RFC) 1750, IETF.

European Union (1992). The OECD guidelines for the security of information systems.

European Union (1993, April). Directive 93/13/EEC of 5 April 1993 on unfair terms in consumer contracts.

European Union (1994, December). Council regulation (EC) no 3381/94. Setting up a community regime for the control of exports of dual-use goods.

European Union (1995, October). Directive 95/46/EC of the European Parliament and of the Council of 24 October 1995 on the protection of individuals with regard to the processing of personal data and on the free movement of such data.

European Union (1996). Communication on illegal and harmful content on the Internet. COM(96) 0487 - C4-0592/96.

European Union (1997a, October). Directive 97/55/EC of European Parliament and of the Council of 6 October 1997 amending directive 84/450/EEC concerning misleading advertising so as to include comparative advertising.

European Union (1997b, May). Directive 97/7/EC of the European Parliament and of the Council of 20 May 1997 on the protection of consumers in respect of distance contracts.

European Union (1997c, November 8). Ensuring security and trust in electronic communication: Towards a european framework for digital signatures and encryption. Communication to the European Parliament, the Council, the Economic and Social Committee and the Committee of the Regions, COM(97)503.

European Union (1997d, December). EU directives 91/250, 96/9 and 92/100 on copyright and related rights in the information society.

European Union (1997e, April 15). A european initiative in electronic commerce. Communication to the European Parliament, the Council, the Economic and Social Committee and the Committee of the Regions, COM(97) 157.

European Union (1997f). The OECD cryptography policy guidelines (1997).

European Union (2000, January 19). Directive 1999/93/EC of the European Parliament and of the Council of 13 December 1999 on a community framework for electronic signatures. *Official Journal of the European Communities L 13*, 12–20. Available from http://www.qlinks.net/comdocs/elsig/en.pdf.

Even, S. (1983). A protocol for signing contracts. *ACM SIGACT News 15*(1), 34–39.

Even, S. and Y. Yacobi (1980, March). Relations among public key signature systems. Technical Report 175, Computer Science Department, Technion, Haifa, Israel.

Feigenbaum, J. (1998). Towards an infrastructure for authorization (position paper). See USENIX (1998). (not in printed version of proceedings; available from http://www.research.att.com/~jf/pubs/usenix-ecommerce98.ps).

Ford, W. and M. S. Baum (1997). *Secure Electronic Commerce*. Upper Saddle River, New Jersey, USA: Prentice Hall.

Fowler, M. and K. Scott (1997). *UML Distilled : Applying the standard object modeling language*. Addison-Welsey, Reading MA.

Fox, D. (1998). Zu einem prinzipiellen Problem digitaler Signaturen. *Datenschutz und Datensicherheit DuD 22*(7), 386–388.

Franklin, M. K. and M. K. Reiter (1995). The design and implementation of a secure auction service. In *Proceedings of the IEEE Symposium on Research in Security and Privacy*, Oakland, CA, pp. 2–14. IEEE TC S&P: IEEE Computer Society Press.

Freier, A. O., P. Karlton, and P. C. Kocher (1996, November). The SSL protocol version 3.0. Technical report, IETF Transport Layer Security Working Group.

Fritsch, L. (1998, August). Sichere anonyme Kommunikation für den elektronischen Marktplatz *SEMPER* — Design und Implementierung in Java. Diplomarbeit, Fachbereich Informatik, Universität des Saarlandes.

FSTC (1995). Electronic check proposal. Technical report, Financial Services Technology Consortium.

Gabber, E., P. B. Gibbons, Y. Matias, and A. Mayer (1997). How to make personalized web browsing simple, secure, and anonymous. See IFCA (1997), pp. 17–32.

Gamma, E., R. Helm, R. Johnson, and J. Vlissides (1995). *Design Patterns - Elements of Object-Oriented Software*. Addison-Wesley-Longman, Reading.

German Government (1997, June). Digital Signature Act (Signaturgesetz — SigG). Available from http://www.iid.de/rahmen, also in an English translation.

Goldstein, T. (1997). The gateway security model in the Java electronic commerce framework. See IFCA (1997), pp. 340–354.

Gosling, J., B. Joy, and G. Steele (1996, August). *The Java^{TM} Language Specification* (1.0 ed.). Sun Microsystems. Appeared also as book with same title in Addison-Wesleys 'The Java Series'.

Haber, S. and W. S. Stornetta (1991). How to time-stamp a digital document. *Journal of Cryptology 3*(2), 99–111.

Harrison, M. A., W. L. Ruzzo, and J. D. Ullman (1976). Protection in operating systems. *Communications of the ACM 19*(8), 461–471.

Hauser, R. and M. Steiner (1995). Generic extensions of WWW browsers. See USENIX (1995), pp. 147–154.

Hauser, R., M. Steiner, and M. Waidner (1996). Micro-payments based on iKP. See SECURICOM (1996), pp. 67–82.

Hauser, R. and G. Tsudik (1996). On shopping incognito. See USENIX (1996), pp. 251–258.

Henry, D., S. Cooke, P. Buckley, J. Dumagan, G. Gill, D. Pastore, and S. La-Porte (1999, June). The emerging digital economy II. Technical report, U.S. Department of Commerce, Economics and Statistics Administration, Office of Policy Development, Washington. Available from http://www.ecommerce.gov/ede/report.html.

Herzberg, A., Y. Mass, Y. Mihaeli, D. Naor, and Y. Ravid (2000). Access control meets public key infrastructure, or: Assigning roles to strangers. In *Proceedings of the IEEE Symposium on Research in Security and Privacy*, Oakland, CA. IEEE TC S&P: IEEE Computer Society Press.

IACR (1996). *Advances in Cryptology — Crypto '96*, Number 1109 in Lecture Notes in Computer Science. IACR: Springer-Verlag, Berlin Germany.

IACR (1998a). *Advances in Cryptology — Crypto '98*, Number 1462 in Lecture Notes in Computer Science. IACR: Springer-Verlag, Berlin Germany.

IACR (1998b). *Advances in Cryptology — Eurocrypt '98*, Number 1403 in Lecture Notes in Computer Science. IACR: Springer-Verlag, Berlin Germany.

IACR (1999). *Advances in Cryptology — Crypto '99*, Number 1666 in Lecture Notes in Computer Science. IACR: Springer-Verlag, Berlin Germany.

IEEE TC S&P (1996). *Proceedings of the IEEE Symposium on Research in Security and Privacy*, Oakland, CA. IEEE TC S&P: IEEE Computer Society Press.

IETF Working Group. Public-key infrastructure (X.509) (PKIX). http://www. ietf.org/html.charters/pkix-charter.html.

IFCA (1997). *Proceedings of the First Conference on Financial Cryptography (FC '97)*, Number 1318 in Lecture Notes in Computer Science, Anguilla, British West Indies. IFCA: Springer-Verlag, Berlin Germany.

ISO/IEC (1990). Information technology — Open Systems Interconnection — The directory: Authentication framework. ISO International Standard 9594-8. Same as ITU-T Rec X.509.

ISO/IEC (1995). Information technology — Open Systems Interconnection — The directory: Authentication framework. ISO International Standard 9594-8:1995. Same as ITU-T Rec X.509v3.

ISO/IEC JTC 1/SC27, N 1105 (1995). Information technology — Security techniques — Non repudiation — Part 1: General model. ISO International Standard 13888-1.

ISO/IEC JTC 1/SC27, N 1106 (1995). Information technology — Security techniques — Non repudiation — Part 1: Using symmetric encipherment algorithms. ISO International Standard 13888-2.

ISO/IEC JTC 1/SC27, N 1107 (1996). Information technology — Security techniques — Non repudiation — Part 1: Using asymetric techniques. ISO International Standard 13888-3.

ISO/IEC TC154 (1999). Electronic data interchange for administration, commerce and transport (EDIFACT) – Application level syntax rules – Part 5: Security rules for batch edi (authenticity, integrity and non-repudiation of origin). ISO Draft International Standard 9735-5:1999. Syntax version number 4.

Jakobsson, M. (1998). A practical mix. See IACR (1998b), pp. 448–461.

Jakobsson, M., D. M'Raihi, Y. Tsiounis, and M. Yung (1999). Electronic payments: where do we go from here. In R. Baumgart (Ed.), *Secure Networking - CQRE [Secure] '99*, Number 1740 in Lecture Notes in Computer Science, pp. 43–63. Springer-Verlag, Berlin Germany. Invited talk.

Jakobsson, M., E. Shriver, B. K. Hillyer, and A. Juels (1998). A practical secure physical random bit generator. In *5th ACM Conference on Computer and Communications Security*, San Francisco, pp. 103–111. ACM Press.

JavaSoft (1996, November). Java native interface specification. Release 1.1.

Jerichow, A., J. Müller, A. Pfitzmann, B. Pfitzmann, and M. Waidner (1998). Real-time mixes: A bandwidth-efficient anonymity protocol. *IEEE Journal on Selected Areas in Communications 16*(4), 495–509.

Kahin, B. (1994). The strategic environment for protecting multimedia. In *Technological Strategies for Protecting Intellectual Property in the Networked Multimedia Environment*, The Journal of the Interactive Multimedia Association Intellectual Property Project, Coalition for Networked Information, MIT, Program on Digital Open High-Resolution Systems, pp. 1–8. Interactive Multimedia Association, John F. Kennedy School of Government.

Katsch, M. E. (1996). Dispute resolution in cyberspace. In *Connecticut Law Review Symposium: Legal Regulation of the Internet*, Number 953 in 28. Available from http://www.umass.edu/legal/articles/uconn.html.

Ketchpel, S. P., H. Garcia-Molina, A. Paepcke, S. Hassan, and S. Cousins (1996). U-PAI: A universal payment application interface. See USENIX (1996), pp. 105–121.

Knott, J. and A. Stemerding (Eds.) (1996). *A Guide to Financial EDI*. EBES/EEG4.

Kocher, P. (1996). Timing attacks on implementations of Diffie-Hellman, RSA, DSS, and other systems. See IACR (1996), pp. 104–113.

Kocher, P., J. Jaffe, and B. Jun (1999). Differential power analysis. See IACR (1999), pp. 399–397.

KRISIS Consortium (1998, May). Key recovery in secure information systems. Final report of EU project KRISIS. Available from http://www.cordis.lu/infosec/src/study9.htm.

Lenstra, A. K. and E. V. Verheul (1999, November). Selecting cryptographic key sizes. 3rd Workshop on Elliptic Curve Cryptography (ECC '99). Revised November 1999, http://www.cryptosavvy.com.

Linington, P. F. (1983, December). Fundamentals of the layer service definitions and protocol specifications. *Proceedings of the IEEE 71*(12), 1341–1345.

Linn, J. (1997). Generic security service application program interface, version 2. Internet Request for Comment (RFC) 2078, IETF.

Lomas, M. (Ed.) (1997). *Security Protocols—International Workshop*, Volume 1189 of *Lecture Notes in Computer Science*, Cambridge, United Kingdom. Springer-Verlag, Berlin Germany.

Low, S. H., N. F. Maxemchuk, and S. Paul (1994). Anonymous credit cards. In J. Stern (Ed.), *2nd ACM Conference on Computer and Communications Security*, Fairfax, Virginia, pp. 108–117. ACM Press.

MANDATE II Consortium (1998, February). MANDATE final report. Draft version 2.0. Available from http://www.cryptomathic.dk/mandate/.

Masaguer, F. F. (1996). Security in electronic trading over open networks: a detailed analysis and comparison. See SECURICOM (1996), pp. 39–66.

MasterCard and Visa (1997, May). *SET Secure Electronic Transactions Protocol* (Version 1.0 ed.). Book One: Business Specifications, Book Two: Technical Specification, Book Three: Formal Protocol Definition. Available from http://www.setco.org/set_specifications.html.

Medvinsky, G. and B. C. Neuman (1993). NetCash: A design for practical electronic currency on the Internet. In V. Ashby (Ed.), *1st ACM Conference on Computer and Communications Security*, Fairfax, Virginia, pp. 102–106. ACM Press.

Menezes, A. J., P. C. van Oorschot, and S. A. Vanstone (1997). *Handbook of Applied Cryptography*. CRC Press series on discrete mathematics and its applications. Boca Raton: CRC Press.

Micali, S. (1997). Certified e-mail with invisible post offices — or — a low-cost, low-congestion, and low-liability certified e-mail system. Presented at RSA 97.

Neuman, C. and G. Medvinsky (1995). Requirements for network payment: The NetCheque Prespective. In *Proceedings of IEEE Compcon '95*, San Francisco.

Neumann, P. G. (1995). *Computer Related Risks*. Reading Massachusetts: Addison Wesley – ACM Press.

Nilsson, H. and D. Pinkas (1999, January). Validation of electronic signatures. White paper, iD2 Technolgies and Bull. http://www.id2.se/whitepapers/ES_validation.pdf.

Nilsson, H., P. Van Eecke, M. Medina, D. Pinkas, and N. Pope (1999, July). Final report of the EESSI expert team. Technical report, European Electronic Signature Standardization Initiative (EESSI), Brussels.

OBI Consortium (1998, June). Open buying on the Internet (OBI) — Technical specifications, release v1.1. Technical report, The OBI Consortium. http://www.openbuy.org.

Open Market (1998, July). Internet commerce: The Open Market Transact solution. Technical white paper, Open Market, Inc. Available from www.openmarket.com.

OTP Consortium (1998, August). Internet open trading protocol (version: 0.9.9). Technical report, The OTP Consortium. http://www.otp.org.

Peat, B. and D. Webber (1997, August). Introducing XML/EDI — The e-business framework. Technical report, The XML/EDI Group. http://www.geocities. com/WallStreet/Floor/5815/guide.htm.

Pedersen, T. P. (1997). Electronic payments of small amounts. See Lomas (1997), pp. 59–68.

Pfitzmann, A., B. Pfitzmann, M. Schunter, and M. Waidner (1997). Trusting mobile user devices and security modules. *IEEE Computer 20*(2), 61–68.

Pfitzmann, A., B. Pfitzmann, and M. Waidner (1991). ISDN-mixes — untraceable communication with very small bandwidth overhead. In *7th IFIP International Conference on Information Security (IFIP/Sec '91)*, pp. 245–258. Elsevier.

Pfitzmann, A. and M. Waidner (1987). Networks without user observability. *Computers & Security 6*(2), 158–166.

Pfitzmann, B. (1996). *Digital Signature Schemes - General Framework and Fail-Stop Signatures.* Number 1100 in Lecture Notes in Computer Science. Berlin: Springer-Verlag.

Pfitzmann, B., M. Schunter, and M. Waidner (1998). Optimal efficiency of optimistic contract signing. In *17th Symposium on Principles of Distributed Computing (PODC)*, New York.

Pfitzmann, B. and M. Waidner (1992). How to break and repair a "provably secure" untraceable payment system. In *Advances in Cryptology — Crypto '91*, Number 576 in Lecture Notes in Computer Science, pp. 338–350. IACR: Springer-Verlag, Berlin Germany.

Pfitzmann, B. and M. Waidner (1996, May). Properties of payment systems — General definition sketch and classification. Research Report RZ 2823 (#90126), IBM Research Division. Submitted for Publication.

Pfitzmann, B., M. Waidner, and A. Pfitzmann (1987). Rechtssicherheit trotz Anonymität in offenen digitalen Systemen. *Computer und Recht 3*(10,11,12), 712–717, 796–803, 898–904. Extended revision in Datenschutz und Datensicherung DuD 14/5–6 (1990) 243–253, 305–315. (English translation available from authors.).

Pointcheval, D. (1998). Strengthened security for blind signatures. See IACR (1998b), pp. 391–405.

Rabin, M. O. (1983). Transaction protection by beacons. *Journal of Computer and System Sciences 27*, 256–267.

Reed, M. G., P. F. Syverson, and D. M. Goldschlag (1998). Anonymous connections and onion routing. *IEEE Journal on Selected Areas in Communications 16*(4), 482–494.

Reiter, M. K. and A. D. Rubin (1998). Crowds: Anonymity for web transactions. *ACM Transactions on Information and System Security 1*(1), 66–92.

Resnick, P. and J. Miller (1996). PICS: Internet access controls without censorship. *Communications of the ACM 39*(10), 87–93.

Rivest, R. L. and A. Shamir (1997). PayWord and MicroMint: Two simple micropayment schemes. See Lomas (1997), pp. 69–88.

Rivest, R. L., A. Shamir, and L. M. Adleman (1978, February). A method for obtaining digital signatures and public-key cryptosystems. *Journal of the ACM 21*(2), 120–126. US Patent 4,405,829: Cryptographic Communications System and Method, Public Key Partners PKP.

RosettaNet (1998). RosettaNet - an overview. http://www.rosettanet.org/ general/overview.html.

Schoder, D., R. E. Strauss, and P. Welchering (1998). *Electronic Commerce Enquête 1997/98, Survey on the business uses of electronic commerce for companies in the German speaking area.* Stuttgart: Konradin Verlag. Executive Research Report.

Schoenmakers, B. (1998). Basic security of the ecash™payment system. In B. Preneel and V. Rijmen (Eds.), *State of the art in applied cryptography*, Number 1528 in Lecture Notes in Computer Science, pp. 338–352. Springer-Verlag, Berlin Germany.

Schoenmakers, B. (1999). A simple publicly verifiable secret sharing scheme and its application to electronic voting. See IACR (1999), pp. 148–164.

Schunter, M. (2000). *Optimistic Fair Exchange*. Ph. D. thesis, Universität des Saarlandes, Saarbrücken.

SECURICOM (1996). *14th Worldwide Congress on Computer and Communications Security Protection*, C.N.I.T Paris-La Defense, France. SECURICOM.

SEMPER Consortium (1996, September). Basic services: Architecture and design. Deliverable D03 of ACTS project AC026, public specification. Available from http://www.semper.org.

SEMPER Consortium (1999a, January). Architecture, services and protocols. Deliverable D10 of ACTS project AC026, public specification. Available from http://www.semper.org.

SEMPER Consortium (1999b, April). Evaluation of the enhanced trial. Deliverable D12 of ACTS project AC026. Available from http://www.semper.org.

State of Utah (1996). Utah digital signature act. Title 46 — Chapter 03 of the Utah Code. Available from http://www.commerce.state.ut.us/web/commerce/digsig/act.htm.

Stüble, C. (2000, May). Development of a prototype for a security platform for mobile devices. Diploma thesis, Fachbereich Informatik, University of Dortmund.

Sun Microsystems (1998). *The Java Wallet™ Architecture White Paper*. Available from http://java.sun.com/products/commerce/docs/.

Turban, E. (1997). Auctions and bidding on the Internet: An assessment. *EM — Electronic Markets 7*(4), 7–11. http://www.electronicmarkets.org.

U. S. National Institute of Standards and Technology NIST (1994a, May). The digital signature standard. Federal Information Processing Standards Publication 186 (FIPS PUB 186).

U. S. National Institute of Standards and Technology NIST (1994b, January). Security requirements for cryptographic modules. Federal Information Processing Standards Publication 140 (FIPS PUB 140).

UBS (1998). Registration for SET (Secure Electronic Transaction) — Application for the supplementary function SET for the UBS Visa Card. Document SETRUBSE - 3.9.98, UBS AG, VISA Center, Flughofstrasse 35, CH-8152 Glattbrugg, Switzerland.

United States. United States' uniform commercial code article 2 — Sales, part 2: Form, formation and readjustment of contracts, § 2-201. Formal requirements; statute of frauds.

University of Leuven (1998). Study for DG XV, European Commission with respect to the legal aspects of digital signatures. Interdisciplinary centre for Law and Information Technology.

USENIX (1995). *First USENIX Workshop on Electronic Commerce*, New York. USENIX.

USENIX (1996). *Second USENIX Workshop on Electronic Commerce*, Oakland, California. USENIX.

USENIX (1998). *Third USENIX Workshop on Electronic Commerce*, Boston, Mass. USENIX.

Wassenar (1996). The Wassenaar arrangement on export controls for conventional arms and dual-use goods and technologies.

Weber, A. (1998). See what you sign. secure implementation of digital signatures. In *Intelligence in Services and Networks: Technology for Ubiquitous Telecom Services (IS&N'98)*, Number 1430 in Lecture Notes in Computer Science, Berlin, pp. 509–520. Springer-Verlag.

Weber, A. (2000). Full bindingness and confidentiality. Requirements for secure computers, and design options. In *8th European Conference on Information Systems ECIS 2000: A Cyberspace Odyssey*. Vienna University of Economics and Business Administration: IEEE.

Widmer, U. and K. Bähler (1997). *Rechtsfragen im Internet - Sichere Geschäftstransaktionen im Internet*. Zürich: Orell Füssli Verlag.

WIPO (1996). Berne convention for the protection of literary and artistic works (1886); WIPO copyright treaty (WCT) (1996); WIPO performances and phonograms treaty (WPPT) (1996). http://www.wipo.org/eng/general/index5.htm.

Zakon, R. H. (1998). Hobbes' Internet timeline v3.3. Internet Request for Comment (RFC) 2235, IETF. See http://www.isoc.org/guest/zakon/Internet/History/HIT.html.

Zentraler Kreditausschuss (ZKA) (1999, March). HBCI — Homebanking computer interface. Version 2.1.

Zhou, J. and D. Gollmann (1996). A fair non-repudiation protocol. See IEEE TC S&P (1996), pp. 55–61.

Zhou, J. and D. Gollmann (1997). An efficient non-repudiation protocol. In *10th Computer Security Foundations Workshop*, pp. 126–132. IEEE Computer Society Press, Los Alamitos.

Glossary

Acquirer   The bank used by the recipient of electronic money.

Audit trail   Logging information which is the basis for an audit of the use of a service or system. The audit trail may contain non-repudiation tokens to resolve disputes. *SEMPER* also provides higher-level transaction records and a transaction browser.

Authentication   A proof of the origin (and integrity) of a message or the identity of a person; in the second case typically combined with establishing a secure channel to that person. Also said for producing or verifying such a proof. Authentication does not imply non-repudiation. See also *Digital signature* and *Message authentication code.*

Business application   Business applications implement specific business processes. In the *SEMPER* context they are built on top of the *SEMPER* services. As there are no restrictions on the implementation of Business Applications by third parties, they are a priori untrusted and not allowed to perform security-critical actions without user authorization.

Business-Item Layer   The Business-Item Layer handles the business items of various nature, such as payments, statements, or information. In particular, it deals with the simple transfer of such items and provides, where necessary, management functionality.

Business process   A business process consists of several linked step, e.g., a purchase process contains an offer, and order, delivery and payment. Many security properties must be ensured for the process as a whole. In *SEMPER*, business processes are represented by *deals.*

Certificate   A certificate is a digitally signed statement about a person or key. *SEMPER* distinguishes three types of certificates: Key certificates link a public key and a person, while attribute certificates link a person or public key and an attribute, typically a property or right. Hybrid certificates combine this, i.e., they link a person, a public key, and an attribute.

Certification authority (CA)   A third party that signs digital certificates.

Certified mail   A fair exchange of a message for a receipt.

Channel   A medium shared by peer entities for communication.

Commerce Layer   The Commerce Layer offers security services to business applications in *SEMPER*, in particular those that offer process orientation. Its main parts are the deal support services and the commerce transaction service. It also maintains the user's security policy.

Commerce transaction   Commerce transactions represent service primitives in the Commerce Layer. A commerce transaction encapsulates a protocol to be executed between the participants of a deal. It is typically a value-added version of a lower-layer transaction, e.g., the simple delivery of a message or a complex payment protocol. Commerce transactions must always exist in the context of a deal.

Conditional access   Access to a service, which is restricted to entities having certain properties or rights.

Confidentiality   Protecting a message against eavesdropping such that it is only meaningful to the intended set of recipients. More generally, any protection of the secrecy of an action.

Container   A data structure used in *SEMPER* to transfer or exchange information and payments. It is structured in the form of a tree. The leaves specify or containing information, statements, or payments. Internal nodes contain security attributes applying to subtrees.

Context   Intuitively, a context means all the prior information relevant for a business transaction. Technically, in *SEMPER* a context is the state of a session, in particular (on the Commerce Layer) of a deal. It evolves from the preferences set by the user, the results of negotiating parameters with business partners, and prior transactions in the same session.

Contract signing   In general, a non-repudiable proof of agreement on a certain text. A fair exchange of two signatures under a contract is a special case.

Credential   A statement about properties or rights of a person, or of the issuers relation (e.g., trust) to this person. A physical credential might be a passport present at time of registration with a RA. For the electronic world, we use it as a synonym of attribute certificate.

Customer   The role of a user with respect to a service provider, typically a buyer with respect to a merchant.

Deal   The Commerce Layer introduces deals as a representation of business processes, i.e., several transactions operating on the same context. A deal contains the representation of an association between the participants, the history of commerce transactions between the participants and private data stored by the participants.

Device   A physical object, such as a personal computer. Usually, a device belongs to the player (or set of players) who relies on it. We also say user equipment.

Digital signature   A digital signature is an electronic analog of handwritten signatures. It is verified against a public key, and if the signature system is secure, this serves as a proof that the signed message originates from someone knowing the corresponding secret key. This should be only one person; whether it is, depends on the security of user equipment and certification.

Directory authority (DA)   A third party that maintains a register of public information about users including their certificates.

Dispute handling   See *Exception handling*.

Electronic money   Electronic money is the electronic analog of conventional money. We typically speak of electronic payments, because the notion of "money" has additional connotations in economics.

Entity   This word has no specific definition in *SEMPER*. We often use it as a vague version of "person", comprising legal entities and persons acting under pseudonyms. We also use it to designate an arbitrary active element in the *SEMPER* architecture (e.g., "the peer entity"); thus an entity could be a manager, a module, a transaction etc.

Exception handling   Exception handling means resolving an exception, i.e., an undesired state noticed by an entity. In a first approach the exception handling bases on the assumption that all parties are honest. If this fails, the parties are in a dispute and a more pessimistic approach must be used, usually involving arbiters and finally courts. Exception handling requires all parties to keep sufficient audit trails. For real disputes, the audit trail has to contain evidence, e.g., non-repudiation tokens.

Exchange   An exchange is a protocol whereby a number of parties can exchange business items (payment, information, vouchers, etc.). In the simplest case these are two transfers. See also *Fair exchange*.

External interface   The interface of a block of the *SEMPER* architecture to callers from outside the block. This is also often called an Application Programming Interface (API).

Fair exchange   A fair exchange is an exchange where it is guaranteed that either all parties obtain the desired items or none. For this, they input their expectations at the start of the transactions. Examples are *Certified mail*, *Fair purchase*, and *Contract signing*.

Fair Internet Trader   The Fair Internet Trader (FIT) is an electronic assistant for interactive person-to-person trade. Such trade ranges from low-value transactions like occasional sales of used items between private persons over medium-value transactions between small businesses offering specialized services, to high-value transactions with strong formal requirements like public procurement. Technically, the FIT is a business application in *SEMPER*.

Fair purchase   A fair exchange of information for a payment.

Generic Payment Service Framework   A *SEMPER* framework enabling business applications to use a variety of payment systems in a transparent manner. In *SEMPER*, it is also called the Payment Block.

Hash function   A function (or family of functions) used to compute a fixed-length digest of any bit string. Unless stated otherwise, a hash function is assumed to be one-way and collision-resistant, meaning that it is infeasible in practice to find the input string given the digest or to find two different bit string with the same digest.

Identification   A process whereby an entity proves its identity.

Integrity protection   The protection of information against unauthorized modification.

Internal interface   The interface that a module (e.g., a specific payment instrument) must offer to fit into *SEMPER*. This is also often called a Service Provider Interface (SPI).

Issuer   In the context of an electronic payment systems it means the bank of the payer. In the context of certificates it means the certification authority.

Layer   A (virtual) collection of services, and of entities in all devices offering these services, that have a similar degree of abstraction.

Liability-cover service   A *SEMPER* service that allows to limit the risk of both key owners and relying parties from compromise of signature keys, e.g., due to *Trojan horses*.

Manager   A manager is a fixed entity in a *SEMPER* block, which provides functions for negotiation and selection of an appropriate module.

Message authentication code (MAC)   A MAC assures the recipient of a message of its origin. However, this is symmetric cryptography, i.e., the sender and the recipient share the key of the MAC function. Hence a MAC does not offer non-repudiation, i.e., it cannot be used to convince a third party of the origin of the message. See also *Digital signature*.

Module   In *SEMPER*, each type of services may be provided by different modules (e.g., different payment systems of crypto libraries). It is expected that modules will come from different providers. A module must support the internal interface of a *SEMPER* block in order to be used by the manager.

Multi-party security   Security without a-priori assumptions that everybody will trust particular entities.

Non-repudiation   Non-repudiation of an event means that one can convince a third party that the event took place. In particular, non-repudiation of origin means that one can prove that a message originated from a certain entity, and non-repudiation of delivery means that one can prove that a message has been delivered.

Non-repudiation token   A non-repudiation token is the information needed for non-repudiation, i.e., the proof needed to convince a third party. These tokens are often necessary for dispute handling.

Optimistic protocol   A protocol where correctness is guaranteed by a third party which is only involved in case of faults.

Payment instrument   An instance of one player's component of a payment system.

Payment manager   Overall controller of an instance of the Generic Payment Service.

Payment system   A collective name for one "way" of making a payment. It consists of protocols, contractual agreements, and data structures.

Payment system provider   A party (such as a financial institution) that makes a payment system available.

Peer entity   Peer entities are two entities of the same block but located on different devices. Usually, we only speak of peer entities if the entities work together to provide a certain service, e.g., two peer managers or two peer entities in a transaction.

Player   The word "player" has no specific meaning in *SEMPER*. It is typically used for is a real-world person or body participating in the electronic marketplace.

Preferences   Settings entered by the user that personalize a program according to his wishes. In *SEMPER*, in particular the user's default choices of security attributes.

Protocol   A description of how a service is provided by means of interactions of peer entities, often using lower layer services.

Public-key infrastructure (PKI)   All entities involved in handling public-key certificates. See *Certification authority, Directory authority* and *Registration authority*.

Purse   Representation of a payment instrument within the Generic Payment Service Framework.

Purse-management application   User application to create and manage purses in the Generic Payment Service.

Registration   Here it usually means the registration of the public key of a signature system. Optimally, an entity (usually a real person) appears in person at a *Registration authority*, proves his or her identity, and signs that he or she wants to accept a certain liability for this key. In return, the participant gets a certificate from an associated *Certification authority*.

Registration authority (RA)   An entity that carries out registration.

Revocation   The process of withdrawing something; typically a public key or a certificate. The reason can be that the key is compromised or lost or was registered by an impostor, or that the key remains valid but some information in the certificate changes (e.g., if it contains an address). An attribute certificate may be revoked if the rights change.

Role   The function of an entity in a certain transaction. All protocols are specified for roles (e.g., "a buyer and a merchant"), but performed by specific entities "playing" the corresponding roles. In a related sense, the word "role" is used in access control.

SECA certificate   A certificate stating that an entity is using a key and accepting liability for it according the specific provisions of the *SEMPER Electronic Commerce Agreement*.

Secure channel   A channel between two entities fulfilling certain security requirement, e.g., authenticity, integrity and/or confidentiality. Note that non-repudiation can typicallly not be fulfilled by a secure channels.

Security attribute   Security attributes are a high-level way to select the security level of a certain service. Examples are confidentiality, non-repudiation and anonymity. In *SEMPER*, security attributes of a transaction are derived from preferences, the surrounding session if there is one, inputs from the caller if it is trusted, and in rare cases from direct user input.

SEMPER Electronic Commerce Agreement (SECA)   The SECA is a model agreement that can be used to regulate (among its subscribers) liability questions and other legal issues which are not or only unsatisfactorily covered by current regulation.

Service   Service generally means the joint functionality of a system or component as offered to its environment. layer to its upper interface. For instance, we speak of the services offered by a *SEMPER* block, or the entire *SEMPER* services.

Session   A session provides a common context to several transactions. Compared with a transaction, a session is longer-lived and atomicity is not required. Sessions can be nested: a session on a higher layer may start several sessions on lower layers (or use existing sessions) and exchange parts of its state with them, e.g., security attributes).

SME   Small and medium size enterprises.

Third party   A third party is an entity supporting a business transaction without being directly involved as a business partner. Typical third-party services are notary services.

TINGUIN (Trustworthy Interactive Graphical User Interface)   Security requires a carefully designed user interface. Important aspects are a uniform look-and-feel for critical steps, and clear indications of "points of no return". In *SEMPER*, this is called TINGUIN. If one had a *Trusted computing base*, a trusted path to the TINGUIN would be implemented, so that the user could not be tricked into taking other windows for the TINGUIN.

Transaction   Intuitively, a transaction in *SEMPER* is one step in a business process. More technically, it should be a transaction in the usual computer-science sense, i.e., atomic. This means that it either finishes successfully or has no effect at all. It should also mean a transition from one consistent state into another, at least for the block providing the transaction. (For instance, a payment transaction keeps the purse states and the states of the bank consistent, but on the higher layers a delivery may have to precede or follow.)

Transaction browser   User application to examine transaction records, e.g., from payment transactions.

Transfer   The process of transferring business items from a sender to a recipient, usually in a secure way. Transferable business items are for example payments, signed statements, and information.

Transfer-and-Exchange Layer   The Transfer-and-Exchange Layer coordinates the secure exchanges and transfers of business items and containers. In particular it handles fairness. See also *Business-Item Layer, Container* and *Fair exchange*.

Trojan horse   A program that contains malicious parts apart from its usual functionality. Viruses are the best-known case. Together with bugs in well-known programs like browsers and emailers that allow outsiders to get code executed on a machine whose user is not intending to load any code, Trojan horses are the main reason why one cannot place unlimited trust in digital signatures at present. See *Liability-cover service, Trusted computing base.*

Trust management   Trust management enables the user to specify policies for using his own certificates and accepting certificates from other parties in business processes, and provides services for selecting the appropriate certificates that satisfy all requirements for a business application.

Trusted computing base (TCB)   The part of the system which enforces the security policies. The TCB should be nontamperable and noncircumventable, i.e., it has to protect itself and its users from malicious applications, in particular *Trojan horses*. As the TCB has to be trusted by definition it's important that the design and the implementation of the TCB is also trustworthy, i.e., it is minimal and verifiable.

User   A user is anyone using the marketplace (e.g., buyer or seller). We also say "user" for the owner of a device, e.g., in *User authorization*.

User authorization The approval of an action (of a program) by the user, typically a human user in the case of consumers and small businesses. Mandatory for security-critical operations such as signing a contract or payments.

Index